The Rehnquist Court and Criminal Justice

The Rehnquist Court and Criminal Justice

Edited by Christopher E. Smith, Christina DeJong, and Michael A. McCall

LEXINGTON BOOKS
Lanham • Boulder • New York • Toronto • Plymouth, UK

Published by Lexington Books
A wholly owned subsidiary of The Rowman & Littlefield Publishing Group, Inc.
4501 Forbes Boulevard, Suite 200, Lanham, Maryland 20706
http://www.lexingtonbooks.com

Estover Road, Plymouth PL6 7PY, United Kingdom

British Library Cataloguing in Publication Information Available

Library of Congress Cataloging-in-Publication Data
The Rehnquist court and criminal justice / edited by Christopher E. Smith, Christina
DeJong, and Michael A. McCall.
    p. cm.
  Includes index.
  ISBN 978-0-7391-4080-2 (cloth : alk. paper)
  1. Criminal justice, Administration of--United States--Cases. 2. United States. Supreme
Court--History. 3. Rehnquist, William H., 1924-2005. I. Smith, Christopher E. II.
DeJong, Christina, 1967- III. McCall, Michael A., 1965-
  KF9223.R44 2011
  347.73'2609--dc23
                            2011030853

⊖™ The paper used in this publication meets the minimum requirements of American
National Standard for Information Sciences—Permanence of Paper for Printed Library
Materials, ANSI/NISO Z39.48-1992.

Printed in the United States of America

Contents

Preface

The announcement in 2010 concerning the impending retirement of Justice John Paul Stevens and President Barack Obama's nomination of Solicitor General Elena Kagan as his replacement served to remind the nation that the U.S. Supreme Court is never a static institution. The nation's highest court changes as its members retire, as it faces a new array of difficult issues, and as its individual justices alter their perspectives on law and society. Such changes affect the Court's decision making and, obviously, its impact on society. As in prior Supreme Court eras, the newly-constituted Roberts Court of the twenty-first century will address novel issues, such as the impact of rapidly-developing technologies on privacy rights, and continuing policy cleavages, such as those embodied in contentious issues such as abortion and campaign finance laws. The ultimate impact of the Roberts Court will eventually be evaluated in retrospect when scholars have time to look back and study the current Court era carefully without the burden of constantly incorporating consideration of ongoing contemporaneous changes in legal issues and judicial personnel.

This volume represents an effort to look at the recent past in order to evaluate the Supreme Court and its justices during an era in which criminal justice issues absorbed a significant portion of the highest court's time and energy. These are issues of importance to all Americans because any individual can come into contact with the criminal justice system through encounters with police and all individuals risk being subjected to searches and arrests, no matter how well they comply with the law. Even innocent people can be drawn into the system through police officers' discretionary decisions, errors by witnesses, and mistakes in official record keeping. Thus constitutional rights affecting criminal justice have special importance for law-abiding citizens as well as criminal offenders.

The Rehnquist Court's attention to important criminal justice topics was attributable to a number of factors, including the nationalization of constitutional rights through the incorporation process of the mid-twentieth century and changes in the Court's composition that perpetuated the Burger Court's conservative efforts to limit the rights-granting decisions of the prior Warren Court era. The Rehnquist Court era was a time when political conservatives had high hopes for dismantling the recognition of rights that they believed hampered the nation's crime control efforts. Although many Rehnquist Court decisions narrowed the scope of constitutional rights, the anticipated counterrevolution did not fully take place. In large part, the complexity of the mixed results of the Rehnquist Court's decisions that interpreted constitutional rights is attributable to the distinctiveness of each justice on the Court. Although we label them as "conservatives" and "liberals" as a matter of convenience, they each display independent tendencies, value preferences, and inconsistencies that distinguish them from one another. Thus we have chosen to examine—and hopefully illuminate—the Rehnquist Court's impact on criminal justice by analyzing each individual justice and his or her approach to decision making (except one—Justice Lewis Powell, who only served for one term during the era).

The authors of this volume were given great freedom to make choices about the cases, issues, and opinions that best illuminate the performance and role of each individual justice. In light of the distinctiveness of each justice and the challenge of revealing the complex elements reflected in the decisions of individual justices, it made little sense to impose a "cookie cutter" framework for each chapter and then try to "shoehorn" each justice into that framework. As a result, there is diversity among the chapters and their approaches—a diversity that appropriately reflects both the distinctiveness of the individual justices and the varied analytical perspectives of the particular scholars who studied each justice.

We owe many debts of gratitude for the assistance required to produce an edited volume. All of the contributors benefit from the resources and collegial support within their respective academic homes. In particular, the editors' home departments, the School of Criminal Justice at Michigan State University and the Department of Sociology at San Diego State University, deserve special acknowledgement. We want to thank the anonymous reviewers for their attention and endorsements. We are especially grateful for extra editorial advice and assistance generously provided by Karen Malmisur, and for invaluable aid from one particularly helpful contributor, Charles F. Jacobs. Finally, we wish to express a special "thank you" to Joseph C. Parry, the editor at Lexington Books, and his staff for their patience, receptivity, and support.

Chapter 1
Introduction:
The Rehnquist Court

Christopher E. Smith and Michael A. McCall

The Rehnquist Court era, spanning the Supreme Court terms from October 1986 to June 2005, began with the Senate confirmation of William H. Rehnquist to be Chief Justice of the United States. President Ronald Reagan selected Rehnquist, who had already served for fourteen years as an associate justice, to become the U.S. Supreme Court's new leader because Rehnquist had established a clear record as a jurist who sought to limit the expansion of constitutional rights and defer to the decisions of elected officials. Because criminal justice cases constitute such a significant portion of the Supreme Court's annual docket, typically 20 to 30 percent of the cases decided by the Court, Reagan and other political conservatives hoped that Rehnquist would lead the Court to expand the authority of law enforcement officials and shrink the scope of rights for criminal suspects, defendants, and convicted offenders. While serving as an associate justice (1972-1986) during the Burger Court era, Rehnquist supported, on average, only 15 percent of individuals' claims in criminal procedure cases during each term (Epstein, Segal, Spaeth, and Walker 2007). Based on Rehnquist's prior performance as an associate justice and his actions as a government attorney, Reagan administration officials had good reason to expect that Rehnquist shared their values and policy preferences. As described by one scholar, in Rehnquist's prior service as a government attorney,

> [H]e supported inherent executive authority to order wiretapping and surveil-lance without a court order, no-knock entry by the police, preventive detention, abolishing habeas corpus proceedings after trial, and abolishing the exclusionary rule. (Davis 1991, 316)

Rehnquist's elevation to chief justice came during a long period in which the intersection of presidential election results and the quirks of fate affecting Supreme Court justices' deaths, resignations, and retirements gave Republican presidents the exclusive opportunity to appoint new justices for a period of twenty-six years (1967-1993). The lone Democrat elected to the White House between the 1968 election and the 1992 election, President Jimmy Carter (1977-1981), never had an opportunity to make a Supreme Court appointment because no justices left the bench while Carter was in office. As a result, the Rehnquist Court era was known as a period in which the Supreme Court's composition became increasingly conservative, with "conservatism" understood to mean a tendency to favor the interests of government and business over the claims of individuals.

Throughout the chapters of this book, the terms "liberal" and "conservative" are used to describe the judicial philosophies and voting patterns of justices who served during the Rehnquist Court era. These terms are vague and problematic when applied to judicial decision makers. The authors follow the standard political science definitions as utilized in the Supreme Court Judicial Database for applying the terms to Supreme Court decisions. With this book's focus on criminal justice issues, "liberal decisions in the area of civil liberties are pro-person accused or convicted of a crime . . . and anti-government in due process and privacy" (Segal and Spaeth 1989, 103). Conversely, conservative decisions in criminal justice cases favor the government's interest in prosecuting and punishing offenders rather than endorse the claims of individuals or expand the definitions of rights (Smith 1999, 26). These classifications, as defined in this way, are useful for analyzing the decision making of Supreme Court justices. They serve as the basis for discerning patterns and detecting inconsistencies in the votes and opinions of individual justices as well as for assessing the directional trends in the Court's decisions on specific issues.

As indicated by the foregoing definitions, the Rehnquist Court era's reputation for conservatism in the realm of criminal justice, driven by compositional changes from the appointment of new justices, was based on the Supreme Court's decisions that reduced the scope of individual rights and expanded the authority of police and prosecutors. During the Rehnquist Court era, the Supreme Court issued full written decisions in more than 450 cases classified in the Supreme Court Judicial Database as concerning "criminal procedure" plus dozens more concerning other aspects of criminal justice related to due process claims, prisoners' rights, and First Amendment issues affecting criminal statutes (Epstein et al. 2007). In examining myriad cases concerning searches, seizures, police questioning, and other topics, the majority of justices often denied the claims of individuals and endorsed the challenged actions undertaken by criminal justice officials. In many respects, much like the preceding Burger Court era (1969-1986), the Rehnquist Court's decisions reacted and responded to the liberal expansion of rights during the Warren Court era (1953-1969). The Warren Court justices issued many landmark rulings affecting criminal justice, such as *Mapp v. Ohio* (1961), applying the exclusionary rule to improper searches undertaken by state and local police and *Miranda v. Arizona* (1966), requiring the reading of specific warnings to suspects prior to custodial questioning. Many cases in the Rehnquist Court era required the justices to look at specific situations and determine whether the principles established in the Warren Court's landmark decisions should be applied, expanded, modified, reduced, or even eliminated. Within the Rehnquist Court, many of these cases produced significant disagreement among the justices. Early in the Rehnquist Court era, two holdover justices from the Warren Court era defended their legacy against the conservatizing changes generally favored by a majority of justices. After these long-serving justices retired, other justices defended the preservation of constitutional rights and, in some cases, succeeded in gathering enough votes to vindicate the claims of criminal defendants and convicted offenders.

The Rehnquist Court era saw the Court majority frequently support expanded government authority in criminal justice at the expense of individual rights. One scholar wrote that "[t]he Rehnquist Court is the most conservative Supreme Court since before the New Deal. Ronald Reagan's efforts to reshape the American judiciary succeeded" (Schwartz 2002, 13). However, the conservative majority never coalesced into a unified group with a shared vision and concerted action aimed at undoing the legacy of the Warren Court era.

On criminal justice issues, the media typically described Chief Justice Rehnquist as having led a Court that primarily continued the conservative trends emerging during the Burger Court era by further reducing restrictions on government in investigating and prosecuting crimes. Comparisons of voting tendencies during the Warren and Rehnquist Courts bolster such claims. For example, as indicated in Table 1.1, decisions from the Warren Court were nearly twice as likely as those from the Rehnquist era to favor criminal defendants and, in specific issue areas, the gap was even greater (Epstein et al. 2007, tables 3-8).

Table 1.1. Comparison of Court Eras: Supreme Court Majority Support for Liberal Outcomes in Criminal Justice Issue Areas [percentages]

	Warren Court 1953-1969	Burger Court 1969-1986	Rehnquist Court 1986-2005
4th Amendment Search and Seizure	58	32	21
5th Amendment Self-Incrimination	56	23	25
6th Amendment Right to Counsel	86	44	24
8th Amendment Capital Punishment	33	53	41

Source: Supreme Court Judicial Database, 1953-2004 Terms. See Smith and Hensley 2005, 166.

Similarly, the median justice on the Warren Court voted liberally in criminal justice cases more than twice as often as did his counterpart on the Rehnquist Court (Smith, McCall, and McCluskey 2005, 27). Most systematic analyses characterize the Rehnquist Court as a period of retrenchment in the protections afforded the criminally accused and tend "to confirm that the image of the Rehnquist Court as conservative on criminal justice cases is justified" (Smith, McCall, and McCluskey 2005, 31).

Although there is evidence to support the characterization of the Rehnquist Court as conservative, there is a risk that such generalizations obscure the complexity of the Court's legacy, especially with respect to myriad issues affecting criminal justice that constitute a significant portion of the Supreme Court's docket each term. The Court also handed down important liberal (pro-accused) rulings in key criminal justice cases (Smith, McCall, and McCall 2005), suggesting that assessing the conservatism of the Rehnquist Court is a more complex task than its general reputation would imply (Smith and Hensley 1993). Indeed, nearly two of every five criminal justice cases decided during the last ten years of the Rehnquist Court favored the individual over government. Many of these liberal decisions were also unanimous ones (e.g., Smith and Dow 2002).

The chapters of this book, in examining the individual justices who served on the Rehnquist Court and their opinions in criminal justice cases, seek to convey the complexities and nuances of the Rehnquist Court era and its impact. Even the most consistently conservative justices support the preservation of constitutional rights for specific issues. As presented in the analyses by the contributors to this book, these justices each played a role in preserving specific rights even as the Court's general patterns of decision making tended to move in a conservative direction. Because each justice was a unique individual, no effort was made to fit each chapter's analysis into a standard format. For each justice, the contributor presents an analysis that seeks to highlight notable aspects of that justice's performance and influence on the Court's criminal justice decisions.

The Justices

Scholars separate and label Supreme Court eras according to the tenures of individual chief justices. In reality, the Court's composition can change significantly during the tenure of a specific chief justice. Thus the use of the phrase "the Rehnquist Court" can convey the misleading impression that the Supreme Court during this era was a single, static entity when there were actually changes occurring during that time period with respect to the identities of the nine justices and the Court's decision making trends. For greater precision, scholars prefer to talk about "natural court periods," time spans in which a single set of nine individuals served as the Supreme Court's justices (Banks 1992). By studying a specific set of individuals, a scholar can make a more accurate assessment of consistency, conflict, and coalitions. However, many natural court periods are very short. For example, when new justices are appointed to the Court in consecutive terms then there will only be a one-term natural court period after the first appointment before a new natural court period begins with the second appointment. During the Rehnquist Court era, excluding the periods of several months between the retirements of specific justices and the confirmation of their successors, there were six natural court periods for the nine-justice Supreme Court, as illustrated in Table 1.2. The dynamics of the justices' interactions and the voting coalitions that form in response to specific cases will change somewhat with the addition of each new justice. Obviously, additional changes affecting decision making can occur as individual justices themselves refine their approaches to constitutional interpretation and adopt new perspectives on specific issues.

Table 1.2. Supreme Court Composition for Nine-Member "Natural Court" Periods during the Rehnquist Era, 1986-2005, by Seniority of Justice

		U.S. Supreme Court Term			
1986	1987-89	1990	1991-92	1993	1994-2004
Brennan	*Brennan*	White	*White*	*Blackmun*	Rehnquist
White	White	*Marshall*	Blackmun	Rehnquist	Stevens
Marshall	Marshall	Blackmun	Rehnquist	Stevens	O'Connor
Blackmun	Blackmun	Rehnquist	Stevens	O'Connor	Scalia
Powell	Rehnquist	Stevens	O'Connor	Scalia	Kennedy
Rehnquist	Stevens	O'Connor	Scalia	Kennedy	Souter
Stevens	O'Connor	Scalia	Kennedy	Souter	Thomas
O'Connor	Scalia	Kennedy	Souter	Thomas	Ginsburg
Scalia	**Kennedy**	**Souter**	**Thomas**	**Ginsburg**	**Breyer**

Boldface: New appointee. *Italics*: Justice in his last natural court. Although Justice O'Connor announced her retirement in July 2005, she continued to serve until January 2006 as a member for the first few months of the Roberts Court. Supreme Court terms run from early October to the end of June in the following calendar year. Kennedy took his judicial oath in February 1988; oaths for all other new appointees noted above were taken in August, September or October of the first year of the term indicated.

The risks of losing sight of the impact of composition changes and differences between natural court periods can loom large if scholars seek to analyze a Supreme Court era by devoting each chapter of a book to a different topical issue. If one focuses on the Rehnquist Court, for example, through separate chapters on affirmative action, abortion, capital punishment, religious freedom, and other topics, the composition changes affecting all of these issues may be subsumed by the discussion of the many cases decided by the Court. By contrast, this book focuses on the individual justices and their opinions for a single general issue area, criminal justice, in order to provide depth of analysis and make composition changes an underlying basis of each chapter's discussion. Among the fourteen justices who served during the Rehnquist Court era, only four justices—Chief Justice William Rehnquist and Associate Justices John Paul Stevens, Sandra Day O'Connor, and Antonin Scalia—served during all nineteen annual terms that comprise the Rehnquist Court era. Service by the other ten justices during this era ranged from one term (Justice Lewis Powell) to eighteen terms (Justice Anthony Kennedy). In focusing on individual justices, each chapter can examine the extent of the justice's tenure during the Rehnquist Court era. Although some books that take this approach may focus solely on those justices who served together and interacted with each other for the longest period of time (e.g., Maltz 2003), this book will focus on all of the justices, except one, because even those who served only four (William Brennan), five (Thurgood Marshall), or seven (Byron White) terms exerted influence over the Court's decisions affecting criminal justice. The lone exclusion is Lewis Powell due to his very brief, single-term tenure on the Rehnquist Court.

The roles of the individual justices within the Rehnquist era are especially intriguing for several reasons. First, the Rehnquist Court included some of the longest-serving justices in Supreme Court history. As indicated in Table 1.3, four of the justices had spent three or more decades on the Court by the end of the era. Three others spent nearly a quarter-century on the Court.

Table 1.3. Tenure of Rehnquist Court Justices

Justice	Appointment Year: Appointing President	Tenure at end of Era or at Retirement within Era
William Brennan	1956: Eisenhower	34 years
William Rehnquist	1971: Nixon	34 years
Byron White	1962: Kennedy	31 years
John Paul Stevens	1975: Ford	30 years
Harry Blackmun	1970: Nixon	24 years
Thurgood Marshall	1967: Johnson	24 years
Sandra Day O'Connor	1981: Reagan	24 years
Antonin Scalia	1986: Reagan	19 years
Anthony Kennedy	1988: Reagan	17.5 yrs
Lewis Powell	1971: Nixon	15.5 years
David Souter	1990: G.H.W. Bush	15 years
Clarence Thomas	1991: G.H.W. Bush	14 years
Ruth Bader Ginsburg	1993: Clinton	12 years
Stephen Breyer	1994: Clinton	11 years

Note: Historically, the average length of service for the 110 individuals who have served on the U.S. Supreme Court (including the nine not-yet-retired justices serving in 2010) was 16 years. Rehnquist was elevated to chief justice by President Reagan in 1986.

Thus, when the Rehnquist Court era began, the new chief justice, albeit one who already had a decade of Supreme Court experience, found himself interacting with four justices who had more seniority (Brennan, White, Blackmun, Marshall). All of these justices were more liberal than Rehnquist in their criminal justice decisions (see Table 1.4), especially Brennan, Marshall, and Blackmun, who used their experience, relationships, interactions, and opinion-writing skills to resist the conservative direction in which Rehnquist sought to lead the Court.

Table 1.4. Percent Support for Liberal Outcomes in "Criminal Procedure" Cases* over the Course of Career, through End of Rehnquist Court Era

Justice	Liberal Voting Percentage
Marshall	80
Brennan	76
Stevens	65
Ginsburg	61
Souter	54
Breyer	54
Blackmun	42
White	33
Kennedy	30
Powell	29
O'Connor	27
Scalia	25
Thomas	21
Rehnquist	17

Source: Calculated from Epstein et al. 2007, 534-36.
*Note: Cases as identified in the Supreme Court Judicial Database. These cases do not include the full range of criminal justice issues addressed by the Rehnquist Court because some criminal justice cases are classified within the Database in other categories, such as prisoners' rights cases classified as "Due Process" and prisoners' rights and obscenity prosecutions classified under "First Amendment."

A second intriguing aspect about the justices on the Rehnquist Court is the divergent voting records of the Republican appointees to the Court. When Ronald Reagan became president in 1981, the Supreme Court included three justices who had been appointed by Republican presidents yet had deeply disappointed political conservatives in the Republican Party. William Brennan, a Democrat who had been appointed by Republican President Dwight Eisenhower in 1956, was one of the leading liberals during the Warren Court era. Eisenhower later referred to his appointment of Brennan as a mistake (Cray 1997, 337). Brennan's biographer observed with respect to the topical area of criminal justice, "Those, like President Eisenhower himself, who would later express surprise at Brennan's activism in criminal cases after he joined the U.S. Supreme Court clearly had not scrutinized his record on the New Jersey court system" (Eisler 1993, 81). Because Brennan so consistently supported the rights claims of individuals in criminal justice and other issue areas, he was the antithesis of what political conservatives wanted President Reagan's appointees to be.

Harry Blackmun, an appointee of Republican President Richard Nixon in 1970, drew criticism from political conservatives for specific opinions he wrote, especially the majority opinion in *Roe v. Wade* (1973) establishing a right of choice regarding abortion, as well as for his increasingly liberal voting record (Greenhouse 2005, 235). As one scholar wrote, Blackmun "surely . . . disappointed" President Nixon because "Blackmun's judicial philosophy evolved into a thoughtful, moderate liberalism" (Davis 1991, 315). Indeed, by the end of his tenure on the Rehnquist Court, his views had evolved so much that he joined his ultra-liberal former colleagues Brennan and Marshall as the only other justice who, at that time, had forthrightly declared his opposition to capital punishment (*Callins v. Collins* 1994). Justice Stevens reached a similar conclusion in the later Roberts Court era (*Baze v. Rees* 2008).

The third Republican, John Paul Stevens, an appointee of President Gerald Ford, did not disappoint his own appointing president, who claimed to be proud of Stevens's work on the Court. However, he clearly was not a political conservative. Initial analyses of Stevens's record prior to the advent of the Rehnquist Court era characterized him as a maverick who was especially independent and, in the eyes of many, somewhat unpredictable (Sickels 1988). It was clear from his initial performance on the Supreme Court that the man who would eventually become the leading liberal in the final years of the Rehnquist Court era took a special interest in protecting rights for prisoners and was sensitive to the importance of rights elsewhere in the justice system (Smith 2007).

Because President Reagan and his advisors were committed to turning the federal judiciary in a more conservative direction, he vowed that he would appoint conservatives to the Supreme Court and other federal courts. For his first appointment in 1981, he sought to fulfill his campaign pledge to appoint the first woman to the Supreme Court. He appointed Sandra Day O'Connor, a former Republican state legislator and state appellate judge in Arizona. She eventually was one of the four justices who served during all nineteen terms of the Rehnquist Court era. Although she disappointed political conservatives with her votes to preserve affirmative action and the right of choice for abortion, her decisions in criminal justice cases were generally conservative.

Reagan's first appointee of the Rehnquist Court era was Antonin Scalia, a federal judge and former law professor who was revered by political conservatives. Scalia has generally pleased his conservative supporters, although there are specific issues in the realm of criminal justice, such as the Sixth Amendment's Confrontation Clause and the role of juries in fact-finding that guides sentencing, that lead him to join the liberals and support the claims of individuals.

Three more Republicans were appointed to the Rehnquist Court in relatively quick succession. Anthony Kennedy was appointed by President Reagan to replace Lewis Powell in 1988. With respect to criminal justice, Kennedy was a conservative appointee replacing a conservative retiree, so his arrival did not significantly shift the voting patterns on the Court. Kennedy was generally conservative in criminal justice cases, although he voted for liberal positions on specific issues. The big change in the Court's composition arrived in the form of President George H.W. Bush's two nominees, David Souter in 1990 and Clarence Thomas in 1991. They were Republican appointees replacing the Rehnquist Court's two most liberal justices, Warren Court holdovers William Brennan and Thurgood Marshall. Thomas immediately established himself as a consistent, outspoken conservative whose decisions were dramatically different from Marshall's in cases concerning constitutional rights. Souter, after initially casting conservative votes in criminal justice cases, then moved in a more liberal direction and became one of the justices most likely to support individuals' rights, albeit much less frequently than his predecessor Brennan and other justices from the Warren Court era (see Table 1.4).

President Bill Clinton rounded out the appointments to the Rehnquist Court by making the first Democratic appointments since 1967 when he nominated respected federal appellate judges Ruth Bader Ginsburg (1993) and Stephen Breyer (1994). Both Ginsburg and Breyer were often supportive of rights claims in criminal justice cases, but with more moderate voting records than the consistent liberals of the Warren Court era.

The interesting dynamic within the Rehnquist Court was the frequent disagreements between the Republicans who often voted in support of individuals' claims in criminal justice—Stevens, Souter, and, especially later in his career, Blackmun—and those who pleased political conservatives by consistently seeking to expand the authority of police and prosecutors—Rehnquist, Scalia, Thomas, O'Connor, and Kennedy. As Mark Tushnet has observed, this rift between the Republican appointees on the Rehnquist Court reflected the changes that occurred in the Republican Party from the 1970s onward (Tushnet 2005). The Republican Party that produced Chicagoan Stevens, Minnesotan Blackmun, and New Hampshirite Souter prior to the 1970s had greater diversity of political orientations, including people who were quite liberal on social issues. As the Republican Party sought to appeal to white southerners and to religious conservatives in the 1970s and 1980s, it became less diverse—and people like Stevens, Blackmun, and Souter came to seem less like the new Republicans, especially in contrast to the most outspoken social conservatives on the Court, Scalia and Thomas. The chapters on these justices will illuminate the differences between these individual Republican appointees.

The Rehnquist Court era is also especially interesting because its final stage was one of the longest natural court periods in Supreme Court history. For eleven terms, from October 1994 through June 2005, the same group of nine individuals served together on the Court. This extraordinary continuity in the Court's composition created a unique opportunity for scholars to monitor voting coalitions and consistency (or the lack thereof) in justices' decisions and agreements with each other. Presumably, these justices also developed relationships and routines for discussing cases, participating in oral arguments, and persuading each other through draft opinions that enhanced their knowledge of each other and their ability to interact strategically to seek votes for their preferred positions.

Another intriguing element of the Rehnquist Court is the role of so-called "swing voters" and their impact on case outcomes. Throughout the Rehnquist Court era, even as the Court's composition changed, the justices were consistently divided into wings composed of four justices who voted in favor of individuals in more than half of criminal justice cases and five justices who voted for the government in two-thirds or more of cases. This characterization takes account of Justice Blackmun's 62 percent support rate for individuals in criminal justice cases during his eight terms on the Rehnquist Court, a liberal voting rate that exceeds the 42 percent mark for his liberal voting throughout his career in cases classified in the Supreme Court Judicial Database as "criminal procedure." The lone exception to this characterization was the 1990 Term in which newcomer David Souter voted in a decidedly conservative fashion in criminal justice cases (Johnson and Smith 1992). However, his support for liberal outcomes quickly increased and remained at a higher level throughout the remainder of his career.

In light of the divisions within the Rehnquist Court, much has been made of the role "swing voters" played in determining the outcomes of cases, especially O'Connor's and Kennedy's control over case outcomes when they decided to desert their usual conservative allies and provide the decisive fifth vote in favor of a liberal outcome (Maveety 2008; Greenburg 2007). The focus on these two justices takes into account their specific roles in preserving interpretations of the Constitution that are vigorously opposed by many political conservatives, such as those concerning the right of choice for abortion (O'Connor and Kennedy), race-based affirmative action in higher education admissions (O'Connor), and the prohibition on the death penalty for juveniles (Kennedy). Although O'Connor and Kennedy were typically regarded as the votes that were potentially "in play" by attorneys who tailored their arguments to fit the interests of one or both of these justices, the actual "swing votes" in criminal justice cases during the Rehnquist Court era show that other justices also cast decisive votes in specific cases for their less-preferred decisional direction.

Table 1.5 shows the "swing votes" in criminal justice cases throughout the Rehnquist Court era. Here "swing votes" are defined as individual justices' outcome-determining votes in 5 to 4 decisions that deviated from the "expected vote." The expected vote in each case is defined as the five justices with the most conservative lifetime voting records in criminal justice cases lining up against the four most liberal lifetime voters to produce a conservative outcome. The identities of the five most conservative and four most liberal justices obviously changed during the Rehnquist Court era as the Court's composition changed. Under these definitions, conservative justices are credited with a swing

Table 1.5. Decisive "Swing Votes" in Criminal Justice Cases. Number of Outcome-Determining Votes by Individual Justices in 5 to 4 Cases that Deviated from the Expected Vote* during the Rehnquist Court Era

Term:	'86	'87	'88	'89	'90	'91	'92	'93	'94	'95	'96	'97	'98	'99	'00	'01	'02	'03	'04	Total
O'Connor	0	2	0	1	2	1	0	0	2	1	1	1	0	1	0	3	2	0	2	**19**
Kennedy	-	0	1	1	1	2	2	2	1	0	1	1	1	0	0	0	1	2	1	**17**
Scalia	2	1	1	2	1	0	1	1	1	0	0	0	1	1	1	0	0	1	3	**17**
Souter	-	-	-	-	6	2	1	0	0	0	1	0	0	0	2	0	0	0	1	**13**
Thomas	-	-	-	-	-	1	0	0	0	0	0	1	0	2	1	0	1	2	3	**11**
Stevens	1	3	2	0	2	0	1	0	0	0	0	1	0	0	0	0	0	0	1	**11**
Blackmun	2	1	2	1	1	1	0	0	-	-	-	-	-	-	-	-	-	-	-	**8**
White	0	3	1	2	0	0	2	-	-	-	-	-	-	-	-	-	-	-	-	**8**
Breyer	-	-	-	-	-	-	-	-	0	0	0	3	0	0	0	1	0	0	2	**6**
Powell	3	-	-	-	-	-	-	-	-	-	-	-	-	-	-	-	-	-	-	**3**
Ginsburg	-	-	-	-	-	-	-	-	0	0	0	0	0	0	1	0	0	0	0	**2**
Brennan	0	0	1	0	0	-	-	-	-	-	-	-	-	-	-	-	-	-	-	**1**
Marshall	0	0	0	0	1	-	-	-	-	-	-	-	-	-	-	-	-	-	-	**1**
Rehnquist	0	1	0	0	0	0	0	0	0	0	0	0	0	0	0	0	0	0	0	**1**

5 to 4 Criminal Justice Cases in which No Justices Switched to Their Less-Frequently Supported Decisional Direction

Number of "Expected Vote Cases"

12	3	8	12	1	0	2	1	1	0	1	3	1	7	4	3	3	6	1

*Note: "Expected vote" is when the five justices during any term who have the most conservative lifetime voting rates in criminal justice cases vote together to produce a conservative outcome. Numbers are of *votes*, not *cases*, because sometimes more than one justice deviated from his or her usual pattern to contribute to a five-member majority supporting his or her less-frequently supported decisional direction. Also included are votes to produce conservative outcomes in those cases in which one or more of the Court's four most liberal justices cast a decisive fifth vote for a conservative outcome. Not all "switch" votes are shown; excluded are those cast in dissent to support each justice's less-frequently supported decisional direction. Source: Calculated from *The Supreme Court Judicial Database*, available online at http://scdb.wustl.edu/index.php.

vote when they provided one of the five votes for a liberal outcome. Liberal justices are credited with a swing vote when they provided one of the five votes for a conservative outcome. In the latter scenario, obviously one or more of the usually conservative voters had also switched sides to become a liberal dissenter in the case and thereby created the need for the remaining conservative justices to attract one or more usually-liberal voters in order to produce a conservative outcome. The "switcher" who dissents is not credited with a swing vote because his or her vote did not determine the case outcome.

One of the interesting nuances revealed in Table 1.5 is that some of the Court's most consistent and outspoken conservatives, Scalia and Thomas, cast decisive votes for liberal outcomes in a number of close cases during the Rehnquist Court era. These cases happened to present issues that struck these text-oriented originalists as clearly calling for the vindication of a specific rights claim by an individual. By contrast, Chief Justice Rehnquist may have been a more outcome-driven conservative as he almost never cast a vote for a liberal outcome in a close criminal justice case. In that respect, he was perhaps the mirror-image of his ultra-liberal counterparts Brennan and Marshall, justices who only infrequently voted against individuals in criminal justice cases.

Rehnquist as Chief Justice

Chief justices can affect the direction a Court takes in both subtle and obvious ways through their roles that Danelski (1968) classically termed social leader and task leader. Collegiality on this small and rather isolated body might depend, in part, on how well the chief justice maintains the group's cohesion. As head administrator the chief justice might attempt to influence the size and content of the Court's docket. It is the chief justice, for instance, who prepares a preliminary list of cases considered to be worthy of discussion, as well as a list of cases that the chief justice believes should be declined summarily. Although the other justices may reject such guides, the opportunity to frame discussions represents a significant power vested in the chief justice. If he casts his vote with the majority, the chief justice's ability to assign who writes the Court's opinion is perhaps the most powerful tool available to the chief justice and one that has received substantial attention from scholars who study the judiciary.

As for Rehnquist specifically, many observers commented on his intellectual prowess and reputation as an effective opinion writer prior to his elevation to chief justice (Davis 1991). Later reviews of him as chief justice almost unfailingly applaud his administrative leadership and widely credit him for being "a well-liked leader" who facilitated the justices' "warm and easy rapport over the years, even though they grappled with the most divisive issues of the time" (Greenburg 2007, 17).

Federal judges appreciated how Rehnquist functioned as a staunch advocate for federal courts who spoke frequently to defend the independence of the judiciary and to criticize both the perceived low pay of federal judges and intrusive congressional oversight. He also actively sought to make the Court's workload more manageable, with apparent success. When Rehnquist first became the chief justice, the Court regularly decided about 150 cases each year with a slightly smaller number of written opinions. Toward the end of Rehnquist's tenure, the Court generated only about eighty written opinions per year. The mix of forces affecting the Court's docket makes it difficult to determine how much of this reduction can be credited to Rehnquist's leadership. However, it is notable that the Court reduced the number of cases it heard and decided at a time when petitions to the Court for review surged from 5,111 in 1986, the Rehnquist Court era's first term, to 8,584 in the era's final 2004 Term (Epstein et al. 2007, 74-75).

Rehnquist's effectiveness as a chief justice was especially notable in his even-handed distribution of the power and burden of writing the Court's opinion in those frequent instances when he was in the majority. Writing just after his elevation to chief justice, Rehnquist (1987, 297) offered insights into his approach to opinion assignment. He noted that he preferred to spread the good cases, assign others as the term progressed based on which justices were current on their other work, and give "everyone approximately the same number of assignments" during any given term. Indeed, Rehnquist distributed a fair share of majority opinions to each individual justice during his tenure as chief justice with two exceptions (Epstein et al. 2007, 652-54). Justice Stevens typically received fewer assignments, probably both because he was the justice least likely to agree with Rehnquist in many cases and because Stevens annually assigned a number of opinions to himself in those cases in which Rehnquist dissented and Stevens assumed the opinion-assigner role as senior justice in the majority. Justice Thomas also received fewer assignments in some years, perhaps because his interpretive approach was often distinctive, even when he agreed with the outcome supported by Rehnquist and the other conservatives.

While collegiality became a hallmark of the Rehnquist Court in part due to the chief justice's assignment practices, little evidence exists to suggest that Rehnquist highly valued consensus. That is, mutual respect did not engender broad agreement on the interpretation of law in a substantial number of cases. Making consensus building a low priority would be consistent with Rehnquist's willingness to dissent as an associate justice during the Burger Court era. It may also be true, however, that it was difficult to build consensus for many of the contentious issues that divided a Court that was split into distinctive wings based on the justices' typical voting patterns.

Conclusion

As indicated by the foregoing discussion, the outcomes produced by the Rehnquist Court were determined by the judicial philosophies, interactions, and votes of the individual justices who served from the 1986 Term through the 2004 Term. Although the Rehnquist Court generally produced conservative outcomes in criminal justice cases, there were many cases in which these outcomes merely represented a disinclination to expand the scope of rights or a move toward a modest diminution of rights established during the Warren Court era. The Rehnquist Court did not engage in a wholesale dismantling of rights in the criminal justice process, despite the expressed desires of some of its members to move in that direction. Although the Rehnquist Court preserved *Miranda* warnings, the exclusionary rule, right to counsel, and other legacies from the Warren Court's landmark decisions, liberal critics raise legitimate questions about whether the cumulative effect of the Rehnquist Court's conservative decisions was to dilute many of these rights and give them a symbolic quality that failed to provide needed, concrete protections for individuals (Smith 1997). Nearly every diminution of a constitutional right in the context of criminal justice carries with it a concomitant expansion of authority for police, prosecutors, and corrections officials. Thus the ultimate impact of the Rehnquist Court on criminal justice flows from the justices' roles in defining the rules, obligations, and protections that shape the treatment and fates of individuals drawn into the justice system.

References

Banks, Christopher P. "The Supreme Court and Precedent: An Analysis of Natural Courts and Reversal Trends." *Judicature* 75 (1992): 262-68.

Cray, Ed. *Chief Justice: A Biography of Earl Warren.* New York: Simon & Schuster, 1997.

Danelski, David. "The Influence of the Chief Justice in the Decisional Process of the Supreme Court." Pp. 147-60 in *The Federal Judicial System: Readings in Process and Behavior,* edited by Thomas P. Jahnige and Sheldon Goldman. New York: Holt, Rinehart and Winston, 1968.

Davis, Sue. "Justice William H. Rehnquist: Right-Wing Ideologue or Majoritarian Democrat?" Pp. 315-42 in *The Burger Court: Political and Judicial Profiles,* edited by Charles M. Lamb and Stephen C. Halpern. Urbana, IL: University of Illinois Press, 1991.

Eisler, Kim Isaac. *A Justice for All: William J. Brennan and the Decisions that Transformed America.* New York: Simon & Schuster, 1993.

Epstein, Lee, Jeffrey A. Segal, Harold J. Spaeth, and Thomas G. Walker. *The Supreme Court Compendium,* 4th edition. Washington, DC: CQ Press, 2007.

Greenburg, Jan Crawford. *Supreme Conflict: The Inside Story of the Struggle for Control of the United States Supreme Court.* New York: Penguin Press, 2007.

Greenhouse, Linda. *Becoming Justice Blackmun.* New York: Times Books, 2005.

Johnson, Scott P., and Christopher E. Smith. "David Souter's First Term on the Supreme Court: The Impact of a New Justice." *Judicature* 75 (1992): 238-43.

Maltz, Earl M., ed. *Rehnquist Justice: Understanding the Court Dynamic.* Lawrence, KS: University Press of Kansas, 2003.

Maveety, Nancy. *Queen's Court: Judicial Power in the Rehnquist Era.* Lawrence, KS: University Press of Kansas, 2008.

Rehnquist, William H. *The Supreme Court: How It Was, How It Is.* New York: William Morrow, 1987.

Schwartz, Herman. "Introduction." Pp. 13-22 in *The Rehnquist Court: Judicial Activism on the Right,* edited by Herman Schwartz. New York: Hill & Wang, 2002.

Segal, Jeffrey A., and Harold J. Spaeth. "Decisional Trends on the Warren and Burger Courts: Results from the Supreme Court Judicial Data Base Project." *Judicature* 73 (1989): 103-107.

Sickels, Robert Judd. *John Paul Stevens and the Constitution.* University Park, PA: Pennsylvania State University Press, 1988.

Smith, Christopher E. "Turning Rights Into Symbols: The U.S. Supreme Court and Criminal Justice." *Criminal Justice Policy Review* 8 (1997): 99-117.

———. "Criminal Justice and the 1998-99 United States Supreme Court Term." *Widener Journal of Public Law* 9 (1999): 23-59.

———. "Justice John Paul Stevens and Prisoners' Rights." *Temple Political and Civil Rights Law Review* 17 (2007): 83-107.

Smith, Christopher E., and Steven B. Dow. "Criminal Justice and the 2000-2001 U.S. Supreme Court Term." *University of Detroit Mercy Law Review* 79 (2002): 189-227.

Smith, Christopher E., and Thomas R. Hensley. "Assessing the Conservatism of the Rehnquist Court." *Judicature* 77 (1993): 83-89.

———. "Decision-Making Trends of the Rehnquist Court Era: Civil Rights and Liberties Cases. *Judicature* 89 (2005): 161-67.

Smith, Christopher E., Madhavi McCall, and Cynthia Perez McCluskey. *Law and Criminal Justice: Emerging Issues in the Twenty-First Century.* New York: Peter Lang, 2005.

Tushnet, Mark. *A Court Divided: The Rehnquist Court and the Future of Constitutional Law.* New York: Norton, 2005.

Cases Cited

Baze v. Rees, 553 U.S. 35 (2008)
Callins v. Collins, 510 U.S. 1141 (1994)
Mapp v. Ohio, 367 U.S. 643 (1961)
Miranda v. Arizona, 384 U.S. 436 (1966)
Roe v. Wade, 410 U.S. 113 (1973)

Chapter 2
William Brennan and Thurgood Marshall: The Mediator & the Absolutist

Lee Ruffin Wilson and Ashlyn Kuersten

Justices William Brennan and Thurgood Marshall comprised one of the most solid, liberal alliances in Supreme Court history. Born just two years apart, the two jurists took very different paths to arrive at the Supreme Court bench. Brennan was an Ivy League graduate who served most of his legal career in the judiciary. Conservative Republican President Eisenhower nominated him to the Court. Eleven years later, Marshall, a civil rights activist, was President Johnson's choice for the Supreme Court. Despite their apparent differences, Brennan, the son of immigrants, and Marshall, the great-grandson of slaves, enjoyed a professional and personal kinship. It is a testament to their mutual respect that Marshall's grandson was named after Brennan (Davis and Clark 1992). When Brennan retired in 1990, Marshall followed him into retirement the next year.

During their years on the Rehnquist Court, the justices regularly dissented from the Court's conservative holdings, particularly in criminal justice cases. However, despite the frequency with which the justices voted together and their shared legacies of liberal judicial activism, Brennan and Marshall were not simply two interchangeable liberal jurists. Their perspectives on criminal justice issues during the Rehnquist era often differed. For example, while both were against the death penalty, Brennan took a more nuanced view than Marshall's dogmatic opposition.

Brennan Biography

William J. Brennan, Jr. was born in 1906 to Irish immigrant parents in Newark, New Jersey, as the second of eight children. His father, who was not well-educated, helped organize a labor union and eventually became a labor leader and Commissioner of Public Safety for Newark. William, Jr. described his origins as "a family that had damned little in the way of wherewithal and a father and a mother who were determined that we would all have educations [even] if they starved" (Hoffman 1990, 21). After earning a degree in economics in 1928 from the Wharton School of the University of Pennsylvania and a degree at Harvard Law School in 1931, Brennan returned to New Jersey where he practiced labor law. During World War II, he was on the staff of the Department of Undersecretary of War, leaving the army as a colonel in 1945. In 1949, Brennan was appointed to New Jersey's Superior Court. After one year on the trial court, he was appointed to the Appellate Division of the Superior Court and, later, the New Jersey Supreme Court in 1952.

Brennan was not a particularly noteworthy state jurist, so many, including Brennan himself, were surprised when President Dwight Eisenhower nominated him in 1956 to replace Justice Sherman Minton on the U.S. Supreme Court. It was almost by happenstance that Brennan came to the attention of the Eisenhower Administration. While serving on the New Jersey Supreme Court, Brennan filled in for that court's chief justice, Arthur Vanderbilt, as a speaker at a Washington, D.C. conference. Herbert Brownell was among those impressed by Brennan's speech on overcrowded court dockets. Brownell was U.S. Attorney General, and when a vacancy arose on the Supreme Court shortly before the 1956 presidential election, Brownell suggested to President Eisenhower that Brennan was an ideal nominee for the Supreme Court seat.

The president was gun-shy about selecting a nominee. His previous choice was not working out as he planned. In fact, Eisenhower considered his appointment of then Chief Justice Earl Warren as one of the biggest mistakes of his administration. President Eisenhower "was rather unenthusiastic about using the courts to impose civil rights on the country" (Walpin 2003, 108). Earl Warren was a career Republican politician, but once seated on the Court he frequently joined his liberal Supreme Court colleagues in opinions broadening individual liberties and civil rights. Warren even authored the opinion in *Brown v. Board of Education of Topeka,* the 1954 decision that desegregated public schools.

Determined to be more successful with the selection of his nominee to replace Justice Minton, the president sought a candidate who met specific criteria. A number of factors made Brennan an appealing choice. Certainly, Eisenhower wanted to place a conservative jurist on the bench. In the wake of the Warren disappointment, Eisenhower said that in the future he would only appoint jurists with proven track records, such as those who had experience on lower federal courts or who had served as state jurists (Walpin 2003, 109). After hearing Brennan speak about judicial backlogs at the Washington conference, Brownell noted Brennan's apparent conservatism, particularly concerning criminal justice matters (Eisler 1993, 85), and recommended him to Eisenhower accordingly.

But Eisenhower was not only seeking to fill the Supreme Court vacancy. He was also campaigning for president and with the election only weeks away, he needed to show bipartisanship. Nominating Democrat Brennan would demonstrate his ability to work across party lines. He also needed to court the Catholic constituency, an increasingly important group for winning the presidency. And William Brennan was a Catholic. There had not been a Catholic on the Court since Justice Frank Murphy died in 1949. The Eisenhower Administration had reportedly confirmed Brennan's qualifications as a Catholic through communication with Cardinal Francis Spellman, a prominent Catholic, and Brennan's own priest (Eisler 1993). His Catholic credentials may have been as important as his judicial ones because Brennan was never asked a "single question about his politics or judicial philosophy" (Biskupic 1997).

After Brennan was identified as a conservative leaning Democratic Catholic with prior judicial experience, Eisenhower gave Brennan a recess appointment to the Supreme Court on October 16, 1956. During the confirmation process, Senator Joseph McCarthy attacked Brennan for what he felt was Brennan's hostility toward governmental efforts to investigate communism. Brennan was confirmed on March 17, 1957, without Senator McCarthy's vote (the only dissent). Nearly a decade later, Thurgood Marshall joined Justice Brennan on the Court.

Marshall Biography

Thurgood Marshall was the first descendant of slaves confirmed to the Supreme Court. His opinions throughout his twenty-four years on the Court demonstrated a constant concern for the "unempowered, the poor, minorities, those outside the mainstream" (Davis and Clark 1992, 7). But his humble beginnings did not portend such an illustrious future.

Marshall was born the second of two sons in 1908 to a railroad porter and a public school teacher in Maryland. His father did not have a formal education but was involved in public life (he served on a grand jury) and read the Constitution to his sons. During college at Lincoln University in Pennsylvania, the oldest black college in America, Marshall and his classmates regularly discussed why minorities "had to take" discrimination (Davis and Clark 1992, 44). At a movie theater, he and six of his colleagues refused the direction of the ushers to take the seats in "nigger heaven" (the balcony section) of the theater. Surprisingly, neither the police nor the theater owners did anything about the students' forced integration. Marshall would claim throughout his life that this event profoundly affected his belief in the efficacy of civil disobedience. Denied admittance into the whites-only University of Maryland Law School, he was accepted into Howard University Law School, a federally-funded public school that did not specify the race of its students. It was here that he began working with lawyers from the NAACP (National Association for the Advancement of Colored People) who used the school as a "legal laboratory" for planning strategy on civil rights cases (48). He also worked as a waiter, bellhop, and a baker to pay tuition. After graduating in 1933, he opened a small law practice in Baltimore but became so involved in local civil rights activities that he eventually became special counsel for the NAACP. He traveled throughout Maryland investigating lynchings and various discrimination issues, as well as staging civil disobedience acts like boycotts of stores to bring attention to inequalities in American society.

The NAACP had become increasingly involved in working toward racial equality. Race riots and lynchings inspired the NAACP and its attorneys to strategize to develop a long-range plan for combating limitations on race equality. One of the strategies developed was to utilize the judicial branch of government, instead of the other political branches, to get such laws overturned. Using the judiciary was simply less expensive. But successes in the judiciary were also ideally premised upon the best legal argument instead of strong political connections, something necessary in lobbying the political branches of government. The NAACP had more of the former than the latter so their strategy was to focus their attention on the judiciary in changing public policy.

Marshall's first major civil rights victory was in 1935 when he won a suit with his mentor and Howard professor, Charles Hamilton Houston, to integrate the University of Maryland's Law School (the school that had denied Marshall admittance because of his race in 1930). By 1944, only ten years after graduating from law school and now in charge of legal strategy for the NAACP, he successfully argued *Smith v. Allwright*, the Supreme Court case that declared unconstitutional the Democratic "white primary." In the following ten years he would successfully argue the 1948 case of *Shelley v. Kraemer* that struck down the legality of racially restrictive housing covenants and two integration cases that would lay the base for future discrimination in education cases.

These cases, however, were but a prelude for his crowning achievement of *Brown v. Board of Education of Topeka* (1954). By striking down all racial segregation in public schools, the Warren Court unanimously overturned the separate-but-equal doctrine in *Plessy v. Ferguson* (1896). Thurgood Marshall became known both to the public and within legal circles as an exceptional attorney because of his successes before the U.S. Supreme Court.

President Kennedy nominated Marshall to the Second Circuit of the U.S. Court of Appeals in 1961. During his tenure there he wrote 150 opinions and the Supreme Court did not reverse a single one of his ninety-eight majority decisions (Davis and Clark 1992, 13). In 1965 he became U.S. Solicitor General under President Johnson and continued his exceptional legal record, winning fourteen of the nineteen cases he argued before the Supreme Court. Many of these cases argued for compliance with the newly enacted Civil Rights Act of 1964. When President Johnson nominated him for the Supreme Court in 1967, Johnson said, "I believe it is the right thing to do, the right time to do it, the right man and the right place" (see Cohen 1999). Certainly the confirmation process of the first black justice was less conflictive than the confirmation of the second (Clarence Thomas) in 1991.

The Warren Era

The Warren Court handed down one historic decision after another, with groundbreaking and far-reaching impact unparalleled during any other Supreme

Court era. However, it was only after Brennan joined the Court that the majority of these revolutionary cases became law. According to one law professor,

> Some idea of what Justice Brennan achieved may be appreciated by consider-
> ing the state of constitutional law when he took his seat . . . At best, the Court
> had no clear direction . . . *Brown v. Board of Education*, just two years old, was
> unimplemented; the equal protection clause was a sleeping giant; free speech
> doctrine was partial and chaotic; criminal procedure was virtually the exclusive
> domain of state law; and the idea of using the Constitution to protect personal
> choice on matters such as contraception and abortion was utopian. (Dorsen
> 1990, 15)

When he arrived on the Warren Court, Brennan began to carve out his legacy as a liberal activist jurist. Brennan and Chief Justice Warren became judicial
allies, and Brennan was an integral player on the Warren Court. Brennan championed individual liberties and civil rights and advocated a broad interpretation
of the Constitution. Of the landmark decisions handed down after he joined the
Warren Court, Brennan said, "We were past the era of using the Constitution to
protect industry and the affluent. We started to get into the area of protecting
individual rights" (Hoffman 1990). Once again, President Eisenhower failed in
his efforts to put a conservative on the Supreme Court.

Brennan's contribution to the Warren Court extended beyond the opinions
he drafted in individual cases. Brennan was a consensus builder and he was often an integral part of Court decisions even when he did not write the majority
opinion (see Schwartz 1994, 219). Throughout his years on the Court, Brennan
used his charm and negotiating skills to first advance his liberal activism, and
then later, during the Burger and Rehnquist eras, to protect the precedents made
by the Warren Court. During his early years on the Supreme Court, Brennan was
an "accomodationist," mediating between "two groups: the absolutists [Black
and Douglas] and the conservatists [Clark and Stewart]" (Coltharp 1997, 35).
This "unmatched ability" (Biskupic 1997) proved useful to Chief Justice Warren, who needed Brennan to build support among the Court's members for Warren's activist expansion of personal liberties and civil rights. To construct majorities, a justice must have a talent for persuasion, but he must also be able to
compromise and create decisions that can reconcile the opposing views of justices such as the liberals Warren, Black, and Douglas, with their more conservative brethren. Brennan often accomplished this balance by writing "opinions
relying on relatively narrow, sometimes technical grounds, gathering a majority
for the disposition of cases when . . . 'the Court seemed hopelessly split into
minor fragments'" (Panel Discussion 1999: Patricia Wald at 29 citing Hopkins).
The compromises Brennan and his liberal colleagues made during these years
were not concessions, but part of Brennan's vision "to plot the path he felt the
law must take and to follow through with a series of opinions that served as
stepping stones toward his ultimate destination" (29).

Several years after the Warren Court decided *Brown v. School Board of Education of Topeka*, the Court heard *Cooper et al. v. Aaron et al.* (1958), wherein the school board and superintendent of a Little Rock school district alleged that Arkansas's governor and state legislature were obstructing efforts to integrate the district's public schools. The Court took the position that the states must obey the Supreme Court's rulings regarding desegregation of public schools. Although the opinion was per curiam, Justice Brennan played "a significant role" (Coltharp 1997, 20) in the decision and is "considered the primary writer" (Biskupic 1997). The opinion cited *Marbury v. Madison* and reiterated that the historic case "declared the basic principle that the federal judiciary is supreme in the exposition of the law of the Constitution" (*Cooper et al. v. Aaron et al.,* 18). While the states bear the primary responsibility for providing public education, the Fourteenth Amendment prohibits "[s]tate support of segregated schools through any arrangement" and applies to the "right of a student not to be segregated on racial grounds" (19). The opinion goes on to volunteer that the three justices who joined the Court since *Brown*, including Brennan, reaffirmed that holding (19). Even though he was not a member of the Court at the time, Thurgood Marshall also played a role in the *Cooper* decision. He represented the African American children who sought to attend the previously all-white high school.

Justice Brennan authored a critical voting rights decision in 1962, in an opinion that demonstrates Brennan's judicial activism and "his abandonment of the restraint canon" (Schwartz 1994, 217). Determining that the federal courts could review challenges to the state legislative district apportionments, the opinion overruled precedent. Brennan's handling of the case "illustrates [his] role as an architect of constitutional jurisprudence and his uncanny ability to tie together a fractured Court" (Panel Discussion 1999: Patricia Wald, 30). Chief Justice Warren described the case as the most important of his time on the Supreme Court (see Schwartz 1994, 218; Biskupic 1997) and assigned Brennan to write the Court's opinion. The majority was not firmly unified, and Brennan used his mediating skills to help sway Justice Stewart and "to write an opinion that pushed the envelope just to the point of what his fellow Justices would accept" (Panel Discussion 1999: Patricia Wald, 33).

Griswold v. Connecticut (1965) is one case in which Brennan laid the foundation for later, more far-reaching holdings before Marshall joined him on the Supreme Court bench. Although Justice Douglas authored *Griswold*, a case that struck down a Connecticut law prohibiting the sale of contraceptives, even to married persons, Brennan supplied the rationale Douglas used in the opinion. While Douglas originally wrote that the statute was unconstitutional because the First Amendment right of association extends to marriage, Brennan proposed the Court resolve the controversy by holding "that a right of privacy could be inferred from the Bill of Rights' specific guarantees" (Schwartz 1994, 219). The right to privacy approach Brennan orchestrated in *Griswold* was expanded in numerous subsequent Supreme Court decisions, including the controversial contraception and abortion cases with which the Burger Court would eventually wrestle (see *Eisendstadt v. Baird* 1972 and *Roe v. Wade* 1973).

The impact of the Warren Court and Justice Brennan on the status of civil rights and individual liberties cannot be overstated. However, in criminal law matters, the liberal-leaning Warren Court "virtually created the field of constitutional criminal justice" (Cole 2000). Justice Brennan, and later Justice Marshall, contributed to the creation of the revolutionary criminal law doctrines, many of which are still relied upon in the criminal justice system and some of which have become part of popular culture (see, for example, *Miranda v. Arizona* 1966).

The Warren Court expanded the application of the Bill of Rights to state criminal defendants and issued rulings that broadly interpreted those rights (see Dorsen 1990, 16 and Cole 2000). Between 1961 and Chief Justice Warren's retirement in 1969, the Supreme Court held that the exclusionary rule for evidence found in violation of the Fourth Amendment also applies to state criminal proceedings (*Mapp v. Ohio* 1961); the Sixth and Fourteenth Amendments require states to provide counsel for poor criminal defendants (*Gideon v. Wainwright* 1963); incriminatory statements elicited by a government agent in the absence of the defendant's attorney deny the defendant his Sixth Amendment right to counsel (*Massiah v. United States* 1964); an accused's statements were inadmissible where the suspect was not read his rights and was denied his request to consult with his attorney during police interrogation (*Escobedo v. Illinois* 1964); and, in *Miranda v. Arizona* (1966), the Court set guidelines for police conduct in the arrest and interrogation of criminal suspects to safeguard the Fifth Amendment right against self-incrimination.

Thurgood Marshall proved to be Brennan's greatest ally during their two years together on the Warren Court. When Thurgood Marshall joined the Supreme Court, Brennan had already been on the Court for over a decade. Before Chief Justice Warren stepped down in 1969, Marshall participated in many of the opinions that created a new approach to criminal jurisprudence. Both Brennan and Marshall supported the Court's decision in the landmark stop and frisk case *Terry v. Ohio* (1968), wherein Chief Justice Warren wrote that a gun discovered on the defendant's person was admissible evidence even though the police officer lacked probable cause to arrest the defendant at the time of the warrantless pat-down. Under specific circumstances, it was reasonable for a police officer to ascertain the presence of weapons.

Marshall's votes during his two years on the Warren Court coalesced with the liberal block of Warren, Black, Douglas, Fortas, and Brennan. This bloc continually emphasized the rights of the accused. In *Barber v. Page* (1968), for example, Marshall wrote the opinion that supported the right of suspects to confront their accusers in preliminary hearings. "The right to confrontation," he wrote, "is basically a trial right" (725).

The Warren Court issued opinions in both civil law and criminal procedure that substantially broadened the rights of individuals under the Constitution. As was the case in *Terry* and *Miranda*, much of the criminal law produced by Chief Justice Warren and his Court concerned the routine interactions of the police with members of the public. The Warren Court steered our criminal justice system toward a broad application of the U.S. Constitution to state criminal procedures. When Warren stepped down in 1969, he left behind liberals Brennan and Marshall on the Court, with the hope that they would continue to build on his legacy.

Burger Years

President Johnson accepted Chief Justice Warren's resignation in 1968 and quickly nominated Associate Justice Abe Fortas to become the new chief justice. After conflict of interest charges were brought against Fortas, he withdrew his name from consideration for chief justice. When Johnson declined to seek a second term and Nixon became president, he began his search for chief justice and chose Burger, who was confirmed in 1969. Nixon had made campaign promises to reverse the leftist direction of the Warren Court by appointing strict constructionists to the Court. Moreover, the Nixon Justice Department was investigating the Court's remaining liberals, hoping to find something to use in impeachment proceedings or to force resignations. Justices Douglas and Fortas came under fire, as did Brennan for a fifteen-thousand dollar real estate investment he had made with several other judges around the country. Because of these investigations, Fortas would eventually resign to prevent possible impeachment proceedings, giving Nixon an extra opening on the Court.

Chief Justice Warren Burger was highly critical of the Warren Court's judicial activism. The Warren Court sought to utilize the government to fix social problems and protect the individual rights of the poor, women, racial minorities, and criminal defendants. When Burger assumed leadership of the Supreme Court, it seemed evident that Burger would disturb the constitutional doctrine Brennan and Marshall helped to create under Chief Justice Warren (Mikva 1988, 815). Despite these predictions, the Burger Court never produced a successful counterrevolution to the expansion of individual liberties and constitutional rights established by the Court during the 1960s. In matters of criminal jurisprudence, the Burger Court issued opinions that occasionally limited and sometimes even expanded decisions handed down by the Warren Court. In the end, during Burger's reign, the Court never managed to make a complete pull to the right (see Alschuler 1987, 1441).

There are many explanations for why the wholesale reversal of the Warren era criminal jurisprudence never occurred. There are those who cite Burger's apparent lack of the leadership and personal skills necessary to guide such an undertaking. Burger "proved singularly incapable of leading the [C]ourt" (Newton 2007) and was "known for long harangues and a less-than-fair approach to assigning opinions" (Taylor 2005). The Burger Court's opinions and their many "anomalies and thin distinctions suggest the Burger Court's reluctance or inability to chart a clean course" (Alschuler 1987, 1441). It is possible that while

Burger and other justices on the Court disagreed with precedent set during the Warren Court era, the conservatives on the Burger Court were limited in their ability to reverse those offensive decisions because they felt obligated to adhere to stare decisis (1452-53). As one writer notes, "The practice of limiting earlier decisions to their facts and of restricting disfavored precedents in arbitrary and disingenuous ways has a venerable history, and some justices may have regarded the limitation [of precedent] by fiat as less destructive of the rule of law than forthright abandonment of disfavored decisions" (1452).

Certainly, the temperament of the members of the Court complicated any attempts by Burger and his conservative colleagues to reverse Warren Court criminal procedure doctrine. In its early years, the Burger Court consisted mostly of members from the Warren era, including liberals Hugo Black, William Douglas, William Brennan, and Thurgood Marshall. Over the course of the Burger years, original members of the Warren Court retired and were replaced by justices nominated by Republican Presidents Richard Nixon, Gerald Ford, and Ronald Reagan. In 1972 four members of the Burger Court were Nixon appointees. For a time, Brennan, who was once the "dominant intellectual figure in the new liberal majority . . . continu[ed] to muster majority support despite the Court's move to the right" (Panel Discussion 1999: Horwitz, 15). Brennan was often able to use his coalition-building skills to protect the Warren Court legacy. In 1984, one scholar "suspect[ed] that when the history of the 1970s is written, it will reveal that Brennan's skills contributed as much as anything to the absence of a counterrevolution" (Tushnet 1984, 1263; see also Newton 2007). To the extent the Warren legacy remained undisturbed by the Burger Court, it is due to "the subtle, effective leadership of . . . [Justice Brennan], who guided the [C]ourt's dwindling liberal bloc to influence well beyond its votes and solidified the work of the Warren Court into a set of accepted norms of American life" (Newton 2007).

During the Burger era, Brennan employed several techniques to protect the legacy of the Warren Court. He used "his negotiating skills to bring the shifting middle of the court . . . closer to the liberal corner" (Serrill 1985). When it became harder for Brennan to gain enough support for a liberal majority, he "cajole[d] the conservative opinion writer . . . to limit the damage to a liberal precedent" (Serrill). After Brennan became the most senior member of the Court, in conference he was able to present his thoughts on a case immediately following Chief Justice Burger. When given the opportunity to designate the opinion's writer, Brennan often "select[ed] a justice who occupied the middle ground" (Serrill). And of course, fellow liberal Thurgood Marshall was an almost constant ally.

While serving on the Burger Court, Brennan and Marshall experienced both frustrations and successes in their efforts to advance (or even just defend) their criminal justice doctrines. However, when it came to the controversial institution of the death penalty, Justices Brennan and Marshall saw complete success (*Furman v. Georgia* 1972), followed by abject failure (*Gregg v. Georgia* 1976). In 1972, in a 5-4 decision, the Supreme Court found the death penalty unconstitutional. Justices Brennan and Marshall were firmly opposed to the death penalty. Brennan worked to put together a majority, writing a draft opinion that "did not go as far as Marshall would have liked, but it was crafted to appeal to the moderates in its conclusion" (Newton 2007). Although won by a narrow margin, the decision to strike down the death penalty was a victory for Brennan and Marshall, particularly since they often found themselves in the minority by that time. Then in 1976 they found themselves in the minority in another death penalty case (*Gregg v. Georgia*). The liberal allies could not prevent the conservative members of the Burger Court from reinstating the death penalty.

The *Gregg* decision demonstrated that judicial activists Brennan and Marshall were losing their ability to gain the votes necessary to create a liberal majority. Increasingly, Justice Rehnquist and his conservative leaning colleagues pulled the Court to the right on many issues, including criminal justice issues. As Chief Justice Burger neared retirement, Brennan and Marshall more frequently dissented from the Court's holdings. The country embraced conservative Republicans Ronald Reagan and George Bush throughout the 1980s, and the Court seemed to follow the conservative mainstream. In 1986, halfway through his second term in office, President Reagan appointed conservative William Rehnquist as chief justice.

Brennan and Marshall's Roles in Criminal Justice Jurisprudence during the Rehnquist Years

During the Burger Court years Brennan and Marshall often managed to hold the liberal ground gained during the Warren Court era. However, Rehnquist's ascension to the position of Chief Justice of the United States in 1986 changed that. The judicial careers of Brennan and Marshall were winding down. Both justices would retire from the Supreme Court within five years of Rehnquist's promotion to chief. Judicial appointments by four Republican presidents (Nixon, Ford, Reagan, and Bush) gradually replaced retiring liberals with conservatives and by the end of the Reagan Administration, only Brennan and Marshall remained as the Court's liberal bloc. The promotion of Rehnquist to chief justice created a vacancy among the associate justices that Reagan filled with the appointment of Justice Antonin Scalia, a staunch conservative. Marshall and Brennan found themselves facing six presumed conservative justices—Rehnquist, White, Blackmun, Powell, Stevens, O'Connor, and Scalia. As the Rehnquist Court continued to move to the right and undo the liberties protected by the Warren Court, Brennan and Marshall were increasingly in the minority.

Rehnquist's appointment certainly tilted the Court toward the right. The new chief justice was critical of the Warren Court's expansion of the protections afforded those accused of crimes. The year before he became chief justice, Rehnquist reported that when he arrived on the Supreme Court, he "felt that my job was . . . to kind of lean the other way" to bring "a halt to . . . the sweeping rulings that were made in the days of the Warren Court" (quoted in Schwartz 1994, 248). In 1986, when he became chief justice, just three members of the Warren Court remained, including Justice Byron White, a more conservative justice than Brennan and Marshall. Most of the Court's members had not participated in the pivotal cases of the liberal Warren Court, and many had no interest in preserving its legacy. Rather than maintaining the Warren Court's broad application of the Constitution to criminal procedure, the Rehnquist Court promised to reverse the Warren Court's history of protecting criminal defendants. Perhaps then more than ever, Brennan and Marshall were likely to be the only votes dissenting from a pro-prosecution Court holding.

Marshall responded to his change in status in characteristic fashion. He described Reagan as the "worst president in my lifetime," a president who had done "zero for civil rights" because on the "racial issue you can't be a little bit wrong anymore than you can be a little bit pregnant or a little bit dead." But "don't worry," he told reporters, "I am going to outlive those bastards" (Davis and Clark 1992, 5). Justices Brennan and Marshall waged a surprisingly effective tug-of-war with the Court's conservatives. While Chief Justice Rehnquist and his conservative brethren, such as Justices Thomas and Scalia, ultimately undermined some of the Warren Court's criminal justice doctrines, the influence of Brennan and Marshall slowed the Court's shift toward conservatism. Despite the Court's shift to the right and the frequency with which they comprised the Court's minority vote, Justices Brennan and Marshall remained as vocal as ever, if not as successful.

One of the most basic issues on which Brennan and Marshall agreed was the conflict involving rights guaranteed by the Fourth Amendment. In *National Treasury Employees Union v. Von Raab* (1989) the U.S. Customs Service required a urinalysis test (in the absence of probable cause) for employees seeking transfers or promotions if their positions involved them in drug enforcement, carrying a firearm, or handling classified material. The majority opinion upheld the warrantless drug testing programs, claiming that mandating warrants would divert "valuable resources." Further, drug tests served a "vaiid public interest" and the test for constitutionality was whether the practice (e.g., the drug test without a warrant) was a reasonable one. Marshall and Brennan dissented but more importantly, they attacked the Court's deference to governmental authority. The Fourth Amendment expressly requires that searches of citizens must be based on probable cause, not unprincipled government authority. In a subsequent decision, *Skinner v. Railway Labor Executives' Association* (1989), a similar case involving mandatory blood and urine tests of all employees, the Marshall-Brennan duo blasted the majority for allowing such searches simply because requiring probable cause was "impracticable." In other words, as they noted, principles were more important than urgency: "History teaches that grave threats to liberty often come in times of urgency, when constitutional rights seem too extravagant to endure" (*Skinner* 1989, 635).

When it came to the disintegration of the *Miranda* protections developed during the Warren Court era, Marshall and Brennan were even more caustic and troubled by the direction of the Rehnquist Court. Rehnquist authored *Duckworth v. Eagan* (1989) that severely limited the application of *Miranda*. Brennan and Marshall dissented with Justice Marshall penning the dissent. In *Duckworth*, the police advised a murder suspect in part "[w]e have no way of giving you a lawyer, but one will be appointed for you, if you wish, if and when you go to court" (198). The majority found that the police "touched all of the bases required by *Miranda*" (203), noting that the Court "never insisted that *Miranda* warnings be given in the exact form described in that decision" (202). In his dissent, Marshall said that the Court was "seriously mischaracterizing" *Miranda* declaring, "I refuse to acquiesce in the continuing debasement of this historic precedent" (*Duckworth* at 214). While *Miranda* did not require police to use specific language to advise a defendant of his right to appointed counsel, Marshall believed that the police should give *Miranda* warnings in a "straightforward fashion" (220), and reminded the present Court of the origins of the *Miranda* doctrine. In *Miranda*, "the Court, speaking through Chief Justice Warren, emphasized repeatedly that the offer of appointed counsel must be 'effective and express.'" (*Duckworth* at 215, citations omitted). Justice Marshall further criticized the *Duckworth* majority for an analysis that "wholly overlooked . . . that the recipients of police warnings are often frightened suspects unlettered in the law, not lawyers or judges or others schooled in interpreting legal or semantic nuance" (216).

Brennan and Marshall were both liberals and judicial activists under almost any definition of the terms. Both justices disagreed with the Rehnquist Court vehemently. However, each justice had a distinctive approach to matters of criminal justice. Both were concerned with the treatment of individuals in the judicial system, but Brennan's philosophy differed from Marshall's more rational approach. Emotion and idealistic notions drove Brennan more than Marshall. Brennan believed that the administration of justice could and should include "qualities other than reason" (Schwartz 1994, 229). To be effective, a judge "reflects upon the values and ideals underlying the legal system, seeks to understand what those ideals require in the practical world" (229-30). Justice Marshall had a more practical view of the criminal justice system. As a Supreme Court justice with a background representing criminal defendants, Marshall had a unique understanding of how the criminal justice system operated at lower levels. His Court opinions reflected an awareness of the nature of the most frequent interactions between police and citizens, including the experience of suspects during investigation and defendants at trial. Marshall spent much of his career combating the effects of racial disparity, and although Brennan did not share this experience, both justices wrote opinions voicing their concern about past and ongoing racial discrimination in America.

For example, in *Ford v. Wainwright* (1986), a majority decision written by Marshall and joined by Brennan, Blackmun, Powell, and Stevens, the Court held that insane death row inmates cannot be executed without violating the principles of the Eighth Amendment's prohibition on cruel and unusual punishments. Marshall argued toward the end of his career that Chief Justice Rehnquist's opinions in criminal justice cases were "incontrovertible evidence of Rehnquist's insensitivity to the problems encountered by members of disadvantaged groups in American society" (Davis 1989, 62). Whereas the Rehnquist Court showed the upmost deference to local police and prosecutors, Marshall argued that the principles embedded in the Constitution were always more important than the needs, costs, or difficulties faced by the government. In following principles, Brennan believed that treating defendants differently than other citizens was just wrong.

While Brennan believed that the Constitution was a "living" document, Marshall took a more textual approach to constitutional interpretation. Moreover, Marshall did not share Brennan's willingness or talent for compromise. The justices usually voted together, and when they wrote separate opinions, it was often because Marshall took a more absolutist approach than Brennan did. Regardless of their occasional philosophical differences, Brennan and Marshall comprised a formidable liberal alliance that worked to extend the longevity of the Warren Court era's criminal jurisprudence in both death penalty law and other criminal matters.

Months after Rehnquist became chief justice, the *New York Times* declared that Justice Brennan was running the Court (Taylor 1987). In the term's five major opinions at that point, Rehnquist was in the minority in each case. When the chief justice is in the minority, the senior majority justice assigns the majority opinion. Thus "[i]t is Justice William J. Brennan Jr., the Court's senior liberal, who has been in charge so far" (Taylor). Of course, this eventually changed, as evidenced by a comparison of Brennan's dissents during the Rehnquist Court against those he made while on the Warren Court. Whereas Justice Brennan cast just three dissenting votes while serving on the Warren Court's 1968 Term, he cast sixty-two dissenting votes in the 1988 Term under Chief Justice Rehnquist (Dorsen 1990, n. 17). In 1968, Brennan filed one dissenting opinion, but filed eighteen dissenting opinions in the 1988 Term. Marshall's record was not much different. At a press conference subsequent to announcing his retirement from the Court, Justice Marshall claimed he only hired clerks who enjoyed working on dissents (Mello 1995, 593, citing Lewis).

Search and Seizure

The exclusionary rule prevents admission into evidence of material gathered by the police in violation of the Fourth Amendment's Warrant Clause. In the 1980s, "conservative hostility to the exclusionary rule" (Dripps 1990, 630) grew in step with the country's so-called "war on drugs." Under Rehnquist, the Supreme Court "significantly narrowed the application of the exclusionary rule and accepted many of the reforms sought by the Reagan Administration" (Clayton and Pickerill 2006, 1417). In search and seizure cases decided by the Warren Court, 59 percent of the rulings favored criminal defendants. During the years Rehnquist was chief justice, the Court decided against the defendants in 78 percent of its search and seizure rulings (1415). Justices Brennan and Marshall did not embrace the Rehnquist Court's Fourth Amendment jurisprudence and in their last years on the bench, the two justices frequently voted in the Court's minority. Often one drafted a dissent that his ally joined.

In *Colorado v. Bertine* (1987), the Supreme Court held that the warrantless inventory search of closed containers in a vehicle impounded by police subsequent to an arrest did not violate the Fourth Amendment. In response to an opinion written by the chief justice, Justice Marshall wrote a dissent in which he distinguished the facts at hand from precedent, noting that the search at issue "cannot legitimately be labeled an inventory" (377). Months later, Brennan and Marshall again found themselves dissenting from a 7-2 search and seizure decision (*United States v. Dunn* 1987). In *Dunn*, Justice Brennan spoke for the two liberal justices. The majority found that the warrantless search of a barn in proximity to a house did not violate the defendant's reasonable expectation of privacy because the barn was outside the home's curtilage and, in any event, the police only peered into (as opposed to entering) the barn. However, Brennan and Marshall believed that the barn was part of the home's curtilage and therefore the police violated the defendant's reasonable expectation of privacy.

California v. Greenwood (1988) was yet another case that "demonstrate[d] the Court's current posture toward privacy interests outside the home" (Herdrich 1989, 994). Once again, the majority of the Court decided in favor of upholding a warrantless search conducted by police. The majority "formulated a new interpretation of privacy by disregarding case law" (1017) and found that the criminal defendant did not enjoy a reasonable expectation of privacy in garbage left for collection on the street outside the home. In a dissent joined by Justice Marshall, Justice Brennan criticized the Court's logic and suggested that the Court's reasoning was disharmonious with American society. "Scrutiny of another's trash is contrary to commonly accepted notions of civilized behavior. I suspect, therefore, that members of our society will be shocked to learn that the Court, the ultimate guarantor of liberty, deems unreasonable our expectation that the aspects of our private lives that are concealed safely in a trash bag will not become public" (*California v. Greenwood* 1988, 45-46). Brennan reminded his colleagues that "[s]o far as Fourth Amendment protection is concerned, opaque plastic bags are every bit as worthy as" other containers and "deserved no less protection," even when used to discard trash (48-49).

Aerial surveillance of a greenhouse within a home's curtilage was at issue in *Florida v. Riley* (1989). While the Court once again upheld a warrantless search, the decision was by a narrower margin. Both Justices Marshall and Stevens joined Brennan's dissent and Justice Blackmun filed his own dissent. The more conservative members of the Court found that the criminal defendant did not have a reasonable expectation of privacy from observation by a government helicopter flying lawfully over the defendant's yard, but Brennan wrote that the aerial surveillance constituted a Fourth Amendment search requiring a warrant. Brennan reminded the Court that the relevant consideration was the defendant's expectation of privacy. It was not enough that the police helicopter flew at a lawful altitude: "Under the plurality's exceedingly grudging Fourth Amendment theory, the expectation of privacy is defeated if a single member of the public could conceivably position himself to see into the area in question without doing anything illegal" (457). The Court should have determined "not whether the police were where they had a right to be, but whether public observation . . . was so commonplace that Riley's expectation of privacy in his backyard could not be considered reasonable" (460). Brennan, who would retire the following year, continued, "[O]ne wonders what the plurality believes the purpose of the Fourth Amendment to be" (461). Justice Brennan suggested that the rising war on drugs might have influenced the Court's decision in *Florida v. Riley* (463), noting,

> It is difficult to avoid the conclusion that the plurality has allowed its analysis of Riley's expectation of privacy to be colored by its distaste for the activity in which he was engaged. It is indeed easy to forget, especially in view of current concern over drug trafficking, that the scope of the Fourth Amendment's protection does not turn on whether the activity . . . is illegal or innocuous.

Justice Marshall also referenced the "war on drugs" in the dissenting opinion he drafted in a case in which the Court considered warrantless police sweeps of public buses (*Florida v. Bostick* 1991). In *Bostick*, armed police officers boarded a bus and asked permission to search some passengers' luggage. Bostick, a passenger on the bus, moved to suppress as evidence the cocaine found in his luggage. The Supreme Court considered whether a Fourth Amendment seizure took place. Justice O'Connor, writing for the majority, said a seizure does not occur when "a reasonable person would feel free to 'disregard the police and go about his business'" (434, quoting *California v. Hodari* 1991). O'Connor noted that if the defendant did not feel free to leave the bus, it was because the bus on which he rode was scheduled to depart, and any feeling of confinement by the defendant "says nothing about whether or not the police conduct at issue was coercive" (*Florida v. Bostick*, 436). The majority remanded the case for further determination of whether a seizure took place, while Marshall was incredulous that "[t]he majority suggests that this latest tactic in the drug war is perfectly compatible with the Constitution" (444). Despite the majority's assertions, Justice Marshall "had his own views of how real people . . . will understand the encounter with the police" (Green and Richman 1994, 376) and thought the police should advise citizens of their right to refuse consent. Marshall was also concerned that bus sweeps like that in *Bostick* "had a particular impact on minority travelers" because police officers looking for drugs targeted "minority groups in disproportionate numbers" (381).

Marshall's own professional experience with the criminal justice system convinced him that the police conduct in *Bostick* would have a coercive effect on bus passengers and such warrantless sweeps should not be part of the "government's drug-war arsenal" (*Florida v. Bostick*, 450). Justice Marshall's argument was similar to that made by Justice Brennan in a dissenting opinion regarding the constitutionality of sobriety checkpoints. Despite a legitimate governmental interest (such as curtailing drug trafficking or preventing drunk driving), "consensus that a particular law enforcement technique serves a laudable purpose has never been the touchstone of constitutional analysis" (*Michigan v. Sitz* 1990, 459). As the Rehnquist Court grew increasingly supportive of the government's crime-fighting tactics and the politicians' "tough on crime" measures, Justices Brennan and Marshall remained true to the search and seizure principles that developed under the Warren Court.

Miranda Rights

Not surprisingly, during the years Rehnquist was chief justice, the Court issued decisions that served to narrow the scope of criminal defendants' *Miranda* rights. Although the Court "stopped short of overruling *Miranda*," in many ways "the Court has moved toward dealing *Miranda* the death of a thousand cuts" (Clayton and Pickerill 2006, 1417). Justices Brennan and Marshall frequently dissented from opinions in which the Court limited the government's obligation to warn criminal defendants of their *Miranda* rights. The opinions issued by Justices Brennan and Marshall in the *Miranda* line of cases were representative of their philosophies in other areas of criminal jurisprudence. Both justices generally tended to favor restraining police conduct in criminal investigations. Justice Brennan felt that the right to remain silent "require[d] vigilant protection if we are to safeguard the values of private conscience and human dignity" (*Colorado v. Connelly* 1986, 176). The less idealistic Justice Marshall often voiced his concerns in a more practical approach. He was ever mindful of the real life circumstances under which most criminal defendants found themselves when dealing with police investigations.

In *Colorado v. Connelly* (1986), the Court found that despite a criminal defendant's mental illness, the defendant's waiver of *Miranda* rights was valid. In the absence of police coercion, the confession was voluntary and therefore admissible at trial. The opinion authored by Chief Justice Rehnquist made the broad pronouncement that "coercive police activity is a necessary predicate to the finding that a confession is not 'voluntary' within the meaning of the Due Process Clause of the Fourteenth Amendment" (167). Justice Marshall joined Justice Brennan's dissent in arguing that to determine the voluntariness of a confession, the Court should consider "the totality of the circumstances surrounding the confession" rather than just "[t]he absence of police wrongdoing" (176). The Court's decision, according to Brennan, "abandons precedent" (179) and "redefines voluntary confessions" (181).

Justices Brennan and Marshall were not always of like minds in deciding criminal justice cases during the Rehnquist Court. In some *Miranda* cases, for example, Marshall dissented while Brennan voted to uphold the admissibility of a confession (see *Illinois v. Perkins* 1990). In *Pennsylvania v. Bruder* (1988), Brennan joined the Court in a per curiam opinion from which Marshall dissented. The Court found that statements made by the defendant at a traffic stop prior to receiving *Miranda* warnings were admissible because ordinary traffic stops do not involve custodial situations that require *Miranda* warnings.

Jury Selection and Race Discrimination

Shortly before Rehnquist became chief justice, the Burger Court decided *Batson v. Kentucky* (1986), a case involving the use of peremptory challenges in jury selection in a racially discriminatory manner. The majority, including Brennan and Marshall, held that when a prosecutor used peremptory challenges to strike all black venire persons, the black criminal defendant could allege an equal protection violation. Chief Justice Burger dissented, and as the senior member of the majority, Brennan did not assign his friend Marshall to write the opinion. Most likely, Brennan, the consensus builder and mediator, knew that Marshall would not write an opinion that the majority of the Court could endorse. Marshall was an absolutist who believed that the only way to end racial discrimination in jury selection was to eliminate peremptory challenges. Brennan did not seem to share Marshall's absolutist position regarding peremptory challenges. Although Brennan joined the *Batson* majority, Brennan did not join Marshall's concurring opinion. Marshall joined the opinion authored by Justice Powell, even calling the ruling "a historic step toward eliminating [a] shameful practice," but he also wrote a separate concurring opinion (*Batson*, 102).

In his *Batson* concurrence, Marshall advocated the elimination of peremptory challenges. To support his position, Marshall described the history of racial discrimination in jury selection, citing statistics documenting the exclusion of blacks from juries (see Anderson 1998, 359). Marshall frequently used history and scientific studies to demonstrate the existence of racial discrimination in the judicial system, particularly in criminal justice cases, including death penalty convictions. As repeatedly seen in his decisions, Marshall's career experiences in the criminal justice system colored his view of how the justice system operated at the lower court levels. Marshall's concurring opinion in *Batson* also reflected his own involvement working in the criminal justice system. He worried that under the *Batson* standard "[p]rosecutors are left free to discriminate against blacks in jury selection provided that they hold that discrimination to an 'acceptable' level" (*Batson v. Kentucky* 1986, 105). Nor did he "share the Court's faith that trial judges could protect this [constitutional] right through ad hoc inquiries into prosecutorial motivations" (Green and Richman 1994, 398).

After *Batson*, Brennan and Marshall participated in several major peremptory challenge decisions handed down under the Rehnquist Court. In *Griffith v. Kentucky* (1987), both justices joined Blackmun's majority opinion voting to expand the application of *Batson* to criminal litigation still under review or not yet final at the time of the *Batson* decision. Although they were in the majority in *Griffith*, a few years later Brennan and Marshall found themselves in the minority when the Rehnquist Court decided another case involving race-based peremptory challenges. The ultraconservative Justice Scalia authored the Court's ruling in *Holland v. Illinois* (1990). A white criminal defendant appealed his conviction after a prosecutor struck black venire members from the jury pool. The Illinois Supreme Court found that the state's use of its peremptory challenges to exclude the black jury members violated neither the defendant's Fourteenth Amendment Equal Protection rights nor his Sixth Amendment right to an impartial jury. In his appeal to the United States Supreme Court, Holland pursued a Sixth Amendment argument but not the Equal Protection claim. Scalia, writing for the Court's conservatives and moderates, held that while a white defendant had standing to challenge the exclusion of all black venire persons, the prosecutor's use of peremptory challenges in that manner did not violate the defendant's Sixth Amendment rights.

Marshall wrote in response that "the majority has so little understanding of our Sixth Amendment jurisprudence" (*Holland v. Illinois,* 504, n. 2). He authored a dissent in which he thoroughly and passionately criticized the majority's logic and its conclusion. Justices Brennan and Blackmun, Marshall's frequent liberal allies, joined his dissent. Marshall's dissent in *Holland,* unlike his opinion in *Batson,* did not call for the elimination of the doctrine of peremptory challenges. However, he still argued forcefully that the prosecutor's conduct violated Holland's Sixth Amendment rights. Again, Marshall "pressed for more constitutional protection against peremptory challenges" (Anderson 1998, 364). The language Marshall used in *Holland* shows his increasing alienation from his brethren on the Rehnquist Court. Marshall says of Scalia's opinion, "[e]ach step in the majority's logic is plain fallacious" and "glosses over not only a few, but quite literally *every single* fair-cross-section case" previously decided by the Court (*Holland v. Illinois* 1990, 500-501). "To reach this startling result," Marshall claimed, "the majority misrepresents the values underlying the fair-cross-section requirement, overstates the difficulties associated with the elimination of racial discrimination in jury selection, and ignores the clear import of well-grounded precedents" (490). In Marshall's view, the purposes of the fair-cross-section requirement of the Constitution included "the goal of ensuring that no distinctive group be excluded from full participation in our criminal justice system" (497). Marshall was mindful of the criminal defendant's right to a fair jury, but he was also concerned that peremptory challenges might prohibit blacks from participating in the justice system as jurors. Furthermore, Marshall proclaimed, "The elimination of racial discrimination in our system . . . is not a constitutional goal that should lightly be set aside" (503-04).

The year after *Holland v. Illinois,* the Supreme Court issued an opinion in a similar peremptory challenge case, this time analyzing the claim under the Equal Protection Clause. Although Marshall's liberal ally Brennan retired before *Powers v. Ohio* (1991), in this case involving racially-based peremptory challenges, Marshall found himself in the majority while Justice Scalia wrote the dissenting opinion. In a 7-2 decision written by Justice Kennedy, the Court held that a criminal defendant could object to a prosecutor's racial discrimination in the exercise of peremptory challenges even if the excluded jurors were not of the defendant's race. *Batson* did not require that the defendant and excluded jurors share a racial identity. The Equal Protection Clause and the Civil Rights Act of 1875 protected potential jurors from being excluded from jury participation sole-ly based on their race. The criminal defendant had third party standing to raise objections to the prosecutor's race-based use of peremptory challenges. Thus, the "Court cleared a major obstacle from the path extending the availability of *Batson* claims to a wide range of litigants" (Koonce 1995, 543). While *Powers* fell short of eliminating peremptory challenges altogether, it seemed that Mar-shall had scored a victory in his last few months on the Court. After all, "*Powers* supposedly protected jurors from exclusion on the basis of their race, and . . . seemed to have the effect of expanding the defendant's *Batson* rights to encom-pass all exclusions of jurors based on race" (Johnson 1993, 39-40; see also An-derson 1998, 364).

In June 1991, the Court made "a dramatic extension of its equal protection jurisprudence" (Anderson, 364). In one of his last major cases, Marshall joined the majority in a case that extended *Batson* to civil litigants (*Edmonson v. Lees-ville Concrete Co., Inc.* 1991). The Court's application of the Equal Protection Clause to jury selection by private litigants was another step toward the elimina-tion of racial discrimination in jury selection although the Court still had not embraced Marshall's argument for the complete elimination of peremptory chal-lenges. Marshall stepped down from the bench just two months after *Powers*.

Death Penalty and the Value of Dissent

Unlike their colleague Justice Harry Blackmun, who changed his stance on the death penalty during his latter years on the Court, Justices Brennan and Mar-shall were consistent in their opposition to the death penalty during their tenures. As Blackmun was exposed to more capital punishment cases during his tenure, he increasingly joined Brennan and Marshall in voting in opposition to uphold-ing death sentences. Ultimately, he announced that he would no longer support capital punishment in any case. But Blackmun's opposition to the death penalty differed from that of Brennan and Marshall. Whereas Blackmun determined that the death penalty could not be carried out in a manner consistent with the Con-stitution, Brennan and Marshall thought the very notion of capital punishment was antipodal to the Constitution.

While Brennan and Marshall did not have identical judicial philosophies, their approaches to criminal justice issues were harmonious with one another and contrasted sharply to the approach of Chief Justice Rehnquist and his con-servative brethren. These liberal justices, during the Rehnquist Court, increa-singly found themselves dissenting from the majority opinion. As their careers came to a close, Brennan and Marshall sided together and against their col-leagues in procedural and substantive criminal jurisprudence. Even though they frequently dissented from the rightward shift of the Burger and Rehnquist Courts, Brennan and Marshall still wrote opinions that influenced the criminal justice system. There is value in dissent, as Justice Brennan argued in a 1985 speech entitled "In Defense of Dissent" (Brennan 1986).

In that speech Brennan asked, "What does . . . a Justice of the Supreme Court of the United States . . . hope to accomplish by dissenting? After all, the law is the law, and in our system . . . it is made by those who command the majority" (Brennan 1986, 429). For various reasons, "The dissenting opinion as an institution within the United States Supreme Court has received both scorn and reverence" (Mello 1995, 606). As Brennan noted in his lecture, some argue "the dissent is an exercise in futility, or worse still, a 'cloud' on the majority decision that detracts for [sic] the legitimacy that the law requires and from the prestige of the institution that issues the law" (Brennan 1986, 429; see also Panel Discussion 1999: Patricia Wald, 10). Moreover, a dissenting vote may be considered an ineffective vote, or even a wasted vote. In some instances, a justice who dissents thereby divests himself of the opportunity to influence the majority opinion toward a more moderate holding that the dissenting justice would find less objectionable. Furthermore, "[c]ollegial lobbying greatly influences the tone and substance of a finished opinion, and thus the future course of law" (Mello 1995, 686). When a justice routinely dissents to the Court's holdings on a particular subject, such as the death penalty, the justice not only relinquishes his negotiating power, but also repeatedly issues opinions that contradict Supreme Court precedent rather than acknowledging and accepting what the Court previously adjudicated as the law of the land (see Mello, 650, 680).

The many dissents authored by Brennan and Marshall during the Rehnquist years nevertheless influenced criminal jurisprudence by providing direction to other courts, litigants, and lawmakers. When the United States Supreme Court determines that the U.S. Constitution entitles a criminal defendant to a certain right, the states may not restrict that right in state court. However, in their own constitutions, the states may provide broader rights to criminal defendants than the protections found in the U.S. Constitution. State courts are often required to determine the scope of a state guarantee, and therefore, there is "continuing state litigation following Supreme Court decisions rejecting federal rights" (Williams 2007, 230; see also Wright 2002, 1431). Justice Brennan encouraged "state courts to interpret their state constitutions to provide greater protection to citizens than the United States Supreme Court may have found in the counterpart federal constitutional provisions" (Panel discussion: O'Hern 1999, 20; see also Wright 2002, 1441; Dorsen 1990, 20). When a Supreme Court ruling addresses a criminal justice issue at the federal level, state courts may use the federal opinion, including dissents, for guidance resolving state constitutionality. "Supreme Court dissents can and do have a significant impact upon state courts . . . on federal questions that may also arise under state constitutions" (Williams 1984, 361; see also Panel Discussion: Patricia Wald 1999, 34). At one time, "[t]he Warren Court's dicta influenced the state courts even more than did its holding" (Wright 2002, 1442), and perhaps in later years Brennan and Marshall hoped their dissents would guide state courts to interpret state constitutional law in a manner consistent with the principles of the Warren Court.

A dissenting opinion serves to point out the weaknesses and limitations in the majority opinion, a function that influences criminal jurisprudence even before the Court writes the majority opinion. Justice Brennan observed that "vigorous debate improves the final product by forcing the prevailing side to deal with the hardest questions urged by the losing side" (Brennan 1986, 430). The author of the majority opinion must be mindful of the arguments raised in dissent. Upon the publication of the Court's opinion, the dissenting opinion can guide the losing party and future litigants toward other forums or arguments that might prove more successful (430). Dissents filed by Supreme Court justices "can also persuade future courts, influence state courts operating under their own constitutions, and provoke Congress" (Panel Discussion 1999: Patricia Wald, 34). These opinions can also serve to reassure the public that the justices decide cases according to their own conscience, thus maintaining independence (Brennan 1986, 434).

In modern Supreme Court history, it is not uncommon to find one or more justices writing dissents. In most instances, the justice simply objects to the Court's rationale in reaching its conclusion or disagrees with the majority's application of the law to the facts of a given case. When a justice disagrees with the precedent that is the basis for subsequent cases, the justice usually nonetheless follows the principle of stare decisis and accepts the precedent as the law of the land, perhaps noting his continued disagreement with the holding of the original case. In these instances, the judge may dissent on other grounds, such as the Court's application of precedent in the instant case or factual distinctions between the case at hand and the precedent.

Less frequently, a justice will refuse to accept the Court's holding and will continue to issue dissenting opinions in all cases on a particular issue. Brennan and Marshall provide perhaps the most notable example of perpetual dissents. In death penalty cases, these justices maintained that capital punishment was unconstitutional and therefore the two Warren Court holdovers dissented in all Supreme Court opinions that upheld a death penalty conviction. Brennan and Marshall always voted to grant certiorari in death penalty cases, a stance that also put them at odds with the Rehnquist Court's conservative-leaning justices. From the Court's 1976 decision in *Gregg v. Georgia* until their retirements, both justices refused to accept the premise that capital punishment is constitutional (see Mello 1995, 593).

When Justice Brennan presented "In Defense of Dissents," he declared that "stare decisis merely provides the background for judicial development of the law" (435). This approach to precedent recognizes that over time some "dissents ripened to majority opinions depend[ing] on societal developments and the foresight of individual justices" (436). While "it must have been apparent to Brennan and Marshall that the Court's decision on the constitutionality of the death penalty was not likely to be soon reversed" (Mello 1995, 650), the justices persisted in dissenting in decisions upholding the death penalty and always issued dissents from the Court's denial of certiorari in death penalty cases. In 1994

Justice Harry Blackmun followed their examples, and from that time forward made his own sustained dissent on capital punishment.

While the increasingly conservative members of the Rehnquist Court embraced the death penalty doctrine, Justices Brennan and Marshall contributed to the ongoing societal debate on the morality of capital punishment. Their perpetual dissent

> in capital penalty cases produced a rich body of legal literature where the issues of morality and ethics have shaken the very core of the doctrine of stare decisis. These Justices' relentless unwillingness to accommodate the views of the majority signals a clarion call to change the law in a certain direction within the capital penalty jurisprudence. . . . The continued dissents by Justices in cases upholding the death penalty perhaps signals that the law of capital punishment is far from being settled. (Ghoshray 2007/08, n. 59)

As Brennan knew, the sustained "dissent constitutes a statement by the judge as an individual: 'Here I draw the line'" (Brennan 1986, 437).

Conclusion

Indeed, the law of capital punishment was far from settled. By the time Brennan and Marshall retired, fifteen states had banned the death penalty. The dissents of Marshall and Brennan in death penalty jurisprudence drew an ever constant line in the sand about capital punishment to which future justices could pay heed. However, throughout the Rehnquist Court era, the Supreme Court position would continue, ultimately, to waver. It was not until the waning years of the Rehnquist Court and the early years of the Roberts Court that capital punishment would be deemed unconstitutional in several circumstances. The Court would ultimately ban the execution of offenders under the age of sixteen (*Thompson v. Oklahoma* 1988), and eventually expand the ban to juveniles of any age (*Roper v. Simmons* 2005). The Court would also prohibit the execution of those with mental retardation (*Atkins v. Virginia* 2002) and the use of the death penalty in child rape cases (*Kennedy v. Louisiana* 2008).

The "perpetual dissents" of Brennan and Marshall ultimately did impact the ongoing decisions on the Court about the death penalty particularly with regard to questions of morality and ethics. They contributed to the debate, most importantly, by forcing later justices to determine just where their line in the sand should be.

References

Alschuler, Albert W. "Commentary: Failed Pragmatism: Reflection on the Burger Court." *Harvard Law Review* 100 (1987): 1436-56.

Anderson, Jose Felipe. "Catch Me if You Can! Resolving the Ethical Tragedies in the Brave New World of Jury Selection." *New England Law Review* 32 (1998): 344-400.

Biskupic, Joan. "Justice Brennan, Voice of Court's Social Revolution, Dies," *Washington Post*, July 25, 1997, 1(A).

Brennan, William J. Jr. "Lecture: In Defense of Dissents." *Hastings Law Journal* 37 (1986): 427-38.

Clayton, Cornell W., and Mitchell Pickerill. "Symposium: Just Right?: Assessing the Rehnquist Court's Parting Words on Criminal Justice: The Politics of Criminal Justice: How the New Right Regime Shaped the Rehnquist Court's Criminal Justice Jurisprudence." *Georgetown Law Journal* 94 (2006): 1385-1425.

Cohen, Adam. "Thurgood Marshall: The Brain of the Civil Rights Movement." *Time*, June 14, 1999. http://www.time.com/time/magazine/article/0,9171,991253,00.html (accessed on November 10, 2010).

Cole, David. "Hear No Evil, See No Evil." *The Nation* (October 9, 2000): 30.

Coltharp, Donna F. "Essay: Writing in the Margins: Brennan, Marshall, and the Inherent Weaknesses of Liberal Judicial Decision-making." *St. Mary's Law Journal* 29 (1997): 1-46.

Davis, Michael, and Hunter Clark. *Thurgood Marshall: Warrior at the Bar, Rebel on The Bench.* New York: Carol Publishing, 1992.

Davis, Sue. *Justice Rehnquist and the Constitution.* Princeton, NJ: Princeton University Press, 1989.

Dorsen, Norman. "A Tribute to Justice William J. Brennan, Jr." *Harvard Law Review* 104 (1990): 15-22.

Dripps, Donald A. "Beyond the Warren Court and Its Conservative Critics: Toward a Unified Theory of Constitutional Criminal Procedure." *University of Michigan Journal of Law Reform* 23 (1990): 591-640.

Eisler, Kim Isaac. *A Justice for All: William J. Brennan Jr. and the Decisions That Transformed America.* New York: Simon and Schuster, 1993.

Ghoshray, Saby. "Illuminating Justice Marshall's Death Penalty Jurisprudence Via the Prism of Dynamic Constitutionalism." *Mississippi College Law Review* 27 (2007/08): 313-34.

Green, Bruce A., and Daniel Richman. "Of Laws and Men: An Essay on Justice Marshall's View of Criminal Procedure." *Arizona State Law Journal* 26 (1994): 369-402.

Herdrich, Madeline A. "Note: *California v. Greenwood*: The Trashing of Privacy." *American University Law Review* 38 (1989): 993-1020.

Hoffman, Matthew. "A Great Judge for the Little Man; William Brennan's Retirement After 34 Years Could Cause a Decisive Shift in the Political Balance of the US Supreme Court," *The Independent (London)*, July 25, 1990, 21.

Hopkins, W. Wat. *Mr. Justice Brennan and Freedom of Expression.* Santa Barbara, CA: Praeger, 1991.

Johnson, Sheri Lynn. "The Language and Culture (Not to say race) of Peremptory Challenges." *William and Mary Law Review* 35 (1993): 21-93.

Koonce, Lance. "*J.E.B. ex rel. T.B.* and the Fate of the Peremptory Challenge." *North Carolina Law Review* 73 (1995): 525-61.

Lewis, Anthony. "Marshall Urges Bush to Pick 'The Best,'" *New York Times*, June 29, 1991, 8(A).

Mello, Michael. "Adhering to Our Views: Justices Brennan and Marshall and the Relentless Dissent to Death as a Punishment." *Florida State University Law Review* 22 (1995): 592-694.

Mikva, Abner J. "The Burger Court Evaluated: Some Good Marks from Unexpected Quarters." *Northwestern University Law Review* 82 (1988): 808-17. (Review of *The Burger Years*, edited by Herman Schwartz, 1987, New York: Viking.)

Newton, Jim. "The Brennan Memos: Brennan Dishes on his Colleagues. Brennan on Burger." *Slate,* January 9, 2007. http://www.slate.com/id/2156940/entry/2157320/ (accessed November 10, 2010).

Panel Discussion. "Panel Discussion: Remembering a Constitutional Hero." *New York Law School Law Review* 43 (1999): 13-36.

Schwartz, Bernard. "Brennan vs. Rehnquist—Mirror Images in Constitutional Construction." *Oklahoma City University Law Review* 19 (1994): 213-50.

Serrill, Michael S. "The Power of William Brennan." *Time,* July 22, 1985: 62.

Taylor, Stuart Jr. "To Reagan's Consternation, Brennan Leads Court in Big Cases," *New York Times*, March 30, 1987. http://www.nytimes.com/1987/03/30/us/to-reagan-s-consternation-brennan-leads-court-in-big-cases.html (accessed on November 10, 2010).

———. "The Rehnquist Court." *National Journal*, May 21, 2005: 1532-39.

Tushnet, Mark. "Review: The Optimist's Tale. The Burger Court: The Counter-Revolution that Wasn't." *University of Pennsylvania Law Review* 132 (1984): 1257-73.

Walpin, Gerald. "Take Obstructionism out of the Judicial Nominations Confirmation Process." *Texas Review of Law and Politics* 8 (2003): 89-112.

Williams, Robert F. "In the Supreme Court's Shadow: Legitimacy of State Rejection of Supreme Court Reasoning and Result." *South Carolina Law Review* 35 (1984): 353-61.

———. "Symposium: Independent State Ground: Should State Courts Depart from the Fourth Amendment In Construing Their Own Constitutions, and if so, On What Basis Beyond Simple Disagreement With the United States Supreme Court's Result?: State Constitutional Methodology in Search and Seizure Cases." *Mississippi Law Journal* 77 (2007): 225-63.

Wright, Ronald F. "Symposium: The Jurisprudential Legacy of the Warren Court: Reform of Criminal Procedure in the States: How the Supreme Court Delivers Fire and Ice to State Criminal Justice." *Washington and Lee Law Review* 59 (2002): 1429-57.

Cases Cited

Atkins v. Virginia, 536 U.S. 304 (2002)
Barber v. Page, 390 U.S. 719 (1968)
Batson v. Kentucky, 476 U.S. 79 (1986)
Brown v. Board of Education of Topeka, 347 U.S. 483 (1954)
California v. Greenwood, 486 U.S. 35 (1988)
California v. Hodari, 499 US 621, 628 (1991)
Colorado v. Bertine, 479 U.S. 367 (1987)
Colorado v. Connelly, 479 U.S. 157 (1986)
Cooper, et al. v. Aaron, et al., 358 U.S. 1 (1958)
Duckworth v. Eagan, 492 U.S. 195 (1989)

Edmonson v. Leesville Concrete Co., Inc., 500 U.S. 614 (1991)
Eisendstadt v. Baird, 405 U.S. 438 (1972)
Escobedo v. Illinois, 378 U.S. 478 (1964)
Florida v. Bostick, 501 U.S. 429, 440 (1991)
Florida v. Riley, 488 U.S. 445 (1989)
Ford v. Wainwright, 477 U.S. 399 (1986)
Furman v. Georgia, 408 U.S. 238 (1972)
Gideon v. Wainwright, 372 U.S. 335 (1963)
Gregg v. Georgia, 428 U.S. 153 (1976)
Griffith v. Kentucky, 479 U.S. 314 (1987)
Griswold v. Connecticut, 381 U.S. 479 (1965)
Holland v. Illinois, 493 U.S. 474 (1990)
Illinois v. Perkins, 496 U.S. 292 (1990)
Kennedy v. Louisiana, 128 S.Ct. 2641 (2008)
Mapp v. Ohio, 367 U.S. 643 (1961)
Marbury v. Madison, 5 U.S. 137 (1803)
Massiah v. United States, 377 U.S. 201 (1964)
Michigan v. Sitz, 496 U.S. 444, 459 (1990)
Miranda v. Arizona, 384 U.S. 436 (1966)
National Treasury Employees Union v. Von Raab, 489 U.S. 656 (1989)
Pennsylvania v. Bruder, 488 U.S. 9 (1988)
Plessy v. Ferguson 163 U.S. 537 (1896)
Powers v. Ohio, 499 U.S. 400 (1991)
Roe v. Wade, 410 U.S. 113 (1973)
Roper v. Simmons, 543 U.S. 551 (2005)
Shelley v. Kraemer, 334 U.S. 1 (1948)
Skinner v. Railway Labor Executives Association, 489 U.S. 602 (1989)
Smith v. Allwright, 321 U.S. 649 (1944)
Terry v. Ohio, 392 U.S. 1 (1968)
Thompson v. Oklahoma, 487 U.S. 815 (1988)
United States v. Dunn, 480 U.S. 294 (1987)

Chapter 3
Byron White:
The Overlooked, Moderate Swing Voter

Mark S. Hurwitz

> White may have functioned as a critical swing vote on the Court for much of his tenure. (Mishler and Sheehan 1996, 195)

While Justice Byron R. White was among the most well-known public figures before he ascended to the Supreme Court, he was fiercely protective of his privacy, both professional and personal, during his time on the Court. Indeed, he seemed to revel in his relative judicial anonymity, while the other justices gained media attention. In this regard, when he was U.S. Deputy Attorney General under President Kennedy he was recognized in public and asked if he was "Whizzer White" the star football player. "I was" was his quiet response; interestingly, it is also claimed that the same thing happened to White in 1959, as he was pondering whether to run then Senator John F. Kennedy's upcoming presidential campaign in Colorado (Hutchinson 1998, 1, 237). Wherever and whenever such occurrences took place, they illustrated how White had a manner of achieving success while flying under the radar, at least after his days as a well-known football star. This relative lack of attention likewise reached scholarly circles. Save for one biography (Hutchinson 1998), there is not all that much written on White's influence on the Court. In fact, in the book *Rehnquist Justice: Understanding the Court Dynamic* (Maltz 2003), an edited volume that delves into the interactions among many of the justices on the Rehnquist Court, Justice White is barely mentioned even though he served for the first seven terms of Rehnquist's tenure in the center seat of the Court.

Additionally, many contradictions surround Justice White. Prior to his service on the Court, White was famously known as "Whizzer White," an All-American football tailback from the University of Colorado in the 1930s, where he led the nation in scoring and became a member of the College Football Hall of Fame. But even then, considering all of his achievements and accolades on the gridiron, there were whispers that he was successful as a collegiate football player only because of the relative lack of talent and competition in the western part of the country at the time. Afterward, White was drafted by the Pittsburgh franchise in the National Football League, where he became the highest paid player in the game his rookie year, despite rumors he would soon leave the game to pursue his education. He went to England as a Rhodes Scholar at Oxford University and then served in the U.S. Navy during World War II.

After the war, he finished law school at Yale and then served as a law clerk for Chief Justice Fred Vinson at the U.S. Supreme Court. He practiced law until he became chair of the John F. Kennedy presidential election campaign in Colorado. After Kennedy's electoral victory, White became deputy attorney general, subordinate in the U.S. Department of Justice only to Attorney General Robert Kennedy. President Kennedy soon appointed White to the Supreme Court in 1962. He served on the high court for over thirty years, earning a reputation for being more conservative than perhaps what would have been expected considering his nomination by a Democratic president.

For these reasons Justice White does not have an easily defined and broadly recognized reputation as is the case of some of the other, better-known justices on the Rehnquist Court. Indeed, it has been difficult to pinpoint White, which perhaps is reason for the relative lack of attention to him. Nevertheless, he appears to have played the role of both moderate justice and swing voter for much of his time on the Court. Furthermore, while serving under three different chief justices, his tenure was among the longest on the Supreme Court. Only nine associate justices in the history of the Supreme Court served longer than White. Accordingly, White provides a critical, if muted and perhaps misunderstood, voice on the Supreme Court.

Biography

Justice White led an accomplished professional life prior to his appointment to the Supreme Court. He attended college in his home state at the University of Colorado. He played both collegiate and professional football, attended Oxford University as a Rhodes Scholar, and was in the Intelligence Division of the U.S. Navy during the Second World War, where he served in the South Pacific. A photograph of White as a law clerk for Chief Justice Vinson taken on the steps of the Supreme Court in the 1946 Term has become almost as commonplace as his formal portraits taken years later as a Supreme Court justice. Indeed, this picture of White as a law clerk adorns the front cover of the book, *Courtiers of the Marble Palace: The Rise and Influence of the Supreme Court Clerk* (Peppers 2006). White would eventually become the first former law clerk to be appointed to a seat on the Supreme Court.

After his year as a law clerk for the chief justice, White returned to Colorado where he practiced law in Denver from 1947-61. During this time he was active in local politics, and though Democratic Party leaders often recruited him, he never ran for elected office himself (Hutchinson 1998). However, he found himself immersed in national politics when he agreed to direct the Kennedy for President Campaign in Colorado in 1960. White and the future president were casual acquaintances from their prewar travels in Europe where White, the Rhodes Scholar, had encountered Kennedy, the son of the U.S. ambassador to Great Britain. Their paths crossed again during the war when Naval Intelligence Lieutenant White wrote the official report on the famous sinking of Kennedy's PT-109 boat in the Pacific (Kramer 1991).

These serendipitous encounters with Kennedy proved exceedingly important for White's ascent in Washington politics. While Kennedy did not carry Colorado in the Electoral College tally, the result in the state was closer than expected. Consequently, White caught the attention of both the president-elect and his brother Robert, who would become President Kennedy's attorney general. White was considered for Secretary of the Army and the Air Force before he was offered and accepted the position of deputy attorney general (Hutchinson 1998). One of the primary tasks confronting Deputy Attorney General White during his first year in the Kennedy Administration was to work on the president's task of filling the many vacancies in the lower federal courts.

President Kennedy was soon presented with a surprise when Justice Charles Whittaker resigned in early 1962 because of poor health after a relatively short tenure on the Supreme Court (Whittaker had been appointed by President Dwight Eisenhower in 1957). While a number of potential names to replace Whittaker were bantered about at both the White House and Department of Justice, including a list of possible nominees prepared by White, in the end the president and attorney general preferred White over all others as Whittaker's successor. After his official nomination by President Kennedy, White received an "exceptionally well qualified" rating from both the American Bar Association (Kramer 1991, 410) and Colorado Bar Association (Hutchinson 1998, 330).

White's confirmation hearing was extremely short, particularly compared to more recent nominations, lasting only ninety minutes. During the hearing, when asked about the controversial issue of judges legislating from the bench, a common criticism of the Warren Court, White responded, "I think it is clear under the Constitution that the legislative power is not vested in the Supreme Court. It is vested in the Congress" (Hutchinson 1998, 331). After receiving unanimous approval from the Senate Judiciary Committee, White's appointment became official later the same day when the Senate confirmed his nomination by voice vote. On April 12, 1962, at the age of forty-four, Justice White received his commission as a Supreme Court justice, where he served for thirty-one terms under Chief Justices Earl Warren, Warren Burger, and William Rehnquist.

Justice White and the Warren Court

Justice White's first seven terms on the Supreme Court occurred during the Warren Court era. When he first became an associate justice the big question about White concerned his ideological place on the Court; that is, would he provide a reliable fifth vote for the liberal voting bloc of Warren-Black-Douglas-Brennan as some either hoped or feared, or would he fall somewhere to the right of the liberals on the Warren Court? While the Warren Court is reputed for carving a liberal path throughout its entire era, in fact, the Supreme Court reached its most liberal point from 1965 to 1968 at the very end of the Warren Court era. Indeed, the Court did not take its extremely liberal turn after the appointment of Justice White; instead, the liberal ideology for which the Warren Court is known took shape after the subsequent appointments of Justice Arthur Goldberg by President Kennedy and then Justices Abe Fortas and Thurgood Marshall by President Lyndon Johnson (see, e.g., McGuire and Stimson 2004). Stated somewhat differently, the real Warren Court began when Goldberg joined the liberal bloc on the Warren Court (Currie 1990), as White never filled this role. Thus, while Justice White was not as conservative as his predecessor, Justice Whittaker, he was not nearly as liberal as any of the justices on that wing's ideological bloc on the Court.

While this fact of White's lack of liberalism is demonstrated by systematic research (see, e.g., Mishler and Sheehan 1996; Epstein, Hoekstra, Segal, and Spaeth 1998), it is also observed in more qualitative analyses. During the Warren Court, for instance, White dissented early and often from some of the more liberal decisions of the day. For instance, in his first term on the Court White dissented from the majority opinion in *Robinson v. California* (1962), a typical Warren Court decision, as White believed there was no Eighth Amendment violation with respect to a state law that criminalized narcotics addiction (Hutchinson 1998). There were numerous other examples where White dissented from liberal rulings of the Warren Court. Most famously, he dissented from the Supreme Court's landmark decision in *Miranda v. Arizona* (1966) and wrote, seemingly in anger, "In some unknown number of cases, the Court's rule will return a killer, a rapist or other criminal to the streets and to the environment which produced him, to repeat his crime whenever it pleases him" (*Miranda v. Arizona* 1966, 542).

At the time when White was gaining a reputation for dissenting from the liberalism of the Warren Court, his voting record during his early years on the Court actually showed him to be a moderate justice, not a conservative one. In fact, White took the liberal position in about 60 percent of the cases during the Warren era. One example of his agreement with a liberal Warren Court ruling was *Griswold v. Connecticut* (1965, 502), where Justice White wrote a separate concurrence emphasizing personal liberty that declared, "In my view, this Connecticut law, as applied to married couples, deprives them of 'liberty' without due process of law." This concurrence is interesting for the simple fact that White was in such strong opposition to the Court's subsequent abortion rulings, which relied on the *Griswold* analysis. Yet, White's concurrence in *Griswold* also shows that he was not always in opposition to liberal opinions from the Warren Court.

Nevertheless, because his voting record was more conservative than that of his more liberal colleagues on the Warren Court, particularly Warren, Black, Douglas, Brennan, Goldberg, Fortas, and Marshall (see Mishler and Sheehan 1996), from a relative perspective his moderate record made it appear as if he were conservative. Though he was not a reliable or consistent liberal during the Warren Court (nor for that matter at any point of his tenure on the Court), it certainly cannot be said that he was a conservative justice. White often disagreed with the liberal positions taken during the Warren Court era; but, White did not provide a consistent conservative vote, as his perceived stance was more a function of his position relative to the liberal majority of the Warren Court. In sum, White's judicial path during the 1960s was far more moderate than is conventionally recognized.

Justice White and the Burger Court

With the departure of Chief Justice Warren in 1969, a distinctive Supreme Court era ended abruptly, as no longer would the Court lend a consistent liberal voice to the polity. To the contrary, President Richard M. Nixon appointed four justices within three years, including Chief Justice Warren Burger as well as Justices Harry Blackmun, Lewis Powell, and William Rehnquist, each of whom proved to be more conservative than the justice he replaced. Consequently, the Supreme Court's decisions turned sharply to the right. Moreover, this trend away from a liberal Court toward a conservative jurisprudence has continued essentially unabated for the forty plus years since the commencement of the Burger Court era.

The changes in the Court's composition led observers at that time to raise questions about White's role on the Court. How would Justice White fare on a Court transformed by appointments made by a president who campaigned on reining in the perceived extremism of the Warren Court? Would White continue to play the role of dissenter as he often did on the Warren Court? Or, would he fit in more comfortably on a bench no longer quite so liberal? Once again, even on the Burger Court it is difficult to place labels on Justice White, a role he seemed to relish throughout his legal career (Hutchinson 1998). In this regard, White continued in his moderate vein, although his slightly liberal voting record diminished on the Burger Court, to the point where he voted liberally about 50 percent of the time—perhaps the very definition of a true moderate justice.

His moderate voting record throughout his tenure on the Court, and particularly during the Burger Court years, may explain why scholars have found it difficult to carve out a distinct legacy for Justice White. For instance, there were times during the Burger Court era when White voted in both a liberal and conservative direction in different cases concerning a specific issue. One example in the criminal justice arena concerns permissible criminal punishments and the death penalty.

Justice White argued that the Court was wrong in *Robinson v. California* to use the Eighth Amendment to override the state's choice about appropriate criminal punishment. One decade later, the Supreme Court revisited the issue of criminal punishments by examining the death penalty. The Court stayed all executions with its decision in *Furman v. Georgia* (1972). White was in the majority in *Furman* contending, along with Justice Potter Stewart, that "this unique penalty [was] so wantonly and so freakishly imposed" that it violated the Eighth Amendment (*Furman v. Georgia* 1972, 310). White did not go so far as some of his colleagues, however, to argue that the death penalty was unconstitutional per se. Consequently, when the Court in *Gregg v. Georgia* (1976) subsequently allowed the resumption of the death penalty if certain procedural safeguards were met, Justice White agreed with that outcome; in fact, he concurred with his more conservative brethren Chief Justice Burger and Justice Rehnquist when he wrote that even greater usage of the death penalty was permissible than the *Gregg* decision implied (see Hurwitz 2008). This death penalty example from the Burger Court provides an additional illustration of the moderate nature of White's jurisprudence.

Another example of Justice White's perceived inconsistency, perhaps more accurately defined as moderation, concerns the issue of personal liberty. As stated earlier in this chapter, White agreed with the majority in *Griswold v. Connecticut* that a substantive due process right protects a married couple's decision about contraception without interference from the state. White then agreed with his colleagues in *Eisenstadt v. Baird* (1972) that the *Griswold* zone of privacy additionally encompassed unmarried couples' contraceptive decisions. Furthermore, White concurred with the majority outcome in *Carey v. Population Services International* (1977), which held that a state could not prohibit minors from gaining access to contraception.

Notwithstanding these various opinions on personal liberty regarding access to contraception, all of which might be perceived as liberal, Justice White staked out a very different position when the issue of abortion confronted the Court. In *Roe v. Wade* (1973, 153), the Court famously or infamously applied the *Griswold* reasoning to abortion, holding, "This right of privacy . . . is broad enough to encompass a woman's decision whether or not to terminate her pregnancy." White disagreed.

In fact, Justice White was one of only two justices to disagree with the *Roe* rationale. In a dissent joined by Justice Rehnquist, White contended, "This issue, for the most part, should be left with the people and to the political processes the people have devised to govern their affairs" (*Roe v. Wade* 1973, 222, Justice White dissenting). That is, legislatures, not courts, should decide this issue. Further, in a statement from his dissent that comported with his testimony before the Senate Judiciary Committee during his confirmation hearings, White seemed to lecture his colleagues for improperly flexing their judicial muscles, stating, "As an exercise of raw judicial power, the Court perhaps has authority to do what it does today; but in my view its judgment is an improvident and extravagant exercise of the power of judicial review that the Constitution extends to this Court" (1973, 222).

These cases show how Justice White was neither consistently liberal nor conservative on the issue of personal liberty. When it came to contraception, White took the perceived liberal position of extending the concept of personal liberty under notions of substantive due process, arguing that the judiciary must protect against legislative attempts to trample upon an individual's zone of privacy. Yet, White was a strong opponent of abortion, taking the perceived conservative position that the political process undertaken by legislatures is the appropriate method to determine when abortion is, and is not, permitted. That is, in Justice White's view the constitutional zone of privacy did not extend to the issue of abortion, and accordingly the judicial process should not arrogate an area better left to legislatures.

Finally, in perhaps the case for which he is best known, White authored the Court's opinion in *Bowers v. Hardwick* (1986), where the majority held that no fundamental right to privacy protects homosexual conduct from leading to criminal prosecution. A year after he passed away, the Supreme Court in *Lawrence v. Texas* (2003) officially overruled Justice White's decision in *Bowers*, when the Supreme Court held that a constitutional right of personal liberty protects private, consensual, sexual activity among adults, as the Court held unconstitutional a state's criminal anti-sodomy law.

Justice White and Criminal Justice during the Rehnquist Court

Just as Justice White began his tenure on the Supreme Court by serving for seven years under Chief Justice Warren, he finished his active duty on the Court with seven years as an associate justice under Chief Justice Rehnquist. From an overall ideological perspective, Justice White continued to become a bit more conservative over time, voting in a liberal direction about 40 percent of the time on average during the Rehnquist Court era. However, the evidence from systematic studies show that Justice White turned somewhat to the left in his final terms (see Mishler and Sheehan 1996), thus rebutting the argument sometimes heard that White would have been even more conservative had he continued on the Court. Indeed, White ended his tenure on the Court voting in a liberal direction in about 50 percent of the Court's cases, evincing a true moderate voice on the Supreme Court.

What about his decisions on the issues of criminal justice in his final years on the Court? Was White a moderate when criminal cases were at stake, or did he show a tendency toward either liberal or conservative outcomes in these types of cases? A review of the Rehnquist Court's criminal justice cases shows that while White was a moderate justice overall, he was somewhat more conservative in criminal justice cases than in other issue areas.

For instance, during his entire Supreme Court career White voted in a liberal direction in one-third of criminal cases. Nevertheless, while this may seem to portend conservative leanings in criminal justice cases, from a relative perspective White's voting record over the course of his tenure was largely similar to a number of moderate justices, including Clark, Harlan, Stewart, and Blackmun, all of whom had liberalism rates in the 30 to 40 percent range. In fact, there were a number of justices who were far more conservative in criminal cases than White (including Burger, Powell, Rehnquist, O'Connor, Scalia, Kennedy, and Thomas), all with liberal voting records at 30 percent or less. Similarly, the liberal justices were far from White's moderate position on criminal cases (Warren, Brennan, Goldberg, Fortas, Marshall, and Stevens) as their liberalism rates were no less than 75 percent, save for Justice Stevens who supported the liberal position in criminal cases 62 percent of the time (Epstein, Segal, Spaeth, and Walker 1994). Once again this demonstrates why White is best characterized as a moderate justice, even when the issue area of criminal justice cases is considered. Justice White's perspective is illustrated by examining a few specific issue areas within the criminal justice field decided during the Rehnquist Court era.

Death Penalty and Post-Conviction Reviews

Perhaps no issue in the field of criminal justice is as salient or controversial as the death penalty. Of course, the Supreme Court's jurisprudence in the death penalty does not begin with the Rehnquist Court, as the seminal cases of *Furman v. Georgia* (1972) and *Gregg v. Georgia* (1976) had already been decided. As stated earlier, Justice White was on the majority side of both *Furman*, which temporarily halted the death penalty in the country until specific procedural safeguards were put in place, and *Gregg*, which reinstated imposition of the death penalty, provided procedural safeguards would prevent arbitrary or capricious executions.

The Rehnquist Court handled a number of death penalty cases, but none seem quite as salient as *McCleskey v. Kemp* (1987), which was issued in the first term of the Rehnquist Court era. Indeed, there was quite a bit of public and scholarly attention given to *McCleskey*, largely because the question of race was infused into the case. Technically, the *McCleskey* decision concerned the introduction of aggravating and mitigating factors during the sentencing phase of a death penalty trial. But, the critical issue concerned the claim that death sentences were imposed in a racially discriminatory manner that violated the Eighth and Fourteenth Amendments. In particular, the petitioner argued that social science research demonstrated the death penalty was unconstitutionally dependent upon the race of the victim. The Supreme Court did not agree. While Justice Powell wrote the majority opinion in *McCleskey*, Justice White joined the Powell's opinion and did not write a separate concurrence.

While the statistical study presented by the defense in *McCleskey* was deemed valid by the Court and tended to show disparities based on race, the study was declared by the Court majority to be insufficient from a legal perspective to invalidate the death penalty imposed upon the petitioner. To show that his death sentence violated either the Eighth Amendment or Equal Protection Clause, the defendant needed to prove the state acted with discriminatory intent in his particular case. In addition to Justices Powell and White, the other justices in the majority were Rehnquist, O'Connor, and Scalia, while the dissenters included the more liberal wing of the Court on death penalty cases, including Brennan, Marshall, Blackmun, and Stevens. While White's voting record showed that he was often more liberal in race discrimination cases than otherwise, the *McCleskey* case illustrates his perceived tendency to find little or no constitutional fault with the criminal justice system.

The Supreme Court later decided three cases on whether the death penalty can be imposed on a defendant with mental incapacities, though Justice White participated in only the first two of them. In the final term of the Burger Court, the Supreme Court held in *Ford v. Wainwright* (1986) that executing a defendant who is insane is unconstitutional. This was a closely divided 5-4 decision in which Justice Marshall wrote the majority opinion. While White did not write his own opinion, he joined in Justice O'Connor's opinion that concurred and dissented in part. Essentially, O'Connor and White felt that the particular state law created an expectation that no person with a mental incapacity could be executed; but, the procedure for appraising defendant's mental state did not satisfy notions of due process, and thus these justices would have remanded the case for a new hearing on mental capacity that comports with the Fourteenth Amendment.

The next decision on this subject was issued during the Rehnquist Court era, and the outcome differed from the *Ford v. Wainwright* decision. In *Penry v. Lynaugh* (1989), the Supreme Court determined that the death sentence of an adult with mental deficiencies was not unconstitutional. Again, Justice White did not write any opinion in this case, though he joined with the majority. The *Penry* outcome was different from the previous *Ford* case because Justice Kennedy voted with the White voting bloc in *Penry*, while his predecessor Justice Powell voted with the Marshall bloc in *Ford*.

In *Atkins v. Virginia* (2002), the final in this line of cases, the Supreme Court again examined the issue of executing mentally deficient individuals. This time, however, with Justice White no longer on the Court and with Justice Stevens writing the majority opinion, the Court ruled that executing mentally deficient individuals violates the Eighth Amendment. Consequently, the *Penry* decision (in which White was in the majority) was overruled.

The Rehnquist Court also confronted the issue of how to handle additional evidence in a death penalty case that is raised after the time for additional appeals has tolled. More particularly, in a death penalty case can claims of actual innocence based on newly discovered evidence be raised after the state's procedural laws bar them? That was the issue in *Herrera v. Collins* (1993), where Chief Justice Rehnquist's opinion for the Supreme Court held that defendant's habeas corpus claim based on new evidence was inappropriate, since habeas corpus was available for reversible errors at trial, not new evidence, even if the newly-discovered evidence proves the defendant is actually innocent.

Justice White concurred in the judgment but expressed his concern about executing an innocent person:

> In voting to affirm, I assume that a persuasive showing of "actual innocence" made after trial, even though made after the expiration of the time provided by law for the presentation of newly discovered evidence, would render unconstitutional the execution of petitioner in this case. To be entitled to relief, however, petitioner would at the very least be required to show that based on proffered newly discovered evidence and the entire record before the jury that convicted him, "no rational trier of fact could [find] proof of guilt beyond a reasonable doubt". (*Herrera* at 529 citing *Jackson v. Virginia*, 443 U.S. 307, 324 (1979))

Justice White's concurrence shows that he believed the defendant had not met that standard, and thus there was no reason to allow the defendant's habeas corpus petition to proceed. While White's concurrence falls against the criminal defendant, it is clear that White's opinion is not nearly as reliant on technical criminal procedure as was the majority opinion. Indeed, it appears White was troubled by the implication that the majority would allow the execution of an innocent person who had been found guilty simply because the time to file appeals had expired. In Justice White's view, it is unconstitutional to carry out a death sentence when newly discovered evidence clearly shows that the defendant is innocent.

Similarly, White spoke out about procedural fairness in post-conviction processes in *Brecht v. Abrahamson* (1993), a murder case in which the defendant was given a life sentence. On behalf of Justices Blackmun and Souter, White's dissenting opinion complained about the majority imposing excessively difficult-to-prove standards on convicted offenders seeking post-conviction relief after demonstrating the existence of constitutional violations in their cases. White's opinion criticized his colleagues for creating too many impediments to the use of the habeas corpus process to correct errors:

> Our habeas jurisprudence is taking on the appearance of a confused patchwork in which different constitutional rights are treated according to their status, and in which the same constitutional right is treated differently depending on whether its vindication is sought on direct or collateral review. (*Brecht v. Abrahamson* 1993, 649)

These examples do not demonstrate that White took a consistent or ideological view of post-conviction processes for the most serious cases. His moderate stance led him to go in different directions on particular legal topics, depending on the specific issue in a case. He also wrote the majority opinion in a 5-4 decision that denied post-conviction relief to a death row defendant who, in White's view, was not permitted to benefit from a new rule of constitutional law that was decided after his conviction and appeals had become final (*Graham v. Collins* 1993).

These disparate death penalty and murder-conviction appeal cases issued during the Rehnquist Court era illustrate Justice White's record as moderate on criminal justice issues. Though he may have leaned toward the conservative side overall, White was not nearly as conservative as Rehnquist, Scalia, and Thomas; clearly, he also was not quite so liberal as Marshall, Brennan, or Stevens. Justice White's voting record placed him in the middle of the Court.

Criminal Punishment in Noncapital Cases

As previously discussed, White's conservative reputation in criminal justice cases is due, in part, to his well-known dissents in prominent Warren Court era decisions such as *Robinson v. California* (1962) concerning the Eighth Amendment and permissible punishments, and *Miranda v. Arizona* (1966) concerning the Fifth Amendment and police practices. As indicated in the foregoing discussion of capital punishment and post-conviction proceedings, White actually took a moderate stance, supporting liberal or conservative outcomes depending on the specific issue raised. Further evidence of White's moderation can be seen in liberal opinions concerning Eighth Amendment issues in noncapital cases. Although White is credited in these examples with adopting the liberal side, in fact, these cases should be seen as White pushing back against the more extreme aspirations of his most conservative colleagues rather than seeking to establish new or enhanced constitutional protections for defendants and prisoners.

In *Harmelin v. Michigan* (1991), a defendant challenged Michigan's criminal sentencing laws that imposed mandatory sentences of life imprisonment without parole for people convicted of possessing 650 or more grams of cocaine, even if they were nonviolent, first offenders. This was the most severe mandatory sentencing for drug offenses of any jurisdiction in the United States. The Rehnquist Court majority, in an opinion written by Justice Scalia, endorsed the Michigan law and found no violation of the proportionality principle within the Cruel and Unusual Punishments Clause of the Eighth Amendment. Scalia wrote an additional section in his opinion, joined only by Chief Justice Rehnquist, which argued against including any proportionality principle as part of the Eighth Amendment for noncapital cases. In other words, Scalia sought to permit states to impose any noncapital sentences in any manner that they wished. White's dissenting opinion on behalf of Justices Blackmun and Stevens took aim, in particular, at Scalia's aspiration to significantly shrink the protective value of the Eighth Amendment. Under Scalia's conceptualization, only tortuous punishments would be barred, not punishments considered disproportionate to the crime. In a particularly memorable criticism, White said of the "dangers" that lurked in Scalia's analysis, "[H]e provides no mechanism for addressing a situation such as that proposed in [a prior proportionality case], in which a legislature makes overtime parking a felony punishable by life imprisonment" (*Har-*

melin v. Michigan 1991, 1018). While Scalia argued that such extreme examples were highly unlikely to occur, White observed, "This is cold comfort indeed, for absent a proportionality guarantee, there would be no basis for deciding such cases should they arise" (1018). Here, White's moderation led him to merely advocate the preservation of constitutional doctrine in the face of unwise suggestions from Scalia about how to further diminish rights for individuals.

White challenged Scalia again in *Wilson v. Seiter* (1991), a case that raised an Eighth Amendment claim about allegedly cruel and unusual conditions involving a prison's food, cells, heating system, and other matters. White concurred with the majority's decision to reject this prisoner's claim. However, he wrote a concurring opinion that challenged Scalia's successful effort in the majority opinion to introduce a new Eighth Amendment standard for all conditions of confinement cases concerning prisons. Scalia selectively utilized case precedent in order to require prisoners to prove "deliberate indifference" on the part of corrections officials, even though that standard had not been used in conditions of confinement cases; it had only applied to specific contexts of medical claims and excessive use of force cases (Smith 2001). Again, White's moderate stance led him to argue for the preservation of the prior standard that objectively examined prison conditions as he criticized the new subjective standard introduced by Scalia. White noted in *Wilson* (1991, 310-11),

> Not only is the majority's intent requirement a departure from precedent, it likely will prove impossible to apply in many cases. The majority's approach is also unwise. It leaves open the possibility, for example, that prison officials will be able to defeat a [lawsuit] . . . simply by showing that the conditions are caused by insufficient funding from the state legislature.

In *Helling v. McKinney* (1993), White seized the opportunity to prevent additional limitations on prison conditions lawsuits. He wrote a majority opinion that accepted the "deliberate indifference" standard but, over the objections of Scalia and Thomas, permitted a prisoner to sue for potential future harms that he could suffer in prison. The case concerned a prisoner who feared severe health consequences from exposure to high levels of second-hand smoke by being confined many hours each day with a chain-smoking cellmate. Scalia and Thomas argued that he could not file a lawsuit until he suffered demonstrable harms to his health. White, speaking for the other justices, sought to prevent further reductions in Eighth Amendment conditions of confinement protections for prisoners.

Search and Seizure

Justice White sometimes held in favor of the government's search authority while at other times ruling that a search was unconstitutional, again demonstrating his moderate mettle. For instance, in a case decided at the end of the first term of the Rehnquist Court, the Supreme Court in *Arizona v. Hicks* (1987) confronted the issue of a warrantless search. In this case, police responded to a shooting and entered into an apartment without a warrant, where they seized a number of weapons. There were no constitutional problems at that point in the police officers' performance of their duties because they entered the apartment under urgent circumstances in which there seemed to be a clear threat to public safety. However, an officer also noticed expensive stereo equipment in the apartment, which he moved in order to take note of the serial numbers. It was determined that the stereo equipment had been stolen. The police then seized the stereo equipment as evidence, and the respondent was subsequently charged with armed robbery. This case received attention because some observers were surprised that Justice Scalia authored the majority opinion. Scalia held that moving the stereo equipment to look for the serial numbers represented an unconstitutional search because no probable cause was shown. In so ruling Scalia wrote, "[T]he Constitution sometimes insulates the criminality of a few in order to protect the privacy of us all" (*Arizona v. Hicks* 1987, 329).

Justice White joined Scalia's majority in *Hicks* along with the most liberal justices on the Court, Brennan, Marshall, Stevens, and Blackmun. White also wrote a separate concurrence in *Hicks* that criticized the dissenters (O'Connor, Rehnquist, and Powell). In White's concurrence, he emphasized that the inadvertent plain view doctrine was not before the Court, a point improperly brought up by the dissenters, and thus the search was unconstitutional. White wrote,

> I join the majority opinion today without regard to the inadvertence of the officers' discovery of the stereo components' serial numbers. The police officers conducted a search of respondent's stereo equipment absent probable cause that the equipment was stolen. (*Arizona v. Hicks* 1987, 334)

Justice White also found himself on the side of the state in other Fourth Amendment cases during the Rehnquist Court era. For instance, earlier in the same term the Court confronted what seemed to be a similar warrantless search to that in *Hicks*, yet the outcome in *Colorado v. Bertine* (1987) was quite different. In *Bertine*, the defendant was arrested for driving under the influence, and his van was impounded. While at the impound lot, the police searched his van without a warrant, seized various items, and subsequently arrested the defendant for several drug crimes. In an opinion by Chief Justice Rehnquist, the Supreme Court held that this was a proper inventory search of an automobile, where there is lesser constitutional protection than exists in one's home. Justice White agreed with Rehnquist's majority opinion allowing the search, though he did not write separately in this case. In fact, only Justices Brennan and Marshall dissented from this case, which was far more typical of a Rehnquist Court ruling on the Fourth Amendment.

The Supreme Court approved another warrantless search in *California v. Greenwood* (1988), and not only was Justice White in the majority, this time White authored the majority opinion. The issue and conclusion in *Greenwood* were rather simple, as White himself provided: "The issue here is whether the

Fourth Amendment prohibits the warrantless search and seizure of garbage left for collection outside the curtilage of a home. We conclude . . . that it does not" (*California v. Greenwood* 1988, 35). According to White, there is no objective expectation of privacy with respect to garbage. White (*California v. Greenwood* 1988, 40-41) continued:

> [R]espondents placed their refuse at the curb for the express purpose of convey- ing it to a third party, the trash collector, who might himself have sorted through respondents' trash or permitted others, such as the police, to do so. Ac- cordingly, having deposited their garbage in an area particularly suited for pub- lic inspection and, in a manner of speaking, public consumption, for the express purpose of having strangers take it . . . respondents could have had no reasona- ble expectation of privacy in the inculpatory items that they discarded.

As might be expected, the dissent by Justices Brennan and Marshall in this 6-2 case (Justice Kennedy did not participate) was extremely critical of Justice White's opinion.

Greenwood was another typical Rehnquist Court decision on search and seizure that provided the state with expanded law enforcement authority, partic- ularly concerning warrantless searches outside the home. In this regard, all three of the cases cited here, *Hicks, Bertine,* and *Greenwood,* are typical of Justice White's jurisprudence in matters of criminal justice. He was not in favor of all warrantless searches; in fact, White seemed to favor Fourth Amendment protec- tion when the search took place in an individual's home. But, White was clearly not interested in liberal positions across the board as Brennan and Marshall would support in these cases.

Conclusion:
Justice White Could Swing with the Best of Them

After Justice White died in 2002, Chief Justice Rehnquist wrote a short tribute to White that was published in the *Stanford Law Review*. Rehnquist (2002, 1) re- flected:

> One's first impression of Byron White—a crushing handshake, a somewhat gruff manner, and a reluctance to talk about his past accomplishments—would have given no hint that he was even a lawyer, say nothing of a Supreme Court Justice. But a Justice he was, for more than thirty years, and a major contributor to the Court's work during that time. He did not fit readily into any ideological mould . . . He will not be remembered as a champion of any particular philoso- phy—indeed, he would not want to be so remembered. He was the balance wheel, and as such an invaluable member of the Court for all of his long tenure.

While tributes often reek of faint praise, Rehnquist's is one tribute that appears very apt. Justice White did not fit any ideological label—he was non-ideological and cast both liberal and conservative votes throughout his tenure. He also was an invaluable justice, serving not only for a long time but also providing an important vote if not voice as the swing vote or, as Rehnquist contended, the balance wheel.

So in the end, what do we make of Justice White? Was he a Kennedy Democrat, somewhat more pragmatic than FDR New Deal Democrats but still a relatively consistent liberal vote on the Supreme Court? Or, was he a bona fide conservative justice, with a judicial voice more akin to a Republican wrapped in a Democrat appointee's clothing? The answer from this analysis appears to be neither. Perhaps the most accurate statement regarding Justice White is that he is best labeled a moderate justice; more particularly, he was a moderate who wielded a good deal of power and authority based on his position as a swing vote on the Court.

In recent years it has become fashionable to discuss how Justice O'Connor sat in the median seat of the Court during her final years, as she consequently wielded much control over the outcomes of many of the Supreme Court's cases. Similarly, on the Roberts Court, Justice Kennedy enjoys the power that comes with being the median justice, commanding the outcome in many cases, particularly those that are closely divided along ideological lines. While he's not often credited with this role, Justice White was regularly the median voter during both the Burger and Rehnquist Courts, though not so much on the Warren Court. During the 1970s, the four Nixon appointees were generally more conservative than White, while the other justices were more liberal (Mishler and Sheehan 1996). The ideological lines were not quite as clear-cut as they are today, since Justice Stewart also appeared to play the role of swing voter during the Burger Court. The arrival of Justice O'Connor combined with the liberalizing trend in Justice Blackmun's voting record made White less frequently the median voter during the final years of the Burger Court.

Interestingly, once the Rehnquist Court era moved forward, Presidents Reagan and Bush generally made conservative appointments, and this put Justice White back in the middle as the critical swing vote on the Court, particularly once Justice Blackmun became a more reliable liberal vote. And, while President Bush's first appointee, Justice Souter, developed into a reliable liberal vote at the end of his tenure on the Court, his voting record when he first was appointed was moderately conservative. Moreover, Justices White and Souter did not overlap in their tenures for very long. Thus, the "Souter mistake," as characterized by political conservatives, did not seem to push Justice White out of the median seat on the Court.

The result is that White's moderate stance and place in the center of the Court's ideological divides on both the Burger and Rehnquist Courts provided him with more power than is often recognized (cf., Blasecki 1990 and Mishler and Sheehan 1996, both of which contended, as I do here, that Justice White served as the median justice for much of his tenure on the Court). For some reason, White's influence on the Supreme Court is often overlooked.

It seems odd that there has been a lack of interest in Justice White, just as it is odd that many fail to credit White for his true influence during his long tenure on the Court. These holes in scholarly and media attention are particularly ironic considering how famous White was prior to his appointment to the Court. It also is surprising to observe so little written or attributed to White, considering how much attention has been paid to the strong liberals of the Warren and Burger Courts such as Brennan and Marshall, and to the powerful conservative voices in Scalia and Thomas, and to the important role that O'Connor and Kennedy have played as the swing voters on the Rehnquist Court. Justice White's position as a moderate who often played the role of median justice, along with his relatively long tenure on the Court, together provide evidence that White owned a more critical voice for both the Court's jurisprudence and judicial outcomes than the conventional wisdom typically acknowledges.

References

Blasecki, Janet L. "Justice Lewis F. Powell: Swing Voter or Staunch Conservative?" *Journal of Politics* 52 (1990): 530-47.

Currie, David P. *The Constitution in the Supreme Court: The Second Century, 1886-1986.* Chicago: University of Chicago Press, 1990.

Epstein, Lee, Valerie Hoekstra, Jeffrey A. Segal, and Harold J. Spaeth. "Do Political Preferences Change? A Longitudinal Study of U.S. Supreme Court Justices." *Journal of Politics* 60 (1998): 801-18.

Epstein, Lee, Jeffrey A. Segal, Harold J. Spaeth, and Thomas G. Walker. *The Supreme Court Compendium: Data, Decisions & Developments.* Washington: CQ Press, 1994.

Hurwitz, Mark S. "Give Him a Fair Trial, Then Hang Him: The Supreme Court's Modern Death Penalty Jurisprudence." *Justice System Journal* 29 (2008): 243-56.

Hutchinson, Dennis J. *The Man Who Once Was Whizzer White: A Portrait of Justice Byron R. White.* New York: Free Press, 1998.

Kramer, Daniel C. "Justice Byron R. White: Good Friend to Polity and Solon." Pp. 407-32 in *The Burger Court: Political and Judicial Profiles,* edited by Charles M. Lamb and Stephen C. Halpern. Urbana, IL: University of Illinois Press, 1991.

Maltz, Earl M. *Rehnquist Justice: Understanding the Court Dynamic.* Lawrence, KS: University Press of Kansas, 2003.

McGuire, Kevin T., and James A. Stimson. "The Least Dangerous Branch Revisited: New Evidence on Supreme Court Responsiveness to Public Preferences." *Journal of Politics* 66 (2004): 1018-35.

Mishler, William, and Reginald S. Sheehan. "Public Opinion, the Attitudinal Model, and Supreme Court Decision Making: A Micro-Analytic Perspective." *Journal of Politics* 58 (1996): 169-200.

Peppers, Todd C. *Courtiers of the Marble Palace: The Rise and Influence of the Supreme Court Clerk.* Stanford, CA: Stanford University Press, 2006.

Rehnquist, William H. "Tribute to Justice Byron R. White." *Stanford Law Review* 55 (2002): 1.
Smith, Christopher E. "The Malleability of Constitutional Doctrine and Its Ironic Impact on Prisoners' Rights." *Boston University Public Interest Law Journal* 11 (2001): 73-96.

Cases Cited

Arizona v. Hicks, 480 U.S. 321 (1987)
Atkins v. Virginia, 536 U.S. 304 (2002)
Bowers v. Hardwick, 478 U.S. 186 (1986)
Brecht v. Abrahamson, 507 U.S. 619 (1993)
California v. Greenwood, 486 U.S. 35 (1988)
Carey v. Population Services International, 431 U.S. 678 (1977)
Colorado v. Bertine, 479 U.S. 367 (1987)
Eisenstadt v. Baird, 405 U.S. 438 (1972)
Ford v. Wainwright, 477 U.S. 399 (1986)
Furman v. Georgia, 408 U.S. 238 (1972)
Graham v. Collins, 506 U.S. 461 (1993)
Gregg v. Georgia, 428 U.S. 153 (1976)
Griswold v. Connecticut, 381 U.S. 479 (1965)
Harmelin v. Michigan, 501 U.S. 957 (1991)
Helling v. McKinney, 509 U.S. 25 (1993)
Herrera v. Collins, 506 U.S. 390 (1993)
Jackson v. Virginia, 443 U.S. 307 (1979)
Lawrence v. Texas, 539 U.S. 558 (2003)
McCleskey v. Kemp, 481 U.S. 279 (1987)
Miranda v. Arizona, 384 U.S. 436 (1966)
Penry v. Lynaugh, 492 U.S. 302 (1989)
Robinson v. California, 370 U.S. 660 (1962)
Roe v. Wade, 410 U.S. 113 (1973)
Wilson v. Seiter, 501 U.S. 294 (1991)

Chapter 4
Harry A. Blackmun:
Counterweight to a Conservative Court

Ashlyn Kuersten and Lee Ruffin Wilson

Justice Harry A. Blackmun was a federal jurist for almost forty years, serving twenty-four of his ninety years of life on the United States Supreme Court. Blackmun joined the Supreme Court in 1970, preceding fellow Nixon nominee William Rehnquist by just two years. During his years on the Supreme Court, Justice Blackmun heard over four thousand cases (Koh 1994) but he was probably best known, of course, as the author of *Roe v. Wade* (1973). Following that decision, he was regularly criticized by his brethren (especially Rehnquist and Scalia) and members of the public who not only disagreed with the decision but also blamed Blackmun for legalizing abortion.

However, Blackmun's contribution to American jurisprudence extends beyond his judicial opinions. Blackmun archived the personal and professional papers he accumulated throughout his lifetime. In 2004, five years after his death, the Library of Congress unveiled Blackmun's extensive collection of "correspondence, diaries, notebooks and notes, speeches, [and] writings" (Blackmun Papers 2005), including drafts of some of the opinions he wrote and memoranda he exchanged with other justices. With the publication of these papers, Justice Blackmun's life became more publicly accessible than any other justice in American history. Indeed, his papers offer the public one of the few windows into a justice's inner thoughts about both the Court and the various justices with whom he worked.

His memos, papers, and the opinions he produced during his lifetime allow an assessment of his contribution to criminal jurisprudence during his years on the Rehnquist Court. From 1986 until he accepted senior status in 1994, Blackmun served the last eight years of his tenure on the Rehnquist Court. Justices Harry Blackmun and William Rehnquist, while nominated by the same president, created two disparate judicial legacies. Both arrived on the Supreme Court with President Nixon's expectation that each justice would help to reverse the leftist trend of the Court's Warren era. While Rehnquist's decisions often showed evidence of the values of a partisan conservative, Justice Blackmun is

widely described as a conservative who converted to liberalism during his Supreme Court years (see Wasby 1995; Greenhouse 2005; Kobylka 2005; Epstein,
Hoekstra, Segal, and Spaeth 1998, 813; Martin and Quinn 2002, 147).

But Blackmun himself took exception to that characterization and once said,
"I haven't changed, the Court has changed under me. . . . It has become more
conservative" (Blackmun Oral History Project, interview July 6, 1994; see also
Koh 1994). It is clear that as one Republican nominee after the next joined the
Court during the Burger Court era and the early Rehnquist Court years, Blackmun's decisions in matters of criminal law became increasingly aligned with the
liberal justices. While Rehnquist continued to follow the course Chief Justice
Burger charted toward a more partisan and conservative Court, Blackmun remained steadfast, demonstrating the same judicial temperament that earned him
an appointment to the Supreme Court when he was an appellate judge. By his
own admission, Justice Blackmun was not guided by a particular philosophy: "I
get disturbed when we have a case that goes off on theory and does injustice to
the litigant. I think we're there to try to do justice to him as well as to develop a
great, overlying cloud of legal theory" (Shaman 1986, 38).

While at the beginning of his career Blackmun's voting behavior was consistent with the more conservative justices, by the end of his tenure and during
the Rehnquist Court era his opinions indicated an increasing concern with the
erosion of civil liberties. Blackmun witnessed the restriction of habeas corpus
during his years on the Court. He became increasingly concerned with the inconsistency of criminal law doctrine, particularly in capital punishment cases.
Blackmun's voting behavior mirrored the changing nature of the Court and was
not a reflection of a changed judicial philosophy or value system. For example,
despite his personal distaste for capital punishment, at the beginning of his career he regularly voted to affirm death sentences and defer to state courts in considering habeas corpus petitions. But as he neared the end of his career and was
confronted with the inequities in the Rehnquist Court's criminal law doctrine,
Blackmun focused on due process and equal rights, ultimately determining that
the death penalty could not be carried out in a manner consistent with either. In
other criminal justice matters, including search and seizure law and jury selection, Blackmun's decisions showed an ideology that was neither liberal nor conservative. While he respected precedent, Blackmun was also willing to reexamine established judicial doctrine. Blackmun maintained his own form of judicial
restraint, ultimately using the liberties guaranteed in the Constitution as the basis
for his judicial decisions, while maintaining concern for the litigants and facts in
each individual case and the real world impact of judicial decision making.

Blackmun's Judicial Beginnings

Attending Harvard on scholarship and a one hundred-dollar loan to be paid back
within three years of graduation, Blackmun paid his bills by installing windows,

tutoring math, working as a janitor, and delivering milk. When he graduated from Harvard with a degree in mathematics in 1929, his admission to Harvard Law School (the only law school to which he applied) was all but guaranteed to him (Greenhouse 2005, 9). Blackmun's journals demonstrate that at times he was discouraged in his study of the law, largely because of his relatively poor performance. After receiving grades back one semester, Blackmun wrote, "I do not know when anything has quite so completely taken the wind out of my sail. . . . Oh, well, life is full of disappointments and I should be getting used to them" (Greenhouse 2005, 12).

As a student, Blackmun discovered the intellectual strengths that would serve him throughout his judicial career. Blackmun excelled in briefing and arguing appellate cases with the moot court team at Harvard. After graduation from law school in 1932, he served an eighteen-month clerkship in Minnesota with John Sanborn, at that time one of seven judges on the Eighth Circuit U.S. Court of Appeals. Following his clerkship, Blackmun entered private practice and in 1950 became in-house counsel at the Mayo Clinic. He described his tenure at the Mayo Clinic as "the happiest decade of my professional life" (Blackmun Oral History Project, interview July 6, 1994), largely because he became immersed in all aspects of the Clinic from reorganizing the management structure, to giving advice on various legal issues, to analyzing the doctors' research papers (Blackmun Oral History Project interview July 6, 1994). In 1959, decades after Judge Sanborn awarded a teenaged Blackmun a prize for his debate on the Constitution and Blackmun served as his law clerk, Sanborn essentially handpicked Blackmun as his replacement on the Eighth Circuit bench. Later that year, President Dwight D. Eisenhower nominated Blackmun to the Eighth Circuit where he would become known as the court's most "studious member" (Reuben 1994, 48).

A federal appellate court judge at fifty-one years of age, Blackmun began interpreting the evolving body of constitutional law produced by the decisions of the U.S. Supreme Court under Chief Justice Earl Warren. Often, the Warren Court's wide-ranging pronouncements on criminal justice matters required extensive translation and interpretation by the lower federal courts. These controversial cases also generated tremendous public scrutiny. Handing down just over two hundred opinions while on the Court of Appeals, Blackmun's approach seemed to emphasize judicial restraint even when he personally disagreed with the outcome. In a 1967 fair housing case that ultimately went to the Supreme Court, a subdivision developer refused to sell a home to a black man solely because of his race (*Jones v. Alfred H. Mayer Co.* 1967). The Civil Rights Act of 1866 clearly barred racial discrimination in the sale of real property, but the question posed to the Court was whether the Act limited action between private parties or applied exclusively to state action. Blackmun found that Congress did not have authority to prevent private discrimination, but privately he noted that "[t]his is the kind of situation, where one does not mind being reversed" (Greenhouse 2005, 30). To his colleague on the Eighth Circuit, he wrote, "The implication [of the opinion] was that we were bound by existing Supreme Court utterances. I am fairly convinced, personally, that fair housing is an important factor in the elimination of the ghetto" (Greenhouse 2005, 30). Indeed, his decision was reversed when the Supreme Court held that the Thirteenth Amendment abolishing slavery, the Fourteenth Amendment's Due Process Clause, and the 1866 Civil Rights Act reflected constitutionally-permissible congressional authority to prohibit private discrimination (*Jones v. Alfred H. Mayer Co.* 1968).

The case of *Pope v. United States* (1967) ultimately gave Blackmun the national attention that would lead him to a seat on the U.S. Supreme Court. Blackmun voted to uphold the death penalty for a multiple-murder conviction after a federal jury rejected the defendant's insanity defense. As described by Greenhouse (2005, 33),

> The defendant, Duane Pope, was a twenty-two-year-old college football star who, (a few days after his college graduation in Kansas) crossed the state line to Big Springs, Nebraska. There he robbed the Farmers State Bank and shot three employees . . . to death. Then he headed west by bus and by plane, gambling in Las Vegas and attending a bullfight in Tijuana, before turning himself in. A federal jury rejected his insanity defense and sentenced him to death under the capital punishment provision of the bank robbery statute. His appeal raised questions about the way the trial court had handled jury selection and about the psychiatric evidence.

In a per curiam decision written by Blackmun, the judges voted to uphold the death sentence. The Eighth Circuit decision indicated that legislatures rather than courts should decide whether the death penalty is an appropriate punishment for serious crimes. The Supreme Court had not yet ruled on the constitutionality of capital punishment. Thus Blackmun concluded it was not the Eighth Circuit's role to decide that question. In his original draft, which hinted at opinions he would later deliver from the Supreme Court, Blackmun expressed his doubts about fairness in the imposition of the death penalty. After two of his fellow judges called Blackmun's original draft and the accompanying negative words about the death penalty "gratuitous," a wounded Blackmun rewrote the opinion (Greenhouse 2005, 34).

In the wake of publicity he received from the *Pope* ruling, Blackmun decided the appeal of a conscientious objector to the military draft. Reluctantly deciding to vacate the conviction of the respondent, Blackmun's concurring opinion included a sentiment widely circulated at the time that "it may be hard [for people such as respondent] to grow up these days. Others, however, seem to manage" (*United States v. Cummins* 1970).

Because of the national attention Blackmun received he became publicly known as tough on crime, a proponent of social order, and a judge who rarely disturbed criminal convictions and sentences. He was considered a conservative, and therefore an ideal candidate as Nixon's third nominee for a seat on the Supreme Court. As will be shown, Justice Blackmun's early positions appeared to comport with many of these expectations, though his jurisprudence ultimately would prove more nuanced and difficult to label.

A Moderate is Confirmed to the Supreme Court

The circumstances of Justice Blackmun's nomination and confirmation to the Supreme Court did not foreshadow the controversial role Blackmun ultimately played in the judiciary. As President Richard Nixon's third nominee to fill the seat left by the resignation of Abe Fortas, Blackmun later joked to Justice Anthony Kennedy that they were both members of the "Number Three Club" (Kennedy was also a presidential third choice to fill a seat on the U.S. Supreme Court after the Reagan Administration's failed nominations of Robert Bork and Douglas Ginsburg). President Nixon nominated Blackmun shortly after the Senate rejected the politically right-wing nominations of G. Harrold Carswell (who had participated in cases in which he had financial interests) and Clement F. Haynesworth, Jr. (who was seen as unsupportive of civil rights claims concerning racial discrimination issues). Just a few years before his own nomination to the Supreme Court, Assistant Attorney General William Rehnquist was assigned the task of vetting Blackmun's record as a judge on the Eighth Circuit U.S. Court of Appeals. Rehnquist's report demonstrated that while Blackmun might not have been a particularly strong conservative, he was at least not an unknown quantity: "I think he can be fairly characterized as conservative-to-moderate in both criminal law and civil rights. He does not uniformly come out on one side or the other, though his tendencies are certainly more in the conservative direction than in the liberal. His opinions are all carefully reasoned" (Greenhouse 2005, 47).

The Nixon Administration clearly aspired to create a conservative Court that would overturn many of the Warren Court's liberal decisions. However, following Nixon's two failed nominations, it was unlikely that Nixon could have pushed a die-hard conservative jurist through the relatively moderate Senate. Blackmun's moderately conservative record was just what Nixon needed to get his nominee through the Senate because Blackmun's opinions on the Court of Appeals reassured liberals that he was not a judicial activist with a conservative agenda. He was easily confirmed by a 94-0 vote in the Senate.

Early Years as a Minnesota Twin

Blackmun arrived on the Court after the close of the Warren Era (1953 to 1969), a period of profound liberalization and reformation of criminal justice law. Many of the opinions handed down during the Warren Court era were extraordinarily controversial, imposed new limits on governmental powers, and endorsed broad interpretations of constitutional rights. Despite selecting a judicial nominee who appealed to both political parties, the right wing hoped that Blackmun would help the Court to change the direction of constitutional jurisprudence concerning criminal justice. President Nixon and the conservative faithful had high expectations for Blackmun and his potential contributions to the anticipated counterrevolution in criminal law under the leadership of Chief Justice Warren Burger.

Initially, Blackmun did not disappoint the conservatives who supported his nomination. He voted as a conservative counterpoint to the Warren Court's liberal approach to defining rights in the criminal justice process. Blackmun was considered the more conservative of the two "Minnesota Twins," the nickname applied to Blackmun and his childhood friend from Minnesota, Chief Justice Burger. Burger, who was appointed to the Court in 1971, was known as a strict constructionist and a critic of the Warren Court's liberal decisions. Blackmun and Burger were extremely close before their joint tenure on the Court. In fact, Blackmun served as best man at Burger's wedding. From all accounts, Burger and Blackmun stayed close, both personally and professionally, for their first few years on the Court. They certainly voted alike. In Blackmun's first year on the Court, he voted with the conservative Burger 96 percent of the time and over the next five years he joined with Burger in 84 percent of his votes.

Critics often characterized Blackmun as "overly sentimental" and claimed that his opinions were not grounded in consistent principles. His early opinions on the Court demonstrate that Blackmun applied his own sense of practicality, even with regard to indigent defendants. In *United States v. Kras* (1973), a decision written in the same year as *Roe v. Wade*, Blackmun voted to uphold a fifty-dollar filing fee for indigent plaintiffs seeking bankruptcy protection, finding the installment payments were "less than the price of a movie and little more than the cost of a pack or two of cigarettes" (*U.S. v. Kras*, 449). Justice Thurgood Marshall's dissenting opinion (460) countered by reprimanding Blackmun for his insensitivity:

> The desperately poor . . . have more important things to do with what little money they have—like attempting to provide some comforts for a gravely ill child, as Kras must do. It is perfectly proper for judges to disagree about what the Constitution requires. But it is disgraceful for an interpretation of the Constitution to be premised upon unfounded assumptions about how people live.

Blackmun was a strong opponent of the judge-made standards that became prevalent during the Warren Court era. He tended to defer to law enforcement in criminal cases and to oppose the exclusionary rule for tainted evidence. For example, he supported the establishment of a good-faith exception to the exclusionary rule in cases of an invalid search warrant in *United States v. Leon* (1984). In a very pragmatic majority opinion, the Court concluded that by allowing some guilty defendants to go free, the public might begin to lose respect for the law. Blackmun's concurring opinion stated that "[i]f a single principle may be drawn from this Court's exclusionary rule decisions . . . . It is that the scope of the exclusionary rule is subject to change in light of changing judicial understanding about the effects of the rule outside the confines of the courtroom" (928).

Indeed, Blackmun often held the conservative line on substantive criminal issues and brought with him an appellate judge's appreciation for the potential abuse of the habeas corpus process by convicted offenders and their attorneys (Reuben 1994). Blackmun's early Supreme Court opinions recognized that post-conviction review of state criminal cases was often used by defense attorneys as a stalling tactic. He initially voted to restrict federal judges' habeas corpus reviews of certain state decisions. For example, he voted to bar defendants from raising Fourth Amendment claims in federal habeas corpus proceedings if the issues were already litigated in the state court (*Stone v. Powell* 1976).

Blackmun's early years on the Burger Court also involved him in cases that produced sweeping changes in death penalty case law. For example, in 1972 the majority of the Court in *Furman v. Georgia* held that the imposition of the death penalty constituted cruel and unusual punishment in violation of the Eighth (and Fourteenth) Amendment. It was a contentious decision (232 pages and nine separate opinions) and created confusion about the Constitution's requirements for proper proceedings in states' capital prosecutions. Justice Blackmun's dissent in *Furman* is probably one of the most elegant explanations of the need for, and difficulties of, judicial restraint. His dissent demonstrated Blackmun's resolve to follow legal precedent even when the results contradicted his personal beliefs. Blackmun argued that the justices who voted with the majority had ignored constitutional principles, writing, "We should not allow our personal preferences as to the wisdom of legislative and congressional action, or our distaste for such action, to guide our judicial decision in cases such as these" (411).

A quick survey of the Court's rulings on the death penalty demonstrates the conflicts and inconsistencies in the criminal case law developed by the Burger Court during this era. Beginning in 1976, the Court handed down decisions that approved some death penalty statutes (see *Jurek v. Texas* 1976; *Proffitt v. Florida* 1976; *Gregg v. Georgia* 1976), invalidated others that mandated death penalties for specific offenses (*Roberts v. Louisiana* 1977) and even created capital sentencing guidelines that seemed incompatible with 1972's *Furman* decision (*Lockett v. Ohio* 1978). In *Lockett,* the Court ruled that Ohio's death penalty statute impermissibly prevented full consideration of mitigating factors. In effect, the decision arguably expanded opportunities for discretionary decision making, the very problem that the *Furman* decision sought to curb.

Justice Blackmun's concurrence in *Lockett* took the factual context of the case into account and argued that capital punishment could not be imposed on a defendant who had only aided and abetted a murder "without permitting any consideration . . . of the extent of her involvement, or the degree of her *mens rea*" (*Lockett* 1978, 613). The female defendant in the case had been sentenced to death although she was sitting in the getaway car and not present at the scene when a pawnshop robbery went awry and the store owner was killed when he struggled to grab a gun from one of the robbers. Blackmun's opinions regarding the Eighth Amendment verified the findings in the report Rehnquist made to Nixon before Blackmun's confirmation hearings—Blackmun was a moderate with conservative leanings.

Blackmun's Criminal Justice Cases during the Rehnquist Court

In matters of criminal justice, Blackmun is probably best known for his opinions on the death penalty. However, his decisions in other areas of criminal law reflect a similar judicial temperament. During the Rehnquist Court years, the justices steadily carved out exceptions to the constitutional protections given to criminal defendants by the Warren Court. While Blackmun at times wrote majority opinions that were joined by stalwart conservatives like Scalia and Rehnquist, he was often part of the minority, joining liberals Marshall and Brennan in dissent. The body of decisions Blackmun made in criminal matters while on the Rehnquist Court cannot be categorized easily as liberal or conservative, but certainly he seemed to become more liberal compared to his increasingly conservative colleagues, as a review of his opinions makes clear.

A Moderate Blackmun and the Right to a Jury

In *Batson v. Kentucky* (1986), one of the last cases from the Burger Court era, the Court ruled that if the prosecution used peremptory challenges to dismiss members of a defendant's race from the jury panel, the defendant had a prima facie case of racial discrimination in violation of the Fourteenth Amendment. Soon the Supreme Court was asked to decide whether *Batson* applied retroactively to cases pending on direct review or not yet final at the time of the *Batson* decision—in other words, whether defendants who were tried before *Batson* but had not yet exhausted their appeals could benefit from the ruling. In 1987, Blackmun authored the majority opinion in *Griffith v. Kentucky*, a case that reviewed the Court's historical treatment of retroactivity and the rationale behind the existing "clear break" exception to retroactivity of new criminal procedural rules like the holding in *Batson*. Ultimately, he declared "a new rule for the conduct of criminal prosecutions is to be applied retroactively to all cases, state or federal, pending on direct review or not yet final" (*Griffith* 1987, 326); thus, the Court abandoned the "clear break" exception.

With his opinion in the *Griffith* case, Blackmun made an important contribution to criminal case law. The ruling ensured that similarly situated defendants would be treated in an equitable fashion. The standard adopted in *Griffith* opened the court system to more appeals by broadening the number of defendants who might benefit from *Batson* and the retroactive application of other Court rulings. Five other justices joined Blackmun in his opinion. Chief Justice Rehnquist and Justice O'Connor joined Justice White's dissent, which hints at the direction the Rehnquist Court was moving. While "the majority's concerns are no doubt laudable," those in dissent expressed hope that "good judgment would . . . win out over blind adherence to the principle of treating like cases alike" (*Griffith* 1987, 330, 332).

Blackmun participated in a series of cases that developed the *Batson* doctrine and resulted in the constitutionalization of the jury selection process. These opinions changed the way juries are selected in trials and consequently altered the rights of criminal defendants. In general, the effect of Blackmun's votes was to restrict the use of peremptory challenges. In two instances, he wrote majority opinions that directly limited the availability of peremptory challenges (*Georgia v. McCollum* 1992 and *J.E.B. v. Alabama ex rel. T.B.* 1994). In other cases, he joined the minority in expressing concern for both a defendant's right to a jury trial and also a citizen's right to sit on a jury (e.g., *Hernandez v. New York* 1991). For example, Blackmun joined Marshall's dissent in *Holland v. Illinois* (1990) when the majority rejected a white defendant's claim that a prosecutor violated the Sixth Amendment when he used his peremptory challenges solely to exclude African Americans from a petit jury. A year later, when a white defendant made a Fourteenth Amendment equal protection claim in a similar case (*Powers v. Ohio* 1991), Blackmun was in the majority when the Court recognized that potential jurors should not be excluded from a jury because of a prosecutor's race-based peremptory challenges and that a criminal defendant has standing to "raise the third-party equal protection claims of jurors excluded by the prosecution" due to their race (415). In the dissent authored by conservative Scalia and joined by Rehnquist, the majority's characterization of *Batson* was "hotly disputed" (Johnson 1993, 37).

In *Georgia v. McCollum* (1992) and *J.E.B. v. Alabama ex rel. T.B.* (1994), Blackmun authored majority opinions that broadened the *Batson* doctrine. Again, his decisions restricted the use of peremptory challenges, although, unlike in the *Holland* case, now that stance put him in the Court's majority. In *McCollum*, Blackmun's opinion reflected his ongoing concern for the effect of racial discrimination on American society, including the judicial system. The defendants were charged with a racially-motivated assault and the state sought to prevent the white defendants from using peremptory challenges in a racially discriminatory way. The trial court denied the state's motion and Georgia's Supreme Court affirmed, citing the historical purpose of peremptory challenges to protect criminal defendants at trial. In a 7-2 decision, the U.S. Supreme Court ruled that equal protection principles covered and restricted a criminal defendant's racially-discriminatory use of peremptory challenges. After noting that over the years, "the Court gradually has abolished race as a consideration for jury service" (*McCollum* 1992, 46), the Court determined it was proper to extend *Batson* to limit criminal defendants' peremptory challenges. Writing for the Court, Blackmun first reasoned that "regardless of who invokes the discriminatory challenge," both the juror and the public are harmed. The juror is "subjected to open and public racial discrimination" and public confidence is undermined by discriminatory selection procedures. According to Blackmun, "Public confidence in the integrity of the criminal justice system is essential for preserving community peace in trials involving race-related crimes" (49). Blackmun also referred to a law review article on the community violence that resulted when two white defendants were acquitted of racial beatings after trials in which the defendants used their peremptory challenges to strike all African American jurors. Surely, Justice Blackmun had contemporary events on his mind when he wrote this opinion. *McCollum* was handed down in June 1992, less than two months after deadly riots occurred in Los Angeles following the acquittals of four police officers accused of beating black motorist Rodney King (49).

Continuing his analysis in *McCollum*, Blackmun determined that racial discrimination by criminal defendants in the use of peremptory challenges constitutes a state action implicating the Equal Protection Clause because in jury selection, "a criminal defendant is wielding the power to choose a quintessential government body" (*McCollum* 1992, 54). Applying *Powers v. Ohio* (1991), Blackmun's opinion then declared that prosecutors have standing to bring an equal protection challenge against a criminal defendant's racially-based peremptory challenges. Therefore, the state could "assert the invasion of the constitutional rights of the excluded jurors in a criminal trial" (*McCollum* 1992, 56). Lastly, Blackmun's opinion weighed the interests protected by *Batson* against any potential harm to the right of criminal defendants to exercise peremptory challenges. According to the opinion, while the Constitution guarantees criminal defendants an impartial jury and a fair trial; peremptory challenges are only a means to that end and are not themselves guaranteed. Using the passionate language that sometimes ruffled his critics, Blackmun noted that "[i]t is an affront to justice to argue that a fair trial includes the right to discriminate against a group of citizens based upon their race" (*McCollum* 1992, 57). Blackmun was concerned not only with the institution of the jury trial, but also with the right of the individual citizen-juror to participate in the judicial system.

By 1992, Blackmun's opinions in death penalty cases routinely favored criminal defendants, yet Blackmun's opinion in *McCollum* arguably served to restrict criminal defendants and their trial attorneys in the jury selection process. Some Court observers criticized Blackmun's opinion, citing the possible effect of limiting criminal defendants' use of peremptory strikes. Blackmun also received strong criticism from his more conservative colleagues who challenged his reasoning. Justice Thomas concurred with the Court's decision but warned that "black criminal defendants will rue the day that this Court ventured down this road that inexorably will lead to the elimination of peremptory challenges" (*McCollum* 1992, 60). Justice O'Connor complained in her dissent about the Court's "remarkable conclusion that criminal defendants being prosecuted by the State act on behalf of their adversary when they exercise peremptory challenges during jury selection" (62). In essence, she could not accept that a defendant's decision could be treated as "state action" in order to come under the limitations imposed by equal protection analysis. The "perverse result" about which O'Connor complained was met with equal hostility by Justice Scalia, who referred to the results as "terminally absurd" (63, 69).

In 1994, Justice Blackmun authored a final opinion in which he extended the *Batson* doctrine. In a paternity action filed by the state on behalf of the mother, the putative father complained that the state used its peremptory challenges to remove men from the jury (*J.E.B. v. Alabama ex rel. T.B.* 1994). The

Supreme Court agreed with the father that the use of peremptory challenges in a gender-based discriminatory manner violated the Equal Protection Clause. Although he rooted the Court's holding in precedent and constitutional theory, Blackmun expressed recognition for the way gender "stereotypes have wreaked injustice in so many other spheres of our country's public life" (140). Blackmun surveyed the historical exclusion of women from jury service and noted that allowing gender discrimination in jury selection would require the Court to "condone the same stereotypes that justified the wholesale exclusion of women from juries and the ballot box" (139). Just as in *McCollum,* where he discussed the harm created by race-based discrimination in preemptory challenges, in *J.E.B.* Blackmun discussed the negative effects of gender-based discrimination on the parties, the jurors, and the community. All are harmed by gender-based discrimination in peremptory strikes that "ratify and reinforce prejudicial views of the relative abilities of men and women" (140).

Blackmun contended in his opinion that the decision was not meant to herald the elimination of the peremptory challenges and insisted that proper voir dire could eliminate the need to rely on "stereotypical and pejorative notions" about gender or race (*J.E.B. v. Alabama ex rel. T.B.* 1994, 143). Despite this assertion, Blackmun continued to be the target of barbed criticism from his conservative colleagues. In a "concurrence that had the tone of a dissent" (Koonce 1995, 531), Justice O'Connor argued that the holding in *J.E.B.* should not apply to peremptory rights exercised by civil litigants and criminal defendants. She noted that adding constitutional restrictions on the use of peremptory challenges might hamper "an important litigator's tool and a fundamental part of the process of selecting impartial jurors" (*J.E.B. v. Alabama ex rel. T.B.* 1994, 148). Conservatives Rehnquist, Scalia, and Thomas dissented from the ruling penned by Blackmun. The chief justice wrote a dissent arguing that the *Batson* doctrine should not include gender-based peremptory challenges, noting the differing natures of gender and race discrimination. He contended that not only do gender and race discrimination enjoy different levels of constitutional scrutiny, but also gender-based peremptory challenges are "generally not the sort of derogatory and invidious acts which peremptory challenges directed at black jurors may be" (156). Rehnquist also joined Justice Scalia's dissent, which in "characteristically withering terms" (Koonce 1995, 533) protested that the majority's reasoning was "largely obscured by anti-male chauvinist oratory" (*J.E.B. v. Alabama ex rel. T.B.* 1994, 160). Scalia alleged that by extending *Batson* to include gender, the majority further restricted the use of peremptory challenges, thus "vandalizing" an important legal tradition (163).

Blackmun's Standards in Search and Seizure Cases

As the Rehnquist Court carved out exceptions to the Fourth Amendment's restrictions on police investigations, Blackmun's decisions in search and seizure cases continued to defy easy categorization. In some cases, Blackmun stayed with the majority in rulings that would limit the application of the Fourth Amendment, but in other cases Blackmun was in the minority, objecting to the Court's efforts to narrow the scope of Fourth Amendment rights.

In *Hodari D.*, Blackmun joined a 7-2 majority opinion authored by Scalia that decided that drugs discarded by a juvenile fleeing police were not the fruit of a Fourth Amendment seizure of the defendant's person *(California v. Hodari D.* 1991). Likewise, a man who ran when he saw a police car was not seized by police for Fourth Amendment purposes when the police car followed him then drove alongside him *(Michigan v. Chesternut* 1988). Blackmun, speaking for a unanimous Court, found that the police conduct "would not have communicated to the reasonable person an attempt to capture or otherwise intrude upon respondent's freedom of movement" (575). While the ruling favored the exercise of police authority, Blackmun narrowed the holding to the specific facts. Rather than formulate a "bright-line rule applicable to all investigatory pursuits" (572), Blackmun said that in determining whether police conduct amounts to a Fourth Amendment seizure, the Court must consider the circumstances of each individual incident.

In 1991, the Court ruled that a bus passenger was not seized for Fourth Amendment purposes when police boarded the bus, interviewed selected passengers, and asked to search the passengers' belongings *(Florida v. Bostick)*. Blackmun joined the dissent, wherein an incredulous Marshall wondered how the majority concluded that a reasonable person would feel free to decline to cooperate with police officers during such a "suspicionless, dragnet style sweep" (444). The three dissenting justices agreed that although this law enforcement tactic might be an effective weapon in the nation's war on drugs, it was an unconstitutional seizure under the Fourth Amendment.

Blackmun's opinions in search and seizure cases also recognized that police need some latitude with which to carry out their law enforcement functions. Blackmun agreed with the majority of the Court that an inventory search of the containers in an impounded vehicle did not exceed the scope of a permissible warrantless search *(Colorado v. Bertine* 1987). However, in his concurring opinion, Blackmun wrote "separately to underscore the importance of having such inventories conducted only pursuant to standardized police procedures" (376). Blackmun worried that, without guidelines, inventory searches could be used as investigatory tools in violation of the Fourth Amendment. In a case where the police had no departmental policy on inventory searches, Blackmun concurred with the majority that contraband found in a locked suitcase in the trunk of an impounded vehicle was inadmissible. The evidence did not fall under the inventory search exception to the Fourth Amendment because the Florida Highway Patrol had no policy governing the search of closed containers *(Florida v. Wells* 1990). While policies calling for the opening of all containers or no containers at all are "unquestionably permissible," Rehnquist wrote, an acceptable inventory search might also allow a police officer the discretion to open the container, depending on "the nature of the search and characteristics of the container itself" (5). Blackmun agreed with the Court's conclusion that the search was improper in the absence of any departmental inventory search policy, but he took exception to what he characterized as the majority opinion's "unnecessary" language about permissible extent of police discretion during an inventory search. He cautioned that the "exercise of discretion by an individual officer, especially when it cannot be measured against objective, standard criteria, creates the potential for abuse" (11). While Blackmun reached the same conclusion as his more conservative colleagues, he worried about the effects of the Court's opinion when judges and police officers interpreted Rehnquist's justifications for discretionary searches of closed containers.

The same year that Blackmun wrote his concurring opinion in *Bertine*, he wrote an opinion in an administrative search case that further broadened the exceptions to the Fourth Amendment's Warrant Clause (*New York v. Burger* 1987). A defendant charged with possession of stolen vehicle parts moved to suppress evidence discovered by police while conducting a warrantless inspection pursuant to an administrative inspection statute. The Court found that the New York statute was constitutional and the defendant—the owner of a junkyard, a closely regulated business—had a reduced expectation of privacy. The government's substantial interest in addressing vehicle theft informed the regulatory scheme under which the search of the junkyard was made. The decision also rejected the notion that the statute was a pretext designed to give the police a means to investigate criminal activity, noting that a warrantless inspection is not necessarily unconstitutional even though it may lead to evidence of crimes not covered by the regulatory scheme. His opinion supported the use of warrantless searches by law enforcement but also expressed again his belief that police should have limited discretion in executing warrantless searches. According to Blackmun, the inspection in *Burger* did not "constitute discretionary acts by a governmental official because the statute limited the time, place, and scope of the inspection" (711).

Although Blackmun was willing to extend the warrantless search exception to administrative searches of closely regulated businesses, he refused to join the Court's holding that the search of a probationer's home without a warrant was protected by a special needs exception to the warrant requirement (*Griffin v. Wisconsin* 1987). The statute under review declared that if the state determined reasonable grounds existed to believe that contraband was in a probationer's home, there was no need for a search warrant. While the majority found that a warrant requirement would interfere with the state's probation system, Blackmun offered a middle of the road alternative. He found that although law enforcement special needs justified a reduced level of suspicion before a probation officer could search a probationer's home, those needs did not justify an exception to the warrant requirement.

In a number of search and seizure cases, Blackmun took a position that limited the individual's expectation of privacy under the Fourth Amendment. In *United States v. Dunn* (1987), Blackmun joined the Court's finding that a warrantless search was proper when police officers stood outside the curtilage of a home and peered inside a barn but did not enter. Similarly, Blackmun agreed with the Court that defendants did not have an expectation of privacy in garbage left for collection outside the home's curtilage (*California v. Greenwood* 1988). In both *Greenwood* and *Dunn*, Blackmun found himself in opposition to liberals Brennan and Marshall, but in *O'Connor v. Ortega* (1987), Blackmun authored a dissent joined by both of those holdovers from the Warren Court era. Concluding that a public employee had a Fourth Amendment expectation of privacy in his office, Blackmun wrote that the expectation of privacy in the workplace was based in part on the "reality of work in modern time," in which aspects of work and home life were increasingly intertwined (739). Again showing an awareness of the practicalities of life for the average citizen, Blackmun chided the plurality for an opinion that revealed "a certain insensitivity" to the realities of life for most working Americans.

After a "series of cases in which the Court vacillated" in its opinions regarding the warrantless search of closed containers in automobiles (Kinports 1998, 234), Blackmun wrote *California v. Acevedo* (1991). In *Acevedo*, Blackmun attempted to address the Court's inconsistent holdings and to articulate, in his words, "one clear-cut rule" governing the constitutionality of such searches (579). Throughout his career, Blackmun demonstrated a willingness to reexamine the Court's approach to a question of law when that approach "bred confusion or . . . led to anomalous results" (579). Blackmun acknowledged in *Acevedo*, that the Court's earlier decisions "troubled courts and law enforcement officers" charged with carrying out the Court's rulings (569). In *Acevedo*, the defendant carried a package out of an apartment that the police knew contained marijuana. The brown paper bag he carried was the same size as marijuana packages previously delivered to the apartment. After watching the defendant place the bag into his car's trunk, the police stopped him. Without first obtaining a warrant, the police removed the bag from the trunk and upon opening it, discovered marijuana. The lower appellate court held that the evidence was inadmissible because while the police had probable cause to believe that the bag contained drugs, they did not have probable cause to inspect the car without a warrant. The Supreme Court disagreed and ruled that the police did not need a warrant to search a container in a movable vehicle when probable cause existed to search the container but not the entire automobile. Although the ruling seemed decidedly pro-police, Blackmun pointed out that if the Court adopted separate rules governing probable cause to search a package in a vehicle and probable cause to search the vehicle itself, the result might actually broaden police powers. He feared that the police might search a car as a way to justify the search of a container in the car.

Blackmun was relatively consistent in voting to limit the power of the police. For example, in a 1987 case police officers obtained a search warrant for a suspect's third floor apartment (*Maryland v. Garrison*). The officers did not realize there was a second apartment on that floor. When executing the warrant for the suspect's dwelling, they searched the respondent's separate apartment where they found and seized contraband. Garrison was ultimately convicted of drug possession. The Supreme Court held that the seized contraband was admissible evidence and "insofar as it authorized a search that turned out to be ambiguous in scope," the warrant still satisfied the particularity requirement of the Fourth Amendment (86). Nor did the execution of the warrant violate the respondent's rights. The majority declared "the need to allow some latitude for honest mistakes . . . by officers in the dangerous and difficult process of making arrests and executing search warrants" (87).

Justices Brennan and Marshall joined Blackmun's dissent in which he argued that, based on the Court's precedents, the search in *Garrison* clearly violated the Fourth Amendment. The warrant was inconsistent with the particularity requirement of the Warrant Clause. If the warrant described only the third-floor apartment of the original suspect, then the search of the respondent's separate apartment was "warrantless and is presumed unreasonable" (*Maryland v. Garrison* 1987, 93). Further, the police conduct did not amount to reasonable error preventing a Fourth Amendment violation, because "the mistakes here, both with respect to obtaining and executing the warrant, are not reasonable and could easily have been avoided" (101). In reaching his conclusion, Blackmun exhibited his typical concern for the particularities of the facts of the case under review. He recited a number of factors that made the police officers' conduct unreasonable. For example, he noted that the police knew it was a multiunit building and after observing seven doorbells and seven mailboxes, still made no effort to determine if there was more than one apartment on the third floor.

His dissent in the 1989 case *Florida v. Riley* demonstrated Blackmun's unique consideration of the specific facts of each case, as well as his ever-present concern for the impact of government actions on citizens' lives. The majority found that observations made from a police helicopter flying at a 400-foot altitude over a greenhouse on residential property did not constitute a search for Fourth Amendment purposes. Any expectation of privacy enjoyed by the defendant was not violated because the helicopter was flying at an altitude allowed by law. In his dissent, Blackmun noted his own belief that for "most American communities it is a rare event when nonpolice helicopters fly over one's curtilage at 400 feet" (467). The proper inquiry, he wrote, was not whether the altitude was lawful, but whether the prosecution proved the facts necessary to show the defendant lacked a reasonable expectation of privacy. Further, Blackmun suggested that the Court establish such a prosecutorial burden of proof specifically for any "helicopter surveillance cases in which flight occurred below 1,000 feet" (468).

Blackmun's opinions on search and seizure reflect his recognition of two important interests. He did not consistently seek to limit police authority because he recognized that the police need some latitude in seeking to collect evidence in various search and seizure situations. On the other hand, he was less inclined than several of his colleagues to expand police authority because he recognized that police needed guidelines in order to reduce the risk of abusing discretionary search authority in ways that would violate citizens' privacy interests. Thus his opinions did not consistently favor either expanded police authority or the protection of individuals from searches.

"Tinkering" with the Death Penalty

The death penalty became one of the most debated issues in American politics beginning in the early 1980s and continuing throughout Blackmun's years on the Rehnquist Court. In 1972, the year *Furman* was decided, the number of inmates on death row was 334. In 1986, the first year of the Rehnquist Court, the number of inmates on death row had soared to 1,781, the highest number in American history to that point. Further, the number of scheduled executions was increasing each year. And with the increase in inmates on death row came an increase in emergency requests for stays of execution, last minute appeals by defense attorneys whose clients had exhausted their post-conviction appellate proceedings in other courts. Justice Blackmun had the Eighth Circuit as his circuit assignment. Thus, he heard requests for stays of execution from the state and federal courts within the boundaries of the circuit in which he first served as a judge. The Missouri Supreme Court was particularly aggressive in expediting the death penalty process within the Eighth Circuit jurisdiction because its justices routinely set execution dates before allowing inmates to exhaust their appeals to the U.S. Supreme Court. Already troubled by the conflicting death penalty decisions developed first under the Burger Court and then under the Rehnquist Court, Blackmun handled numerous last-minute requests for stays as part of his circuit duties.

The question of the fairness of the death penalty was brought front and center to Harry Blackmun's conscience. As a matter of course, he granted stays for any inmate who had yet to seek review by the U.S. Supreme Court, a policy consistent with Blackmun's wariness of the Rehnquist Court majority's narrow view of procedural safeguards and its restriction of habeas corpus rights.

By the time Chief Justice Warren Burger retired from the Court in 1986, Justice Blackmun was clearly and publicly reevaluating the legalities of the death penalty. Directly following William Rehnquist's elevation to chief justice, Blackmun spoke at the Eighth Circuit's Annual Conference and specifically addressed the imposition of the death penalty. In a speech to the lower federal court judges, Blackmun called the 1985 Term "the most difficult" of the sixteen prior terms for which he had served on the Supreme Court (Greenhouse 2005). He noticed the increasingly hostile public comments to his dissent in *Darden v. Wainwright* (1986), a case in which he wrote that the majority opinion "reveals a Court willing to tolerate not only imperfection but a level of fairness and reliability so low it should make conscientious prosecutors cringe" (189). In response to this statement, Chief Justice Burger, Blackmun's "Minnesota Twin," fired back in his concurring opinion: "The dissent's suggestion that this Court is motivated by impatience with Darden's constitutional claims is refuted by the record; the thirteen years of judicial proceedings in this case manifest substantial care and patience. Our rejection of Darden's claims . . . is once again based on a thoughtful application of the law to the facts of the case. At some point, there must be finality" (188).

Soon after Rehnquist became chief justice, the Court decided a Georgia death penalty case (*McCleskey v. Kemp* 1987). The case was based primarily on the Baldus study, an empirical study of two thousand Georgia murder cases in the 1970s that demonstrated racial disparities in the manner in which the death penalty was imposed in that state. In Georgia, black defendants who killed white victims had the highest likelihood of receiving the death penalty. Specifically, black defendants who killed whites were 4.3 times more likely to receive a death sentence than those defendants whose victims were black. In *McCleskey*, the black defendant was sentenced to death for killing a white Georgia police officer. McCleskey's attorneys argued that the sentence violated the Equal Protection Clause of the Fourteenth Amendment because the Baldus study's statistical analysis showed that, as a black defendant convicted of killing a white victim, he had an increased likelihood of receiving the death penalty. A five-member majority of the Court found that there was no merit to the claim that the state had "enacted or maintained the death penalty statute because of an anticipated racially discriminatory effect" (298). The Court held that general trends did not prove the existence of discrimination in the decision of the jury that decided the defendant's particular case.

Further, the Court held that the petitioner's claim questioned the very principles that "underlie our entire criminal justice system" (*McCleskey v. Kemp* 1987, 315). Thus McCleskey's argument potentially could be extended to apply to other types of criminal sentences as well as to claims based on unexplained discrepancies correlating to membership in other minority groups and even to gender (Yarbrough 2000, 240). In the majority's view, the statistics cited by the defendant failed to show intentional discrimination. In addition, the majority worried that if racial disparities in death sentences could be used as evidence of constitutional violations then "we could soon be faced with similar claims as to other types of penalties" (*McCleskey v. Kemp* 1987, 303).

Blackmun's dissent blasted the majority by first arguing that the empirical inconsistencies in capital punishment found by the study at least deserved attention from the Court. Similar to his dissent in *Darden*, he marveled at the low level of scrutiny the majority of justices applied to a death penalty case:

> The Court today seems to give a new meaning to our recognition that death is different. Rather than requiring 'a correspondingly greater degree of scrutiny of the capital sentencing determination,' *California v. Ramos* 1983, 998-99, the Court relies on the very fact that this is a case involving capital punishment to apply a *lesser* standard of scrutiny under the Equal Protection Clause. The Court concludes that 'legitimate' explanations outweigh McCleskey's claim that his death sentence reflected a constitutionally impermissible risk of racial discrimination. (*McCleskey v. Kemp* 1987, 347-48)

Blackmun also criticized the Georgia prosecutor's broad discretion in deciding whether to seek the death penalty, referencing the Baldus study findings that prosecutors were five times more likely to seek the death penalty in cases involving black defendants and white victims (compared to black defendant-black victim cases), and three times less likely to seek the death penalty in white defendant and black victim cases.

Most pointed, however, was Blackmun's criticism of the majority's concern that if it allowed racial discrimination claims to influence the Court's judgment in death penalty cases, the Court would broaden the scope of allowable constitutional challenges in not only death penalty cases, but in other types of cases as well. Blackmun wrote,

> One of the final concerns discussed by the Court may be the most disturbing aspect of its opinion. Granting relief to McCleskey in this case, it is said, could lead to further constitutional challenges. That, of course, is no reason to deny McCleskey his rights under the Equal Protection Clause. If a grant of relief to him were to lead to a closer examination of the effects of racial considerations throughout the criminal justice system, the system, and hence society, might benefit. (*McCleskey v. Kemp* 1987, 365; citations omitted)

Justice Blackmun's growing concern over the constitutionality of the death penalty culminated with the *McCleskey* case. By 1987, the year after Rehnquist's confirmation as chief justice, Blackmun abandoned the notion that the death penalty could be implemented in a way consistent with notions of fairness and due process. Notes from his papers in a decision a few years later (*Sawyer v. Whitley* 1992) indicate that Justice Blackmun had begun evaluating cases that would act to "explain how [his] views on the death penalty have evolved [because] of the [Court's] dismantling of the writ of habeas corpus" (Blackmun Papers 2005: Dangel Memorandum). Indeed, one of Blackmun's clerks wrote that one draft of Blackmun's concurrence in *Sawyer* was intended "as a personal statement" on the state of habeas and the death penalty (Blackmun Papers 2005: Ward Memorandum). Blackmun concluded that the Court's standard was wrong, but he joined Justice Stevens in upholding the death penalty even as he voiced his disapproval of the Court's increasingly conservative decisions that he felt were narrowing the scope of constitutional protections for criminal defendants. Most importantly, he indicated that he was particularly concerned with the constitutionality of the death penalty. He wrote in his concurring opinion (*Sawyer v. Whitley* 1992, 351)

> to express my ever-growing skepticism that, with each new decision from this Court constricting the ability of the federal courts to remedy constitutional errors, the death penalty really can be imposed fairly and in accordance with the requirements of the Eighth Amendment.

Also by this time, he demonstrated in both his opinions and several interviews that he was willing to reconsider his previously held positions that were not intellectually sustainable, particularly positions he had taken on various issues involved in habeas corpus claims. Clearly, in its very first years the Rehnquist Court seemed poised to continue the Burger Court's efforts to limit the availability of habeas corpus, a rights-protecting mechanism that was expanded by the Warren Court's decisions. Blackmun once complained that the Court "has wandered a long way down the road in expanding traditional notions of habeas corpus" (*Hensley v. Municipal Court* 1973, 353; see also *Braden v. 30th Judicial Circuit Court* 1973). However, his orientation toward habeas corpus changed as the Court under Rehnquist made restrictions on habeas corpus become more broadly stated as legal rules rather than as restrictions on petitions through case-by-case evaluations of frivolous filings by convicted offenders. As the Rehnquist Court's criminal law jurisprudence developed, Blackmun responded with an increased willingness to accept habeas corpus claims and to expand habeas rights.

In 1989, for example, he dissented from the majority's decision that "arbitrarily impose[d] procedural obstacles to . . . send a man to a presumptively unlawful execution because he or his lawyers did not raise his objection at what is felt to be the appropriate time for doing so" (*Dugger v. Adams* 1989, 412-13). In 1990, Justice Blackmun joined the dissent wherein the adamantly-liberal Justice Brennan noted the Rehnquist Court's "growing hostility toward Congress' decision to authorize federal . . . review of state criminal convictions [and its] curtailing the writ of habeas corpus by dramatically restructuring retroactivity doctrine" (*Butler v. McKellar* 1990, 417). Blackmun also parted company with the Rehnquist Court majority's inclination to create procedural burdens for habeas defendants. Blackmun joined Justice Marshall's dissent in noting that "the very essence of the Great Writ is our criminal justice system's commitment to suspending 'conventional notions of finality of litigation . . . where life or liberty is at stake and infringement of constitutional rights is alleged'" (*McCleskey v. Zant* 1991, 517-18, quoting *Sanders v. United States* 1963, 8).

More and more often as the decade wore on, Blackmun voted with the minority, joining liberals Brennan and Marshall, who opposed the majority's politically conservative positions in death penalty cases. He voted to ban the death penalty for juvenile defendants (*Stanford v. Kentucky* 1989) and for the mentally retarded (*Penry v. Lynaugh* 1989). In those opinions, he spoke of standards of decency and questioned whether executing juveniles and those with mental retardation served any legitimate purpose of criminal punishment.

In 1993, as Blackmun neared the end of his tenure, the Court handed down its opinion in *Herrera v. Collins* holding that an inmate could not present late evidence of innocence and receive a writ of habeas corpus and, thus, a stay of execution. Blackmun's dissent eloquently articulated his growing concerns about the legality of the death penalty:

> I have also expressed doubts about whether . . . capital punishment remains constitutional at all. Of one thing, however, I am certain. Just as an execution without adequate safeguards in unacceptable, so too is an execution when the condemned prisoner can prove that he is innocent. The execution of a person who can show that he is innocent comes *perilously close to simple murder*. (*Herrera v. Collins* 1993, 446; emphasis added)

This case was the clearest indication yet that Blackmun had given up on the concept of a constitutionally-permissible death penalty. According to Blackmun, "Nothing could be more contrary to contemporary standards of decency . . . or more shocking to the conscience . . . than to execute a person who is actually innocent" (430; citations omitted).

Blackmun's opposition to capital punishment differed from that expressed by Justices Brennan and Marshall, who viewed the death penalty as cruel and unusual punishment forbidden by both the Eighth and Fourteenth Amendments. Justice Blackmun found the application of death penalty sentencing as simply too arbitrary and capricious, directed by economic and racial disparities instead of judicial fairness. His law clerk, Andrew H. Schapiro, proposed that Blackmun publicly abandon efforts to create a constitutional death penalty based on his experiences in thirty years on the federal bench.

In the 1993 Term, Justice Blackmun directed his law clerks to draft a dissent expressing his opposition to the death penalty and then find a case in which to use it. As the clerks kept track of death penalty cases that Blackmun could potentially use as his vehicle, a highly emotional opinion that would demonstrate the lack of fairness of the death penalty was drafted with blanks to be filled in when the right case was found. In February 1994, just two months before announcing his retirement, Blackmun found his vehicle in a decision denying certiorari review in *Callins v. Collins*. He filed the lone dissenting opinion that stated that he felt "morally and intellectually obligated simply to concede that the death penalty experiment has failed" (*Callins v. Collins* 1994, 1145). Blackmun wrote,

> Twenty years have passed since this Court declared that the death penalty must be imposed fairly, and with reasonable consistency, or not at all, see *Furman v. Georgia*, and, despite the effort of the States and courts to devise legal formulas and procedural rules to meet this daunting challenge, the death penalty remains fraught with arbitrariness, discrimination, caprice, and mistake. . . . Rather than continue to coddle the Court's delusion that the desired level of fairness has been achieved and the need for regulation eviscerated . . . From this day forward, I no longer shall tinker with the machinery of death. (*Callins* 1143-45)

He made clear that he would support vacating all death penalty sentences from that moment onward, mirroring the earlier stance of Justices Brennan and Marshall. The Court Clerk's office was told to attach to every death penalty decision the standard phrase of dissent for Justice Blackmun: "Adhering to my view that the death penalty cannot be imposed fairly within the constraints of the Constitution" (see, for example, *Stansbury v. California* 1994, 327). Nonetheless, the inmate, Bruce Callins, was executed in 1997.

The emotional and personal language Blackmun used in opinions like *Herrera* and *Callins* subjected him to critics' claims that he opposed the death penalty because of his own personal abhorrence of capital punishment, and his decisions were no longer based on solid legal principles. He also was criticized for employing an ad hoc evaluation of each individual case and defendant instead of utilizing broad constitutional principles. Blackmun distinguished himself as a justice prone to making extremely personalized, even sentimental remarks to an extent not usually seen in the opinions of other Supreme Court justices (Rosen 1994). Personal remarks in legal opinions are nothing new but can be considered a "remarkable spectacle" if a justice speaks to a reader "without any pretense of dispassionate neutrality" and argues that his (or her) opinions are based on law and not personal attitudes and opinions (Greenhouse 2005, 232).

Certainly, a review of Justice Blackmun's decisions over the twenty-four years of his tenure on the Court demonstrates his increasing unwillingness to decide cases in support of the death penalty. The personal and emotional remarks contained in his later opinions written in opposition to the death penalty are often cited as proof that Blackmun opposed the death penalty because of his morality. However, even when his judicial decisions routinely upheld or even expanded the death penalty, his diaries, notes, and opinions indicated that he never supported the death penalty personally. In *Furman v. Georgia* (1972), one of his earliest Supreme Court opinions on the matter, Blackmun not only voted to uphold the death sentence but also chastised his colleagues for allowing their personal beliefs to interfere with their judicial duty to base decisions on legal reasoning. He also made a passionate and eloquent description of his own privately-held objection to the death penalty:

> Cases such as these provide for me an excruciating agony of the spirit. I yield to no one in the depth of my distaste, antipathy, and, indeed, abhorrence, for the death penalty, with all its aspects of physical distress and fear and of moral judgment exercised by finite minds. That distaste is buttressed by a belief that capital punishment serves no useful purpose that can be demonstrated. For me, it violates childhood's training and life's experiences, and is not compatible with the philosophical convictions I have been able to develop. It is antagonistic to any sense of 'reverence for life.' Were I a legislator, I would vote against the death penalty for the policy reasons argued by counsel for the respective petitioners and expressed and adopted in the several opinions filed by the Justices who vote to reverse these judgments. (*Furman v. Georgia* 1972, 405-6)

Conclusion

By the end of his tenure with the Rehnquist Court, Blackmun was called the "most empathetic justice of recent times" (Lazarus 1998, 39), a criticism or a compliment for the justice, depending on one's perspective. Even after he was firmly ensconced in his Supreme Court position, Justice Blackmun identified with the average citizen and had an awareness of the realities of life for those less fortunate. "There is another world 'out there,' the existence of which the Court, I suspect, either chooses to ignore or fears to recognize" (*Beal v. Doe*

1977, 463). Indeed, working as a janitor, a milkman, and even as a ranch hand at one point to pay for his education showed him how most Americans lived and this recognition was evident in his opinions in criminal cases (Yarbrough 2007). His opinions showed "in the treatment of little people, what I hope is a sensitivity to their problems" (Rosen 1994, 13).

Throughout his career, he was aware of the practical ramifications of Court decisions. His decision in *Roe*, he told reporters, was a "step that had to be taken down the road toward the full emancipation of women." He hired more female law clerks than any other justice—even more than did Sandra Day O'Connor, who became the first female justice on the Supreme Court. He championed affirmative action programs and derided his fellow justices by writing in *Wards Cove Packing Co. Inc., v. Atonio* (1989, 662), "One wonders whether the majority still believes that race discrimination . . . is a problem in our society, or even remembers that it ever was."

Although articulated recognition of disadvantaged Americans was not common among members of the Rehnquist Court, Blackmun continued to acknowledge the realities of society and to take heed of the effect the Court's decisions had on citizens. In criminal justice cases, his concern for the practical implications of the Court's decisions on the public showed in his opinions. His opposition to the death penalty was based, in part, on his recognition of the inequalities that existed in death penalty sentencing. His own experiences on the Court and various empirical studies proved to him that issues of racial disparity, poverty, lack of education, and minimal legal assistance for indigent defendants were at the heart of many death penalty sentences, thereby making them unconstitutional in his view. To Blackmun, the death penalty was simply an unworkable penalty for states to carry out fairly.

Throughout his time on the Supreme Court bench, Blackmun continued to demonstrate the same reluctance to disturb precedent that he showed as an appellate judge. He often explained his rulings by relying on the factual distinctions between the case at hand and precedent. In a 1978 memo from Justice Blackmun to Chief Justice Burger, he wrote,

> At the end of your opinion, however, I sense a shift to the plurality position in *Woodson*, namely, that to be constitutional a capital sentencing statute must permit consideration of age, prior record, prospects for rehabilitation, and character . . . For me the point of taking a non-triggerman case was that there might be some broader agreement on the necessity of considering some factor distinctive to non-triggermen, namely, the degree of involvement. (Blackmun Papers 2005: Memorandum from Blackmun to the Chief Justice)

One critic suggests that Blackmun's style of making decisions with an emphasis on the individual characteristics of each case allowed Blackmun's personal antipathy "toward capital punishment to shape his decisions, in the sense that it may be easier to approve the punishment in the abstract than as applied to an individual defendant particularly when a clear, controlling legal standard is present" (Pearson and Wells 2005, 1190).

By waiting for the right death penalty case to declare that the penalty could not be executed in a manner consistent with the Constitution, and that therefore he would vote to vacate any future death sentences, Blackmun opened himself up to severe criticism from his colleagues. In his concurrence to the Court's denial of *certiorari* in *Callins*, Justice Scalia noted that Blackmun chose *Callins* because of its emotional and moral content and because the case was

> one of the less brutal of the murders that regularly come before us—the murder of a man ripped by a bullet suddenly and unexpectedly, with no opportunity to prepare himself and his affairs, and left to bleed to death on the floor of a tavern . . . It looks even better next to some of the other cases currently before us which Justice Blackmun did not select as the vehicle for his announcement that the death penalty is always unconstitutional—for example, the case of the 11-year old girl raped by four men and then killed by stuffing her panties down her throat . . . How enviable a quiet death by lethal injection compared with that! (*Callins* at 1142-43; citations omitted)

Justice Blackmun announced his retirement from the Supreme Court just a few weeks before former President Richard Nixon died. At an April 6, 1994, press conference announcing Blackmun's move to senior status, President William J. Clinton described Blackmun's contribution to the Supreme Court. In his judicial decision making, "he found the human dimension and struck the right balance" (*New York Times* 1994). Clinton said that "Blackmun's identification was firmly and decisively with the ordinary people of this country, with their concerns" (*New York Times* 1994). Blackmun's response to these presidential words of praise for his legacy—"[i]t's been a great ride, and I'm indebted to the nation . . . for putting up with the likes of me" (*New York Times* 1994).

President Clinton nominated Justice Stephen Breyer to replace Blackmun on the Court, and a nearly unanimous Senate confirmed Breyer. Five years later, in 1999, Justice Harry Blackmun died following complications from hip surgery. In a eulogy delivered at his memorial service, Justice Breyer praised Blackmun's "humane judicial vision" (Gearan 1999). At the funeral procession, a light blue Volkswagen Beetle carried the late Justice's remains to Arlington National Cemetery. For many years, Blackmun drove a similar car to work every day at the highest court in the land. Perhaps Justice Blackmun's primary contribution to American jurisprudence is the uncommon humanity and humility he brought to Supreme Court decision making.

References

Blackmun Oral History Project, 2004-2005. Interviews with Harry A. Blackmun, interviewer Harold Hongju Koh, July 6, 1994 through December 13,

1995.   http://lcweb2.loc.gov/diglib/blackmun-public/series.html?ID=D10 (accessed September 29, 2010).

Blackmun Papers. "The Papers of Harry A. Blackmun," Library of Congress, Manuscript Reading Room, 2005. http://www.loc.gov/rr/mss/blackmun/ (accessed September 29, 2010).

Epstein, Lee, Valerie Hoekstra, Jeffrey A. Segal, and Harold J. Spaeth. "Do Political Preferences Change? A Longitudinal Study of U.S. Supreme Court Justices." *Journal of Politics* 60 (1998): 801-18.

Gearan, Anne. "Justice Lauded for Humane, Judicial Vision," March 10, 1999. http://www.sddt.com/News/article.cfm?SourceCode=199903101c (last accessed January 27, 2011).

Greenhouse, Linda. *Becoming Justice Blackmun: Harry Blackmun's Supreme Court Journey.* New York: Times Books, 2005.

Johnson, Sheri Lynn. "The Language and Culture (Not to say race) of Peremptory Challenges." *William and Mary Law Review* 35 (1993): 21-93.

Kinports, Kit. "Symposium: Justice Blackmun's Mark on Criminal Law and Procedure." *Hastings Constitutional Law Quarterly* 26 (1998): 219-70.

Kobylka, Joseph F. "Tales From the Blackmun Papers: A Fuller Appreciation of Harry Blackmun's Judicial Legacy." *University of Missouri Law Review* 70 (2005): 1075-1132.

Koh, Harold Hongju. "Justice Blackmun and the 'World Out There.'" *Yale Law Journal* 104 (1994): 23-31.

Koonce, Lance. "J.E.B. ex rel. T.B. and the Fate of the Peremptory Challenge." *North Carolina Law Review* 73 (1995): 525-61.

Lazarus, Edward. *Closed Chambers: The Rise, Fall, and Future of the Modern Supreme Court.* New York: Times Books, 1998.

Martin, Andrew D., and Kevin M. Quinn. "Dynamic Ideal Point Estimation via Markov Chain Monte Carlo for the U.S. Supreme Court, 1953-1999." *Political Analysis* 10 (2002): 134-53.

New York Times. "The Supreme Court; Statements on Retirement of Blackmun from Court," April 7, 1994: 24(A).

Pearson, Martha Dragich, and Christina E. Wells. "Symposium: Reflections on Judging: A Discussion Following the Release of the Blackmun Papers." *Missouri Law Review* 70 (2005): 965-71.

Reuben, Richard C. "Justice Defined: It Takes More Than a Single Opinion to Understand How Legal Reasoning and Personal Experience Shape a 24-year Career." *American Bar Association Journal* 80 (July 1994): 46-50.

Rosen, Jeffrey. "The Emotional Jurisprudence of Harry Blackmun; Sentimental Journey." *New Republic* 210, 18 (May 2, 1994): 13-14, 17-18.

Shaman, Jeffrey. "The Evolution of a Realist." *American Bar Association Journal* 72 (June 1986): 38-41.

Wasby, Stephen L. "Justice Blackmun and Criminal Justice: A Modest Overview." *Akron Law Review* 28 (1995): 125-86.

Yarbrough, Tinsley E. *The Burger Court.* Santa Barbara, CA: ABC-Clio Press, 2000.

———. *Harry A. Blackmun: The Outsider Justice.* New York: Oxford University Press, 2007.

Cases Cited

Batson v. Kentucky, 476 U.S. 79 (1986)
Beal v. Doe, 432 U.S. 438 (1977)
Braden v. 30ᵗʰ Judicial Circuit, 410 U.S. 484 (1973)
Butler v. McKellar, 494 U.S. 407 (1990)
California v. Acevedo, 500 U.S. 565 (1991)
California v. Greenwood, 486 U.S. 35 (1988)
California v. Hodari D., 499 U.S. 621 (1991)
California v. Ramos, 463 U.S. 992 (1983)
Callins v. Collins, 510 U.S. 1141 (1994)
Colorado v. Bertine, 479 U.S. 367 (1987)
Darden v. Wainwright, 477 U.S. 168 (1986)
Dugger v. Adams, 489 U.S. 401 (1989)
Florida v. Bostick, 501 U.S. 429 (1991)
Florida v. Riley, 488 U.S. 445 (1989)
Florida v. Wells, 495 U.S. 1 (1990)
Furman v. Georgia, 408 U.S. 238 (1972)
Georgia v. McCollum, 505 U.S. 42 (1992)
Gregg v. Georgia, 428 U.S. 153 (1976)
Griffin v. Wisconsin, 483 U.S. 868 (1987)
Griffith v. Kentucky, 479 U.S. 314 (1987)
Hensley v. Municipal Court, San Jose-Milpitas Judicial District, 411 U.S. 345 (1973)
Hernandez v. New York, 500 U.S. 352 (1991)
Herrera v. Collins, 506 U.S. 390 (1993)
Holland v. Illinois, 493 U.S. 474 (1990)
J.E.B. v. Alabama ex rel. T.B., 511 U.S. 127 (1994)
Jones v. Alfred H. Mayer Co., 379 F.2d 33 (1967)
Jones v. Alfred H. Mayer Co., 392 U.S. 409 (1968)
Jurek v. Texas, 428 U.S. 262 (1976)
Lockett v. Ohio, 438 U.S. 586 (1978)
Maryland v. Garrison, 480 U.S. 79 (1987)
McCleskey v. Kemp, 481 U.S. 279 (1987)
McCleskey v. Zant, 499 U.S. 467 (1991)
Michigan v. Chesternut, 486 U.S. 567 (1988)
New York v. Burger, 482 U.S. 691 (1987)
O'Connor et al. v. Ortega, 480 U.S. 709 (1987)
Penry v. Lynaugh, 492 U.S. 302 (1989)
Pope v. United States, 419 U.S. 544 (1975)
Powers v. Ohio, 499 U.S. 400 (1991)
Proffitt v. Florida, 428 U.S. 242 (1976)
Roberts v. Louisiana, 431 U.S. 633 (1977)
Roe v. Wade, 410 U.S. 113 (1973)
Sanders v. United States, 373 U.S. 1 (1963)
Sawyer v. Whitley, 505 U.S. 333 (1992)
Stanford v. Kentucky, 492 U.S. 361 (1989)
Stansbury v. California, 511 U.S. 318 (1994)
Stone v. Powell, 428 U.S. 465 (1976)
United States v. Cummins, 425 F.2d 646 (1970)

United States v. Dunn, 480 U.S. 294 (1987)
United States v. Kras, 409 U.S. 434 (1973)
United States v. Leon, 468 U.S. 897 (1984)
Wards Cove Packing Co., Inc., et al. v. Atonio, et al., 490 US 642 (1989)

Chapter 5
William H. Rehnquist: Leadership & Influence from the Conservative Wing

Michael A. McCall

In January 1972, William Hubbs Rehnquist became the one hundredth jurist to sit on the U.S. Supreme Court. He continued serving until his death in September 2005. Spanning more than a third of a century, Rehnquist's tenure more than doubled the average length of time for a justice to hold a seat on the high court and ranked him as one of the longest-serving members in Supreme Court history.

During these years on the Court, Rehnquist helped decide over four thousand cases including several hundred that collectively reshaped the landscape of American criminal justice. The justices broke new ground in precedent-setting cases regarding capital punishment, search and seizure, habeas corpus, self-incrimination, the right to counsel, and other areas over the course of Rehnquist's three decades on the Supreme Court. Perhaps the more apt metaphor is that in recent decades the Supreme Court, first under Chief Justice Burger and then under Rehnquist, often filled in ground previously excavated. This is to say that many of the opinions Rehnquist supported and wrote tended to carve out exceptions to or set other limitations on the substantive and procedural rights of criminal defendants that the more liberal Warren Court (1953-1969) had articulated and expanded. If the Warren Court can be characterized fairly as often giving primacy to protecting individual rights and preserving safeguards for the criminally accused, the years in which Rehnquist served reflect a pendulum swing toward favoring government interests in criminal justice. From this perspective, the Rehnquist Court era tended to emphasize social order and government's responsibility to protect individuals from crime. The Rehnquist Court also placed an increased burden on defendants who claimed that their constitutional rights had been violated.

The contrast between the Warren Court and the later Burger and Rehnquist Courts aligns with Herbert Packer's (1968) classic analysis identifying two competing models of our criminal justice system. One perspective's definition of justice centers on government's treatment of those brought into the system and champions the *importance of due process* (i.e., Warren Court). The other approach (i.e., Burger and Rehnquist Courts) emphasizes that the *control of crime* through prevention, investigation, and punishment is central to our understanding of justice and reflects a basic obligation of the government. Of course, Rehnquist's values and jurisprudence cannot be placed neatly and completely into only one of these two categories. However, his proclivity to favor social control serves as a framework for much of the discussion in this chapter and represents a significant part of his judicial legacy.

Some of Rehnquist's influence in criminal justice derives from his role as chief justice. Although the Court's norms of egalitarianism, deliberativeness, and majority rule encourage considering the position of chief justice as being "first among equals" (*primus inter pares*), chief justices possess notable powers such as assigning who writes the Court's opinions (when the chief justice is in the majority). Rehnquist had numerous opportunities to exert such influences during his lengthy, nineteen-year service as Chief Justice of the United States. Moreover, while throughout American history chief justices could expect to lead the same group of eight associate justices for only about a year or two before a death or resignation changed the Court's membership, the final decade of Rehnquist's service was characterized by a historic degree of stability. From 1994 to his death in 2005, Rehnquist met with the same group of justices—Breyer, Ginsburg, Kennedy, Thomas, O'Connor, Scalia, Souter, and Stevens—to decide the most important cases facing the nation.

Several factors, then, suggest that Rehnquist possessed a unique opportunity to profoundly affect criminal justice in the United States. He served at a time when the Court and the nation increasingly grappled with determining the proper balance between efficient, effective crime controls on the one hand, and procedural and substantive protections on the other. This dynamic time period may have provided the context for abrupt changes in some of the Court's interpretations. Crime, criminal justice, and the fear of crime became increasingly common topics in national politics and private life (McCall 2004). In addition, membership on the Court became more conservative. Also, Rehnquist's lengthy tenure on the bench and his position as chief justice for nearly two decades assured at least the chance to guide a slower evolution in the Court's interpretation in those issue areas where a majority might find smaller, incremental changes more palatable. The longevity of Rehnquist's last natural court provided an unprecedented number of possibilities for a single group of nine justices to make such adjustments, if desired, by repeatedly returning to a particular statutory or constitutional issue.

Few legacies of long-serving office holders can be contained fully in a single chapter, and this seems especially true regarding Rehnquist. As one former law clerk to Chief Justice Rehnquist conceded, the range, complexities, and importance of issues ruled on during Rehnquist's lengthy time on the bench make it impossible for one person to adequately assess his legacy (Bradley 2005). Certainly, no attempt is made here to provide an exhaustive list of Rehnquist's influential opinions and actions. Instead, this chapter seeks to provide a better understanding of some of the *context* of Chief Justice Rehnquist's criminal justice legacy. Consequently, this endeavor examines Rehnquist's unusual path to the bench, general patterns characterizing Rehnquist and his Court, and specific trends emerging in his written opinions in select criminal justice issue areas.

The following section maps Rehnquist's rise to the Court by synthesizing information drawn from various biographies (e.g., Urofsky 2006), compendia on the Court (Epstein, Segal, Spaeth, and Walker 2007; Witt 1990), analyses of the Rehnquist era (e.g., Hensley 2006; Yarbrough 2000), and Rehnquist's (1987, 1999, 2005) own accounts of certain events. Some aspects of Rehnquist's journey are common ground for many of the Court's members, while others differentiate Rehnquist from most of his colleagues. At times some of these early experiences seem to reveal views that Rehnquist later defended on the bench. Then, qualities often said to characterize Rehnquist are discussed with particular consideration given to his conservatism, presumed "preference for deference," and support of law enforcement. Subsequent attention is focused on Rehnquist's positions—and especially his written opinions—in select Fourth Amendment cases. Search and seizure law represents a frequent destination for the recent Court and something of an area of specialization for Rehnquist. Then, the concept of "negative rights" illuminates some of Rehnquist's positions in a range of other issue areas. Brief, concluding remarks summarize key features of Rehnquist's legacy in criminal justice issues. This book's focus on the Rehnquist Court requires that primary weight be given to Rehnquist's opinions written as Chief Justice. However, some of his dissents as well as his positions as an associate justice are discussed to provide a richer account of Rehnquist's views and influence.

Path to the Bench

Rehnquist grew up in a relatively wealthy Milwaukee suburb and in a conservative household in which Republican leaders such as Alf Landon, Wendell Willkie, and Herbert Hoover were admired. He stayed in the Midwest to begin his undergraduate studies. World War II, however, interrupted Rehnquist's collegiate career as he enlisted in the Army Air Corps and served as a weather observer in North Africa.

Following his military service, Rehnquist benefited from educational assistance provided by the GI Bill. He completed his bachelor's program in political science at Stanford University, where he also earned a master's degree. After obtaining a second M.A. degree at Harvard, he returned to Stanford for his legal training. An impressive student, Rehnquist graduated first in his Stanford Law School class in 1952, just a couple of places ahead of his classmate and future Supreme Court colleague, Sandra Day O'Connor. At the age of twenty-eight,

Rehnquist's résumé could boast of service in World War II, prestigious academic honors (e.g., Phi Beta Kappa, law review, Order of the Coif), and four degrees from two of the nation's most respected universities.

Rehnquist was rewarded for his law school record with an offer to clerk for U.S. Supreme Court Justice Robert Jackson. The clerkship left a lasting imprint on Rehnquist (Rehnquist 1987) and might have shaped and revealed his beliefs in numerous ways. Some argue that a memorandum to Justice Jackson that he wrote as a clerk depicts some of the political and constitutional views Rehnquist held at that time. The memo concerned the landmark desegregation case of *Brown v. Board of Education* (1954) that was then being considered by the Court. In the memo, Rehnquist encouraged upholding the infamous "separate but equal" doctrine that the Court enunciated in *Plessy v. Ferguson* (1896), and that permitted racial segregation in public schools. Rehnquist later asserted that he wrote the memo from Justice Jackson's point of view rather than from his own, with the intention of preparing Jackson for discussions with other Justices.

Elsewhere Rehnquist unquestionably expressed his personal views—and passionately in terms of his opposition to the Warren Court's expansion of defendant rights—in an article he wrote shortly after his clerkship. In that article he vehemently criticized what he saw as the undue influence of liberal law clerks working for justices on the Warren Court. Rehnquist charged that the majority of clerks at that time possessed a liberal bias that caused them to slant the material they presented to the justices who were attempting to determine which applications would be granted a writ of certiorari and heard by the Court. Rehnquist (1957, 75) complained that most of his fellow clerks possessed a

> 'liberal' point of view . . . [characterized by] extreme solicitude for the claims of Communists and other criminal defendants, expansion of federal power at the expense of State power, great sympathy toward any government regulation of business—in short, the political philosophy now espoused by the Court under Chief Justice Earl Warren.

These pointed words would prove predictive of the reputation Rehnquist acquired years later on the bench for limiting defendants' rights (Tomkovicz 2006) and supporting states' powers in federalism issues (Epstein and Walker 2004, 319-447), including the strong tendency to favor state (rather than federal) regulation of business (Hagle and Spaeth 1993).

After his clerkship, Rehnquist married and moved to Phoenix where he went into private practice and became active in local politics and the Republican Party. Rehnquist joined Arizona Senator Barry Goldwater's 1964 presidential campaign as an advisor. Although Goldwater lost by a substantial electoral margin, his campaign messages on curbing the expansion of federal authority over states and balancing individual liberty with social order would echo years later in many of Rehnquist's decisions on the Court, as discussed later in this chapter. In 1968 Richard Nixon repeated versions of these messages in his successful presidential campaign. Nixon excelled at linking the themes by focusing on increasing crime rates and social unrest while criticizing what he depicted as liberal, federal policies hampering attempts by state and local governments to control crime. His rhetoric often targeted the Supreme Court (Baker 1983; McCall 2004, 43-61) and its then-recent decisions—such as *Miranda v. Arizona* (1966) requiring police to inform suspects of certain rights prior to a custodial interrogation—that many critics saw as "coddling criminals and hamstringing the police" (Stephens and Scheb 1999, 601). In short, "Nixon made 'law and order' the center piece of his campaign, blaming rising crime rates on the Warren Court's liberal activism and the Johnson Administration's 'soft-on-crime' law enforcement policies" (Clayton and Pickerill 2006, 1389).

Once elected, President Nixon appointed Rehnquist to be assistant attorney general for the Office of Legal Counsel at the Department of Justice; this is the same position to which Nixon appointed Antonin Scalia five years later. From the Office of Legal Counsel—the constitutional arm of the Department of Justice and what *Newsweek* called "a kind of mini Supreme Court" and "the most important government office you've never heard of" (Klaidman, Taylor, and Thomas 2006, 34)—Rehnquist provided legal advice to the president and attorney general. In 1971 Nixon nominated Rehnquist to the Supreme Court to fill the seat vacated by John Harlan II.

The memorandum written by Rehnquist when he clerked for Justice Jackson advocating that the Court affirm its ruling in *Plessy* became public during Rehnquist's confirmation hearings as a nominee for associate justice (Liptak 2005). Some senators during the confirmation hearings and various Court scholars afterwards (e.g., Boles 1987; Hutchinson 1979; Kluger 1975) challenged Rehnquist's explanation that the memo reflected Jackson's views rather than his own. Despite these and other objections (Taylor 1986), the Senate confirmed Rehnquist by a vote of 68-26. Just a few days earlier only one Senator voted against confirming Lewis Powell to the bench. This illustrates the relative contentiousness of Rehnquist's first nomination process.

A decade and a half later in 1986, President Reagan nominated Rehnquist for chief justice to replace the retiring Warren Burger. By this point, Rehnquist had a substantial voting record on the Court including several important cases in which he supported expanding police powers. Among many others, these included easing the criteria regarding how officers could establish probable cause (*Illinois v. Gates* 1983), broadening what would be deemed a reasonable search of vehicles without a warrant (*New York v. Belton* 1981; *United States v. Ross* 1982), noting exceptions to *Miranda* (*New York v. Quarles* 1984), and creating a 'good-faith exception' to the exclusionary rule justifying the seizure of evidence by police despite a defective warrant (*United States v. Leon* 1984).

It is not surprising, then, that many police unions and agencies backed Rehnquist's nomination to be chief justice. Hinting at the types of warrant exceptions that Rehnquist helped create, one endorsement submitted to the Senate on behalf of several law enforcement organizations gave support to Rehnquist as someone who would "help advance the needs of our law enforcement community to be able to act quickly, when necessary, to protect our citizens against law breakers" (Burden 1986, 1150).

Of course, Rehnquist's record on criminal justice issues did not please all who were interested in the Court. Several civil rights and civil liberties groups mobilized to oppose his nomination. While ultimately the Senate approved Rehnquist's elevation to chief justice, his confirmation vote was one of the closest in American history for a chief justice nominee. Among all those ever confirmed as chief justice by a recorded vote, only Roger Taney (1835) received a lower percent of votes cast (65.9 percent) than did Rehnquist (66.3 percent).

Rehnquist's nomination as chief justice was also unusual in that he became only the third sitting associate justice to be confirmed to the Court's leadership position. President Reagan, by pursuing the less commonly employed strategy of promoting from within to fill the chief justice's chair, opened the associate justice position that Rehnquist had occupied. Reagan nominated Antonin Scalia to that post. Scalia, often characterized as being one of the most conservative members of the Court and perhaps especially so in criminal justice cases (Smith 2003, 170-71), faced only moderate opposition and was unanimously confirmed by the Senate. Rehnquist's simultaneous nomination may have shielded Scalia as opponents tended to focus their scrutiny on Rehnquist.

Rehnquist in Context

This chapter section explores certain dimensions characterizing Rehnquist in relationship to his Court. While understanding that broad assessments of ideological preferences must be treated as general tendencies given the complexities of case facts and variation of issues addressed by the Court, these snapshots depict a conservative Rehnquist on a conservative-leaning Court. The general scope of Rehnquist's conservatism is plotted not only by his lack of support for many of the Court's liberal decisions, but also by his willingness to dissent from some conservative rulings that, apparently in his estimation, should have been even more conservative. On some criminal justice issues, Rehnquist's position eventually found majority support which, coupled with his elevation to chief justice, led him from being "a lone voice on the conservative fringe of the Court to a position at the heart of a solidly ensconced conservative majority" (Spaeth 2005, 108). These patterns suggest that Davis (1984, 89) was correct when she predicted more than a quarter century ago that Rehnquist might "emerge as the leader of a dominant conservative bloc in the Court."

Discussion then returns to the socio-political context of Rehnquist's original nomination to the bench by examining how well his oft-cited preference for deference and support for law enforcement comport with early law-and-order messages of his appointer, Richard Nixon. The brief review helps explain why it is often asserted that of Nixon's four conservative appointments (Rehnquist, Burger, Blackmun, and Powell) to the Supreme Court, "Rehnquist comes closest to

Nixon's desire for a restraintist justice who would support decentralization of federal power" (Hagle and Spaeth 1993, 501), and why Rehnquist likely will be remembered as "the one who best lived up to Nixon's pledge to name 'law and order' conservatives to the bench" (Savage 2005, 20).

The Stalwart Conservative

By the time Rehnquist took the oath of office as associate justice in 1972, some of the liberal justices who had served on the earlier Warren Court had been replaced and a more conservative majority had emerged. Rehnquist's appointment continued the pendulum swing to the right as he quickly established his conservatism in the area of criminal justice by voting conservatively in eighteen of the nineteen criminal procedure cases during his first term (Spaeth 2005, 109). In time, other liberal holdovers from the Warren era including Justices Brennan and Marshall would retire, and more conservative justices (e.g., Scalia and Thomas) would enter. The general conservative drift of the Court partially explains why Rehnquist joined or concurred with the majority in nearly five of every six cases during his lengthy career (see Urofsky 2006).

Predictably, Rehnquist frequently voted with those justices commonly considered to be his ideological companions. One analysis of the Court finds that Chief Justice Rehnquist voted with Justice Scalia in about six of every seven criminal justice cases heard from 1995-2003 (Smith, McCall, and McCluskey 2005, 30), and he posted nearly the same level of agreement with both Justices Thomas and O'Connor. These justices, often joined by Justice Kennedy, typically found themselves in the majority of the Court's numerous, conservative criminal justice decisions.

Rehnquist, however, also produced an unusual pattern of dissents. Despite serving with other conservatives, Rehnquist often filed the only dissent in a given case. On the Burger Court, for example, Rehnquist solo dissented five and a half times more frequently than did Justice Powell who came onto the Court the same day as Rehnquist (Spaeth 2005, 110). By the time he was elevated to chief justice, Rehnquist had written more lone dissents (fifty-four) than any other jurist in Supreme Court history (Hensley 2006, 56-59). Separate dissents by Rehnquist were especially likely when the majority ruled in favor of federal authority at a cost to state sovereignty.

It must have surprised some when Rehnquist disagreed with an otherwise unanimous Court and filed a sole dissent in his very first written opinion (*Cruz v. Beto* 1972). Such votes were not rare from Rehnquist especially early in his career when as "an associate justice he would go off on his own, and his most extreme views emerged" (Kramer, quoted in "Rehnquist Court" 2005, 34).

Rehnquist seemed willing to break at least partially from conservative majorities to express his view that the Court's decision was not conservative enough. The 1981 case of *New York v. Belton* illustrates this and another trait common in Rehnquist's opinions—his expressed desire to overturn *Mapp v.*

Ohio (1961) and its application of the exclusionary rule to the states. In 1981, Rehnquist, then an associate justice, agreed with the Court's judgment in *Belton* that a warrant is not required for police to search the entire passenger compartment of a vehicle after making a lawful arrest of an occupant of the automobile. However, in his concurring opinion Rehnquist indicated his disappointment with the Court for not broadening its ruling by overturning *Mapp*.

Such tendencies apparently prompted some of Rehnquist's law clerks to nickname him the Lone Ranger (Nannes 2006; Tribe 2005). Rehnquist's willingness through concurring and dissenting opinions to separate himself from decisions—the general direction of which he often endorsed—helps explain why some evaluations suggest that Rehnquist's seemingly entrenched positions limited his influence on the bench, at least early in his career (e.g., Rydell 1975). For example, Shapiro (1976, 293) charges that "the unyielding character of his ideology has had a substantial adverse effect on his judicial product" while Davis (1984, 89) notes that Rehnquist emerged as the Court's "most conservative member, with a propensity to dissent alone, [and that] he has often been perceived by observers as somewhat isolated."

Considering Rehnquist's long-term influence, however, generates a fuller and somewhat less damaging appraisal on at least three counts. First, his departure from the conservative bloc rarely supported a narrow, liberal majority and this was especially true in cases dealing with criminal justice issues. That is, his dissents tended not to alter directly the overall conservative direction of the Court's opinion. Second, after becoming chief justice, Rehnquist seemed to temper his more maverick tendencies as an associate justice by reducing the rate at which he wrote dissenting opinions, and especially solo dissents ("Rehnquist Court" 2005, 34; Spaeth 2005, 110). This meant Rehnquist maintained the power to assign who wrote the majority opinion in many of the Court's criminal justice decisions. Third, Rehnquist influenced the eventual direction of the Court on some issues *through* his dissents by suggesting different interpretations upon which he and others later would draw. As Harvard Law Professor Laurence Tribe notes, "even in lone dissent, he has helped define a new range of what is possible" (quoted in Urofsky 2006). Although Rehnquist never succeeded in convincing the Court to overturn *Mapp*, support for several of his other positions increased over time as "the standards from many of Rehnquist's earlier dissenting opinions in criminal justice cases became the law" during his tenure as chief justice (McCall and McCall 2006, 369). Perhaps, as the title of one law review article suggests, this was Rehnquist's reward for his patience and power (Greenhouse 2003).

Suggesting Rehnquist's influence among other forces, most analyses rank the Rehnquist Court era among the more conservative Supreme Court eras in modern times. This is not to suggest that his Court spoke with a single, conservative voice. Indeed, the Rehnquist Court decided an unusually high number of criminal justice cases by a single vote. Of the nonunanimous criminal justice decisions during Rehnquist's last ten terms, for example, more than two of every five ended in the slimmest of majorities. Rehnquist did not participate in four of these eighty-two cases due to his battle with thyroid cancer.

In nineteen of these criminal justice cases spread across the last ten terms of the Rehnquist Court era, the four members of the liberal bloc were able to attract a single member of the conservative bloc (usually, Sandra Day O'Connor). Rehnquist and Scalia were the only justices not to join the liberal bloc to form a single 5-4 liberal majority in criminal justice cases during that period. Moreover, Scalia—unlike Rehnquist—did vote with the majority to produce liberal outcomes in other configurations, such as by joining Thomas and three of the Court's liberals. Strikingly, during the last ten terms of his service on the high court, Chief Justice Rehnquist was not part of a single 5-4 majority that supported claims of criminal defendants.

In the narrowly decided criminal justice cases during that period, Rehnquist supported the government's interest in investigating and prosecuting criminal offenders in seventy-seven of his seventy-eight votes cast. While his fellow members of the conservative wing averaged nearly fifteen liberal votes each in these split decisions, Rehnquist held for the accused and against the government only once. Even then his position fell in the minority such that his vote did not help produce a liberal decision. In that case (*Muscarello v. United States* 1998) a thin majority upheld the application of a punishment-enhancement statute for carrying a firearm in connection with a drug offense. Frank Muscarello drove his truck to a place where he illegally distributed marijuana and police found a firearm locked in the vehicle's glove box. The Court reasoned this to be "carrying" a firearm under the statute, triggering the law's five-year mandatory sentence.

Rehnquist, Scalia and Souter joined Ginsburg's dissent. The four asserted that while "carrying" can have many meanings, the Court should confine its interpretation to the "undoubted meaning of that expression in the relevant context" (*Muscarello*, 140). Noting that other means were available to lengthen Muscarello's sentence, the dissenters encouraged a narrow interpretation of the statute, leaving to Congress any broadening of the law that the legislature might have intended (140-42). Thus, Rehnquist's single liberal vote in these narrow-margin cases better reflects his deference to elected officials and his stated desire to exercise judicial restraint than a goal to restrict the lengths of sentences.

The Nixon Nominee: Projecting Deference, Law-and-Order

When Nixon promised during his 1968 campaign to appoint conservatives to the federal bench, he surely knew of the chief executive's inability to control the behavior of judges and justices once confirmed with life-tenure. After all, it was Eisenhower, the last Republican president before Nixon, who considered the appointments of Warren and Brennan to be among his most regretted choices made in the Oval Office (Eisler 1993). The risk of such a "nomination mistake" was potentially high when Nixon tapped Rehnquist, who lacked a judicial track record by having never served previously as a judge. Although several factors other than judicial experience affect nomination to the bench (Smith 1999, 245-58), thirteen of the sixteen justices whose service overlapped with that of Rehnquist did have such prior experience as a state or federal judge (Lewis Powell, Byron White, and William Douglas did not).

The gamble paid off as Rehnquist's positions often comported with Nixon's policy goals of reining in the perceived activism of the Warren Court. For instance, in a law review article written early in his career, Rehnquist (1976, 695) criticized judicial activists as those who rely on "some other set of values [than] those which may be derived from the language and intent of the framers" and who improperly "second guess Congress, state legislatures, and state and federal administrative officers concerning what is best for the country" (698).

Rehnquist's judicial vision was shaped largely by the importance he gave to the specific words of statutory and constitutional provisions under review as he understood the legislative history of the texts (Davis 1989, 1984; Epstein and Walker 2007, 27-28; Urofsky 2006). This type of textualist or strict constructionist approach to interpreting law tends to inhibit decisions that might broaden the scope of specific protections over time. If specific safeguards and rights are not seen to exist clearly within the original context of the provision, judges, according to Rehnquist, should leave it to legislators to enunciate such protections with new laws.

While Rehnquist based many of his conservative decisions on his presumed narrow reading of statutes and intent, at times he cited the same justification for some of his less frequent liberal votes in criminal justice cases. For example, in both *United States v. Maze* (1974) and *Ball v. United States* (1985), he voted to reverse the criminal conviction and asserted that the federal government failed to show that the defendant's alleged behavior violated the specific terms of the relevant statute.

To be clear, critics question whether Nixon truly desired the exercise of judicial restraint or if he simply sought conservative activism under the guise of restraint (Boles 1987; Clayton and Pickerill 2006; Dean 2001). Some scholars assert that nearly all justices are activists in pursuing their own goals (Tushnet 2005) while others warn that a position on restraint versus activism may reflect an attempt to justify policy choices rather than reveal an underlying judicial philosophy (Baum 2001, 158). Several assessments challenge the depiction of Rehnquist as exercising restraint, maintaining instead that he was a conservative activist during his first years on the high court (e.g., Boles 1987; Powell 1982; Shapiro 1976) and continued to be throughout his career (e.g., Schwartz 2003). Charges include that while Rehnquist may not have rewritten legislative provisions, he often based his analysis on his preferred and creative interpretations of intent and not necessarily on the actual intent of legislators (Davis 1984, 115). In assessments of Rehnquist's first few years on the Court, Shapiro (1976, 299) bemoaned Rehnquist's "unwarranted relinquishment of federal responsibilities and deference to state law and institutions, to tacit abandonment of evolving protections of liberty and property" while Powell (1982) argued that Rehnquist repeatedly misinterpreted or misrepresented history regarding the original intent of the framers of the Constitution.

Whereas it would be difficult and controversial to attempt to measure fully Rehnquist's judicial activism or restraint, greater ease and agreement exist regarding his preference for deference. Rehnquist established a reputation early in his career for deferring to the judgment of legislatures in several areas of the law, and for criticizing the bench when it did not. In his famous dissent in *Trimble v. Gordon* (1977), Rehnquist chastised the Court for using the Equal Protection Clause of the Fourteenth Amendment to threaten state legislatures' authority. He complained that neither the original Constitution nor the Civil War amendments made "this Court into a council of revision, and they do not confer on this Court any authority to nullify state laws which we merely felt to be inimical to the Court's notion of the public interest" (772). As chief justice, he continued to urge the Court to afford greater deference and flexibility to state legislators, courts, and criminal justice officials both as a member of the majority (e.g., *Sandin v. Conner* 1995) and in dissent (e.g., *Thompson v. Keohane* 1996; *Rompilla v. Beard* 2005). On occasion, he called for deference to lawmakers despite his misgivings about the wisdom of law they had made (e.g., Rehnquist's sole dissent in *Chandler v. Miller* 1997).

Compared to other recent justices, Rehnquist may have been the most restrained in terms of his reluctance to strike down state laws as unconstitutional (Epstein and Walker 2007, 37; Hagle and Spaeth 1993, 500; Howard and Segal 2004, 138). His regard for restraint and states' rights seemed rooted in a majoritarian philosophy that viewed the people as the ultimate guardians of individual rights and the source of governmental authority (Devins 2004; Engelken 2007; Rehnquist 1980). Cautioning judges not to tinker endlessly with the decisions of elected officials, he favored the democratic process over judicial actions to produce the most desirable policies (Rehnquist 1976, 698). One assessment made during the final years of his Court service noted, "Rehnquist is mistrustful of judges substituting their judgments of contested constitutional rights for the judgments of popularly elected representatives and thus urges a strong presumption of constitutionality for acts of government challenged in such cases" (Whittington 2003, 16).

This perspective produced a restrictive interpretation of constitutional protections. In several opinions Rehnquist "stresses majority rule and the elected officials' accountability via the electoral process while de-emphasizing the notion that the Constitution protects certain individual rights regardless of the will of the majority" (Davis 1984, 91).

Rehnquist frequently insisted that the constitutional rights that do exist are further limited to what some might term "negative rights" (Savoy 1991). In this sense, he asserted that while the Constitution identifies specific protections *from* government, the Due Process Clause, for example, confers "no affirmative right to governmental aid, even when such aid may be necessary to secure life, liberty, or property interests of which the government itself may not deprive the individual" (*DeShaney v. Winnebago* 1989, 196; see also *Webster v. Reproductive Health Services* 1989, 491; *Harris v. McRae* 1980, 317-18). As subsequent sections of this chapter will illustrate, Rehnquist employed similar logic regarding due process claims in criminal justice cases.

Rehnquist also tended to interpret the scope of the Equal Protection Clause of the Fourteenth Amendment more narrowly than did most of his colleagues on the bench. Asserting that this Civil War amendment was intended to address racial discrimination, he often dissented when the majority sought to heighten the scrutiny afforded sex discrimination claims based on the clause (e.g., *Frontiero v. Richardson* 1973; *Craig v. Boren* 1976; see also Davis 1984). Rehnquist's support for defendants' equal protection claims did not necessarily increase in criminal justice cases even when the demographic characteristic under review was race. For example, in the mid-1980s Rehnquist dissented when the majority held in *Batson v. Kentucky* (1986) that prosecutors could not use peremptory challenges to remove African Americans from juries during voir dire (jury selection process) for reasons of race. More specifically, the Court ruled that the burden fell on the prosecutor to demonstrate that the particular peremptory challenge was applied for race-neutral reasons. Attorneys possess a set number of peremptory challenges whereby they can excuse a potential juror. Historically, no reason had to be given as the challenges do not require the approval of trial judges, and courts gave wide latitude to attorneys in how they chose to use these challenges. Just two decades before *Batson*, the Court ruled that purposeful race discrimination in the use of peremptory challenges in criminal cases would violate equal protection guarantees but placed the burden of proving such discrimination on the defense (*Swain v. Alabama* 1965). Typically, it would be extremely difficult to prove a case of discriminatory intent; by shifting the burden to prosecutors, the ruling in *Batson* made these protections more available and increased the role of judges who would be called upon to evaluate whether reasons given by prosecutors were truly race-neutral.

In his dissenting opinion, Rehnquist exemplified his frequent focus on specific constitutional wording by maintaining that even the purposeful use of challenges to exclude African Americans from the jury in a particular case would not violate the Equal Protections Clause as long as prosecutors also used the challenges in other cases to exclude whites when the defendant was white, Asians when the defendant was Asian, and so on (*Batson v. Kentucky* 1986, 137-38). Although Rehnquist elsewhere emphasized the intent behind constitutional provisions, he appeared to have been satisfied here with focusing on the word "equal" and dismissed the majority's position that "the exclusion of black citizens from service as jurors constitutes a primary example of the evil the Fourteenth Amendment was designed to cure" (*Batson v. Kentucky* 1986, 85). In the final year of the Rehnquist Court, he again disagreed with the majority in another case in which the Court found the prosecutor's use of peremptory challenges to be racially discriminatory (*Miller-El v. Dretke* 2005). Again, Rehnquist dissented and sought greater latitude for prosecutors and greater deference to the lower court judges.

Whether or not Rehnquist's opinions manifested judicial restraint, his crime-control posture was clear and consistent. Many of Rehnquist's votes aligned with Nixon's law-and-order campaign promises to curb the expansion of defendants' rights and to offset Warren Court decisions that had "gone too far in weakening the peace forces as against the criminal forces" (Nixon 1968).

While the next section of this chapter examines in more detail select opinions written by Rehnquist illuminating some of these issues, brief observations here demonstrate his law-and-order credentials and frequent role in expanding or preserving the powers of law enforcement. Consider, for instance, one list identifying forty-four key decisions in which the Supreme Court upheld investigative powers of the state (Schmalleger 2008, 155). This list resembles others commonly found in criminal justice textbooks and includes categories familiar to many students of policing and the courts (e.g., various exceptions to the warrant requirement/exclusionary rule, "no-knock" searches, use of police informants, seizure of abandoned material, custodial interrogations absent *Miranda*). Nearly three-fourths of these cases were decided when Rehnquist was on the bench.

Rehnquist voted with the majority to support the authority of law enforcement in thirty-one of the thirty-two listed cases in which he participated. His remarkably strong tendency to favor crime control interests over due process interests persisted despite the wide range of issues raised by these precedent-setting cases. The near-absence of a Rehnquist dissent was especially striking given that the Court was often sharply divided; only four of the thirty-two opinions reviewed were unanimous while five- or six-member majorities decided more than half of the cases.

Rehnquist's single break with the majority in these thirty-two cases clarifies rather than clouds his pro-law enforcement stance. In *Thompson v. Keohane* (1996), Thompson confessed to murder during a lengthy interrogation by state troopers. A recording of the confession was played at trial and the jury voted to convict. Thompson asserted that the taped confession should have been suppressed because he was not read his *Miranda* rights. The trial court denied his motion, stating that the *Miranda* requirements were not triggered because Thompson technically was not "in custody." Lower federal courts denied Thompson's petition for review, holding that the custody issue was a question of fact and that state determinations on such questions are presumed to be correct.

The majority on the U.S. Supreme Court, however, ruled that such "in custody" decisions, which are made to determine if *Miranda* warnings are required, actually involve "mixed questions" of law and fact. In part, according to the majority opinion, questions regarding circumstances of the interrogation are factual and on these, state rulings are presumed correct, and an independent re-· view by the federal habeas court is not warranted. However, the majority held that the issue also raised questions related to whether a reasonable person felt able to leave the interrogation. This presented questions of law and fact according to the Court and, as such, was a matter to be determined by federal court.

Rehnquist disagreed and joined Justice Thomas's dissent. The two argued that

> [t]he state trier of fact is best situated to put himself in the suspect's shoes, and consequently is in a better position to determine what it would have been like for a reasonable man to be in the suspect's shoes. Federal habeas courts, often reviewing the cold record . . . are in an inferior position to make this assessment. (*Thompson v. Keohane* 1996, 119)

Thus Rehnquist's position in *Thompson* did not run counter to his general law-and-order voting pattern. While the majority preserved the role of the trial court in making certain determinations regarding *Miranda*, much of the ruling broadened the avenue of appeal and the role of federal courts. Rehnquist's rejection of that position was consistent with both his deference to the states and his views of limited constitutional protections afforded the accused. Although such tendencies in Rehnquist's record are illuminating, a fuller appreciation of the former chief justice's legacy requires attention to be focused on decisions in specific issue areas.

Rehnquist and the Fourth Amendment: A Search for Reasonableness

Safeguards housed in the Fourth Amendment address the critical initial stages of the criminal process involving law enforcement efforts to investigate crimes, gather evidence, and arrest or otherwise detain suspects. Provisions in the amendment protect against unreasonable searches and seizures and stipulate the characteristics of a lawful warrant. Furthermore, the amendment's declaration that people have the right "to be secure in their persons, houses, papers, and effects" is often cast as a foundation to our constitutional right to privacy.

While the amendment bars certain rogue behaviors by police, its ambiguous language (e.g., what is "probable cause") has required frequent judicial clarification of its meaning. Indeed, search and seizure cases were among the most common types of criminal justice cases decided by the Court when Rehnquist was an associate justice (Bradley 1985) and then again later when he served as chief (Smith 2003, 166; Smith, McCall, and McCluskey 2005, 22).

Increasing the need for interpretation, the amendment does not address how the criminal justice system should respond when police violate these protections. The Supreme Court established the now-famous remedy, the exclusionary rule, in 1914 (*Weeks v. United States*). Initially a limit only on federal authorities that forbade prosecutors in trials from introducing evidence obtained through an unreasonable search or seizure, the exclusionary rule was applied to the states nearly a half century later in the landmark case of *Mapp v. Ohio* (1961).

Mapp offended Rehnquist's judicial sensibilities. Fond of casting himself as a strict constructionist (Whittington 2003), Rehnquist characterized the exclusionary rule as merely "a judicially created remedy rather than a personal constitutional right" (*California v. Minjares* 1979, 924). Often heralding the importance of judicial restraint and states' rights, Rehnquist likely saw *Mapp* as an act of judicial policymaking forced onto states.

For Rehnquist, excluding evidence represented only one of the possible ways to deter police from violating Fourth Amendment protections, and clearly he thought that it was not the preferred option in most instances. For example, he unsuccessfully argued that the threat of civil lawsuits could deter police misconduct sufficiently to make the exclusionary rule unnecessary at least in some instances (*California v. Minjares*, 1979, 925-26).

Although never able to persuade a majority of justices to support his call to overturn *Mapp*, Rehnquist succeeded in limiting the scope of Fourth Amendment protections and the use of the exclusionary rule in other ways. For example, Chief Justice Rehnquist wrote in *Arizona v. Evans* (1995) that there was no need to exclude evidence resulting from a faulty search warrant when officers based their actions on a clerical mistake by court employees. Suppression of evidence was unnecessary in the absence of intentional misconduct by officers. Similarly, and again writing for the majority, Rehnquist refused to retroactively apply a higher standard regarding warrantless searches of vehicles near the border (*United States v. Peltier* 1975). He found that because agents had acted properly given the standards at the time of the actual search, there was no rogue behavior to rein in and, thus, no justification for applying the exclusionary rule.

Determinations of the constitutionality of searches and seizures, especially warrantless ones, ultimately reflect the weights given to opposing sides of a balancing scale. The value of governmental interests and the appropriateness of steps taken by law enforcement to achieve those interests are measured against the individual's privacy interests. Rehnquist's opinion in *Michigan Department of State Police v. Sitz* (1990) reveals his calculus and familiar support for the state side of the equation. The chief justice held that a particular highway sobriety checkpoint program was reasonable given the state's interest in preventing drunk driving, the limits on police discretion in deciding who would be stopped (a seizure), and the brief period of each stop (limited intrusion into privacy), assuming officers did not detect signs of intoxication.

Much of Rehnquist's influence on Fourth Amendment interpretations might be conceptualized in terms of how he defined and redefined the characteristics of elements commonly weighed against each other in search and seizure cases. As discussed below, Rehnquist was instrumental in: bolstering the authority of arresting officers to conduct searches; raising the bar for what would be considered a protected search under the Fourth Amendment; relaxing standards for establishing probable cause and reasonable suspicion; and identifying conditions that lowered the degree of privacy individuals might expect.

Changing Thresholds

Soon after coming onto the bench, Rehnquist began playing an important role in limiting the reach of the Fourth Amendment by clarifying and strengthening the "search incident to a valid arrest" exception to the warrant requirement. Writing for the Court in *United States v. Robinson* (1973) and in *Gustafson v. Florida* (1973), Rehnquist held that officers could conduct a full search of an individual incident to a lawful custodial arrest without a search warrant. While these searches assist police in preserving evidence and disarming arrestees before taking them into custody, Rehnquist held that there was no need to justify such searches by demonstrating the probability of actually finding weapons or evidence on the arrestee, and courts generally should defer to the judgment of police officers in these instances.

Rehnquist also found that, in some circumstances, probable cause justifies the warrantless entry of a home—generally a more protected area (*United States v. Santana* 1976). Rehnquist wrote that police, with probable cause to arrest but without an arrest warrant, could pursue a suspect into her home where she was arrested and searched. Rehnquist held that officers did not violate the Fourth Amendment because they first attempted to arrest the suspect in a public place (doorway to her home) before she retreated into her house. The attempted arrest based on probable cause permitted police to engage in "hot pursuit" and thereby enter the home without a warrant.

As mentioned earlier in this chapter, Rehnquist joined the Court's majority to expand the area in which police could search incident to a lawful arrest of a person occupying a vehicle to include the vehicle's entire passenger compartment (*New York v. Belton* 1981). Years later, Chief Justice Rehnquist extended this logic and police power in *Thorton v. United States* (2004), a case in which the defendant had already exited his car by the time the police officer made contact. After an ensuing valid arrest, the officer searched the vehicle without a warrant. The Court, per Rehnquist, found that the search did not violate the Fourth Amendment even though initial contact was made outside the car. The search remained incident to a valid arrest as such a search might aid in preserving potential evidence and protecting the officer's safety.

Notably, Rehnquist rejected otherwise similar, warrantless searches when not predicated on an arrest. In one of only two liberal Fourth Amendment decisions written by Rehnquist after he became chief justice, he found a full, warrantless car search to be unconstitutional when it followed a mere traffic citation rather than an arrest (*Knowles v. Iowa* 1998). Unlike a custodial arrest, issuance of a citation did not create the safety and evidentiary concerns necessary to offset privacy considerations. Thus, a warrantless search was not reasonable.

In other cases Rehnquist shortened the reach of Fourth Amendment protections by narrowing the definition of a "search." While common parlance might characterize many types of law enforcement activities as searches, the Court considers both the nature of police conduct and the scope of an individual's interest (i.e., expected privacy) in determining if an investigative exploration rises to the level of a Fourth Amendment search (Clancy 2006, 12). Rehnquist's consideration of these elements often resulted in an activity being classified as something less than a constitutionally protected search. If actions do not qualify as a search, then such an investigative exploration by law enforcement certainly could not be considered an unreasonable search. Consequently, constitutional protections requiring probable cause and a warrant would not be triggered.

Along this line, Rehnquist joined the Court majority to rule that the Fourth Amendment was not violated when, without a warrant, police: rummaged through garbage left at the street curb (*California v. Greenwood* 1988), surveyed an open field (*Oliver v. United States* 1984), used a drug-sniffing dog at an airport (*United States v. Place* 1983), or engaged in aerial surveillance from public airspace under certain conditions (*Florida v. Riley* 1989; *California v. Ciraolo* 1986; *Dow Chemical v. United States* 1986). In these cases, the Court's reasoning supported by Rehnquist tended to hinge on how state interests outweighed the defendants' diminished expectation of privacy.

Writing for the Court in *United States v. Knotts* (1982), Rehnquist further illustrated his position that not all searches rise to the level of a constitutionally protected search. In *Knotts*, officers in Minnesota—without a warrant but believing that one of the defendants was purchasing chloroform to manufacture illegal drugs—placed a radio transmitter in a container of chloroform that was sold to that defendant. The officers used the radio transmissions to follow the defendant to a cabin, secured a search warrant, entered the cabin, and discovered a drug laboratory. Rehnquist and the Court rejected the defendants' claim that the warrantless monitoring violated their reasonable expectation of privacy and the Fourth Amendment. The surveillance, according to Rehnquist, amounted to police following a car on a public street. Rehnquist held that such monitoring was not a search and that travelers on public roads do not have the requisite level of privacy expectation.

Because of Rehnquist's otherwise high threshold for what constitutes a protected search and his usual view that travelers on public roads should rationally anticipate diminished privacy, he surprised many judicial experts with his majority opinion in *Bond v. United States* (2000). The petitioner rode a Greyhound bus that stopped at a checkpoint in Texas where officials routinely verified the immigration status of passengers. A Border Patrol agent entered the bus and squeezed several pieces of soft-side, canvass luggage in the overhead storage area. In the bag belonging to Bond, the agent felt a brick-like object. Bond consented to a search of the bag at which point the officer discovered illegal drugs. Bond sought to have the evidence suppressed, arguing that the agent's initial manipulation of the bag was a search, and that the lack of individualized suspicion made it an unreasonable one. Chief Justice Rehnquist, writing for a seven-member majority and despite his nearly unwavering support for law enforcement in other nonunanimous search and seizure cases (Bradley 2006; McCall and McCall 2006), agreed and ruled that the evidence should be excluded. Rehnquist was persuaded that Bond demonstrated an expectation of privacy: his bag was closed and opaque. While Bond should anticipate that other passengers might move the bag, it was not reasonable to expect that law enforcement officers would touch the item in such an exploratory fashion. Rehnquist found that the agent's tactile (as opposed to visual) inspection constituted a warrantless Fourth Amendment search, and that the lack of individualized suspicion made it an unconstitutional one.

While vehicle-related searches (with the exception of *Bond*) provided fertile soil for Rehnquist to express his high threshold for what constituted a protected search because of the typically diminished expectation of privacy, his opinions in such cases also revealed his willingness to afford officers considerable latitude by using what some critics might call a rather low standard of reasonableness regarding police behavior. If the actions by law enforcement are reasonable, then Fourth Amendment prohibitions against an "unreasonable search" do not apply. For instance, writing for the majority in *Florida v. Jimeno* (1991), Chief Justice Rehnquist held that when a motorist consents to a car search after being told that the officer suspected that the driver might be carrying illegal drugs, it is reasonable to expect that the officer would look in containers that might contain drugs. This was true whether or not the driver thought he was consenting to a search of all items in the vehicle.

In another consensual car search (*Ohio v. Robinette* 1996), the Court considered whether motorists must be informed of their right to leave and essentially to withdraw permission given to police to conduct the search. Chief Justice Rehnquist's majority opinion rejected such a requirement. The critical issue for Rehnquist centered on the reasonableness of the officer's behavior, and not on the degree of knowledge that the suspect had of his rights.

At times Rehnquist relied on the routine nature of a search as an indicator of its reasonableness. He at least implicitly reasoned that routine searches are more limited in scope, and thereby less intrusive, than non-routine ones. The lower level of intrusion into privacy reduces the weight of the state interest necessary to justify the search. The routine border search—where government interests are clear (i.e., national security and interdiction of contraband) and most travelers anticipate at least some scrutiny—offered something of a perfect context for Rehnquist. Indeed, "the U.S. Supreme Court, in a collection of opinions largely authored by Chief Justice Rehnquist, has defined the threshold question for suspicionless border searches as whether the search is routine or not" (Coletta 2007, 974). Writing for the Court in *United States v. Flores-Montano* (2004), Chief Rehnquist upheld the reasonableness of a suspicionless border stop that included the removal and search of a car's gas tank. Such border stops and searches were routine, not physically intrusive, and individuals could expect a lower level of privacy while crossing an international border (*Flores-Montano*, at 154-55). These factors and the uniqueness of state interests prompted Rehnquist to give considerable latitude to border patrol and customs officials as he helped carve out the Court's "border exception" to Fourth Amendment requirements (e.g.,

United States v. Montoya de Hernandez 1985; *United States v. Ramsey* 1977; *United States v. Sokolow* 1989).

Elsewhere, even in the absence of such pressing national interests, Rehnquist found that police acted reasonably when conducting warrantless searches providing that officers followed departmental policies that routinized such searches and regulated police discretion. For example, in *Colorado v. Bertine* (1987) police impounded the van of Steven Bertine after arresting him for driving under the influence of alcohol. During an inventory search of the vehicle, police opened a closed backpack taken from the van and found illegal drugs and drug paraphernalia. Facing narcotics and other charges, Bertine sought to have the drug evidence excluded by arguing that the warrantless inventory search violated the Constitution. The police, Bertine argued, simply should have listed a closed backpack in the vehicle inventory. Chief Justice Rehnquist, writing for the Court majority, disagreed. Rehnquist found that Bertine failed to show that police opened the backpack for investigative purposes rather than for inventorying its contents; intent to investigate likely would require a higher threshold for cause and a warrant. Of considerable importance to Rehnquist, the officers followed standardized caretaking procedures regarding inventory searches as established by their department. This, coupled with the lack of demonstrated bad faith (searching for evidence of possible illegal acts rather than to inventory items), made the search reasonable and the subsequent seizure of contraband lawful.

However, just three years later in *Florida v. Wells* (1990), Chief Justice Rehnquist clarified the limits on officers' discretion while conducting inventory searches. Wells, who was stopped for speeding and then arrested by a state trooper for driving under the influence, had a locked suitcase containing marijuana in the trunk of his vehicle. After impounding the car and during a warrantless inventory search, an officer instructed that the locked case be forcefully opened. Writing again for the Court, Rehnquist found this search to be unconstitutional. For Rehnquist, the critical difference from *Bertine* was that in *Wells* there were no routine procedures requiring officers to open closed containers for inventory purposes. Rehnquist found that the absence of standardized criteria for determining when containers can be opened gives officers excessive discretion that can lead to fishing for evidence under the pretext of conducting an inventory search. Notably, Rehnquist's assessment in both cases was driven more by issues regarding the reasonableness of police actions than by concerns for protecting a person's privacy.

Rehnquist's written opinions often made it easier for law enforcement officials to reach certain thresholds that, in turn, allowed police greater latitude to search and seize items and suspects. He wrote in *Maryland v. Pringle* (2003) that an officer finding drugs and a large amount of money in a car had probable cause to arrest all persons in a vehicle. Rehnquist held that the original stop for speeding was legitimate and that seeing money and drugs gave the officer probable cause to believe a crime had been or was being committed. Rehnquist asserted individualized suspicion was unnecessary as it was reasonable to believe that any or all of the occupants of the car had knowledge of the drugs.

Rehnquist articulated one of his most influential standards just prior to becoming chief justice in an informant-tip case (*Illinois v. Gates* 1983). Police received by letter an anonymous tip that Lance and Susan Gates were dealing in illegal drugs. The letter purported to list the street on which the Gates lived, where the couple purchased the drugs, and other details. Police surveillance and other investigative steps verified certain details noted in the tip. With a search warrant based on the partially corroborated anonymous tip, police discovered large amounts of marijuana and other evidence. The trial judge suppressed the evidence, finding that police lacked sufficient probable cause and should not have been issued a warrant. The tip failed to pass the existing two-pronged test for using information from an anonymous source. Under this standard, to use a tip in establishing probable cause, the informant's basis of knowledge had to be verified, and facts needed to sufficiently establish the veracity or reliability of the informant. Of course, here, police could not verify the basis of knowledge of an anonymous informant. Writing for the Court, Rehnquist determined that the two-prong test was unworkable, too restrictive, and needlessly hampered police. In its place, the Court adopted a "totality of circumstances" test. With this new standard, probable cause could be established from the sum total of related factors even when a specific element of the "two prongs" was absent.

Although Rehnquist authored the *Gates* opinion as an associate justice, this more generous formula for establishing probable cause made frequent appearances during the Rehnquist Court era. Writing as chief justice, Rehnquist used this standard to find that agents had a reasonable basis to suspect Andrew Sokolow and his companion were transporting illegal drugs (*United States v. Sokolow* 1989). Among other things, Sokolow acted nervously, paid for airplane tickets in cash, provided incorrect names for who would be traveling and checked no luggage. Agents detained the couple and later obtained a search warrant based on the reaction of drug dogs to a bag which turned out to contain cocaine. While no single factor provided evidence of wrongdoing to justify the stop, Rehnquist and the Court held that the circumstances in their totality did provide such reasonable suspicion.

The Rehnquist Court returned to a totality of circumstances analysis in a case involving the search of a probationer's home (*United States v. Knights* 2001). As a condition of probation, Knights had agreed to submit to a warrantless search of his residence if officers had reasonable suspicion that he was involved in illegal activity. Officers argued they had such suspicion (regarding vandalism), searched Knights' home, and discovered materials used to make bombs. Rehnquist held for the unanimous Court that the circumstances, collectively, provided officers with reasonable suspicion that Knights was engaged in vandalism. This, coupled with the probation agreement, justified the search.

Rehnquist's opinion for a bare majority found that officers had sufficient suspicion under the totality of circumstances to stop and frisk a man in a known high crime area who ran away when he saw uniformed officers. Rehnquist wrote that while flight is not indicative of wrong doing, it is suggestive, and that while simply being in a high crime area does not generate reasonable suspicion, it does when coupled with flight. Rehnquist asserted, "The determination of reasonable suspicion must be based on common sense judgments and inferences about human behavior," and intimated that this type of totality analysis best allows for that (*Illinois v. Wardlow* 2000, 676).

As indicated by the foregoing examples, Rehnquist's positions on the totality standard and elsewhere tended to recast thresholds central to Fourth Amendment considerations and did so in ways that favored crime control interests over those of the accused. Rehnquist's interpretations commonly garnered majority support in part because he so consistently articulated them.

Consistency and Its Limits

In his almost unfailing support of the state's interest in controlling crime, Rehnquist played a critical role in the pendulum swing after the Warren Court era toward an expansion of police powers through broader latitude afforded officers to conduct searches and to seize evidence and suspects. Despite Rehnquist's conspicuous failure to convince a Court majority to radically reconstruct criminal procedural law by overturning *Mapp*, Rehnquist repeatedly helped reduce the frequency of situations requiring a warrant by finding many police practices to be reasonable, and individual privacy expectations to be limited.

As chief justice, Rehnquist controlled who wrote the Court's position in search and seizure cases with remarkable regularity. Toward the end of his career, he almost always found himself in the majority when the Court considered the Fourth Amendment, dissenting in only five search and seizure cases decided during his last natural court period, 1994-2004 (Arledge and Heck 2005; McCall and McCall 2006). In his final years and despite health problems, Rehnquist continued to craft the Court's search and seizure jurisprudence. Amazingly, during the last four terms of the Rehnquist era, the chief justice authored half (six of twelve) of the search and seizure opinions that the Court produced in cases in which he participated, representing nearly a third (six of nineteen) of all the criminal justice opinions written by Rehnquist during that time.

Closer scrutiny, however, reveals that Rehnquist may have been less influential than his rate of opinion writing suggests. While Rehnquist wrote several Fourth Amendment opinions in his last four years, nearly all (five of six) were unanimous decisions. On the one hand, this may indicate skill on the part of the chief justice to forge consensus. On the other hand, these cases may have involved less contentious, relatively straightforward issues to interpret, reflecting what Rehnquist (1987, 297) once wrote regarding his tendency to assign some of the most boring cases to himself. None of Rehnquist's Fourth Amendment opinions from his final four terms came in split (5-4) decisions. In contrast, more than a third of Rehnquist's opinions in cases raising other criminal justice issues during this period (five of thirteen) represented the narrowest of majorities. The mix of issues and complexities of Court dynamics make it difficult to interpret this contrast confidently. One possibility is that Rehnquist's strongly held views on the Fourth Amendment made him poorly positioned to facilitate the compromises that are often necessary to maintain fragile, five-member majorities.

Moreover, while almost never in the minority in Fourth Amendment cases after 2001, Rehnquist dissented in important cases, both during and before the last natural court period (1994-2004). Often these were close decisions. Had Rehnquist been able to attract another vote or two, the outcome would have pivoted. For example, Rehnquist was unable to convince his colleagues in 2004 that a search, based on a defective warrant but with a proper warrant application, was reasonable. Contrary to his position, a five-member majority ruled the application did not save the search, nor did it protect officers against a resulting lawsuit (*Groh v. Ramirez* 2004).

Chief Justice Rehnquist also cast a dissenting vote in the much-discussed case of *Kyllo v. United States* (2001). The Court ruled that the use of a thermal imager to detect heat emissions from a house (an indicator of using lamps to grow marijuana) constituted a search requiring a warrant. This split decision produced the rare instance of Chief Rehnquist joining a dissent written by Justice Stevens. Rehnquist and the other dissenters contended that sensing heat external to the home was similar to using a trained dog to detect the aroma of drugs, a practice the Court upheld in a previous Rehnquist decision (*United States v. Place* 1983). Furthermore, while years earlier the Court agreed with Rehnquist that an electronic transmitter used to track a container was not a search (*United States v. Knotts* 1982), the majority was unwilling to treat the technology used in *Kyllo* that way.

Dissents joined or written by Rehnquist often repeated themes common to the chief justice's perspective expressed in cases in which he was in the majority. For example, when the Court held that a hospital could not constitutionally test the urine of patients for drugs and then turn the results over to police without the patients' knowledge or consent, Rehnquist joined Scalia's dissent arguing that the event of real interest as they saw it—reporting the results—was not a search (*Ferguson v. City of Charleston* 2001). Similarly, Rehnquist's dissenting opinion in *Indianapolis v. Edmond* (2000) echoed his stances taken on similar searches: brief, routine, discretionless stops at police roadblocks that are minimally intrusive and promote a significant state interest are reasonable. The six-member majority, however, found that such stops that use drug-sniffing dogs at a highway checkpoint to discover and interdict illegal drugs was not sufficiently tied to a narrow state interest or a special need to be constitutional without a warrant. As one expert put it after reviewing the late chief justice's record, "When it comes to the Fourth Amendment, the police have had no greater friend on the Supreme Court than William Rehnquist" (Bradley 2006, 103).

Negative Rights and the Defense of State Judgment

It is not heresy to suggest that many constitutional rights are "negative rights" in the sense that amendments often stipulate protections *from* certain governmental abuses without necessarily mandating that government positively provide something. Yet, justices regularly interpret the Constitution as requiring federal and state authorities to provide some substantive or procedural benefit. Rehnquist was one of the members of the Court who was least likely to read statutes or the Constitution so broadly. This limited receptivity to negative rights served as a helpful companion to Rehnquist's deference to state judgments and to his majoritarian proclivities. Narrowly interpreting what is positively required of government, he typically supported state policies and interests against such claims.

It is unsurprising given Rehnquist's view of states' rights that he tended to interpret narrowly the Due Process and Equal Protections Clauses of the Fourteenth Amendment. The Due Process Clause is used to selectively incorporate protections in the Bill of Rights and apply them as guarantees against abusive actions of states. In the hands of other justices that clause was used to expand rights at the expense of state authority. Rehnquist saw the Equal Protection Clause as having limited applicability given his interpretation of the intent of those drafting the Amendment.

In addition to seeing relatively few positive rights ensconced in the Fourteenth Amendment, Rehnquist found that government often bore little obligation to act in a variety of cases. His positions tended to portray a very restricted view of prisoners' rights, and liberty interests more generally, that might otherwise trigger due process protections in the interpretive approaches of other justices. Similarly, some might be tempted to characterize Rehnquist as setting rather miserly parameters to the constitutional right to counsel and protections against self-incrimination. While his decisions specifically limiting congressional acts do not hang neatly on the negative rights framework, discussion of a sample of his positions in this category further reveals his protection of state policing powers and helps explain these otherwise atypical, liberal votes.

Prisoners' Rights and Liberty Interests

While the Court's interpretations of the Fourth Amendment's search and seizure protections disproportionately affect the early stages of criminal justice, its decisions regarding prisoners' rights and the death penalty shape policies that are more relevant late in the criminal process. Here, Rehnquist's perspective on what constituted punishment and liberty interests tended to shrink the sphere of potential due process claims under the Fifth and Fourteenth Amendments. However, as evidenced near the end of this section and late in his life, some of Rehnquist's definitions of Eighth Amendment "cruel and unusual punishments" lost favor among the Court's majority.

We see in hindsight that Rehnquist's first written opinion was predictive of his pattern of combining deference to state and local criminal justice authorities and a narrow interpretation of what government is constitutionally required to provide. The Court in *Cruz v. Beto* (1972) held that Texas discriminated against a Buddhist prisoner by denying him opportunities, similar to those afforded prisoners practicing other religions, to pursue his faith. In his solo dissent, Rehnquist argued that the petitioner failed to show that the absence of specific religious services was intended to punish him for his beliefs or impaired his religious freedom. Against all of the other justices, Rehnquist maintained that prisons are not constitutionally obligated to provide facilities for any particular type of service, that prison administration might be burdened by such demands and, therefore, prison authorities were best positioned to determine if such provisions should be offered (*Cruz v. Beto* 1972, 323-26).

Rehnquist adopted similar positions elsewhere, rejecting several claims by prisoners that state laws or the Constitution mandated governmental action. For instance, Chief Rehnquist held that a prison disciplinary committee was not obligated to allow a prisoner to call certain witnesses when charged with misconduct in prison (*Sandin v. Conner* 1995). The penalty of thirty days in a segregation unit did not sufficiently deprive the prisoner of liberty under Rehnquist's reading of the Due Process Clause to trigger entitlement to more elaborate hearing rights. Dissenters criticized Rehnquist's majority opinion for abandoning previously established standards and for limiting the scope of the Fourteenth Amendment's liberty interests, arguing that the misconduct charge led to a more constrained form of incarceration, and that without a more detailed hearing process the determination of misconduct could negatively affect parole chances.

Predictably, Rehnquist tended to see even fewer liberty interests (and thus fewer due process protections) in cases not involving an immediate threat of incarceration. For example, Chief Rehnquist voted to support the constitutionality of a sex offender registry program (*Smith v. Doe* 2003). Specifically, he joined the majority in upholding the retroactive application of registration requirements. According to Rehnquist and the Court, this did not run afoul of the Constitution's Ex Post Facto Clause because actions stemmed from a civil regulation intended to protect the public rather than to further punish those registered. Three dissenters countered that the program constituted a severe deprivation of the offender's liberty (e.g., required registration, limits on changing residences, public dissemination of certain information) and that the program was at least as much a criminal as a civil program in that it placed requirements only on those convicted of relevant criminal offenses.

In that same year, Rehnquist wrote for a unanimous Court to hold that individual hearings are not necessary before publicly posting information about a registered sex offender (*Connecticut Department of Public Safety v. Doe* 2003). Writing much earlier for the Court, he also found no due process violation when police posted flyers listing "active shoplifters," even if the information was incorrect (*Paul v. Davis* 1976). In this instance, Rehnquist ruled that a person's reputation is not a liberty or property protected by the Due Process Clause.

Rehnquist also frequently argued for shortening the appeals process and for greater finality of cases, especially those involving death row inmates. Over the course of his career, Rehnquist helped the conservative majority significantly reduce prisoners' access to the courts through a series of federal habeas review decisions (Lane 2005). These and other non-automatic appeals serve as an important protection against some kinds of grievous errors that may have occurred at trial. Rehnquist effectively reduced post-conviction remedies by enlarging the list of errors that do not trigger review and by placing a greater burden on the individual prisoner for demonstrating the existence of errors.

In perhaps his most influential habeas holding, Rehnquist substantially curbed appeals by barring review in most instances of any issue not raised previously at the appropriate stage in the criminal process (*Wainwright v. Sykes* 1977). He further shifted the burden onto the prisoner in his 5-4 majority opinion in *Brecht v. Abrahamson* (1993). In response, a dissenting Justice White warned that many state decisions would become unreviewable. Rehnquist also wrote for the Court to limit habeas review by denying a petitioner a late-filing (*Pace v. DiGuglielmo* 2005), by finding that neither the Constitution nor relevant statutes entitled prisoners to certain types of hearings (*Hill v. Lockhart* 1985), and by holding that the existence of new evidence does not require the courts to review a claim of actual innocence (*Herrera v. Collins* 1993).

Although Rehnquist usually succeeded in leading a Court that "made it harder for civil rights plaintiffs, prisoners, and Death Row inmates to win claims in federal courts" (Savage 2005, 21), he failed to muster a majority in a few closely watched cases decided in his final years. He dissented when the Court held that the death penalty constituted cruel and unusual punishment when the offender is mentally retarded (*Atkins v. Virginia* 2003) and when the offender was a juvenile when committing the capital offense being punished (*Roper v. Simmons* 2005). The majority in each of these cases found the practices to be cruel and unusual in part due to evolving social standards. Rehnquist and other dissenters were unconvinced that a national consensus against such executions existed. Rehnquist criticized the majority for referring to the movement away from such executions in other countries and for abandoning earlier Court interpretations of cruel and unusual punishment. Thus, late in his career Chief Justice Rehnquist found himself in the minority in significant decisions that might portend additional changes in the direction of capital punishment (Shin 2007). Moreover, in both cases the Court rejected many of the prior standards and positions that Rehnquist supported regarding the execution of youthful (*Stanford v. Kentucky* 1989) and mentally retarded offenders (*Penry v. Lynaugh* 1989).

As we will see, similar patterns emerge in other issue areas, in which Chief Rehnquist failed to garner majority support for his positions in potentially landmark cases late in his life. Whether or not these decisions meant that Rehnquist "lost control" of his Court (Arledge and Heck 2005; Greenhouse 2004), the findings are striking and complicate the assessment of his criminal justice legacy.

Right to Counsel and Self-Incrimination

Rehnquist tended to narrowly interpret rights even where the Constitution seems to recognize a "positive right," such as the Sixth Amendment's right to the assistance of defense counsel. Indeed, he may have been the most aggressive member of his Court in attempting to limit the reach of the right to counsel (Tomkovicz 2006).

The decision that the Sixth Amendment requires government to provide counsel when felony defendants cannot afford an attorney was applied to the states by the Warren Court (*Gideon v. Wainwright* 1963). Although Rehnquist never expressed the same level of hostility to *Gideon* as he did toward *Mapp* and *Miranda* (Bradley 2005), he frequently voted to restrict the reach of this landmark case and was generally successful in this effort for most of his career. For example, writing for the Court in *Ross v. Moffitt* (1974), Rehnquist refused to extend the right to state-provided counsel to indigents in appeals. Rehnquist reasoned that such appellants would have an extensive case file by that point and, consequently, they would not be denied meaningful access to the Courts (a constitutional interpretation and threshold used in *Gideon*). This decision significantly guided the Court until *Halbert v. Michigan* in 2005.

The Court often relied on Rehnquist's 1979 majority opinion in *Scott v. Illinois* in which he held that there was a constitutional requirement to provide indigents with counsel only when actual incarceration occurred. Scott, without an attorney, had been convicted of shoplifting and was fined although he could have been sentenced to jail. Rehnquist held that because there was no deprivation of liberty, there was no constitutional violation. Elsewhere, Chief Justice Rehnquist wrote for a narrow majority holding that the Sixth Amendment protection was "offense-specific." This permitted police to question defendants on matters related to but different from the actual charged offense without raising right-to-counsel concerns (*Texas v. Cobb* 2001).

However, Chief Justice Rehnquist fell in the minority in a series of Sixth Amendment cases late in his career. In *Alabama v. Shelton* (2002) the Court departed from the rationale in *Scott* and extended the right to counsel to those receiving a suspended sentence and probation because such impositions could result in the actual deprivation of liberty (i.e., later revocation and imprisonment). Rehnquist's influence on the Sixth Amendment suffered another blow during his last term when the majority referred to his decision in *Ross* as a justification for extending indigents' right to counsel to the application-to-appeal stage (*Halbert v. Michigan* 2005). That same year, a narrow majority in *Rompilla v. Beard* (2005) overturned a death sentence due to ineffective counsel. Chief Justice Rehnquist joined Justice Kennedy's dissent arguing that the right to counsel does not require defense attorneys to pursue a particular strategy.

In the area of self-incrimination, Rehnquist demonstrated his strong disregard for *Miranda* and his inclination to frame issues in terms of negative rights soon after joining the bench in *Michigan v. Tucker* (1974). The Court, per Rehnquist, allowed the testimony of a witness whose identity was discovered as a result of a statement the defendant made after receiving only part of the *Miranda* warnings. The police questioning, according to Rehnquist, did not violate self-incrimination protections because the warnings were merely prophylactic measures and "these procedural safeguards were not themselves rights protected by the Constitution but were instead measures to insure the right against self-incrimination were protected" (444). Because *Miranda* warnings are not an absolute right, their value and reasonableness can be measured against other interests, such as the state's interest in public safety. Indeed, in *New York v. Quarles* (1984) Rehnquist's majority opinion held that there were circumstances in which "judicially imposed strictures of *Miranda* are inapplicable" (653), thereby establishing the public safety exception to *Miranda*.

Later, Rehnquist reasoned as chief justice that because the warnings are merely an instrument to protect the "real" constitutional rights specified in the Fifth Amendment, it is not necessary to exclude incriminating statements made by a suspect just because mistakes were made by police in delivering the warnings, including mistakes that make it unclear that one has the right to an attorney during questioning (*Duckworth v. Eagan* 1989). Similarly, Rehnquist asserted in one of his first opinions as chief justice that the Constitution does not guarantee the right to make a reasonable, voluntary confession (*Colorado v. Connelly* 1986). In this case, a mentally ill person approached an officer and began confessing to murder. A psychiatrist testified that at times the defendant could understand and waive his *Miranda* rights, but that his psychosis probably motivated him to confess. The trial court excluded the incriminating statements as involuntary. Mirroring his logic in some of the Fourth Amendment cases discussed previously, Chief Justice Rehnquist held that the purpose of excluding involuntary confessions is to deter police abuse. Absent such misconduct, there was no constitutional protection regarding suppression. Rehnquist wrote, "Only if we were to establish a brand new constitutional right—the right of a criminal defendant to confess to his crimes only when totally rational and properly motivated—could respondent's present claim be sustained" (166).

Although the Court typically agreed with the chief justice when he voted for a restrictive view of self-incrimination protections, the majority rejected his position in a 2004 case (*Missouri v. Seibert*) regarding *Miranda* rights. Here, an officer obtained a confession from Seibert after about a half hour of questioning without *Mirandizing* her. After a twenty-minute break, the officer returned, informed Seibert of her rights which she waived, and resumed questioning her with the intent to have her repeat her earlier statements made before being *Mirandized*. The Court held that under such circumstances the *Miranda* warnings were ineffective, and that police using such a "question-first" strategy would *Mirandize* a suspect only after obtaining a confession. Both the pre-warning and post-warning confessions were ruled inadmissible despite the views of Rehnquist and others in the minority.

Reserving General Crime Control for States

Given the number of times that Rehnquist sought to constrict self-incrimination protections and to weaken the muscle of *Miranda*, it surprised many observers when the chief justice authored the Court's decision in *Dickerson v. United States* (2000) that struck down a federal statute that purported to overrule *Miranda*. A long-ignored congressional statute stated that a suspect's confession could be admitted in federal criminal cases providing it was voluntarily given and listed several factors for determining voluntariness. One factor involved having received *Miranda* warnings, but the statute stipulated that the absence of any one factor would not necessarily denote an involuntary confession. That is, *Mirandizing* a suspect before questioning might not be necessary. Three decades after Congress enacted the statute, a lower court relied on it to uphold a conviction based on incriminating statements made by a suspect before being *Mirandized*. Chief Justice Rehnquist's decision overturned the conviction, and reaffirmed the *Miranda* ruling as being rooted in the Fifth Amendment and beyond the reach of the legislature's authority to weaken by statute.

This defense of *Miranda* in light of Rehnquist's record is probably best understood in two ways. First, Rehnquist's opinion included a lengthy list of *Miranda* exceptions that the Court had previously established. As Professor Weisberg characterized Rehnquist's tone in *Dickerson*, the decision is "a begrudging acknowledgement" that the Court was not ready to overturn *Miranda*, with "a side argument that enough limitations have been placed on *Miranda* that it's not so harmful a decision anymore, and that in fact the police can deal with it pretty easily" (quoted in "The Rehnquist Court" 2005, 33). Second, Rehnquist often voted to curb what he saw as overreaching by Congress. The desire to bridle a legislature that attempted to encroach into the judiciary's sphere of influence may have exceeded his dislike for *Miranda*.

Rehnquist cast several other votes to limit congressional power in the criminal justice system. His position tended to flow from a narrow interpretation of Congress's power to regulate commerce rather than illustrating a "negative rights" interpretation. This helps to explain why in these cases, unlike in most others, Rehnquist appears to vote against crime control efforts. For instance, in a decision delivered for a slim, five-member majority in *United States v. Lopez* (1995), Rehnquist held the Gun-Free School Zones Act to be unconstitutional. The federal statute criminalized gun possession within one thousand feet of a school. Sharply criticizing Congress, Rehnquist wrote that the Constitution gave the legislature specific authority to regulate interstate commerce, not general police powers like those enjoyed by the states. This was the first case in a half century to find that Congress exceeded its constitutional authority under the Commerce Clause. In many ways the decision repeated the position on state versus national authority that Rehnquist took in a lone dissent twenty years before (*Fry v. United States* 1975). Rehnquist also joined the majority in *Printz v. United States* (1997) to overturn certain portions of the Brady Handgun Violence Prevention Act that required state law enforcement officials to run background checks on those applying to purchase a handgun. He also wrote for the majority to overturn another act of Congress (Violence Against Women Act), finding the link between gender-motivated crime and interstate commerce to be too tenuous (*United States v. Morrison* 2000).

As in some other previously noted areas, however, the Court majority opposed Chief Justice Rehnquist's position on this type of issue near the end of his service on the bench. Rehnquist was part of the minority when a divided Court upheld the federal government's authority to enforce prohibitions on controlled substances in a state whose voters passed a law permitting the use of marijuana for medical purposes (*Gonzales v. Raich* 2005). Rehnquist joined a dissent written by Justice O'Connor that cast the decision as inconsistent with Court precedent and as offsetting a key advantage of federalism—allowing voters in different states to experiment with different policies. The point nearly parallels a charge Rehnquist made years before against the selective incorporation process for applying constitutional protections against the states. In a case involving the right of the press and public to attend criminal trials, a solo dissent by Rehnquist complained that such actions by the Court give it too much power over the administration of justice and can "smother a healthy pluralism" (*Richmond Newspapers v. Virginia* 1980, 606).

Conclusion

Rehnquist's legacy as an influential decision maker affecting criminal justice cannot be evaluated fully by estimating his proclivity to rule in favor of the interests of law enforcement or by calculating the probability that his position would garner majority support in the Court. Rather, it seems more meaningful to understand how Rehnquist directed an evolutionary process in which he changed conversations in the judiciary by bringing back to the Court's conference table a renewed focus on several of his priorities: limits to individual privacy expectations; more expansive notions of the appropriateness of police actions while viewing narrowly the appropriateness of federal involvement in criminal justice; and constitutional interpretations tending to restrict the obligations of government in stages ranging from investigation (search and seizure) to interrogation (self-incrimination) to detention (prisoner rights and deprivation of life, liberty).

Rehnquist unquestionably played a crucially important role as a leader of the Court while it established criminal justice precedents that often reversed or recast earlier ones articulated during the Warren Court years. Perhaps more importantly, Rehnquist succeeded in redirecting criminal justice debates by shifting thresholds and reconstructing definitions that became central to many subsequent cases. Rehnquist forged majorities that reconsidered the constitutional meaning of core concepts including, among others, what represented a search covered by the Fourth Amendment and what was reasonable police behavior.

The impact of each shift was not limited to a specific case, but rather tended to have lasting significance as the Court repeatedly returned to refine such definitions and thresholds.

Yet, the Court also rejected Rehnquist's rationales in some areas and seemed to do so with increased frequency in his final years and in some of the most-watched cases. Over Rehnquist's objections, the majority was unwilling to permit the further dilution of *Miranda* (e.g., *Missouri v. Siebert* 2004), or to extend to prosecutors greater latitude to dismiss prospective jurors (*Miller-El v. Dretke* 2005). Although Rehnquist expanded the deference given to state and local criminal justice officials and practices, the majority established tighter limits on that deference than Rehnquist preferred. While Rehnquist's preference for deference, at least implicitly, often rested on the presumed value he gave to majoritarianism and voters' will, he took issue with the majority's interpretation of public will and evolving decency standards when the Court struck down certain death penalty practices (*Atkins v. Virginia* 2003; *Roper v. Simmons* 2005).

Moreover, in his near record-setting tenure and almost two decades as chief justice, Rehnquist failed to marshal sufficient support to overturn *Gideon* or *Mapp*. Even the core of the *Miranda* ruling and the exclusionary remedy it established regarding certain pre-warning confessions not only survived decades of Rehnquist assaults, but they also eventually received Rehnquist's grudging recognition of their constitutional importance (*Dickerson v. United States* 2000).

However, it would be misguided to consider either Rehnquist's chief justiceship or his final years on the bench simply as squandered opportunities to lead a conservative Court dominated by Republican appointments to a stronger reversal of previously established protections for criminal defendants and prisoners. Such characterizations err in treating as monolithic the often-fractured conservative interests on his Court in criminal justice issues (Davis 1991; Tushnet 2005), and thereby ignore the dynamics of the institution in which more centrist justices like Sandra Day O'Connor and Anthony Kennedy easily could provide a decisive swing vote in many cases.

For these and other reasons, the Court under Rehnquist might be remembered like the Burger Court as a potential conservative counter-revolution that never quite became the conservative juggernaut in criminal justice—a prospect that many on the right had desired and many on the left had feared (Blasi 1983; Yarbrough 2000). While much of Rehnquist's conservative jurisprudence that he began to stake out early in his career eventually gained majority support and the weight of constitutional law, the Court also produced important pro-defendant decisions, usually over his objections. Adapting the famous phrase *"primus inter pares"* (first among equals) often used to describe chief justices, Rehnquist may have been the first or leading voice in crafting many of the Court's positions on criminal justice issues, but his eight colleagues at any given time were equal to the task of expressing views that challenged his interpretation.

References

Arledge, Paula C., and Edward V. Heck. "Votes and Opinions in Fourth Amendment Cases, 1994-2004: Is it Rehnquist's Court?" Paper prepared at the annual meeting of the Southwestern Political Science Association, New Orleans, LA, March 2005.

Baker, Liva. *Miranda: Crime, Law and Politics.* New York: Athenaeum, 1983.

Baum, Lawrence. *The Supreme Court,* 7th edition. Washington, DC: CQ Press, 2001.

Boles, Donald. *Mr. Justice Rehnquist, Judicial Activist: The Early Years.* Ames, IA: Iowa State University Press, 1987.

Blasi, Vincent. *The Burger Court: The Counter-Revolution That Wasn't.* New Haven, CT: Yale University Press, 1983.

Bradley, Craig. "Two Models of the Fourth Amendment." *Michigan Law Review* 83 (1985): 1468-1501.

———. "Rehnquist's Legacy." *Jurist.* September 3, 2005. www.jurist.law.pitt.edu/forumy/2005/09/rehnquists-legacy.php (accessed February 4, 2010).

———. "Rehnquist and the Fourth Amendment: Be Reasonable." Pp. 81-105 in *The Rehnquist Legacy,* edited by Craig Bradley. Cambridge: Cambridge University Press, 2006.

Burden, Ordway P. "Statement on Behalf of The Honorable William H. Rehnquist Associate Justice of the Supreme Court for Chief Justice of the Supreme Court of the United States." Pp. 1148-50 in *U.S. Senate Judiciary Committee, Rehnquist Confirmation Hearings* (July 29, 1986). Washington, DC: Government Printing Office.

Clancy, Thomas K. "What is a 'Search' within the Meaning of the Fourth Amendment?" *Albany Law Review* 70 (2006): 1-42.

Clayton, Cornell W., and Mitchell Pickerill. "The Politics of Criminal Justice: How the New Right Regime Shaped the Rehnquist Court's Criminal Justice Jurisprudence." *Georgetown Law Review* 95 (2006): 1385-1425.

Coletta, Christine A. "Laptop Searches at the United States Borders and the Border Search Exception to the Fourth Amendment." *Boston College Law Review* 48 (2007): 971-1007.

Davis, Sue. "Justice Rehnquist's Judicial Philosophy: Democracy v. Equality." *Polity* 17 (1984): 88-117.

———. *Justice Rehnquist and the Constitution.* Princeton, NJ: Princeton University Press, 1989.

———. "The Supreme Court: Rehnquist's or Reagan's?" *Western Political Quarterly* 44 (1991): 87-99.

Dean, John W. *The Rehnquist Choice: The Untold Story of the Nixon Appointment That Redefined the Supreme Court.* New York: Free Press, 2001.

Devins, Neal. "The Majoritarian Rehnquist Court?" *Law and Contemporary Problems* 67 (2004): 63-80.

Eisler, Kim Isaac. *A Justice for All: William J. Brennan, Jr. and the Decisions That Transformed America.* New York: Simon & Schuster, 1993.

Engelken, Sheri J. "Majoritarian Democracy in a Federal System: The Late Chief Justice Rehnquist and the First Amendment." *Harvard Public Policy Review* 30 (2007): 695-726.

Epstein, Lee, Jeffrey A. Segal, Harold J. Spaeth, and Thomas G. Walker. *The Supreme Court Compendium: Data, Decisions, and Developments*, 4th edition. Washington, DC: CQ Press, 2007.

Epstein, Lee, and Thomas G. Walker. *Constitutional Law for a Changing America: Institutional Powers and Constraints*, 5th ed. Washington, DC: CQ Press, 2004.

———. *Constitutional Law for a Changing America: Rights, Liberties, and Justice*, 6th edition. Washington, DC: CQ Press, 2007.

Greenhouse, Linda. "The Last Days of the Rehnquist Court: The Rewards of Patience and Power." *Arizona Law Review* 45 (2003): 251-67.

———. "The Year Rehnquist May Have Lost His Court," *New York Times*, July 5, 2004, 1(A).

Hagle, Timothy M., and Harold J. Spaeth. "Ideological Patterns in Justices' Voting in the Burger Court's Business Cases." *Journal of Politics* 55 (1993): 492-505.

Hensley, Thomas R. *The Rehnquist Court: Justices, Rulings, and Legacy*. Santa Barbara, CA: ABC-CLIO, 2006.

Howard, Robert M., and Jeffrey A. Segal. "A Preference for Deference? The Supreme Court and Judicial Review." *Political Research Quarterly* 57 (2004): 131-43.

Hutchinson, Dennis J. "Unanimity and Desegregation: Decision-making in the Supreme Court, 1948-1958." *Georgetown Law Journal* 68 (1979): 1-96.

Klaidman, Daniel, Stuart Taylor Jr., and Evan Thomas. "Palace Revolt." *Newsweek* (February 6, 2006): 34.

Kluger, Richard. *Simple Justice: The History of Brown v. Board of Education and Black America's Struggle for Equality*. New York: Random House, 1975.

Lane, Charles. "A Look at a Rehnquist Legacy," *Washington Post*, June 6, 2005: 17(A).

Liptak, Adam. "The Memo That Rehnquist Wrote and Had to Disown," *New York Times*, September 11, 2005, 5(A).

McCall, Madhavi M. and Michael A. McCall. "Chief Justice William Rehnquist: His Law-and-Order Legacy and Impact on Criminal Justice." *Akron Law Review* 39 (2006): 323-72.

McCall, Michael A. "Urban Policing Levels and the Localization of Law-and-Order Politics." PhD diss., Washington University in St. Louis, 2004.

Nannes, John M. "The 'Lone Dissenter.'" *Journal of Supreme Court History* 31 (2006): 1-4.

Nixon, Richard M. "Richard M. Nixon Presidential Nomination Acceptance Speech, Republican National Convention, August 8, Miami Beach, Florida." Pamphlet: Nixon Agnew Campaign Committee, 1968.

Packer, Herbert. *The Limits of Criminal Sanction*. Stanford, CA: Stanford University Press, 1968.

Powell, Jefferson. "The Compleat Jeffersonian: Justice Rehnquist and Federalism." *Yale Law Review* 91 (1982): 1317-70.

"Rehnquist Court: Roundtable Discussion." *Stanford Lawyer* 72 (2005): 30-36.

Rehnquist, William H. "Who Writes Decisions of the Supreme Court?" *U.S. News and World Report*, December 13, 1957: 74-75.

———. "The Notion of a Living Constitution." *Texas Law Review* 54 (1976): 693-706.

———. "Government by Cliché." *Missouri Law Review* 45 (1980): 379-93.

———. *The Supreme Court: How It Was, How It Is*. New York: William Morrow, 1987.

———. "Reflections on the Practice of Law (1953-1999)." *The Record of the Association of the Bar of the City of New York* 54 (1999): 411-20.

————. "One-on-One with the Chief." Interview by Mike Egan. *Stanford Lawyer* (Spring 2005): 26-29.

Rydell, John R. "Mr. Justice Rehnquist and Judicial Self-Restraint." *Hastings Law Journal* 26 (1975): 875-915.

Savage, David G. "Chief Justice, 80, Led Court on a Conservative Path," *Los Angeles Times*, September 4, 2005, 21(A).

Savoy, Paul. "Time for a Second Bill of Rights." *The Nation* (June 17, 1991): 815-16.

Schmalleger, Frank. *Criminal Justice: A Brief Introduction*, 7th ed. Upper Saddle River, NJ: Pearson Prentice Hall, 2008.

Schwartz, Herman, ed. *The Rehnquist Court: Judicial Activism on the Right*. New York: Hill and Wang, 2003.

Shapiro, David L. "Mr. Justice Rehnquist: A Preliminary View." *Harvard Law Review* 90 (1976): 293-357.

Shin, Helen. "Is the Death of the Death Penalty Near? The Impact of *Atkins* and *Roper* on the Future of Capital Punishment for Mentally Ill Defendants." *Fordham Law Review* 76 (2007): 465-516.

Smith, Christopher E. *Courts, Politics and the Judicial Process*, 2nd ed. Belmont, CA: Wadsworth, 1999.

————. "The Rehnquist Court and Criminal Justice: An Empirical Assessment." *Journal of Contemporary Criminal Justice* 19 (2003): 161-81.

Smith Christopher E., and Madhavi McCall. "Criminal Justice and the 2001-2002 United States Supreme Court Term." *Michigan State DCL Law Review* 2 (2003): 413-46.

————. "Criminal Justice and the 2002-2003 United States Supreme Court Term." *Capital University Law Review* 22 (2004): 859-99.

Smith, Christopher E., Madhavi McCall, and Cynthia Perez McCluskey. *Law and Criminal Justice: Emerging Issues in the Twenty-First Century*. New York: Peter Lang, 2005.

Spaeth, Harold J. "Chief Justice Rehnquist: Poster Child for the Attitudinal Model." *Judicature* 89 (2005): 108-15.

Stephens Jr., Otis H., and John M. Scheb II. *American Constitutional Law*, 2nd ed. Belmont, CA: West/Wadsworth, 1999.

Taylor, Stuart. 1986. "President asserts he will withhold Rehnquist Memos," *New York Times*, August 1, 1986, 8 (A).

Tomkovicz, James. "Against the Tide: Rehnquist's Efforts to Curtail the Right to Counsel." Pp. 129-55 in *The Rehnquist Legacy*, edited by Craig Bradley. Cambridge: Cambridge University Press, 2006.

Tribe, Laurence. "Tribe Reflects on Supreme Legacies." Interview by Robb London. *Harvard Law School Bulletin,* September 13, 2005.

Tushnet, Mark. *A Court Divided: The Rehnquist Court and the Future of Constitutional Law*. New York: W.W. Norton, 2005.

Urofsky, Melvin I., ed. *Biographical Encyclopedia of the Supreme Court: The Lives and Legal Philosophies of the Justices*. Washington, DC: CQ Press, 2006.

Whittington, Keith E. "William H. Rehnquist: Nixon's Strict Constructionist, Reagan's Chief Justice." Pp. 8-33 in *Rehnquist Justice: Understanding the Court Dynamic*, edited by Earl M. Maltz. Lawrence, KS: University of Kansas Press, 2003.

Witt, Elder. *Congressional Quarterly's Guide to the U.S. Supreme Court*. 2nd ed. Washington, DC: CQ Press, 1990.

Yarbrough, Tinsley E. *The Rehnquist Court and the Constitution*. Cambridge: Oxford University Press, 2000.

Cases Cited

Alabama v. Shelton, 535 U.S. 654 (2002)
Arizona v. Evans, 514 U.S. 1 (1995)
Atkins v. Virginia, 536 U.S. 304 (2003)
Ball v. United States, 470 U.S. 856 (1985)
Batson v. Kentucky, 476 U.S. 79 (1986)
Bond v. United States, 529 U.S. 334 (2000)
Brecht v. Abrahamson, 507 U.S. 619 (1993)
Brown v. Board of Education of Topeka, Kansas, 347 U.S. 483 (1954)
California v. Ciraolo, 476 U.S. 207 (1986)
California v. Greenwood, 486 U.S. 35 (1988)
California v. Minjares, 443 U.S. 916 (1979)
Chandler v. Miller, 520 U.S. 305 (1997)
Colorado v. Bertine, 479 U.S. 367 (1987)
Colorado v. Connelly, 479 U.S. 157 (1986)
Connecticut Department of Public Safety v. Doe, 538 U.S. 1 (2003)
Craig v. Boren, 429 U.S. 190 (1976)
Cruz v. Beto, 405 U.S. 319 (1972)
DeShaney v. Winnebago County, 489 U.S. 189 (1989)
Dickerson v. United States, 530 U.S. 428 (2000)
Dow Chemical Co. v. United States, 476 U.S. 227 (1986)
Duckworth v. Eagan, 492 U.S. 195 (1989)
Ferguson v. City of Charleston, 532 U.S. 67 (2001)
Florida v. Jimeno, 500 U.S. 248 (1991)
Florida v. Riley, 488 U.S. 445 (1989)
Florida v. Wells, 495 U.S. 1 (1990)
Frontiero v. Richardson, 411 U.S. 677 (1973)
Fry v. United States, 421 U.S. 542 (1975)
Gideon v. Wainwright, 372 U.S. 335 (1963)
Gonzales v. Raich, 545 U.S. 1 (2005)
Groh v. Ramirez, 540 U.S. 551 (2004)
Gustafson v. Florida, 414 U.S. 260 (1973)
Halbert v. Michigan, 545 U.S. 605 (2005)
Harris v. McRae, 448 U.S. 297 (1980)
Herrera v. Collins, 506 U.S. 390 (1993)
Hill v. Lockhart, 474 U.S. 52 (1985)
Illinois v. Gates, 462 U.S. 213 (1983)
Illinois v. Wardlow, 528 U.S. 119 (2000)
Indianapolis v. Edmond, 531 U.S. 32 (2000)
Knowles v. Iowa, 525 U.S. 113 (1998)
Kyllo v. United States, 533 U.S. 27 (2001)
Mapp v. Ohio, 367 U.S. 643 (1961)
Maryland v. Pringle, 540 U.S 366 (2003)
Michigan v. Tucker, 417 U.S. 433 (1974)
Michigan Department of State Police v. Sitz, 496 U.S. 444 (1990)
Miller-El v. Dretke, 545 U.S. 231 (2005)
Miranda v. Arizona, 384 U.S. 436 (1966)
Missouri v. Seibert, 542 U.S. 600 (2004)

Muscarello v. United States, 524 U.S. 125 (1998)
New York v. Belton, 453 U.S. 454 (1981)
New York v. Quarles, 467 U.S. 649 (1984)
Ohio v. Robinette, 519 U.S. 33 (1996)
Oliver v. United States, 466 U.S. 170 (1984)
Pace v. DiGuglielmo, 544 U.S. 408 (2005)
Paul v. Davis, 424 U.S. 693 (1976)
Penry v. Lynaugh, 492 U.S. 302 (1989)
Plessy v. Ferguson, 163 U.S. 537 (1896)
Printz v. United States, 521 U.S. 898 (1997)
Richmond Newspapers v. Virginia, 448 U.S. 555 (1980)
Rompilla v. Beard, 545, U.S. 374 (2005)
Roper v. Simmons, 543 U.S. 551 (2005)
Ross v. Moffitt, 417 U.S 600 (1974)
Sandin v. Conner, 515 U.S. 472 (1995)
Scott v. Illinois, 440 U.S. 367 (1979)
Smith v. Doe, 538 U.S. 84 (2003)
Stanford v. Kentucky, 492 U.S. 302 (1989)
Swain v. Alabama, 380 U.S. 202 (1965)
Texas v. Cobb, 532 U.S. 162 (2001)
Thompson v. Keohane, Warden, et al., 516 U.S. 99 (1996)
Thorton v. United States, 541 U.S. 615 (2004)
Trimble v. Gordon, 430 U.S. 762 (1977)
United States v. Flores-Montano, 541 U.S. 149 (2004)
United States v. Knights, 534 U.S. 112 (2001)
United States v. Knotts, 460 U.S. 276 (1982)
United States v. Leon, 468 U.S. 897 (1984)
United States v. Lopez, 514 U.S. 549 (1995)
United States v. Maze, 414 U.S. 395 (1974)
United States v. Montoya de Hernandez, 473 U.S. 531 (1985)
United States v. Morrison, 529 U.S. 598 2000)
United States v. Peltier, 422 U.S. 531 (1975)
United States v. Place, 462 U.S. 696 (1983)
United States v. Ramsey, 431 U.S. 606 (1977)
United States v. Robinson, 414 U.S. 218 (1973)
United States v. Ross, 456 U.S. 798 (1982)
United States v. Santana, 427 U.S. 38 (1976)
United States v. Sokolow, 490 U.S. 1 (1989)
Wainwright v. Sykes, 433 U.S. 72 (1977)
Webster v. Reproductive Health Services, 492 U.S. 490 (1989)
Weeks v. U.S., 232 U.S. 383 (1914)

Chapter 6
John Paul Stevens: A Liberal Leader & His Roles on the Court

Christopher E. Smith

At the conclusion of the Rehnquist Court era in 2005, Justice John Paul Stevens had served on the Supreme Court for nearly thirty years. He was one of the longest-serving and most prolific opinion-writing justices in Supreme Court history. Despite the existence of hundreds of his written opinions, Stevens's approach to judicial decision making was not easily classifiable by scholars. After being appointed to the Supreme Court by President Gerald Ford in 1975, Stevens initially gained a reputation as a maverick (Canon 1991). He did not consistently vote with either the Court's most liberal justices or its most conservative justices. He was perceived as charting his own course and he reinforced this perception by writing many concurring and dissenting opinions, often presenting a unique perspective.

During the Rehnquist Court era, Stevens established himself as the Supreme Court's leading liberal after the retirements of Justices William Brennan, Thurgood Marshall, and Harry Blackmun in the first years of the 1990s. Through his judicial opinions supporting the preservation and expansion of individuals' rights in the criminal justice process, Stevens distinguished himself by playing several important roles for the Supreme Court. This chapter will discuss those roles as well as explore the reasons that Stevens emerged as such a strong voice for the protection of the rights for criminal suspects, defendants, and convicted offenders.

John Paul Stevens was born in Chicago in 1920, the son of a wealthy hotel owner and the grandson of the founder of a large insurance company. As an undergraduate, he studied literature at the University of Chicago. During World War II, he served as a U.S. Navy officer in Hawaii working as part of a team of specialists who focused on breaking Japanese codes. After the war, he graduated at the top of his class at Northwestern University's law school. He worked as a law clerk for Justice Wiley Rutledge at the U.S. Supreme Court immediately after graduation from law school (Ray 2008). Except for a brief stint in Washington, D.C. in the early 1950s, where he served as counsel to a congressional committee dealing with antitrust issues, he was an attorney in Chicago until his appointment to the federal bench.

Stevens, a life-long Republican, was a respected lawyer in Chicago with a reputation as an expert on antitrust law. He came to local prominence in 1969 through his appointment as the chief counsel for a committee that investigated allegations of corruption on the Illinois Supreme Court. Stevens's investigation and presentation of the case led to the resignations of two justices from the court (Manaster 2001). Soon afterward, with the support of Senator Charles Percy, President Richard Nixon appointed Stevens to a seat on the Seventh Circuit U.S. Court of Appeals in 1970. Stevens served on the appellate court for five years before President Ford appointed him to replace retiring Justice William O. Douglas on the Supreme Court in 1975.

Most observers initially expected Stevens to shift the Supreme Court in a conservative direction. He was a Republican private practice attorney with experience in corporate law who replaced one of the most liberal justices in Supreme Court history. Douglas had been appointed by Democratic President Franklin Roosevelt and his opinions helped to develop and expand the definitions of constitutional rights throughout the Warren Court era. Contrary to original expectations, Stevens eventually established a liberal voting record in constitutional rights cases, especially in certain categories of criminal justice cases (Farnsworth 2005, 73).

Stevens (2002, 33) described his own approach to constitutional interpretation as reflecting an "understanding of the Constitution as containing broad grants of power to respond to social and economic changes that were unforeseen in the Eighteenth Century." He analogized the Constitution to "an instruction manual explaining how a newly created entity can assemble and exercise governmental power to achieve its goals set forth in the Preamble" (33). This particular description of his approach to constitutional interpretation was intended to articulate his disagreement with his colleagues Antonin Scalia and Clarence Thomas who espouse originalism as the proper approach to deciding constitutional issues. Stevens concluded this particular description of his approach by endorsing the propriety of rights-protecting decisions in criminal justice that were not constrained by narrow readings of either the words or original intentions of the Constitution: "In my judgment the decisions that contributed to the evolution of the doctrines concerning coerced confessions [and] the provision of counsel to indigent defendants . . . . —even though they sometimes stretched the language of the Constitution—fairly ensured that the powers and freedoms specified by the Framers would be effective in today's world" (33).

The independence and liberalism of Stevens during the Rehnquist Court era is well illustrated by Ward Farnsworth's descriptive comparison of Stevens and Rehnquist with respect to criminal justice cases from the 1994 Term through the 1999 Term. According to Farnsworth (2003, 162):

> Stevens voted for the defendant approximately 85% of the time. . . . Stevens wrote or joined dissents in favor of defendants or convicts 64 times, including

18 times by himself. Rehnquist dissented in favor of defendants five times and never by himself. Rehnquist dissented in favor of the government 21 times; Stevens dissented in favor of the government in a criminal case just once during this period.

Scholars have described Stevens as being a judge "who eschews theory in favor of practical reason . . . [and who] deliberately makes decisions that would create the most reasonable results on the facts as he understood them" (Farnsworth 2003, 178). According to Pamela Karlan (1996, 522), Stevens's "opinions reflect a tough-minded realism." Although he was praised for his "love of fairness in each individual case," he was also criticized because "his jurisprudence also will be associated with doctrinal unpredictability [and] a certain ad hoc quality" (Farnsworth 2003, 179). On the other hand, Frederick Schauer (1996) argues that Stevens avoided the creation of doctrinal rules that gave clear guidance to judges in subsequent cases because he preferred to develop standards that would assist with the case-by-case evaluation of the various situations that can give rise to legal disputes. Stevens's preference for standards instead of rules reflected "a general desire to avoid wrong decisions, and to get each case as right as he can" (557).

William Popkin identified another element of Stevens's decision making that was especially important for criminal justice. In his opinions, Stevens advanced the position that "the [C]ourt should protect *individual dignity* . . . [through] creative application of constitutional principles, such as due process and equal protection" (*emphasis in original*) (Popkin 1989, 1090). Indeed, in a prisoners' rights case argued during Stevens's first months as a Supreme Court justice, he signaled his concern for human dignity and a broad, natural rights-based conception of liberty that he applied to all people, including criminal offenders. In his dissenting opinion in *Meachum v. Fano* (1976), joined by Justices William Brennan and Thurgood Marshall, Stevens objected to the majority's denial of hearings for prisoners prior to their transfers to correctional institutions with more difficult living conditions and fewer privileges. According to Stevens (*Meachum* 230-33):

> The Court's holding today, however, appears to rest on a conception of "liberty" which I consider fundamentally incorrect. The Court indicates that a "liberty interest" may have either of two sources. According to the Court, a liberty interest may "originate in the Constitution," . . . or it may have its "roots in state law." [citation omitted] Apart from those two possible origins, the Court is unable to find that a person has a constitutionally protected interest in liberty. If man were a creature of the State, the analysis would be correct. But neither the Bill of Rights nor the laws of sovereign States create the liberty which the Due Process Clause protects. . . . I had thought it self-evident that all men were endowed by their Creator with liberty as one of the cardinal unalienable rights . . . I think it clear that even the inmate retains an unalienable interest in liberty at the very minimum, the right to be treated with dignity—which the Constitution may never ignore.

In addition to his emphasis on human dignity and his fact-based, case-by-case approach to developing standards rather than broad rules, Stevens was notable for his assertiveness in presenting his views in concurring and dissenting opinions. Robert Nagel (2003, 510) described Stevens as "a justice who exhibits considerable self-confidence, both about his views of proper public policy and about using judicial power." Even during his first decade on the Supreme Court, Stevens stood out for the number of opinions that he wrote. One scholar who analyzed the Burger Court era noted that Stevens "wrote a large number of concurring and dissenting opinions, authoring more of these than any of his colleagues in each of the [Burger] Court's last six terms" (Canon, 1991, 344). Stevens continued to be a prolific opinion writer throughout the Rehnquist Court era. By the time he entered the final year of the Rehnquist era, Stevens had written more dissenting and concurring opinions than any other justice in Supreme Court history (Epstein, Segal, Spaeth, and Walker 2007, 636).

Life Experience and an Orientation toward Protecting Rights

One critic has argued that because none of the later Rehnquist Court era's justices represented criminal defendants in their pre-judicial careers as attorneys, they did not fully understand and appreciate the importance of constitutional rights in the context of criminal justice (Fortunato 1999). Although Thurgood Marshall, who retired in 1991, had experience in criminal justice, the biographies of the justices who served through the remainder of the Rehnquist era did not indicate any involvement in criminal cases. In reality, however, there was at least one justice who had experience in criminal cases through pro bono work: John Paul Stevens. Stevens (1998) made a specific reference to pro bono cases as the source of his understanding of criminal justice when he said:

> In closing, I want to express my thanks to the Chicago Bar Association for the many lessons about the law that I learned during my active membership in the Association. Association assignments taught me that prisoners are human beings and some, though not all, of their claims have merit; . . . that the intangible benefits of *pro bono* work can be even more rewarding than a paying client.

One particular pro bono case, as well as other life experiences, apparently helped Stevens develop a sensitivity to the need for open access to the courts, the protection of rights, and the prevention of abuses in the criminal justice process. Nathaniel Nathanson, who had been one of Stevens's favorite law school professors at Northwestern, was appointed by the U.S. Supreme Court to represent Arthur LaFrana. LaFrana had confessed to the murder of a theater cashier in 1937 but later pursued a pro se claim that his confession had been involuntary (Stevens 2004). In arguing before the Supreme Court in 1951, Nathanson also represented two other Illinois prisoners who sought to raise claims about coerced confessions. In a 7-2 decision authored by Chief Justice Fred Vinson, the U.S. Supreme Court remanded the cases to the Illinois courts to determine whether the petitioners' claims could be examined under the state's Post-Conviction Hearing Act. If not, then the U.S. Supreme Court said that the petitioners could present their claims in a U.S. district court (*Jennings v. Illinois* 1951).

According to Stevens (2004), "Because Nat's extensive experience in litigation had primarily involved appellate advocacy, he asked me to handle the investigation and trial of the confession issue [in LaFrana's case]." Stevens represented LaFrana in an evidentiary hearing before an Illinois trial court, and the Illinois Supreme Court subsequently examined the case. In *People v. LaFrana* (1954), the Illinois Supreme Court described the evidence presented in the case:

> According to defendant's testimony, when he refused to confess the captain hit him repeatedly with fists and with a night stick. His hands were then handcuffed behind him and he was blindfolded. A rope was put in between the handcuffs and he was suspended from a door with his hands behind him and his feet almost off the floor. While he was hanging from the door, he was repeatedly struck until he lapsed into unconsciousness. When he lost consciousness he was taken down from the door and when he regained consciousness he would be hung back up on the door and again questioned and struck. After about fifteen minutes of this treatment he agreed to sign a confession. He was taken downstairs to the captain's office where he signed a confession. (585)

LaFrana's version of events was corroborated by a newspaper photograph taken the following day that showed cuts and bruises on his face as well as swelling around his eye. In addition, the county physician who examined him at the jail the following week testified that the abrasions on his wrists could have been caused by hanging him over a door but could not have been caused by normal use of handcuffs.

According to Stevens (2004), the Illinois Supreme Court decision "led to LaFrana's release" after serving seventeen years in prison. Clearly, Stevens never forgot the case because he declared in a speech, "What I learned from that case no doubt had an impact on my work on the Supreme Court" (Stevens 2004). Indeed, a close examination of his speeches reveals that Stevens regularly made reference to the case without always presenting its details. For example, in the printed version of a speech to the Chicago Bar Association, Stevens (2002) cited the *LaFrana* case in the footnotes when he said, "It was a few years after my graduation [from law school], in the course of pro bono representation of an inmate who had been in prison since 1937, that I learned that some of those interrogations did, in fact, involve brutal and indefensible police conduct." In another speech, he cited *LaFrana* without describing it when he acknowledged that in Chicago during the Depression "less prosperous criminals were sometimes treated brutally by Chicago police officers seeking confessions of guilt" (Stevens 1991).

Justice Stevens's experience with the *LaFrana* case and other pro bono cases in Chicago distinguished him from his Rehnquist Court colleagues with respect to his acknowledgement of personal recollections about the risks that criminal justice officials may engage in abusive conduct and violate the rights of criminal suspects, defendants, and convicted offenders (Smith 1997).

Justice Stevens's concerns about keeping courts open and available for the claims of convicted offenders can be attributed, in large part, to one important episode in his life. In 1969, Stevens came into the public eye through his role as the chief investigator for a special commission appointed to investigate allegations of conflicts-of-interest among Illinois Supreme Court justices, specifically financial links between certain justices and interests with cases before the court (Manaster 2001). After highly-publicized commission hearings in which Stevens played a quasi-prosecutorial role, two justices resigned from the Illinois Supreme Court.

The investigation of financial conflicts-of-interest among the Illinois Supreme Court justices began with allegations circulated by Sherman Skolnick, a man of modest means who suffered from paralysis due to polio. His parents had sued over the mishandling of a $14,000 stock fund that had been set up to provide for the care of their disabled son—and they lost in the Illinois Supreme Court (Manaster 2001). Skolnick said afterward, "We went all the way to the state Supreme Court . . . and lost. I vowed to my parents that I would devote my life to helping others in the courts" (4).

Because Skolnick did not have affluence, social status, political connections, or formal education in law, he was the type of person that government officials could easily dismiss as a misguided crackpot. As summarized years later by scholars, Skolnick, "[a]n eccentric gadfly, who was otherwise invisible to the political establishment, pleaded and pushed for his complaints to be heard. The lesson is that, once in a while, the conspiracy theorist is correct" (Danner and Samaha 2006, 2052).

The example of Sherman Skolnick taught John Paul Stevens about the need to keep courts accessible, even to litigants who cannot afford attorneys, in order to permit people to raise their claims. According to Justice Stevens (2001, xi),

> [M]y reaction to so-called pro se petitions—those filed by lay litigants without the assistance of counsel—is also markedly different from that of any of my colleagues . . . . My memory of the unexpected merit that we found in the allegations made by Sherman Skolnick has remained a powerful reminder that categorical prohibitions against repetitive filings can create a real risk of injustice . . . . [A]t virtually every Court conference I find myself dissenting from three or four orders imposing special burdens on this disfavored class of litigants.

Justice Stevens himself has pointed to the importance of his pro bono experiences, including the *LaFrana* case, and the memory of Sherman Skolnick as affecting his understanding of the need for access to the courts and the importance of protecting constitutional rights in the criminal justice process. One additional life experience had a profound effect on his understanding of criminal justice (Smith 2007a). Stevens's father was convicted of embezzlement in the 1930s and the Illinois Supreme Court later overturned his conviction (Lane 2005). Justice Stevens's father, Ernest J. Stevens, completed construction of the world's largest hotel, the Stevens Hotel (now the Chicago Hilton and Towers Hotel) in 1927. When the Great Depression hit, Ernest Stevens encountered severe financial problems. He borrowed money from the insurance company run by his father and brother in order to pay the financial obligations of the Stevens Hotel Company. In a highly-publicized case, Ernest Stevens was charged and convicted for the crime of embezzlement as a result of his loans from his family's insurance business where he served as a member of the Board of Directors. Through the appeals process, the Illinois Supreme Court overturned the conviction because it found that "[i]n this whole record there is not a scintilla of evidence of any concealment or fraud attempted" (*People v. Stevens* 1934, 160). The Illinois Supreme Court observed that it may have been an unwise business transaction for the insurance company to make its capital available to the hotel company, but the court concluded that no evidence was ever presented to show that anyone in the Stevens family personally pocketed any money from these transactions. In sum, the appellate court concluded that the prosecution never presented evidence to show that "the defendant feloniously and fraudulently converted [the money] to his own use," a necessary element to sustain a conviction for embezzlement (160).

At the time of his father's trial, one might presume that the fourteen-year-old future justice was keenly aware that the prospect of imprisonment hung over his father's head. Indeed, Stevens initially told an interviewer that the experience had taught him "that the criminal justice system can misfire sometimes" because "it seriously misfired in that case" (Rosen 2007, 54). In a later interview, however, Stevens said that upon further reflection he did not believe that the trial had an impact on him as a teenager because he never believed his father, whom he admired greatly, would actually go to prison (Stevens 2010). He acknowledged, however, that when he later became an attorney, he could look back on his father's case as a reminder about the risk of errors in the justice system. It was a memory that helped to cement his concern about the importance of protecting procedural rights and maintaining access to appellate processes in criminal cases (Smith 2007a).

Stevens's Supreme Court clerkship with Justice Wiley Rutledge during the 1947 Term also gave him personal experience with criminal justice issues. Stevens worked closely with one of the Court's most rights-oriented justices. In his later speeches and judicial opinions, Stevens continued to quote and cite Rutledge in advocating the importance of procedural rights (Amann 2006). Scholars examining Rutledge's papers have connected memoranda by Stevens the law clerk on the treatment of habeas corpus and other issues in the aftermath of World War II with Justice Stevens's later pro-rights judicial opinions concerning criminal suspects, convicted offenders, and, especially, detained terrorism suspects (Thai 2006).

The Roles of John Paul Stevens
in Criminal Justice Cases

In a speech at the University of Chicago in 1991, Justice Stevens did not mince words in explicitly criticizing the Rehnquist Court majority for its decisions during the preceding term that had, in his view, improperly diminished the rights of individuals in the context of criminal justice (Simon 1995, 226):

> In a totally unnecessary and unprecedented decision, the Court placed its stamp of approval on the use of victim impact evidence to facilitate the imposition of the death penalty (*Payne v. Tennessee* 1991). The Court condoned the use of mandatory sentences that are manifestly and grossly disproportionate to the moral guilt of the offender (*Harmelin v. Michigan* 1991). It broadened the powers of the police to invade the privacy of individual citizens and even to detain them without any finding of probable cause or reasonable suspicion (Stevens 1991).

Although Stevens was outspoken in this criticism of his colleagues, this criticism did not demonstrate that he would automatically support individuals' rights claims in criminal justice cases. As noted in one article, "Justice Stevens' Fourth Amendment opinions are often less protective of defendants' rights than [are the opinions of] other justices" who are considered to be the liberals of the Rehnquist Court era (Bleich, Powell, Feinberg, and Friedland 2007, 29). For example, Stevens wrote the majority opinion that declined to recognize the use of a drug-sniffing dog as a "search" (*Illinois v. Caballes* 2005). He also dissented against a Scalia-authored majority opinion that invalidated as an improper warrantless search the use of a thermal imaging device pointed at a house to detect heat sources that might be "grow lights" for marijuana plants (*Kyllo v. United States* 2001). Stevens did not see any Fourth Amendment problem with those police actions (Bleich et al. 2007). Thus, in contrast to Fourth Amendment cases, several observers note that Stevens was especially protective of *procedural* rights, an orientation that was consistent with the opinions that he helped to construct while learning the law in the chambers of Justice Rutledge during the 1947 Term (Amann 2006; Ray 2008).

While Stevens stands out as a defender of constitutional rights in the context of criminal justice during the Rehnquist Court era, albeit with a mix of issues for which he endorsed governmental authority, his most distinctive contributions stem from his various roles on the Court during this era (Smith 2006).

Senior Justice in the Majority

The retirements of senior colleagues in the first seven terms of the Rehnquist Court era eventually placed Stevens in the position of being the most-frequent senior justice in the majority when Chief Justice Rehnquist dissented. The remaining Warren Court era justices retired in 1990 (William Brennan), 1991 (Thurgood Marshall), and 1993 (Byron White). In addition, Justice Stevens's lone remaining senior colleague from the Burger Court era, other than Chief Justice Rehnquist, was Harry Blackmun, who retired in 1994. Thus Stevens was the senior justice in the majority for one case during the 1992 Term as White and Blackmun performed that role for a combined total of fourteen additional cases. During the 1993 Term, Stevens assigned seven majority opinions as senior associate justice and Blackmun assigned eleven opinions for the eighteen cases in which Rehnquist dissented. Beginning in the 1994 Term and continuing through the ten subsequent years of the Rehnquist era, Stevens made majority opinion assignments in a total of 138 cases while Justice O'Connor made four opinion assignments and Justice Scalia made two such assignments in the 144 cases in which Chief Justice Rehnquist dissented or, in his final term, was absent due to illness.

From among the 146 cases for which Stevens was senior justice in the majority during the Rehnquist Court era, Stevens assigned the majority opinion to himself in fifty-one cases (Epstein et al. 2007, 653-54). He used the opportunity in a number of these cases to craft important opinions affecting criminal justice.

In *Atkins v. Virginia* (2002), Justice Stevens was the self-assigned author of the majority opinion declaring that the execution of mentally retarded offenders violates the Eighth Amendment. The opinion emphasized the vitality of the *Trop v. Dulles* (1958) standard for assessing the Eighth Amendment's Cruel and Unusual Punishments Clause through the evolving standards of contemporary society. The opinion reflected Justice Stevens's efforts to narrow the applicability of capital punishment (Liebman and Marshall 2006). Ultimately, during the Roberts Court era, Stevens announced (*Baze v. Rees* 2008),

> I have relied on my own experience in reaching the conclusion that the imposition of the death penalty represents "the pointless and needless extinction of life with only marginal contributions to any discernible social or public purposes. A penalty with such negligible returns to the State [is] patently excessive and cruel and unusual punishment violative of the Eighth Amendment" (quoting *Furman v. Georgia* 1972, 312).

Justice Stevens assigned to himself the majority opinion in *Rasul v. Bush* (2004) declaring that federal courts have jurisdiction over challenges to the legality of detentions of foreign nationals at Guantanamo Bay, Cuba. This self-assigned opinion represented one of the Supreme Court's first responses to assertions of executive authority by the Bush Administration that imposed indefinite incommunicado detentions as part of the "War on Terrorism." The Court's opinion in *Rasul*, as well as the accompanying decision in *Hamdi v. Rumsfeld* (2004), forced the Bush Administration to modify its unilateral assertions of unchecked authority and begin developing a plan to introduce elements of due process into cases concerning terrorism suspects detained in the United States and at Guantanamo Bay.

In yet another example, a self-assigned majority opinion by Stevens reasserted congressional authority under the Commerce Clause to regulate the cultivation of marijuana under the Controlled Substance Act (*Gonzales v. Raich* 2005). In the previous decade, the Court's conservative justices had sought to assert their support for states' authority by limiting congressional power to enact federal statutes related to criminal justice (*United States v. Lopez* 1995; *Printz v. United States* 1997; *United States v. Morrison* 2000). Stevens has been described as "a vigorous dissenter from the[se] Rehnquist [era] federalism decisions" so that the opportunity to restore congressional legislative authority under the Commerce Clause was presumed to have been "by far the sweetest [decision] for him" of the 2004 Term (Greenhouse 2005).

His frequent formal role as senior justice in the majority also gave him the opportunity to assign majority opinions to Anthony Kennedy, Sandra Day O'Connor, or other justices who typically supported conservative outcomes when he may have thought such assignments might help to retain their participation in a five-member majority. Studies of the Supreme Court have found patterns of opinion assignments to members of the majority who are ideologically distant from the opinion assigner (Maltzman, Spriggs, and Wahlbeck 2000). For example, one of the rare cases in which Clarence Thomas has been assigned the task of writing the opinion for a five-member majority came through an assignment by Stevens when Thomas supported a liberal outcome. In *United States v. Bajakajian* (1998), Thomas provided the decisive fifth vote in the Supreme Court's lone decision protecting a convicted offender's Eighth Amendment right against excessive fines. Similarly, Stevens assigned the majority opinion in *Roper v. Simmons* (2005) to Anthony Kennedy, the lone conservative to join the four liberals in striking down the application of the death penalty to offenders who committed their capital crimes prior to the age of eighteen. Earlier in the Rehnquist Court era, Stevens had written a plurality opinion barring the execution of offenders who committed murders prior to age seventeen (*Thompson v. Oklahoma* 1988). The Court's decision in *Roper* effectively extended Stevens's logic in the earlier case to further limit the application of capital punishment.

Advocate for Adversarial System and Right to Counsel

Justice Stevens stands out among the Rehnquist Court justices as a strong advocate of the right to counsel. In this role, he reminded his colleagues about the justice system's presumed reliance on adversarial process and the need to ensure that defendant's interests are protected through professional representation and zealous advocacy. In his dissent in *McNeil v. Wisconsin* (1991), for example, a jailed defendant facing armed robbery charges was represented by a public defender at his bail hearing. While in jail, he was questioned about a separate murder case. The majority held that his Sixth Amendment right to counsel was offense-specific so that no rights were violated by questioning the suspect outside the presence of counsel on separate charges as long as he had waived his right to counsel after being informed of his *Miranda* rights. Stevens complained that "as a symbolic matter, today's decision is ominous because it reflects a preference for an inquisitorial system that regards the defense lawyer as an impediment rather than a servant to the cause of justice" (*McNeil v. Wisconsin* 1991, 183).

In other examples, Justice Stevens expressed strong disagreement with the majority's conclusion that no Sixth Amendment violation occurred when an appointed counsel in a capital case failed to reveal that he had previously represented the murder victim (*Mickens v. Taylor* 2002). He also objected to the prosecutor's action in directly communicating with an indicted, jailed defendant in order to gain incriminating statements. Instead, Stevens would strictly enforce the right to counsel at the moment that adversarial proceedings begin. Despite the fact that the defendant waived his right to counsel during questioning, Stevens characterized the prosecutor's actions as unfair and unethical because he, in effect, went behind the defense attorney's back when seeking to question the defendant (*Patterson v. Illinois* 1988).

Defender of the Right to Trial by Jury

Justice Stevens, a former trial attorney and a judicial officer who demonstrated significant concern about procedural rights, was especially outspoken and influential with respect to the right to trial by jury. In *Lewis v. United States* (1996), the justices divided into three opinions with the dissent by Stevens, joined by Justice Ginsburg, representing the strongest defense of an entitlement to trial by jury. The Stevens opinion argued that the right to trial by jury existed in all cases for which the maximum penalty could be six months or more of incarceration. By contrast, the five-member majority said that no such right existed when the defendant faced charges for petty offenses, even if conviction of multiple counts of those petty offenses could result in sentences that, when served consecutively, run for many, many years. A concurring opinion by Justices Kennedy and Breyer agreed with Stevens about the entitlement to a jury for any sentence of incarceration for six months or more, but it accepted the judge's authority to preempt the jury trial right through a pretrial promise to limit the sentence to less than six months even if the defendant were to be convicted of multiple counts. Stevens felt strongly that judges should not possess the discretionary authority to control the existence of a Sixth Amendment right to trial by jury. That right should belong to the defendant.

Early in the Rehnquist Court era, Stevens wrote a dissent in *Walton v. Arizona* (1990) that argued for a right to have juries, instead of judges, make factual determinations in capital cases to determine the existence of aggravating factors. He argued that the jury's role in determining critical facts was well-recognized in 1791, when the Sixth Amendment was ratified. He further argued that the Court's decision incorporating the right to trial by jury in *Duncan v. Louisiana* (1968) similarly emphasized that the jury was an important safeguard against both overzealous prosecutors and compliant judges.

A decade later, Stevens saw his view come to fruition as the Court reinforced the fact-finding role of juries in rejecting judges' authority to make post-trial factual determinations that would affect punishments under sentencing guidelines statutes. In *Apprendi v. New Jersey* (2000) and *United States v. Booker* (2005), self-assigned majority opinions by Stevens were key building blocks in a series of cases that limited the ability of judges to enhance criminal sentences. Any facts used in sentencing must have been found by the jury during trial and not rest on a post-trial finding by the judge. These decisions reinforced the important role of juries and called into question the delegation of fact-finding authority to judges in sentencing guidelines.

Guardian of Prisoners' Rights

Justice Stevens stands out among the justices as an advocate of legal protections for convicted offenders. As one scholar observed, "Throughout his tenure, Stevens took the lead in denouncing the majority's deferential stance [toward prison administrators]" (Canon 1991, 370-71). During the Rehnquist Court era, among the justices who participated in more than five prisoners' rights cases, Stevens supported prisoners' claims most frequently, in 72 percent of the eighteen cases (Smith and Corbin 2008, 187).

Justice Stevens issued notable dissenting opinions on behalf of the recognition of prisoners' rights in contexts of transfers and searches during the Burger Court era (Smith 2006, 734). He continued this advocacy throughout the Rehnquist Court era. In the seminal case of *Turner v. Safley* (1987), Justice O'Connor's majority opinion established an influential and enduring three-part test for the recognition of prisoners' rights. The most notable aspect of the test was its deferential posture that nearly forbade judges from looking critically at prison policies and practices that collide with prisoners' assertions of rights (Smith 2009). Stevens feared that the deferential standard created by O'Connor and the majority would invite prison officials to create pretextual excuses for interfering with prisoners' rights. Writing on behalf of Justices Brennan, Marshall, and Blackmun, Stevens was harshly critical of O'Connor's test and its likely effect of denying the recognition of prisoners' constitutional rights. Stevens wrote,

> But if the standard can be satisfied by nothing more than a "logical connection" between the regulation and any legitimate penological concern perceived by a cautious warden . . . it is virtually meaningless. Application of the standard would seem to permit disregard for inmates' constitutional rights whenever the

imagination of the warden produces a plausible security concern and a deferential trial court is able to discern a logical connection between that concern and the challenged regulation. Indeed, there is a logical connection between prison discipline and the use of bullwhips on prisoners; and security is logically furthered by a total ban on inmate communication not only with other inmates but also with outsiders who conceivably might be interested in arranging an attack within the prison or an escape from it. (*Turner v. Safley* 1987, 100-101)

In *Lewis v. Casey* (1996), Stevens complained that the majority opinion by Justice Scalia ignored the facts developed in the case in order to seize the opportunity to impose excessively strict standing requirements on prisoners as a means to reduce their access to legal research materials. In a case concerning prison regulations that prevented prisoners from receiving certain publications, Stevens argued that "general speculation that some administrative burden might ensue should not be sufficient to justify a meat-ax abridgment of the First Amendment rights of either a free citizen or a prison inmate" (*Thornburgh v. Abbott* 1989, 433).

In *Hudson v. McMillian* (1992), Stevens argued that the majority employed an excessively high subjective standard in cases in which prisoners were injured by prison officials' use of force. In this case, a shackled prisoner suffered facial injuries and damage to his teeth when struck by corrections officers who were supposed to walk him down the hallway of the prison. In order to prove a rights violation, the majority required the prisoner to prove that officials used force "maliciously and sadistically for the very purpose of causing harm." By contrast, Stevens asserted that the prisoner should only be required to prove that the use of force produced "an unnecessary and wanton infliction of pain." Stevens's argument reflected his desire to use objective tests to identify Eighth Amendment violations instead of subjective tests that demanded proof of the intentions or state of mind of corrections officials (Smith 2001). Stevens illustrated this theme in a Burger Court era opinion by saying,

> The Court improperly attaches significance to the subjective motivation of the [prison officials] as a criterion for determining whether cruel and unusual punishment has been inflicted. Subjective motivation may well determine what, if any, remedy is appropriate against a particular [official]. However, whether the constitutional standard has been violated should turn on the character of the punishment, rather than the motivation of the individual who inflicted it. Whether the conditions in Andersonville [the Civil War-era prisoner-of-war camp where 13,000 Union soldiers died from disease and starvation] were the product of design, negligence, or mere poverty, they were cruel and inhuman. (*Estelle v. Gamble* 1976, 116-17)

Sometimes a majority of justices supported the analysis put forward by Stevens. In two self-assigned majority opinions, Stevens prevailed in detailing specific protections for prisoners. In *Schlup v. Delo* (1995), Stevens concluded that death row prisoners need only show that a constitutional violation "probably resulted" in a miscarriage of justice. They were not required to fulfill the more demanding "clear and convincing evidence" standard when seeking judicial consideration of newly discovered evidence purporting to show their innocence. Justice Stevens's opinion in *Hope v. Pelzer* (2002) rejected qualified immunity claims by Alabama corrections officers who hoped to avoid being sued for chaining prisoners to an iron bar in the prison yard all day in high temperatures and without adequate access to water or bathroom facilities. Stevens concluded that the officials should have known that their actions clearly violated the Eighth Amendment prohibition on cruel and unusual punishments.

Even when Stevens joined a unanimous majority opinion to reject prisoners' rights claims related to visitation policies, he insisted on writing a concurring opinion to emphasize the continuing importance of prisoners' rights (Smith 2007b). Stevens wrote:

> It is important to emphasize that nothing the Court's opinion today signals a resurrection of [outdated doctrines denying the existence of prisoners' rights]. . . . To the contrary, it remains true that the "restraints and the punishment which a criminal conviction entails do not place the citizen beyond the ethical tradition that accords respect to the dignity and intrinsic worth of every individual." (*Overton v. Bazzetta* 2003, 128)

In effect, Stevens wanted to remind lower court judges about the continued existence of rights for prisoners and to deter them from seeing a unanimous decision rejecting a prisoners' rights claim as signaling a retreat on the protection of rights.

Detector of Racial Discrimination

With the retirements of Warren Court holdovers William Brennan and Thurgood Marshall early in the Rehnquist Court era, Justice Stevens stepped forward to become the Court's strong voice against racial discrimination and unequal treatment in the criminal justice system. Early in the Rehnquist Court era, Stevens signaled that he viewed racial discrimination as so constitutionally unacceptable that it must be stopped even if stopping discrimination would adversely affect other kinds of policy goals within criminal justice. *McCleskey v. Kemp* (1987) concerned the use of statistics to prove the existence of racial discrimination in the administration of the death penalty in Georgia. A five-member majority on the Court refused to permit defendants to submit strong statistical evidence showing that African American defendants charged with killing white victims were many times more likely to receive the death penalty than were other racial combinations of perpetrators and victims. At the time of the case, Stevens did not assert that the death penalty was unconstitutional, yet he argued that capital punishment must give way to the paramount goal of eliminating racial discrimination in the criminal justice system. According to his dissenting opinion:

The Court's decision appears to be based on a fear that the acceptance of McCleskey's claim would sound the death knell for capital punishment in Georgia. If society were indeed forced to choose between a racially discriminatory death penalty (one that provides heightened protection against murder "for whites only") and no death penalty at all, the choice mandated by the Constitution would be plain. (*McCleskey v. Kemp* 1987, 367)

In *Purkett v. Elem* (1995), Stevens wrote the dissenting opinion (joined only by Justice Breyer) against a per curiam opinion concerning racial discrimination in peremptory challenges. Stevens objected to the majority effectively permitting trial judges to accept weak, pretextual excuses for prosecutors' discretionary exclusion of potential jurors of a specific race. In this case with an African American defendant facing trial on robbery charges, the prosecutor used peremptory challenges to exclude African American jurors by claiming that their curly hair and moustaches made them seem as if they would not be good jurors. Justice Stevens was very skeptical of such efforts to create all-white juries. He wrote,

It is not too much to ask that a prosecutor's explanation for his strikes be race neutral, reasonably specific, and trial related. Nothing less will serve to rebut the inference of race-based discrimination . . . . The Court's unnecessary tolerance of silly, fantastic, and implausible explanations . . . demeans the importance of the values vindicated by our decision in *Batson* [*v. Kentucky* 1986]. (*Purkett v. Elem* 1995, 775, 778-79)

In another example, Stevens was the lone dissenter in *United States v. Armstrong* (1996), a case concerning allegations of racial discrimination by the Los Angeles U.S. Attorney's Office in selecting which defendants to prosecute for crack cocaine offenses. The decision about whom to prosecute had significant implications because the prison sentences for crack cocaine offenses were much longer than the sentences for similar offenses involving powder cocaine. The other justices refused to permit anecdotal evidence to provide the basis for discovery involving the prosecutor's records. However, Stevens used his solo dissent to lay out troubling statistics about differential impacts of federal cocaine investigations and prosecutions on African Americans and whites:

Finally, it is undisputed that the brunt of the elevated federal penalties falls heavily on blacks. While 65% of the persons who have used crack are white, in 1993 they represented only 4% of the federal offenders convicted of trafficking in crack. Eighty-eight percent of such defendants were black . . . . [B]lacks on average received sentences 40% longer than whites. (*United States v. Armstrong* 1996, 479-80)

Stevens saw a sufficient basis to justify defense attorneys' access to prosecutors' records in order to examine whether this pattern of prosecutions was driven by discriminatory policies and decisions. In effect, unlike any other justices on the Rehnquist Court in 1996, he believed it was more important to investigate and eradicate racial discrimination in the criminal justice system than to protect the sanctity of the prosecutor's files.

Stevens was similarly unique in 2005 when the Supreme Court ruled that courts should apply the strict scrutiny standard in evaluating equal protection claims about California's use of racial segregation in cells at its corrections processing center (*Johnson v. California* 2005). The majority remanded the case for further consideration in light of its specification of the test to be applied under the Equal Protection Clause. Justices Thomas and Scalia dissented and advocated the application of the deferential rational basis standard from *Turner v. Safley* (1987), the test applied in many other prisoners' rights cases. In effect, Thomas and Scalia were willing to accept racial segregation during prisoners' initial classification period in the California corrections system because the state claimed that the practice was necessary to prevent racial and gang violence. Justice Stevens also dissented, but for entirely different reasons. He looked closely at the facts of the case and the justifications presented by California and argued that the Supreme Court should forthrightly rule that the state had violated the Equal Protection Clause by using racial segregation in its prisons. He criticized the majority for wasting time by remanding the case for further consideration because such a remand could imply that a lower court might recognize a compelling state interest to justify the segregation, even under the strict scrutiny test. Stevens was the lone justice to declare that racial segregation imposed by state government constituted a clear-cut violation of the Equal Protection Clause and must cease, no matter what the purported justification.

Justice Stevens demonstrated a unique understanding about and sensitivity to the ways in which behavior in poor neighborhoods may be understandable even when it clashes with the expectations of law enforcement officials and judges. His concern about police officers' assumptions emerged in *Illinois v. Wardlow* (2000). In this case, the Supreme Court majority ruled that an individual's flight at the sight of police officers in a high-crime area could serve as a consideration to justify a stop-and-frisk under the doctrine established in *Terry v. Ohio* (1968). The *Terry* case established officers' authority to undertake brief, warrantless searches for weapons in the outer clothing when people's behavior raises reasonable suspicions that criminal activity is afoot and the public is in danger. Justice Stevens, concurring in part and dissenting in part from the majority opinion, expressed a view that undoubtedly caused consternation for some criminal justice officials:

> Among some citizens, particularly minorities and those residing in high crime areas, there is also the possibility that the fleeing person is entirely innocent, but, with or without justification, believes that contact with the police can itself be dangerous, apart from any criminal activity associated with the officer's sudden presence . . . . For such a person, unprovoked flight is neither "aberrant" nor "abnormal." (*Illinois v. Wardlow* 2000, 132)

As indicated by the foregoing examples, Justice Stevens asserted his views, often in solitary dissenting opinions, about circumstances in which decisions by police, prosecutors, and corrections officials can clash with equal treatment and realistic understandings of the role of race in society. While one would expect Thurgood Marshall, the Court's first African American justice, to demonstrate understanding of the types of insensitive treatment and discrimination that he encountered in his own life, it is notable and, indeed, remarkable that a Republican lawyer, such as Stevens, who grew up in a affluent family, would assertively speak out about such issues. Stevens's sensitivity to racial discrimination in various criminal justice contexts and his willingness to illuminate this issue through strong, solo dissents made him unique among the justices in the final fifteen years of the Rehnquist Court era.

Conclusion

By the end of the Rehnquist Court era, Justice Stevens was the most prolific author of concurring and dissenting opinions in the U.S. Supreme Court. His 901 concurring and dissenting opinions exceeded the numbers of such opinions authored by justices such as Douglas (640) and Holmes (86) who had more years of service on the Court. Although more than two dozen justices over history had written more majority opinions than the number written by Stevens (362) at the end of the Rehnquist era (Epstein et al. 2007, 635-37), Stevens was unique in his assertiveness and desire to explain his views for cases in which he disagreed with the majority's reasoning. Presumably, his effort to write explanatory opinions and criticisms of the majority's reasoning indicated a desire to shape law and policy (Maltzman et al. 2000). In some instances, such as prisoners' rights, Stevens appeared to be trying to hold the line against further erosion of constitutional rights. His opinions warned against weak legal standards that showed too much deference to decisions by corrections officials or imposed excessively burdensome standards of proof on prisoners who claimed that their rights had been violated. For other issues, such as right to counsel, trial by jury, and other procedural rights, Stevens sought to push the Court to fulfill his vision of the Constitution's promise, presumably fueled, at least in part, by his own experiences in personally seeing the importance of due process in his pre-Court life and career. With respect to issues of race, Justice Stevens attempted to warn and educate his colleagues in order to avoid the perpetuation of unjust consequences stemming from majoritarian perspectives that can be insensitive to unequal treatment in the criminal justice system.

The impact of Justice Stevens on criminal justice in the Rehnquist Court era was not limited to being a vigorous dissenter who advocated on behalf of greater protection for constitutional rights. He also enjoyed notable successes in cases that shaped law and policy. For example, he was credited with limiting the scope of capital punishment, both in his own opinion forbidding its application to mentally retarded defendants in *Atkins v. Virginia* (2002) and in his presumed cultivation of and opinion assignment to Justice Anthony Kennedy in the Court's divisive case that forbade the execution of youthful offenders who commit murders prior to the age of eighteen (*Roper v. Simmons* 2005). His leadership in *Rasul v. Bush* (2004) helped to block unilateral assertions of absolutist presidential power intended to deny specific terrorism suspects any procedural or substantive protections under American law. His impact was also clear in the Supreme Court's decisions that reasserted the primacy of juries as fact-finders and thereby diminished aspects of sentencing guideline schemes. A Stevens dissent (*Walton v. Arizona* 1990) set the foundation for his later self-assigned opinions that strengthened the jury's role (e.g., *Apprendi v. New Jersey* 2000). In these and other examples, Stevens's role as a leader and conscience of the Court enabled him to influence the development of specific issues as well as create a legacy of ideas for future justices to consider when they encounter his numerous judicial opinions.

References

Amann, Diane Marie. "John Paul Stevens, Human Rights Judge." *Fordham Law Review* 74 (2006): 1569-1606.

Bleich, Jeff, Daniel Powell, Aimee Feinberg, and Michelle Friedland. 2007. "Justice John Paul Stevens: A Maverick, Liberal, Libertarian, Conservative Statesman on the Court." *Oregon State Bar Bulletin* 67 (2007): 26-31.

Canon, Bradley C. "Justice John Paul Stevens: The Lone Ranger in a Black Robe." Pp. 343-74 in *The Burger Court: Political and Judicial Profiles*, edited by Charles M. Lamb and Stephen C. Halpern. Urbana, IL: University of Illinois Press, 1991.

Danner, Allison Marston, and Adam Marcus Samaha. "Judicial Oversight in Two Dimensions: Charting Area and Intensity in the Decisions of Justice Stevens." *Fordham Law Review* 74 (2006): 2051-79.

Epstein, Lee, Jeffrey A. Segal, Harold J. Spaeth, and Thomas G. Walker. *The Supreme Court Compendium*, 4th edition. Washington, DC: CQ Press, 2007.

Farnsworth, Ward. "Realism, Pragmatism, and John Paul Stevens." Pp. 157-84 in *Rehnquist Justice: Understanding the Court Dynamic*, edited by Earl M. Maltz. Lawrence, KS: University Press of Kansas, 2003.

———. "Signatures of Ideology: The Case of the Supreme Court's Criminal Docket." *Michigan Law Review* 104 (2005): 67-100.

Fortunato, Stephen. "The Supreme Court's Experience Gap." *Judicature* 82 (1999): 251-54, 300.

Greenhouse, Linda. "The Rehnquist Court and Its Imperiled States' Rights Legacy," *New York Times,* June 12, 2005. 3 (Sect. 4).

Karlan, Pamela S. "Cousins' Kin: Justice Stevens and Voting Rights." *Rutgers Law Journal* 27 (1996): 521-41.

Lane, Charles. "Finding Justice on a Small Scale," *Washington Post,* June 5, 2005: 1(D).

Liebman, James, and Lawrence C. Marshall. "Less Is Better: Justice Stevens and the Narrowed Death Penalty." *Fordham Law Review* 74 (2006): 1607-82.

Maltzman, Forrest, James F. Spriggs II, and Paul J. Wahlbeck. *Crafting Law on the Supreme Court: The Collegial Game*. New York: Cambridge University Press, 2000.

Manaster, Kenneth A. *Illinois Justice: The Scandal of 1969 and the Rise of John Paul Stevens*. Chicago: University of Chicago Press, 2001.

Nagel, Robert F. "Six Opinions by Mr. Justice Stevens: A New Methodology for Constitutional Cases?" *Chicago-Kent Law Review* 78 (2003): 509-30.

Popkin, William. "A Common Law Lawyer on the Supreme Court: The Opinions of Justice Stevens." *Duke Law Journal* 1989, 5 (1989): 1087-1161.

Ray, Laura Krugman. "Clerk and Justice: The Ties That Bind John Paul Stevens and Wiley B. Rutledge." *Connecticut Law Review* 41 (2008): 211-64.

Rosen, Jeffrey. "The Dissenter," *New York Times Magazine*, September 23, 2007: 50.

Schauer, Frederick. "Justice Stevens and the Size of Constitutional Decisions." *Rutgers Law Journal* 27 (1996): 543-61.

Simon, James F. *The Center Holds: The Power Struggle Inside the Rehnquist Court*. New York: Simon & Schuster, 1995.

Smith, Christopher E. *The Rehnquist Court and Criminal Punishment*. New York: Garland, 1997.

——. "The Malleability of Constitutional Doctrine and Its Ironic Impact on Prisoners' Rights." *Boston University Public Interest Law Review* 11 (2001): 73-96.

——. "The Roles of Justice John Paul Stevens in Criminal Justice Cases." *Suffolk University Law Review* 39 (2006): 719-44.

——. "Justice John Paul Stevens and Prisoners' Rights." *Temple Political and Civil Rights Law Review* 17 (2007a): 83-107.

——. "Prisoners' Rights and the Rehnquist Court Era." *Prison Journal* 87 (2007b): 457-76.

——. "Justice Sandra Day O'Connor and Corrections Law." *Hamline Law Review* 32 (2009): 477-97.

Smith, Christopher E., and Anne Corbin. "The Rehnquist Court and Corrections Law: An Empirical Assessment." *Criminal Justice Studies* 21 (2008): 179-91.

Stevens, John Paul. "The Bill of Rights: A Century of Progress." Address, University of Chicago Centennial Celebration and Bicentennial of the Bill of Rights. October 25, 1991.

——. Address, Chicago Bar Association's 125th Anniversary Dinner and Celebration. September 16, 1998.

——. "Foreword." Pp. ix-xii in *Illinois Justice: The Scandal of 1969 and the Rise of John Paul Stevens*, by Kenneth Manaster. Chicago: University of Chicago Press, 2001.

——. "Judicial Activism: Ensuring the Powers and Freedoms Conceived by the Framers for Today's World." *Chicago Bar Association Record* 16 (2002): 25-33.

——. "Random Recollections." Nathaniel L. Nathanson Memorial Lecture. University of San Diego. April 7, 2004.

——. Interview by Christopher E. Smith, July 29, 2010. Washington, DC. Tape recording on file with author.

Thai, Joseph. "The Law Clerk Who Wrote *Rasul v. Bush*: John Paul Stevens' Influence from World War II to the War on Terror." *Virginia Law Review* 92 (2006): 501-32.

Cases Cited

Apprendi v. New Jersey, 530 U.S. 466 (2000)
Atkins v. Virginia, 536 U.S. 304 (2002)
Batson v. Kentucky, 476 U.S. 79 (1986)
Baze v. Rees, 553 U.S. 35 (2008)
Duncan v. Louisiana, 391 U.S. 145 (1968)
Estelle v. Gamble, 429 U.S. 97 (1976)
Furman v. Georgia, 408 U.S. 238 (1972)
Gonzales v. Raich, 545 U.S. 1 (2005)
Hamdi v. Rumsfeld, 542 U.S. 507 (2004)
Harmelin v. Michigan, 501 U.S. 957 (1991)
Hope v. Pelzer, 536 U.S. 730 (2002)
Hudson v. McMillian, 503 U.S. 1 (1992)
Illinois v. Caballes, 543 U.S. 405 (2005)
Illinois v. Wardlow, 528 U.S. 119 (2000)
Jennings v. Illinois, 342 U.S. 104 (1951)
Johnson v. California, 543 U.S. 499 (2005)
Kyllo v. United States, 533 U.S. 27 (2001)
Lewis v. Casey, 518 U.S. 343 (1996)
Lewis v. United States, 518 U.S 322 (1996)
McCleskey v. Kemp, 481 U.S. 279 (1987)
McNeil v. Wisconsin, 501 U.S. 171 (1991)
Meachum v. Fano, 427 U.S. 215 (1976)
Mickens v. Taylor, 535 U.S. 162 (2002)
Miranda v. Arizona, 384 U.S. 436 (1966)
Overton v. Bazzetta, 539 U.S. 126 (2003)
Patterson v. Illinois, 487 US 285 (1988)
Payne v. Tennessee, 501 U.S. 808 (1991)
People v. LaFrana, 122 N.E.2d 583 (Ill. 1954)
People v. Stevens, 193 N.E. 154 (Ill. 1934)
Printz v. United States, 521 U.S. 898 (1997)
Purkett v. Elem, 514 U.S. 765 (1995)
Rasul v. Bush, 542 U.S. 466 (2004)
Roper v. Simmons, 543 U.S. 551 (2005)
Schlup v. Delo, 513 U.S. 298 (1995)
Terry v. Ohio, 392 U.S. 1 (1968)
Thompson v. Oklahoma, 487 U.S. 815 (1988)
Thornburgh v. Abbott, 490 U.S. 401 (1989)
Trop v. Dulles, 356 U.S. 86 (1958)
Turner v. Safley, 482 U.S. 78 (1987)
United States v. Armstrong, 517 U.S. 456 (1996)
United States v. Bajakajian, 524 U.S. 321 (1998)
United States v. Booker, 543 U.S. 220 (2005)
United States v. Lopez, 514 U.S. 549 (1995)
United States v. Morrison, 529 U.S. 598 (2000)
Walton v. Arizona, 497 U.S. 639 (1990)

Chapter 7
Sandra Day O'Connor:
Influence from the Middle of the Court

Madhavi M. McCall

Justice Sandra Day O'Connor was appointed to the United States Supreme Court in 1981 by President Ronald Reagan and confirmed by the Senate in a 99-0 vote to become the first woman to serve on the nation's highest court. Justice O'Connor spent twenty-five years on the bench, greatly influencing the rights of the criminally accused in those years. Indeed, O'Connor often cast the deciding vote in many types of cases, leading Erwin Chemerinsky (2001, 877) to contend, "O'Connor is in control. In virtually every area of constitutional law, her key fifth vote determines what will be the majority's position and what will be the dissent. Lawyers who argue and write briefs to the Court know they are, for all practical purposes, arguing to an audience of one."

This chapter examines Justice O'Connor's decisions and votes in significant criminal justice cases and her unique behavioral characteristics that helped shape the way the Court operates. This chapter cannot adequately cover O'Connor's full impact on American jurisprudence. Indeed, over the course of her career on the high court, O'Connor participated in more than 2,800 cases, wrote 276 majority opinions, 109 dissenting opinions, and seventy-five concurring opinions. Her distinction as the first female on the high court, her role as a swing voter, her longevity on the Court, and her influence on Court norms of behavior contribute to her historical significance. Unable to cover all of these aspects of her career, this chapter instead, following a brief biography and review of her judicial philosophy, concentrates on those areas of criminal justice law where her role was particularly pronounced. Specifically, this chapter examines some of her votes in women's rights, Fourth Amendment, death penalty, and federalism cases.

The case selection here illustrates different aspects of O'Connor's career. First, Justice O'Connor consistently ruled in favor of women's rights and was instrumental in preserving women's abortion rights (Huhn 2006). Second, in Fourth Amendment cases, O'Connor rather consistently ruled in a conservative manner except in cases dealing with warrantless, suspicionless, drug related searches. This distinction in her voting record provides a nice example of her view that government should be given a great deal of leeway in crime control, but that personal privacy concerns should be adequately protected against state actions (Zalman and Shartsis 2003). Third, Justice O'Connor's death penalty jurisprudence is reviewed. Justice O'Connor was an extremely strong supporter of the legitimacy of the death penalty during the early part of her career but her strong support seemed to weaken toward the end of her career. Thus these cases illustrate well her evolution as a justice (Baca 2001). Fourth, this chapter considers her votes in criminal justice related federalism cases because Justice O'Connor was central to the process of returning some power back to the states (Chemerinsky 2001). She was a member of the "federalism five" and her vote was critical to determining not only the outcome of cases, but also the contours of Court doctrine (Maveety 2008, 60). Finally, this chapter concludes its analysis with a brief look at the impact of her retirement.

Biography

Justice Sandra Day O'Connor was born on March 26, 1930, in El Paso, Texas (Biskupic 2005, 11). She spent most of her childhood in Texas with her grandparents but often spent summers in Arizona on her family's ranch (O'Connor and Day 2002). She earned her bachelor's degree in 1950 and, two years later, her law degree from Stanford University. Justice O'Connor graduated with honors from Stanford's Law School and was ranked third in her graduating class (Chief Justice William Rehnquist was ranked first in the same graduating class). Prevalent gender discrimination during the 1950s made it very difficult for her to get a job as a lawyer although she was offered several jobs as a legal secretary (Smith, McCall, and McCluskey 2005). Declining such offers, she accepted the position as a deputy county attorney in San Mateo, California.

Following her marriage to John Jay O'Connor III in 1952, O'Connor and her husband lived in West Germany from 1954 to 1957, returning to Arizona in 1957. In Arizona, O'Connor raised three sons before becoming heavily involved in Republican Party politics. O'Connor was assistant attorney general of the state in 1965 and was appointed to the state senate in 1969. She won election to the state senate in 1970 and later served as the senate legislative majority leader. Her rise in state politics continued in 1979 when she was appointed to the Arizona Court of Appeals. She served on the Court of Appeals until 1981 when President Ronald Reagan nominated her to be the first female United States Supreme Court Justice following the retirement of Justice Potter Stewart in June of 1981. The Senate confirmed her without objection and she became the first woman to sit on the nation's highest court, and one of three women to date to serve on the Supreme Court. O'Connor announced her retirement from the Supreme Court in 2005 and was replaced by Justice Samuel Alito on February 1, 2006. After Justice O'Connor retired, she remained active in public affairs. For instance, she was a member of the Iraq Study Group and spoke out strongly against the practice in many states of electing justices to sit on states' supreme courts.

Justice O'Connor came to the bench with a strong belief in states' rights. As a child, she noted that the federal government was not capable, in her view, of adequately regulating the western ranch lands and concluded that local citizens could better resolve local issues (O'Connor and Day 2002). Her experience as an elected state official furthered her belief in the value of limited federal involvement in local affairs. Not surprisingly, she became a staunch state's rights advocate. She played a central role and cast crucial votes in the federalist revolution initiated by the Rehnquist Court (Huhn 2006). Indeed, although there are earlier cases, the sustained state's rights doctrine started in 1992 with O'Connor's majority decision in *New York v. United States*. In abortion cases, while O'Connor voted to uphold a woman's right to choose, she also held that state governments should have wide latitude to regulate abortion.

O'Connor's decisions to defer to the actions and views of local actors often led to rulings limiting individual rights. Thus, although O'Connor was often labeled as a swing vote (Martin, Quinn, and Epstein 2005), she was rather conservative and consistently ruled against individual rights and liberties (Smith, McCall, and McCluskey 2005). Nevertheless, O'Connor garnered the label of swing voter because following the appointment of Justice Breyer in 1994 and until the death of Chief Justice Rehnquist in 2005, the Court consisted of five conservatives including O'Connor (the other conservatives were Chief Justice Rehnquist and Justices Scalia, Thomas, and Kennedy) and four liberals (Justices Breyer, Ginsburg, Souter, and Stevens) (Smith, McCall, and McCluskey 2005; Martin, Quinn, and Epstein 2005; Maveety 2008; Toobin 2007). In order for the liberal bloc to prevail in cases, they had to pull one of the conservatives away from his or her typical voting patterns. Justice O'Connor, along with Justice Kennedy, was more likely than other conservatives to occasionally join the liberal bloc.

Because O'Connor's vote often decided case outcomes—and even early in her career she often found herself in the middle of deep ideological splits on the Court—she quickly became the Court's most influential justice (Biskupic 2005). Her ability to join, and frequently create, the Court's minimal winning coalition, allowed Justice O'Connor to have the final say in the outcomes of several cases and the direction of the law. For instance, in abortion cases, O'Connor crafted the undue burden test allowing greater state regulation of abortion while nevertheless preserving the right to choice (see *Planned Parenthood of Southeastern Pennsylvania v. Casey* 1992). In death penalty cases, particularly late in her career, Justice O'Connor expressed concern that states were not adequately protecting a defendant's procedural due process rights (e.g., *Rompilla v. Beard* 2005). Thus, although generally deferential to state action, O'Connor occasionally reined in state action and, by doing so, acquired the label of swing justice.

As a result of her position as a centrist on the court, the Court shifted decidedly to the right when Justice Samuel Alito replaced her on the bench (Martin,

Quinn, and Epstein 2005). For instance, O'Connor's liberal voting record from the start of her career in criminal justice cases through her retirement was a bit higher than 30 percent. During the 2006-2007 Supreme Court Term, Justice Alito's first full year on the bench, Alito voted for the criminal defendant in only three cases out of twenty-two, for a liberal voting rate of only 14 percent (McCall, McCall, and Smith 2008). Thus it appears that several cases in which O'Connor was the swing vote may be vulnerable to reversal in the Roberts Court era (Martin, Quinn, and Epstein 2005). Her presence on the Court as well as her retirement left a large imprint on the state of American jurisprudence.

Beyond deference to state actors and her role as the court's center, O'Connor's decisions as well as her dissenting and concurring opinions suggest that her preference was to decide cases on narrow grounds rather than handing down sweeping decisions (Huhn 2006; Maveety 2008). She relied heavily on fact-based decision making and considered the context of cases before articulating a position (Maveety 1996). For instance, her concurring opinion in *J.E.B v. Alabama ex rel. T.B.* (1994), a sex discrimination case, argued that while prosecutors may not discriminate during jury selection, it is permissible for defense attorneys to do so. In *Lawrence v. Texas*, the 2003 case that held that states may not restrict the rights of same-sex adults to engage in private, non-commercial sexual behavior, O'Connor's concurring opinion found the Texas law to be unconstitutional, but on narrow equal protection grounds and not based on the due process argument used by the others in the majority (Justices Kennedy, Ginsburg, Breyer, Souter, and Stevens) (Maveety 2008, 44). In both cases, O'Connor sought to limit the scope of the majority's decision by narrowing the reach through her reasoning.

Moreover, in addition to her tendency to make decisions based on "narrow issues of fact" (McFeatters 2005, 95), O'Connor is also credited with helping establish new court norms of judicial behavior. Some authors assert Justice O'Connor was more influential in directing these judicial norms than even Chief Justice Rehnquist (Maveety 2008), and thus the Court belonged to "Queen Sandra" (3). Primarily, O'Connor is responsible in large part for the Court's increasing use of "individual level judicial making" in which justices are more apt to write separate concurring opinions rather than merely sign on to the Court's majority opinion (O'Brien 2005; Maveety 1996, 2008). O'Connor used these individual opinions to shape the development of the law and the resulting legal doctrine (Maveety 1996), a practice evident, as noted above, in her concurring opinions in both *Lawrence* and *J.E.B.* Indeed, although historically the justices of the United States Supreme Court attempt to forge consensus, O'Connor championed the notion that concurring opinions can be used effectively in shaping the application of the holding and the implementation of the law by the lower courts. Indeed, she once stated that unanimity, "recorded at the expense of strong, conflicting views, is not desirable in a court of last resort" (O'Connor 2003, 120). Further, she often used concurring opinions to articulate pragmatic policy stances that reflected an understanding of the practical issues involved in implementation of court decisions. Her successful use of concurring opinions to shape the law and judicial debates led other justices to follow this practice making Justice O'Connor instrumental in altering the Court's institutional norms of behavior (Maveety 2008).

Indeed, some scholars assert that the Rehnquist Court justices acted as if they belonged to a "judicial choir" where separate concurring and dissenting opinions—often with other justices joining these opinions—are considered collectively to make up a choir (Maveety 2008, 37). The justices, while singing different parts of the song, form a complete musical offering with the dissenting and concurring opinions filling in vital details regarding the state of the law. Justice O'Connor's actions are largely responsible for this development (40).

Ironically, although O'Connor largely championed the use of individual opinions to clarify the law, she is also credited as being an accommodationist judge (Maveety 1996), using the skills she acquired while a state legislator to build consensus among her colleagues and create winning coalitions (Biskupic 2005). She often circulated memos and draft opinions in an attempt to foster collegiality and produce decisions that attracted support from her colleagues (Maveety 2008). One study of judicial memo writing tendencies found Justice O'Connor was one of the most active justices in terms of memo circulation (Maveety 2008). Perhaps one of the byproducts of O'Connor's collegial style, her consensus building tendencies, and her ability to accommodate the views of other justices in her decisions, was that in important cases she was most often in the majority. In fact, of the thirteen cases identified as the most significant of the Rehnquist Court years, O'Connor wrote four decisions, co-authored one decision, and was in the majority in all but three cases (Maveety 2008, 66). Her participation as a majority opinion writer in five of thirteen cases indicates that she was able to steer the Court, to garner working majorities, and to serve as a decisional pivot point on substantive issues among justices who tended to be rather split along conservative—liberal lines.

Clearly, Justice O'Connor's impact on the bench is greater than merely the sum of all the votes she cast over the years. Unfortunately as noted, space in this chapter cannot address adequately the full consequence of her service on the bench. As one author joked, "[I]t's Sandra Day O'Connor's country: the rest of us just dance to her fiddle" (Greve 2004, 227). By carefully examining a sampling of issues and cases, one can understand her role as the justice often casting the pivotal, deciding vote, as well as her general view that cases should be decided narrowly. She also believed that justices should be restrained and modest in their decisions, and that justices should use concurring and dissenting opinions to fully explore the complex legal issues involved in cases.

Women's Rights

Within her first few years on the bench, Justice O'Connor found herself in the middle of an evenly divided Court on a case concerning equal protection arguments about university enrollment for men and women (Biskupic 2005). The case, *Mississippi University for Women v. Hogan* (1982), challenged a nursing school's women-only policy for earning degrees. During conference, O'Connor cast her first vote to support the equal protection of men and women, earned the opportunity to write the majority's decision, and established early in her career that she brought a different perspective to the law than the male justices (Biskupic 2005, 138-39). This chapter does not cover O'Connor's general equal protection jurisprudence; instead, discussion explores her votes in women's rights cases as related to criminal justice.

Justice O'Connor's influence in women's rights cases was perhaps most profound in abortion cases. Simply put, Justice O'Connor was instrumental in preserving the right to an abortion and was a central voice in the abortion debate. She joined the liberal justices in holding that a woman does have a right to choice but also joined the conservatives in articulating the position that states should have great latitude in regulating abortion options. Early in her career as an associate justice, O'Connor dissented in two high profile abortion cases (*Akron v. Akron Center for Reproductive Health* 1983; *Thornburgh v. American College of Obstetricians and Gynecologists* 1986) and filed a concurring opinion in a third (*Hodgson v. Minnesota* 1990) in which she clearly expressed her view that states can regulate abortions as long as the states do not place an undue burden on the right to choice. Although O'Connor was heavily criticized by numerous women's groups for approving regulations on abortion (Biskupic 2005), her "undue burden" test became the Court standard in *Planned Parenthood of Southeastern Pennsylvania v. Casey* (1992) in an opinion coauthored by Justice O'Connor and considered by many scholars to be among the most significant of the Rehnquist Court era (Maveety 2008). In *Casey*, O'Connor helped to craft a pragmatic, relatively functional policy that shows a consideration of the role of policy implementation in constitutional debates (Maveety 2008, 71). The "undue burden" standard is somewhat defined, and the standard is workable at the lower court level. It is safe to conclude that O'Connor's presence was vital to retaining abortion as a constitutional right, even if as a right it became much more highly regulated than during the years immediately following *Roe v. Wade* (1973). As one author stated, "Sandra Day O'Connor saved *Roe v. Wade*" (Huhn 2006).

Indeed, the ruling in *Stenberg v. Carhart* (2000) and aftermath of that case provide an example of the vital role O'Connor played in maintaining abortion rights. Relying again on the undue burden standard, the Court overturned Nebraska's Partial-Birth Abortion Ban in *Stenberg*. The Partial-Birth Abortion Ban outlawed a type of late term abortion under all circumstances unless the procedure was necessary to save a woman's life. The law did not allow a woman to obtain an abortion even if her health was endangered by the continued pregnancy. The Supreme Court found in a 5-4 vote, with Justices Stevens, Ginsburg, Breyer, Souter, and O'Connor in the majority and Justices Thomas, Scalia, Kennedy, and Chief Justice Rehnquist in dissent, that the Nebraska Partial-Birth Abortion Ban placed an undue burden on a woman's abortion rights by failing to provide for a health exception. Justice Breyer's majority opinion noted that physicians may refuse to perform abortions even when a woman's life is at risk for fear of prosecution, further unconstitutionally limiting a woman's access to an abortion.

Justice O'Connor provided the fifth vote to overturn the Nebraska law, but, as was her practice, handed down a concurring opinion that was narrower in scope than the majority's ruling (Huhn 2006). She argued in her concurrence that Nebraska's law could be constitutional if it concerned only post-viability abortions and contained a health exception. O'Connor thus provided the state with practical instructions on how to alter the law in order to attract her vote and pass constitutional muster. Later events, however, made O'Connor's concurrence less relevant than it otherwise might have been.

Specifically, following the decision in *Stenberg* in 2000 and the election of President George W. Bush, the federal government passed the federal Partial-Birth Abortion Ban, a law similar in content to the Nebraska law found unconstitutional by the Court in *Stenberg*. The federal ban—like the Nebraska law— did not contain a health exception; consequently, several federal lower courts refused to enforce the federal law and the Supreme Court let these lower court decisions stand. However, Justice O'Connor's retirement and the appointment and confirmation of Justice Alito changed that calculus. As a member of the Third Circuit U.S. Court of Appeals, Justice Alito had dissented in *Planned Parenthood v. Casey* (1991), arguing against abortion rights in strong terms, and, went further than any other judge on the Third Circuit by holding that women must notify their husbands before getting an abortion. Shortly after Alito was sworn in as associate justice, the Court granted certiorari to *Gonzales v. Carhart* (2007) and *Gonzales v. Planned Parenthood* (2007), two cases challenging the constitutionality of the federal Partial-Birth Abortion Ban. It was clear, given the timing of the decision to grant certiorari and Alito's prior written opinions that the conservatives in *Stenberg* finally had a fifth vote to overturn the decision.

Indeed, the outcome in *Gonzales v. Planned Parenthood* and *Gonzales v. Carhart*, while not a surprise, nevertheless pointed to the profound impact one justice can have on the direction of the Court and the direction of American legal jurisprudence. In a 5-4 vote, the Court overturned *Stenberg v. Carhart* and concluded that the lack of a health exception in the federal Partial-Birth Abortion Ban was not an unconstitutional restriction on the right to choice. Moreover, a close reading of the case and Justice Kennedy's majority opinion strongly suggested that the undue burden standard established in *Planned Parenthood v. Casey* (1991) was no longer applicable and put the Court very close to overturning *Roe v. Wade* (1973).

Beyond abortion, O'Connor filed a concurring opinion in *J.E.B. v. Alabama ex rel. T.B.* (1994) in which a 6-3 majority held that sex discrimination in the realm of jury selection was unconstitutional. While the case in *J.E.B* dealt with the use of peremptory challenges to strike potential male jurors in a paternity case, the case nonetheless reaffirmed that sex-based discrimination could only be constitutional if the state had an exceedingly persuasive justification. Justice O'Connor's concurring opinion in this case again pointed to her penchant for

narrowing the scope of court rulings. Here, O'Connor argued the use of peremptory challenges to discriminate on the basis of sex was unconstitutional when
used by the state, but not unconstitutional when used by defense attorneys.

Finally, in *Atwater v. City of Lago Vista* (2001), while Justice O'Connor did
not vote to uphold the rights of women per se, her vote suggested some gendered decision making (Zalman and Shartsis 2003). The *Atwater* case dealt with
a full custodial arrest and jailing of an individual for a non-jailable misdemeanor
charge. Gail Atwater was driving in her subdivision with her two young children
(ages three and five) in the front seat. They were not wearing seatbelts—an offense punishable by only a twenty-five dollar fine. An officer stopped Atwater
and yelled at her and told her that she was a bad mother. The officer threatened
to arrest her and stated that Atwater was going to jail. Further, and behavior that
seems particularly to have offended Justice O'Connor, the officer refused to let
Atwater take the children to a friend's home and threatened to arrest the children
as well. Neighbors eventually intervened and the children were not arrested.
Atwater was booked and remained in jail for about one hour. The Supreme
Court's five-person majority concluded that the Fourth Amendment did not prohibit the warrantless arrest for a misdemeanor crime that was not eligible for a
jail sentence.

Justice O'Connor was not a member of the five-person majority and instead
filed an uncharacteristically harsh dissent. Consistent with her general approach
to cases, O'Connor was very sensitive to the facts of the case, attempting to decide the case in the context in which the constitutional questions were placed.
She noted in great detail the irrational behavior of the officer and argued forcefully that because of the officer's unreasonable behavior, the facts of the case
strongly suggested that Atwater's Fourth Amendment rights had been violated.
Moreover, O'Connor noted that a practical consequence of the Court's sweeping
ruling was that individuals could be placed under custodial arrest for crimes as
minor as littering. O'Connor explicitly rejected the majority's announcement of
the categorical rule that the Fourth Amendment did not prohibit warrantless arrests of individuals committing non-jailable offenses and instead insisted that the
majority's all-encompassing approach was not reasonable under the Fourth
Amendment. Because much of O'Connor's decision making in this case appeared to reflect a very strong consideration of the case-specific facts, some
judicial scholars have concluded that her position in this case may stem partially
from her empathy for Atwater (Zalman and Shartsis 2003).

Fourth Amendment

Justice O'Connor's Fourth Amendment jurisprudence was relatively consistent,
and she ruled for conservative outcomes in the majority of cases. She participated in ninety-two Fourth Amendment cases as an associate justice and voted
to support individuals' claims in only twenty-four cases (Zalman and Shartsis

2003). Her views on the Fourth Amendment were evident early in her career when she wrote the majority decision in *Michigan v. Long* (1984). The case expanded the conditions under which police officers may search the passenger compartment of cars. O'Connor's opinion for a six-person majority found that an officer may search passenger compartments during a police detention of a motorist if the officer reasonably believes the motorist or vehicle passengers are dangerous. These searches can be conducted without a search warrant to ensure officer safety. The permissible areas of a car that may be searched absent a search warrant were expanded to the car's trunk in *California v. Acevedo* (1991), a case in which O'Connor joined the six-person majority decision. O'Connor wrote the majority decision in *United States v. Place* (1983) that held that briefly detaining luggage to allow narcotics detention dogs to sniff the luggage did not violate the Fourth Amendment. In *INS v. Lopez-Mendoza* (1984), her 5-4 opinion found that illegally obtained evidence does not have to be excluded during deportation hearings. Her concurring opinion in *Florida v. Riley* (1989) agreed with the majority position that a police officer's naked-eye observations from a helicopter did not constitute a search for which a warrant is needed. Justice O'Connor's decision for a five-person majority in *County of Riverside v. McLaughlin* (1991) was very controversial and held that judges can wait up to forty-eight hours before determining if probable cause for a warrantless arrest exists. The decision allows individuals to be held for forty-eight hours before a neutral magistrate must determine that the arrest was valid. Also in 1991, O'Connor's majority opinion in *Florida v. Bostick* (1991) held that an officer's request to search a bus passenger's luggage was not a seizure under the Fourth Amendment and thus was constitutionally permissible. Finally, she dissented from the majority decision in *Kyllo v. United States* (2001), which ruled that the use of thermal imagers without a search warrant by police violated the Fourth Amendment because individuals have a reasonable expectation of privacy to the level of measurable heat coming from their property. In short, O'Connor often ruled against individual liberties in Fourth Amendment cases.

Although Justice O'Connor's votes in Fourth Amendment cases were fairly conservative, she tended to be rather liberal in cases that dealt with warrantless, suspicionless searches related to drug abuse detection. Her votes in *Vernonia School District v. Acton* (1995), *Walker Chandler v. Zell Miller* (1997), *City of Indianapolis v. Edmond* (2000), *Bond v. United States* (2000), *Ferguson v. City of Charleston* (2001), and *Board of Education of Independent School District No. 92 of Pottawatomie County v. Earls* (2002) all suggest that while she was broadly in favor of allowing states latitude under the Fourth Amendment, that latitude stopped when the state conducted warrantless, suspicionless searches to detect drug users. Indeed, of the twenty-four instances in which O'Connor voted for individuals' claims in Fourth Amendment cases, six dealt with the issue of drug-related warrantless searches in which government officials lacked individualized suspicion. In each of these cases, O'Connor's viewpoint was based in large part on the case facts and the lack of suspicion regarding the individuals in question. Thus, rather than handing down sweeping rulings dealing with the applicability of the Fourth Amendment to warrantless searches generally, the policy outcomes of her votes were more modest (Sunstein 1999), ruling against state action only as specifically related to the lack of suspicion for these defendants and under these circumstances.

Starting with *Vernonia School District v. Acton* (1995), Justice O'Connor filed a dissent against a majority opinion that found the warrantless, suspicionless drug testing of student athletes to be constitutional. The school district argued, and the majority agreed, that the widespread drug abuse problem among its student athletes justified random drug testing of these individuals. O'Connor argued this position was unreasonable under the Fourth Amendment because the school lacked individualized suspicion to conduct testing. Sounding almost like a Warren Court liberal, O'Connor noted,

> It cannot be too often stated that the greatest threats to our constitutional freedoms come in times of crisis. But we must also stay mindful that not all government responses to such times are hysterical overreactions; some crises are quite real, and when they are, they serve precisely as the compelling state interest that we have said may justify a measured intrusion on constitutional rights. The only way for judges to mediate these conflicting impulses is to do what they should do anyway: stay close to the record in each case that appears before them, and make their judgments based on that alone. Having reviewed the record here, I cannot avoid the conclusion that the District's suspicionless policy of testing all student athletes sweeps too broadly, and too imprecisely, to be reasonable under the Fourth Amendment. (*Vernonia School District*, 596)

Seven years later in *Board of Education of Independent School District No. 92 of Pottawatomie County v. Earls* (2002) when the Court extended the decision in *Vernonia* to allow the suspicionless drug testing of all students engaged in extra-curricular activities, O'Connor again filed a dissenting opinion arguing that *Vernonia* was wrongly decided. Even more strongly worded than her dissent in *Vernonia*, in *Earls* O'Connor found drug testing of students engaged in extra-curricular activities not only unreasonable, but also capricious and perverse. She argued,

> *Vernonia* cannot be read to endorse invasive and suspicionless drug testing of all students upon any evidence of drug use, solely because drugs jeopardize the life and health of those who use them. Many children, like many adults, engage in dangerous activities on their own time; that the children are enrolled in school scarcely allows government to monitor all such activities. (*Board of Education of Independent School District No. 92 of Pottawatomie County v. Earls*, 844-45)

In *Walker Chandler v. Zell Miller* (1997), an eight-person majority, including Justice O'Connor, found a drug testing program of political candidates for state office to be unconstitutional. O'Connor joined a seven-person majority in *United States v. Bond* (2000) to hold that officers' manipulation of luggage on a bus without passenger consent and without individualized suspicion violated the Fourth Amendment. A smaller majority of only six justices joined Justice O'Connor's opinion in *City of Indianapolis v. Edmond* (2000) that found that roadblocks used for the crime control purpose of discovering drugs are unconstitutional. The case dealt with the use of vehicle checkpoints to interdict illegal drugs. Stops were not conducted out of a concern for driver safety—as is the case with sobriety stops—but were conducted only to catch criminals. O'Connor found this scheme unreasonable under the Fourth Amendment:

> We decline to suspend the usual requirement of individualized suspicion where the police seek to employ a checkpoint primarily for the ordinary enterprise of investigating crimes. We cannot sanction stops justified only by the generalized and ever-present possibility that interrogation and inspection may reveal that any given motorist has committed some crime. (*Edmond*, 44)

These cases are all instances in which Justice O'Connor refused to join decisions allowing broad police latitude to investigate crimes but instead held that the Fourth Amendment does require individualized suspicion. Rather than allow police general access to investigate large numbers of citizens because it is statistically likely that one or more of those citizens may have committed a criminal offense, O'Connor strongly asserted that the justices should not stretch the meaning of exceptions to the warrant requirement to this extent. It is, again, an example of her predilection for more judicially restrained opinions.

Finally, in *Ferguson v. City of Charleston* (2001), O'Connor joined a six-person majority finding a Fourth Amendment violation for a drug testing program of pregnant women without their consent by a public hospital when those results were then turned over to local law enforcement. Women found to have abused drugs could be prosecuted for drug-related offenses, including child abuse, upon the birth of their babies. The Court held that because the purpose of the program was general crime control, suspicionless searches were unconstitutional in this context. O'Connor's vote in this case reflected not only her general view that police should not be able to search absent some individualized suspicion, but also might have reflected gendered decision making and possible sympathy for the plight of the pregnant women. Overall, as noted, O'Connor's liberal voting rate in Fourth Amendment cases remained quite low making her consistency in rulings dealing with drug detection noteworthy.

Eighth Amendment

Justice O'Connor's decisions early in her career showed her to be a staunch supporter of states' ability to implement death penalty decisions without federal interference. For instance, Justice O'Connor wrote the dissenting opinion in *Enmund v. Florida* (1982) in which she argued that felony murder qualifies for the death penalty, even in situations where the defendant was an accomplice to the murders and did not participate in the actual killings. The ruling in *Enmund* was a bit ambiguous and did not provide direct guidance as to which types of accomplices may be death eligible (Taylor 1987). Five years later, in *Tison v. Arizona* (1987), O'Connor's earlier stance in dissent would become the Court's majority opinion. O'Connor's opinion for only five justices found that even those defendants who do not participate in the murder and without intent to kill can still qualify for the death penalty if they participated substantially in the accompanying felony and showed a reckless disregard for human life. The *Tison* decision served to severely limit the protections offered to defendants under *Enmund*. It also served to clarify that, while not all accomplices to felonies can be subjected to the death penalty, those who exhibit a "reckless disregard for human life" by "knowingly engaging in criminal activity known to carry a grave risk of death" are potentially culpable to the extent that their participation can be considered death eligible (Taylor 1987).

Enmund and *Tison* illustrate several points regarding O'Connor's early death penalty jurisprudence and her general judicial style. First, it is possible that because O'Connor wrote an individual dissenting opinion in *Enmund*, she was tapped to write the majority opinion in Tison—validating her use of individual concurring and dissenting opinions. Second, her *Tison* opinion, while certainly expanding conditions under which felonies were death eligible, nonetheless attempted to establish workable standards for use by the lower courts to facilitate implementation of *Tison*. Third, O'Connor's preference for handing down decisions that rely heavily on the case facts was clear. In *Tison,* her decision did not establish categorically that all accomplices to felonies leading to death are eligible for the death penalty nor did she categorically exclude any groups of offenders. For juvenile offenders, for instance, the decision suggested that some juvenile accomplices who showed a reckless disregard for human life and were shown to be mentally culpable could be death eligible. Finally, O'Connor did not appear to have any philosophical objections to the death penalty generally.

Indeed, a year following her dissent in *Enmund*, O'Connor wrote the majority opinion in a case holding that it was not an Eighth Amendment violation to let jurors know through jury instructions that governors can commute life sentences. Rather, O'Connor noted that letting jurors know that life sentences can be commuted allows them to consider a defendant's potential future dangerousness and make capital punishment decisions accordingly. In 1983, she voted with the majority to uphold a death sentence where the trial judge had imposed a death sentence after finding aggravating circumstances that the jury, which had recommended a life sentence for the defendant, had not (*Barclay v. Florida* 1983). O'Connor wrote the decision in *Strickland v. Washington* (1984) finding that a defendant had not received inadequate counsel during capital sentencing, and O'Connor voted with the majority in *Wainwright v. Witt* (1985), allowing jurors to be dismissed from service based solely on their objection to the death penalty if it was determined that the jurors' death objections would interfere with their duties as jurors. O'Connor wrote the Court's decision in *Smith v.*

Murray (1986) and held that a defense attorney's choice to remove claims from state appeals precluded later federal habeas review of those claims. Even before her decision in *Tison*, the general direction of her death penalty jurisprudence was evident.

Indeed, as perhaps an even stronger indication that O'Connor favored decisions upholding death sentences, O'Connor provided the fifth conservative vote in the controversial case of *McCleskey v. Kemp* (1987). In *McCleskey*, the Supreme Court held that statistics strongly indicating racial bias in the implementation of the death penalty were not sufficient evidence to hold the death penalty unconstitutional. She, along with the rest of the majority, held that even though academic research clearly indicated that black defendants were significantly more likely to receive the death penalty than white defendants, absent evidence of racial bias in any specific case, general racial bias in the criminal justice system did not render a specific death sentence unconstitutional.

In addition, Justice O'Connor dissented in *Booth v. Maryland* (1987) and voted to allow victim impact statements when deemed appropriate by the state legislature. She also wrote for the majority in *Penry v. Lynaugh* (1989) that the mentally retarded are not automatically exempt from the death penalty. Finally, although O'Connor provided an important fifth vote in *Thompson v. Oklahoma* (1988) and found that the death penalty for those committing crimes under the age of sixteen violates the Eighth Amendment, she also provided a fifth vote in *Stanford v. Kentucky* (1989) to allow the execution of those committing crimes at the ages of sixteen and seventeen.

In the first decade of her service as an associate justice, Justice O'Connor strongly favored letting death penalty decisions stand and believed death penalty decisions should be made following consideration of individual case facts. She strongly resisted handing down rules that would categorically include or exclude defendants from capital sentence consideration (except her ruling in *Thompson* barring the death penalty for juveniles committing capital offenses at the age of sixteen). She was also the deciding vote in several high profile death penalty decisions (e.g., *Tison, McCleskey, Thompson,* and *Stanford*).

However, later in her career, O'Connor's voting pattern suggested that she became increasingly troubled by the implementation of the death penalty at the state level. In a speech in 2001 O'Connor expressed doubt about whether states were taking sufficient care to make certain that innocent people were not sitting on death row (Baca 2001). Perhaps the fear that improper implementation of the death penalty was resulting in wrongful convictions, as evidenced by the over one hundred innocent individuals released from prison in the last decade, led Justice O'Connor (and Kennedy) to place greater emphasis on proper procedure and due process. Thus, she appeared to have come full circle during her career on the bench, casting vital conservative death penalty votes early (although see *Caldwell v. Mississippi* 1985; *Skipper v. South Carolina* 1986; *Ford v. Wainwright* 1986 for examples of her more liberal tendencies even at the start of her career) and pivotal, liberal death penalty votes in the last decade of her tenure on the bench.

For example, in 1995, Justice O'Connor cast an important, liberal swing vote in a death penalty case. The case, *Schlup v. Delo,* dealt with the necessary standard of proof required by a defendant to assert actual innocence in habeas corpus petitions. In this case, Lloyd Schlup, convicted of murder by a jury, argued that evidence existed to cast doubt on his guilt and presented the Court with signed witness statements that indicated Schlup was not involved in the murder. With these documents, Schlup petitioned the Supreme Court for a writ of habeas corpus, asserting that his claim of actual innocence must be heard so that the state did not execute an innocent man. The Court, in an opinion by Justice Stevens and joined by the remaining three liberals and Justice O'Connor, found that the standard then used for actual innocence claims was far too strict; the majority voted to reduce the defendant's burden in making actual innocence claims. Stevens argued that the Court must balance the need for finality in cases with the need to prevent the miscarriage of justice and thus, while *Schlup* lays out a standard that is still difficult for defendants to use successfully, it nonetheless is less stringent than the previous standard.

O'Connor cast another important death penalty swing vote during the 2001-2002 Term in *Kelly v. South Carolina* (2002). William Kelly was charged and convicted of a death eligible crime. During sentencing, the prosecution presented evidence suggesting that Kelly, if released, would still pose a threat to society. The defense attorney then sought jury instructions informing the jury that Kelly would not be eligible for parole. This information could have assuaged the concerns of jurors who might otherwise fear that Kelly could pose a danger to society in the future. The judge did not instruct the jury that Kelly would serve without the possibility of parole and the jury handed down a death sentence. The Supreme Court majority found for Kelly and concluded that the South Carolina courts had failed to follow the precedent established by the Supreme Court in *Simmons v. South Carolina* (1994). Justice Souter's opinion held that capital defendants are entitled to instructions informing the jury when defendants are not eligible for parole if given life sentences. Justices Stevens, O'Connor, Ginsburg, and Breyer joined Souter in the decision.

In a landmark case, Justice O'Connor, along with Justice Kennedy, cast votes ruling that mentally retarded offenders were not eligible for the death penalty in *Atkins v. Virginia* (2002). The 6-3 opinion by Justice Stevens overturned *Penry v. Lynaugh* (1989), a case written by Justice O'Connor. Indeed, although O'Connor had written in *Penry* that mentally retarded defendants were not automatically exempt from the death penalty, she joined the majority decision in *Atkins* holding that it is unconstitutional to execute those deemed to be mentally retarded. The majority found that executing mentally retarded defendants was contrary to the "evolving standards of decency that mark the progress of a maturing society" (*Atkins*, 309, quoting Chief Justice Earl Warren in *Trop v. Dulles* 1958). The majority concluded that a national consensus had emerged that these defendants should not be executed, the mentally retarded could not aid in their own defense, and the execution of the mentally retarded did not serve any penological purpose (*Atkins*, 316-20). It was a seminal liberal ruling of the sort not often seen or expected from the conservative-leaning Rehnquist Court. Interestingly, this was one of the few instances during O'Connor's career when her vote supported the creation of a judicial rule regarding exclusion of an entire group of individuals from death penalty eligibility. Given that handing down decisions which are not judicially modest or restrained went against O'Connor's general practice and, given that the vote came in a case overturning her own earlier ruling, it appeared that she did not have merely a passing concern that death sentences were meted out unfairly by the state.

Although Justice O'Connor voted in *Atkins* that the death penalty was not a constitutional punishment for the mentally retarded offender, she would not extend the logic of *Atkins* to individuals who commit capital crimes while under the age of eighteen. Rather, in *Roper v. Simmons* (2005), while a majority of five justices—the four liberals plus Kennedy—held that the death penalty is not a constitutional punishment for juvenile offenders, O'Connor voted with the dissenters to find that the death eligibility of juvenile offenders should be determined using case-by-case analysis. The two cases well illustrate O'Connor's death penalty views. While she supported the punishment of death generally, her concern during the later years of her tenure appeared to deal strictly with ensuring that death cases were adjudicated with care by the states. In *Atkins*, O'Connor's vote suggested she did not believe that the mentally retarded could adequately aid in their defense, thus making a death sentence unconstitutional. However, in *Roper*, O'Connor found that juvenile defendants may be able to aid in their own defense; thus the particular mental capacities of any specific juvenile offender should be decided at the state level to determine which juvenile defendants are death eligible and which are not—consistent with her vote in *Stanford v. Kentucky* (1989) a decade and a half earlier.

Roper aside, the importance of Justice O'Connor's vote in death penalty cases was clearly evident in *Rompilla v. Beard* (2005), a very controversial case in which O'Connor cast a deciding vote to hold that a capital defendant had not received adequate counsel during trial. The case represented only the third time in twenty years that that the Supreme Court ruled that a capital defendant received constitutionally deficient assistance of counsel (Greenhouse 2005). Ronald Rompilla was charged and convicted for the first degree murder of bar owner James Scanlon. During sentencing, the prosecutors presented three aggravating factors justifying a death sentence: Rompilla committed a felony murder, the crime was committed with torture, and Rompilla had a history of felony convictions. During the penalty phase, Rompilla's lawyer provided some mitigating evidence consisting mostly of testimony from Rompilla's family requesting mercy from the jury. However, the attorney did not present any evidence regarding Rompilla's mental capacity and mental retardation, childhood traumas, health, or substance abuse. In a petition for habeas corpus relief, Rompilla argued that because his counsel had failed to present other mitigating evidence, he had received ineffective assistance of counsel and, as a result, his death sentence was unconstitutional.

Writing for the five-person majority including Stevens, O'Connor, Ginsburg, and Breyer, Justice Souter found merit in Rompilla's arguments and the
majority concluded that the defense was deficient under the Court's *Strickland v.
Washington* (1984) standard. Justice Souter argued that defense counsel did not
even examine documents that the prosecution had already indicated would be
used against Rompilla to show aggravation. The Court found that merely presenting testimony from five family members as evidence of mitigation was constitutionally insufficient. In short, defense counsel was unprepared to adequately
respond to the prosecution's evidence of aggravating circumstances.

Although Justice O'Connor cast a fifth, liberal vote in this case, her concurring opinion suggested that she reached her conclusions on more narrow
grounds than the rest of the majority. O'Connor asserted that the Court's decision in *Rompilla* did not represent a new rule or modification of the *Strickland*
standard (a case in which she wrote the majority opinion) or the codes of conduct for defense counsel. Rather, O'Connor found a *Strickland* violation specific
to this case. O'Connor noted that defense counsel is not generally required to
review all case documents, but in this instance, because the prosecutor had already alerted the defense that the documents would be used to show aggravation, failure to review the evidence constituted ineffective assistance of counsel.
Interestingly, and as noted earlier, O'Connor's use of a concurring opinion here
was aimed at narrowing the scope of the decision and also at providing lower
courts with additional guidance on how the Court decision should be implemented.

Given O'Connor's place as the swing vote in *Rompilla*, and her insistence
that the decision did not establish new guidelines for a definition of an adequate
defense, it was unclear at the time of the decision what long-term influence the
ruling would have. However, the 5-4 decision in *Schriro v. Landrigan* (2007), a
case where Justice Alito was the swing vote during the 2006-2007 Term, demonstrated that O'Connor's retirement has had and will have a substantive effect
on this area of the law. In *Landrigan*, an Arizona jury found Jeffrey Landrigan
guilty of felony murder. During sentencing, Landrigan asked his ex-wife and
birth mother not to testify on his behalf and they agreed. No other mitigating
evidence was presented and Landrigan was sentenced to death. Landrigan appealed, arguing his attorney's failure to present any mitigating evidence, beyond
counsel's attempts to present the testimony of his birth mother and ex-wife, resulted ineffective assistance of counsel. The United States Supreme Court, in an
opinion by Justice Thomas, determined that Landrigan's ineffective assistance
of counsel claim failed under the *Strickland* standard. While the majority acknowledged that Landrigan's attorney failed to prepare sufficiently for the sentencing phase, they nevertheless found counsel's actions sufficient. The dissenters argued in favor of granting Landrigan constitutional relief, citing defense
counsel's lack of preparation. The minority noted, for instance, that defense
counsel did not obtain a psychological examination of Landrigan. While
O'Connor's case-by-case approach might not have changed the outcome in *Landrigan*, her vote in *Rompilla*, when compared to the majority reasoning in *Lan-*

drigan, suggested that she was more open to ineffective assistance arguments in death penalty cases than her replacement.

Generally, the death penalty cases decided by the Supreme Court over the course of Justice O'Connor's career and her votes in those cases indicated that she was a strong supporter of the death penalty but that she generally lived up to her view that Supreme Court decisions should be modest in scope and should not establish categorical rules. Her individual opinions in several cases also suggested that she felt Court decisions should provide clear guidelines through which lower courts can implement Supreme Court doctrine. Her death penalty decisions further indicated that she was more open than other conservatives to arguments by capital defendants that state death penalty procedures violate procedural due process rights. Hence, she became increasingly concerned about the procedure used to implement the death penalty at the state level in the last decade of her tenure on the Court. Overall, while still a conservative death penalty supporter, Justice O'Connor (along with Justice Kennedy) provided liberal, swing votes in capital punishment cases more frequently than other members of the conservative bloc and for that reason, her retirement from the Court is likely to have an impact on this area of the law.

Federalism

Justice O'Connor, as noted, was considered one of the "federalism five" (Maveety 2008, 60), a group of justices that included O'Connor and Chief Justice Rehnquist and Justices Thomas, Scalia, and Kennedy who strongly supported states' rights and consistently ruled in favor of states over the federal government in federalism cases (Huhn 2006). Several federalism cases support this characterization with O'Connor providing the fifth vote needed for a conservative outcome. Four of those cases, *United States v. Lopez, United States v. Morrison, Printz v. United States*, and *Tennessee v. Lane*, dealt explicitly with criminal justice issues and are covered in this section. A fifth case, *Gonzales v. Raich*, will conclude our discussion of federalism and provide, through Justice O'Connor's dissenting opinion, a revealing look at her views on federalism.

In *United States v. Lopez* (1995), Justice O'Connor joined the other four members of the "federalism five" to rule that Congress had exceeded its authority under the Commerce Clause in enacting the Gun-Free School Zones Act of 1990. The case was significant because it marked the first time since 1937 that the Court held that Congress had overstepped its Commerce Clause powers and strongly signaled that the Court was committed to states' rights (Kelso and Kelso 2001, 927). The Gun-Free School Zones Act made it a federal crime to have a firearm in a school zone and was passed by Congress under its powers to regulate interstate commerce. In 1992, a twelfth-grade student brought a gun and bullets to school and the student was charged with violating the federal law. After being found guilty, on appeal, Lopez challenged his conviction, arguing that the Gun-Free School Zones Act was an unconstitutional exercise of congressional power under the Commerce Clause because bringing a gun to school did not involve interstate commercial activity. Therefore, the regulation of gun possession in a school zone was a state responsibility. The Supreme Court agreed with Lopez.

Writing for the majority, Chief Justice Rehnquist concluded that the Court's precedents permitted Congressional regulation only in terms of those activities that have a substantial effect on interstate commerce, while the regulation of activities without a substantial effect on interstate commerce must be left to the states. In this case, the federal government asserted several arguments in defense of the statute: the costs of crime generally affect interstate commerce; people are less willing to travel to areas perceived as unsafe, therefore interstate travel and commerce depend on public safety; and guns in schools impede the educational process and eventually have a negative impact on the national commerce. The Court majority found these arguments unpersuasive. Chief Justice Rehnquist concluded that, if the Gun-Free School Zones Act were allowed to stand, it would be

> difficult to perceive any limitation on federal power, even in areas such as criminal law enforcement or education where States historically have been sovereign. Thus, if we were to accept the Government's arguments, we are hardpressed to posit any activity by an individual that Congress is without power to regulate. (*U.S. v. Lopez* 1995, 564)

Although voting with the Court's majority, Justice O'Connor joined a concurring opinion written by Justice Kennedy articulating a more modest position than the one suggested by Rehnquist's opinion. Kennedy's concurring opinion sought to limit the majority's ruling by calling for more practical Commerce Clause jurisprudence (Maveety 2008, 70). Kennedy argued that adherence to precedent necessitated giving Congress more leeway to act than that allowed by the majority opinion. Kennedy asserted that the Court, while responsible for preserving the balance between the federal government and state governments, should enter into Commerce Clause questions only when the federal activity has egregiously overstepped proper boundaries. Justice Kennedy, along with Justice O'Connor, suggested that the decision in *Lopez* reflected more the case facts than an actual reversal by the Court of its Commerce Clause precedents.

Regardless of Kennedy and O'Connor's characterization of the case, *United States v. Lopez* (1995) marked a departure from the normal deference the Court had given Congress since the 1930s on commerce power issues. Indeed, in dissent, Justices Breyer, Ginsburg, Souter, and Stevens pointed out that the Court's deference to Congress was long-standing and the Court's established standard was to uphold congressional activity that is rationally related to commerce, as determined by legislative judgment. Writing separate dissenting opinions, Justices Breyer, Souter, and Stevens were highly critical of the majority's position. Justice Breyer accused the majority of substituting its judgment for that of the legislature. Justice Souter noted that judicial activism of the type exhibited by the majority has been a discredited approach to judicial decision making since the late 1930s and should not have been revived in this case. Justices Breyer and Stevens both argued that Congress can regulate gun possession in schools because the country's welfare depends on children receiving a quality education free from fear of school violence. The case was significant because it purported to limit congressional ability to enact legislation under the Commerce Clause.

Although Kennedy and O'Connor argued in *Lopez* that the case outcome was driven by case facts and did not represent a significant change in Supreme Court doctrine, the new evolution of the Commerce Clause that started in *Lopez* was expanded in *United States v. Morrison* (2000), another case in which Justice O'Connor's fifth vote was crucial to the majority. Congress passed the Violence Against Women Act in 1994 to allow victims of gender-motivated violence to bring civil lawsuits against their attackers in federal court. The question in *Morrison*, similar to the question in *Lopez*, was whether or not Congress exceeded its authority under the Commerce Clause by passing legislation related to violent crimes under the commerce doctrine.

The case started in 1994 when Christy Brzonkala, a student at Virginia Polytechnic Institute (Virginia Tech), claimed she was sexually assaulted by Antonio Morrison and James Crawford, also students at Virginia Tech. In 1995, Brzonkala sued Morrison, Crawford, and Virginia Tech (for its handling of the case following her complaints) in federal court, but the district court dismissed her case by holding that part of the Violence Against Women Act was unconstitutional as enacted under the Commerce Clause. The Court of Appeals reinstated her petition and the Supreme Court agreed to review the case. The justices held the law to be unconstitutional.

Writing for the same five-person majority as in *Lopez*, Chief Justice Rehnquist claimed that sexual assault does not have a substantial effect on interstate commerce. What differentiates this case from *Lopez*, however, was that in this case Congress conducted years of studies documenting the effect sexual assault has on commerce. Rehnquist, however, noted that just because Congress says an activity has an effect on commerce that does not necessarily make it true. In this instance, the Court majority discounted the congressional findings. Instead, they substituted their own judgments and engaged in the type of judicial activism typically condemned by the conservative majority. Justice O'Connor's vote with the majority provided a fifth, crucial vote for overturning almost seventy years of Court precedents deferring to Congress and its use of the commerce power. Moreover, unlike *Lopez*, *Morrison* is not a gender-neutral case but rather involved a statute intended to permit female victims of violent crime to win monetary damages in civil court. Some court observers thus thought that O'Connor might remove herself momentarily from the federalism revolution in order to provide legal relief for the victims of sexual assault (Biskupic 2005, 291). O'Connor did not. Instead, consistent with her vote in *Lopez*, she voted to overturn part of the Violence Against Women Act.

Objections by the "federalism five" to congressional action viewed as infringing on state powers were not limited to Congress's use of the Commerce Clause. In *Printz v. United States* (1997), the five-person *Lopez* and *Morrison* majority, in a decision written by Justice Scalia, found provisions of the Brady Handgun Violence Prevention Act to be unconstitutional. The Brady bill was passed in 1993 to mandate background checks and waiting periods before handguns could be purchased. Because the law could not be fully implemented by the federal government in a timely manner, Congress required states to help carry out some of the act's provisions on an interim basis. The majority ruled that this interim measure was unconstitutional. The ruling limited congressional ability to partner with states to implement federal laws, even under a temporary mandate. Again, Justice O'Connor provided a fifth vote for the conservative side.

These cases, even though not written by Justice O'Connor, demonstrated her preference for local officials solving local problems. Indeed, *United States v. New York* (1992), while not a criminal justice case, makes these views further evident as O'Connor questioned the constitutionality of the Low-Level Radioactive Waste Act enacted by Congress to force states to take responsibility for their own radioactive waste. Reviving the Tenth Amendment and basing her opinion on notions of state sovereignty, O'Connor (188) noted:

> States are not mere political subdivisions of the United States. State governments are neither regional offices nor administrative agencies of the Federal Government. . . . Whatever the outer limits of that sovereignty may be, one thing is clear: The Federal Government may not compel the States to enact or administer a federal regulatory program.

While the preceding cases indicate that Justice O'Connor was generally a supporter of states' rights, in *Tennessee v. Lane* (2004) O'Connor once again exhibited her more moderate tendencies. She cast a deciding liberal vote and showed why she was considered a powerful player on the Court. The Court found in *Lane* that states are not exempt from complying with the federal Americans With Disabilities Act (ADA) in a case that concerned the ability of a disabled person to access the court system. George Lane, a paraplegic, brought suit against Tennessee for failing to comply with the ADA when he had to crawl up stairs in order to get to a hearing in court. Tennessee claimed state sovereign immunity but the Court, in an opinion by Justice Stevens and joined by Justices Souter, Ginsburg, Breyer, and O'Connor found that the state must abide by the ADA, especially when failure to do so violates a person's due process right to access to judicial proceedings.

Finally, O'Connor's consistent view that states' rights under the federalism doctrine should be upheld was evident in her dissenting opinion in *Gonzales v. Raich* (2005). The case concerned the constitutionality of federal actions to effectively stop the implementation of California's Compassionate Use Act allowing the medicinal use of marijuana. The majority of six, in an opinion by Justice Stevens, found the action by Congress to be consistent with its powers under the

Commerce Clause. Votes by Justices Stevens, Breyer, Ginsburg, and Souter for the majority were not surprising as all four of these justices had supported the congressional use of the Commerce Clause in *Lopez* and *Morrison* as well. Votes by Chief Justice Rehnquist and Justices O'Connor and Kennedy in dissent and in favor of greater state latitude to regulate citizen welfare were also consistent with their votes in *Lopez* and *Morrison*. Justices Scalia and Thomas, typically staunch supporters of states' rights, here voted to allow congressional regulation, suggesting that these justices may have been more concerned with banning marijuana use than with maintaining a consistent position with regard to federalism.

Indeed, Justice O'Connor's dissenting opinion questioned the majority's failure to adhere to the precedents established in *Lopez* and *Morrison*, noting, "In my view, the case before us is materially indistinguishable from *Lopez* and *Morrison*" (*Gonzales v. Raich* 2005, 70) and therefore, the outcome should not have differed. Citing the Federalist Papers, O'Connor noted:

> We would do well to recall how James Madison, the father of the Constitution, described our system of joint sovereignty to the people of New York: "The powers delegated by the proposed constitution to the federal government are few and defined. Those which are to remain in the State governments are numerous and indefinite . . . The powers reserved to the several States will extend to all the objects which, in the ordinary course of affairs, concern the lives, liberties, and properties of the people, and the internal order, improvement, and prosperity of the State." (*Gonzales v. Raich* 2005, 90, citing The Federalist No. 45, 292-93)

Unlike Justices Scalia and Thomas, Justice O'Connor's strong support for the general principle that states should be allowed to regulate the public welfare continued to be evident in this case.

Conclusion

Justice O'Connor's tenure on the Supreme Court of the United States was memorable for a variety of reasons. Of course, the distinction she holds as being the first woman on the Court makes her a historic figure of enduring importance. Beyond this, however, there were numerous, substantive reasons that contributed to her significance as a justice and that led many commentators to conclude that power on the Court belonged, not to Chief Justice Rehnquist, but rather to Justice O'Connor (Chemerinsky 2001; Greve 2004; Biskupic 2005; Toobin 2007; Maveety 2008). As one author stated about Justice O'Connor, "She was the deciding vote across a range of legal issues coming before the justices and her doctrinal and policy positions determined many minimally winning majorities" (Maveety 2008, 3).

First, Justice O'Connor's overall record was one of a conservative justice and thus she shared and asserted the views of the president who appointed her, Ronald Reagan. To the extent that President Reagan expected her to consistently vote to support conservative outcomes, one can presume that Reagan would have been generally pleased with her voting record. In criminal justice cases, for example, Justice O'Connor voted with the conservative side around 70 percent of the time. While her voting record in other areas of the law—areas not covered in this chapter such as affirmative action, establishment of religion, women's rights not related to criminal justice, and redistricting cases—might cast some doubt on her conservative credentials, in criminal cases she was generally consistent.

Second, and maybe more important, Justice O'Connor could occasionally be convinced by the liberal justices that the state or federal government had simply gone too far by committing due process violations. During the last natural Rehnquist Court era in which the Court's composition did not change from 1994 to 2005, this tendency—one not shared by Chief Justice Rehnquist and Associate Justices Thomas and Scalia—garnered her the label of swing voter and led commentators to consider her the most influential member of the Court (Biskupic 2005). Indeed, as this chapter illustrates, O'Connor was a swing vote in cases dealing with a woman's right to choice, death penalty cases where she felt states had not enacted enough protections to ensure proper implementation of capital punishment, and Fourth Amendment cases in which states lacked individualized suspicion when conducting warrantless searches. Although her voting record overall was, again, one of a strong and consistent conservative, Justice O'Connor seemed to place greater value on procedural due process than her conservative brethren.

Justice O'Connor's strong role as a swing voter and her occasional moderate tendencies, were clearly evident when one considers cases likely to be overturned in the aftermath of her retirement. Indeed, one author noted before she retired, "[I]f O'Connor steps down it would be the judicial equivalent of an earthquake. Replacing her with either a consistent conservative or liberal would affect the majorities on a broad range of issues" (Kirkland 2004). Although she was replaced with another conservative justice, her moderate tendencies created a likelihood that several cases in which she was the median voice may now pivot in the opposite direction. For instance, and as noted earlier, she cast the deciding vote in *Stenberg v. Carhart*, holding that states can only restrict certain late term abortion procedures if they do not place an "undue burden" on women by refusing to add a health exception to the restrictions. The case has already been overturned through Justice Alito's vote in *Gonzales v. Carhart* establishing that such health exceptions were unnecessary. Her vote in *Rompilla v. Beard* that a death row inmate had received unconstitutionally deficient assistance of counsel was not supported by Justice Alito's view of the Sixth Amendment, suggesting that her position in *Rompilla* may be subject to reversal. Indeed, several 5-4 cases in which O'Connor voted with the liberal justices are no longer safe; her retirement likely set into motion compositional changes that will strongly influence the future direction of the law.

Third, O'Connor was a critical member of the five-person majority that ruled relatively consistently in favor of states' rights in federalism cases. In federalism cases, she was a strong supporter of state sovereignty and interpreted the Commerce Clause as well as the Tenth and Eleventh Amendments to overturn or limit federal legislation and regulations. Her votes in *Lopez, Morrison, Printz,* and *Raich,* along with her opinion in *New York,* indicate that she truly felt local officials are better equipped to solve local problems. She was willing to articulate that position even when doing so resulted in overturning decades of Court precedents. To that extent, especially in federalism cases, O'Connor states' rights views superseded the value she placed on precedent, although her vote to support Kennedy's concurring opinion in *Lopez* suggested that she was not willing to go as far as Chief Justice Rehnquist in returning power back to the states.

Fourth, and maybe her greatest contribution to the Court, Justice O'Connor embodied the notion of judicial restraint and judicial modesty when handing down decisions (Sunstein 1999). Labeled by one author as the Court's "Chief Pragmatist" (Maveety 2008, 121), O'Connor used a fact-based, balancing approach for judicial decision making in which few categorical rules were established and decisions were sensitive to the context and case facts of any given situation. Her individual opinions, while adding complexity to the Court's decisions, also often reflected her minimalist judicial philosophy by seeking to limit the reach of the majority's decision. Instead, she articulated positions that were more practical for the purposes of implementation. Ultimately, by the time she retired and left the Court, she was praised "as an enviable judicial minimalist . . . as a model justice . . . as a jurist with practical values" (Maveety 2008, 108).

Overall, Justice O'Connor had a tremendous impact on the Rehnquist Court and she leaves behind an impressive legacy. She helped to shape the judicial norms used today. She also helped lead the Court's conservative movement while at the same time preserving abortion options for women and establishing an emphasis on collegiality within an ideologically fractured Supreme Court (Maveety 2008). Justice O'Connor helped to redefine the role of the justice as a person who should consider the practical consequences of legal decisions. Her legacy goes far beyond the fact that she was the first woman on the Court, and to view her only in those terms substantially undervalues the extent to which she influenced the Supreme Court and American legal jurisprudence.

References

Baca, Maria Elena. "Sandra Day O'Connor Speaks in Minneapolis." *Minneapolis Star Tribune,* July 3, 2001.
Biskupic, Joan. *Sandra Day O'Connor: How the First Woman on the Supreme Court Became Its Most Influential Justice.* New York: Harper Collins, 2005.

Chemerinsky, Erwin. "Justice O'Connor and Federalism." *McGeorge Law Review* 32 (2001): 877-93.

Greve, Michael. "The Term the Constitution Died." *Georgetown Journal of Law and Public Policy* 2 (2004): 227-40.

Kelso, Charles, and R. Randell Kelso. "Sandra Day O'Connor: A Justice Who Has Made a Difference in Constitutional Law." *McGeorge Law Review* 32 (2001): 915-55.

Kirkland, Michael. "Peering into the Court's Future." LEXIS/NEXIS Library News File, August 27, 2004.

Huhn, William. "The Constitutional Jurisprudence of Sandra Day O'Connor: A Refusal to 'Foreclose the Unanticipated.'" *Akron Law Review* 39 (2006): 373-415.

Martin, Andrew, Kevin Quinn, and Lee Epstein. "The Median Justice on the United States Supreme Court." *North Carolina Law Review* 83 (2005): 1275-1317.

Maveety, Nancy. *Justice Sandra Day O'Connor: Strategist on the Supreme Court.* New York: Rowman & Littlefield, 1996.

———. *The Queen's Court.* Lawrence, KS: University of Kansas Press, 2008.

McCall, Michael, Madhavi McCall, and Christopher Smith. "Criminal Justice and the 2006-2007 United States Supreme Court Term." *University of Missouri, Kansas City Law Review* 76, 4 (2008): 993-1043.

McFeatters, Ann Carey. *Sandra Day O'Connor: Justice in the Balance.* Albuquerque, NM: University of New Mexico Press, 2005.

O'Brien, David. *Storm Center: The Supreme Court in American Politics.* New York: W.W. Norton, 2005.

O'Connor, Sandra Day. *The Majesty of the Law: Reflections of a Supreme Court Justice.* New York: Random House, 2003.

O'Connor, Sandra Day, and H. Alan Day. *From Cattle Ranch to the Supreme Court: Lazy B: Growing Up on and Cattle Ranch in the American Southwest.* Random House: New York, 2002.

Smith, Christopher, Madhavi McCall, and Michael McCall. "Criminal Justice and the 2005-2006 Supreme Court Term." *New Mexico Law Review* 35, 1 (2005): 123-60.

Smith, Christopher, Michael McCall, and Madhavi McCall. "Criminal Justice and the 2004-2005 Supreme Court Term." *University of Memphis Law Review* 36, 4 (2006): 951-1011.

———. "Criminal Justice and the 2005-2006 Supreme Court Term." *Quinnipiac Law Review* 25, 3 (2007): 495-546.

Smith, Christopher, Madhavi McCall, and Cynthia McCluskey. *Law and Criminal Justice: Emerging Issues in the Twenty-first Century.* New York: Peter Lang, 2005.

Sunstein, Cass. *One Case at a Time: Judicial Minimalism on the Supreme Court.* Cambridge, MA: Harvard University Press, 1999.

Taylor, Stuart. 1987. "Justices Seem to Widen Death Penalty," New York Times, April 22, 1987. http://www.nytimes.com/1987/04/22/us/supreme-court-roundup-justices-seem-to-widen-death-penalty.html (accessed July 15, 2010).

Toobin, Jeffrey. *The Nine: Inside the Secret World of the Supreme Court.* New York: Doubleday, 2007.

Zalman, Marvin, and Elsa Shartsis. "A Roadblock Too Far? Justice O'Connor's Left Turn on the Fourth." *Journal of Contemporary Criminal Justice* 19 (2003): 182-203.

Cases Cited

Akron v. Akron Center for Reproductive Health, 462 U.S. 416 (1983)

Atkins v. Virginia, 536 U.S. 304 (2002)
Atwater v. City of Lago Vista, 532 U.S. 318 (2001)
Barclay v. Florida, 463 U.S. 939 (1983)
Board of Education of Independent School District No. 92 of Pottawatomie County v. Earls, 536 U.S. 822 (2002)
Bond v. United States, 529 U.S. 334 (2000)
Booth v. Maryland, 482 U.S. 496 (1987)
Caldwell v. Mississippi, 472 US 320 (1985)
California v. Acevedo, 500 U.S. 565 (1991)
City of Indianapolis v. Edmond, 531 U.S. 32 (2000)
County of Riverside v. McLaughlin, 500 U.S. 44 (1991)
Enmund v. Florida, 458 U.S. 782 (1982)
Ferguson v. City of Charleston, 532 U.S. 67 (2001)
Florida v. Bostick, 501 U.S. 429 (1991)
Florida v. Riley, 488 U.S. 445 (1989)
Ford v. Wainwright, 477 U.S. 399 (1986)
Gonzales v. Carhart, 550 U.S. 124 (2007)
Gonzales v. Raich, 545 U.S. 1 (2005)
Hodgson v. Minnesota, 497 U.S. 417 (1990)
INS v. Lopez-Mendoza, 468 U.S. 1032 (1984)
J.E.B v. Alabama, 511 U.S. 127 (1994)
Kelly v. South Carolina, 534 U.S. 246 (2002)
Kyllo v. United States, 533 U.S. 27 (2001)
Lawrence v. Texas, 539 U.S. 558 (2003)
McCleskey v. Kemp, 481 U.S. 279 (1987)
Michigan v. Long, 463 U.S. 1032 (1984)
Mississippi University for Women v. Hogan, 458 U.S 718 (1982)
New York v. United States, 505 U.S. 144 (1992)
Penry v. Lynaugh, 492 U.S. 302 (1989)
Planned Parenthood v. Casey, 947 F.2d 682, 3rd Cir. (1991)
Planned Parenthood of Southeastern Pennsylvania v. Casey, 505 U.S 833 (1992)
Printz v. United States, 521 U.S. 898 (1997)
Roe v. Wade, 410 U.S 113 (1973)
Rompilla v. Beard, 545 U.S. 374 (2005)
Roper v. Simmons 543 U.S. 551 (2005)
Schlup v. Delo, 513 U.S. 298 (1995)
Schriro v. Landrigan, 550 U.S. 465 (2007)
Simmons v. South Carolina, 512 U.S. 154 (1994)
Skipper v. South Carolina, 476 US 1 (1986)
Smith v. Murray, 477 U. S. 527 (1986)
Stanford v. Kentucky, 492 U.S 361 (1989)
Stenberg v. Carhart, 530 U.S. 914 (2000)
Strickland v. Washington, 466 U.S. 668 (1984)
Tennessee v. Lane, 541 U.S. 509 (2004)
Thompson v. Oklahoma, 487 U.S 815 (1988)
Thornburgh v. American College of Obstetricians & Gynecologists, 476 U.S 747 (1986)
Tison v. Arizona, 481 US 137 (1987)
Trop v. Dulles, 356 U.S 86 (1958)
United States v. Lopez, 514 U.S. 549 (1995)
United States v. Morrison, 529 U.S. 598 (2000)

United States v. New York, 505 U.S. 144 (1992)
United States v. Place, 462 U.S. 696 (1983)
Vernonia School District v. Acton, 515 U.S 646 (1995)
Wainwright v. Witt, 469 US 412 (1985)
Walker Chandler v. Zell Miller, 520 U.S. 305 (1997)

Chapter 8
Antonin Scalia:
Outspoken & Influential Originalist

Christopher E. Smith and Madhavi M. McCall

When President Ronald Reagan nominated Antonin Scalia for a seat on the U.S. Supreme Court in 1986, he selected a highly experienced legal professional with an established reputation for conservative positions on various issues. Scalia had experience as a private practice attorney, a prominent law professor at the University of Virginia and the University of Chicago, a federal government attorney in Republican administrations, and a federal appellate judge on the U.S. Court of Appeals for the District of Columbia Circuit.

Scalia went through the confirmation process with little scrutiny or criticism because liberal senators focused their attention on the simultaneous nomination to elevate William Rehnquist to be chief justice. In light of Scalia's forceful and influential performance on the Supreme Court, Joseph Biden, a member of the Senate Judiciary Committee during Scalia's confirmation hearings, expressed regret years later that he had not subjected Scalia to greater scrutiny and voted against the nomination (Biskupic 2009). Unanimously confirmed by the Senate, Scalia became the Senior Associate Justice on the Roberts Court after Justice Stevens retired in June 2010. This chapter will examine selected aspects of Justice Scalia's approach to criminal justice issues during the Rehnquist Court era and his influence on specific areas of law.

In criminal justice cases, Justice Scalia's voting record indicated that he usually opposed the claims of individuals and, instead, favored the interests of police, prosecutors, and corrections officials. During the Rehnquist Court era, for cases classified in the Supreme Court Judicial Database as "criminal procedure" cases, Scalia supported the government in 74.7 percent of cases (Epstein, Segal, Spaeth, and Walker 2007, 536). Among the Rehnquist Court justices, only Justice Thomas was less likely to support the claims of individuals. Scalia's voting record reflected the results of the commitments and priorities that shaped his judicial decision making.

Scalia's Priorities

Justice Scalia claimed to be committed to an originalist approach to constitutional interpretation (Scalia 1989). He sought to have his interpretation of constitutional provisions to be guided by the meaning of those provisions in the eyes of the authors and ratifiers of the Constitution, Bill of Rights, and Fourteenth Amendment. This approach required him to take seriously both the words and history of the country's fundamental document. Observers have labeled Scalia as following "textualist jurisprudence" in which "primacy must be accorded to the text, structure, and history of the document" (Rossum 2003, 35). Scalia saw the use of textualist and originalist approaches to interpretation as the means to prevent judges from imposing their own values into constitutional interpretation. For Scalia, originalism was the antidote for improper judicial activism. Indeed, he was so harshly critical of his colleagues' flexible interpretive approaches that he spoke of them as if they were a cancer on the body of jurisprudence. In Scalia's words, "American constitutional evolutionism has, so to speak, metastasized, infecting courts around the world" (Scalia 2007, 45).

As indicated by the foregoing example, in advocating his approach and his priorities, Scalia became known for being blunt and sarcastic in criticizing his colleagues. His language could be harshly accusatory, as when he and Thurgood Marshall disagreed about whether a white defendant could assert a Sixth Amendment jury trial right to complain about the systematic exclusion of African American jurors: "Justice Marshall's dissent rolls out the ultimate weapon, the accusation of insensitivity to racial discrimination—which will lose its intimidating effect if it continues to be fired so randomly" (*Holland v. Illinois* 1990, 486). Scalia also used biting sarcasm, as when he criticized inconsistencies he perceived in the Court's death penalty jurisprudence through its emphasis on individualized decision making and the use of aggravating and mitigating factors:

> To acknowledge that "there perhaps is an inherent tension" between this line of cases and the line stemming from *Furman* [v. *Georgia* 1972] . . . . is rather like saying that there was perhaps an inherent tension between the Allies and the Axis Powers in World War II. And to refer to the two lines as pursuing "twin objectives," . . . is rather like referring to the twin objectives of good and evil. They cannot be reconciled. (*Walton v. Arizona* 1990, 664)

Justice Scalia's interpretive approach and outspokenness often placed him in opposition to the views of his Rehnquist Court colleagues who, except for Justice Thomas, did not follow an originalist theory. For example, Scalia's commitment to constitutional interpretation by original intent clashed directly with the Supreme Court's established test for cruel and unusual punishment under the Eighth Amendment. Chief Justice Earl Warren famously declared in *Trop v. Dulles* (1958) that judges must define cruel and unusual punishment according to "the evolving standards of decency that mark the progress of a maturing society" (100). The *Trop* standard, with its explicit acceptance of evolving contemporary values, was the antithesis of originalism. Scalia saw this approach to the Eighth Amendment as inviting judges to insert their own values into constitutional decision making. Indeed, the words "cruel and unusual punishments" in the Eighth Amendment have no inherent meaning. Judges must determine the meaning of the words. Even scholars with no sympathy for the interpretive approach of Justice Scalia have acknowledged that the "broad language of the cruel and unusual punishment clause must be seen . . . . as a jurisdictional provision that invited the courts to construct a set of rules" (Feeley and Rubin 1998, 206). Thus, Justice Scalia, along with Justice Thomas, another self-proclaimed originalist, often disagreed with their liberal, non-originalist colleagues in cases concerning capital punishment and prisoners' rights.

Justice Scalia was among the justices who expressed support for a renewal of states' governmental autonomy. Under a vision of federalism shared by Rehnquist and O'Connor, he supported a roll back of the expansive federal law-making authority that began in the late 1930s with Supreme Court deference to wide-ranging congressional activity, especially statutory enactments under the Commerce Clause. In *Printz v. United States* (1997), Scalia wrote the majority opinion invalidating a portion of the Brady Handgun Violence Prevention Act that required local sheriffs to assume temporary responsibility for enforcing federal background check requirements for handgun purchasers. Scalia's opinion emphasized the concept of "dual sovereignty" under the Constitution and applied his interpretation of the framers' original intent to reject the imposition of such federal requirements on state and local officials. Scalia also voted with the majority to limit congressional lawmaking in criminal justice by invalidating the Gun-Free School Zones Act in *United States v. Lopez* (1995) and the Violence Against Women Act in *United States v. Morrison* (2000).

Justice Scalia also sought to limit the number of cases decided by the U.S. Supreme Court and other federal judges. In his first speech to the American Bar Association after being confirmed for the Supreme Court, Scalia focused on his desire to "be a judge, not a case processor" (Taylor 1987, 12), and he bemoaned the deterioration of the prestige of the "natural aristocracy" of the federal judiciary due to overly burdensome caseloads (Taylor 1987, 1). He sought to use jurisdictional doctrines, such as standing requirements, as a means to keep litigants out of the federal courts (Schultz and Smith 1996). By imposing limitations on litigants' access to courts, Scalia could also seek to limit opportunities for judicial decisions that might expand constitutional rights and shape public policy. This was a means to advance his expressed opposition to judicial activism by liberal judges. During the Rehnquist Court era, there was a precipitous drop in the number of decisions produced by the Supreme Court each year even as the number of petitions requesting Court action rose significantly. Presumably, Scalia's role in discussions and voting decisions on granting petitions for a writ of certiorari played a part in this reduction in activity by the nation's highest court. In the first three terms of the Rehnquist Court era (1986 Term through the 1988 Term), the justices received an average of 5,335 cert petitions and granted review to an average of 165 cases each term. By contrast, during the final three terms of the Rehnquist Court era (2002 Term through 2004 Term), the justices accepted an average of only eighty-six cases each term from among an average of 8,953 petitions (Epstein et al. 2007, 74-75). Presumably, Chief Justice Rehnquist and other justices may have also withheld their votes to grant review as a means to reduce the Court's involvement in law and policy issues.

Individually, Scalia stood out among his colleagues for taking a hard line against permitting post-conviction reviews in criminal cases. Most strikingly, Scalia's interpretation of the Constitution precluded any right for a convicted offender to have newly-discovered evidence of innocence presented in court, or even to avoid execution for a capital offense merely because he was innocent. In a concurring opinion in *Herrera v. Collins* (1993), Scalia wrote, "There is no basis in text, tradition, or even in contemporary practice (if that were enough), for finding in the Constitution a right to demand judicial consideration of newly discovered evidence of innocence brought forward after conviction" (427-28). Later, during the Roberts Court era, Scalia explicitly articulated the starkest implication of this viewpoint: "This Court has *never* held that the Constitution forbids the execution of a convicted defendant who has had a full and fair trial but is later able to convince a habeas court that he is 'actually' innocent" (*In re Davis* 2009).

Scalia criticized his colleagues for taking the vague constitutional phrases "due process of law" and "cruel and unusual punishments" and using them to create or expand rights. Thus, while some of the other justices would undoubtedly use one or both of these phrases to justify post-conviction review opportunities and prevent the execution of the innocent, Scalia was not so inclined. His orientation toward constitutional rights with a focus on the words and original intentions, which he asserted could help to prevent excessive exercises of judicial power, made him appear accepting of the inevitability of uncorrected errors in the criminal justice process. Scalia rested his view on the textual articulation of rights in the Bill of Rights and Fourteenth Amendment and the absence of a specific provision addressing the right of innocent people to be free from punishment after erroneous convictions in proceedings for which the full range of procedural trial rights had been provided.

Justice Scalia's resistance to post-conviction appellate reviews also reflected his commitment to the perpetuation of capital punishment and states' authority to determine the circumstances in which the ultimate punishment would apply. Early in his Supreme Court career, Scalia demonstrated this commitment in an exceptionally controversial challenge to the constitutionality of capital punishment. In *McCleskey v. Kemp* (1987), the Court was presented with a detailed statistical study indicating that race was an important factor in determining which defendants were sentenced to death in Georgia. As summarized in Justice Brennan's dissenting opinion:

> [B]lacks who kill whites are sentenced to death at nearly 22 times the rate of blacks who kill blacks, and more than 7 times the rate of whites who kill

blacks. In addition, prosecutors seek the death penalty for 70% of black defendants with white victims, but for only 15% of black defendants with black victims, and 19% of white defendants with black victims. [Georgia] has executed seven persons. All of the seven were convicted of killing whites, and six of the seven executed were black. [E]xecution figures are especially striking in light of the fact that, during the period encompassed by the Baldus study, only 9.2% of Georgia homicides involved black defendants and white victims, while 60.7% involved black victims. (*McCleskey v. Kemp* 1987, 367)

In deciding the case, Scalia cast one of the five pivotal votes to reject the constitutional challenge that alleged systemic racial discrimination in violation of the Equal Protection Clause. The narrow majority of justices concluded that it would not recognize statistical evidence of discrimination to prove equal protection violations in capital punishment cases, despite the fact that such evidence was accepted in seemingly less compelling contexts such as alleged racial discrimination in jury selection and employment discrimination. Justice Powell's majority opinion rationalized the imposition of a greater burden of proof of specific discrimination in each particular capital case because of the importance of maintaining discretion in the criminal justice process. In dissent, Justice Stevens expressed the fear that the majority's rationalizations simply reflected that their commitment to the continuation of capital punishment was a greater priority than equal protection concerns about the eradication of racial discrimination in the justice system.

Justice Powell subsequently admitted that "[m]y understanding of statistical analysis . . . ranges from limited to zero" (Jeffries 1994, 439), thus raising concerns that the Court's decision rested on a lack of comprehension concerning the validity and strength of the social science evidence showing the existence of racial discrimination. Was Scalia's rejection of the discrimination claim similarly based on a possible failure to understand fully the social science evidence? It was subsequently revealed that Scalia had no such difficulty understanding the statistics. Thus his commitment to capital punishment seemed especially strong as an influence over his decision making.

Several years after the *McCleskey* decision, Justice Thurgood Marshall died and his papers became available in the Library of Congress. Dennis Dorin, a political science professor from the University of North Carolina-Charlotte, found within the Marshall Papers a revealing memorandum written by Scalia and circulated internally within the Court at the time of its deliberations in *McCleskey* (Dorin 1994). In the memorandum, Scalia acknowledged his recognition of the existence of discrimination within the criminal justice system. Unlike Powell's later admission about a lack of comprehension of the quantitative evidence, Scalia did not claim to have any difficulty understanding or accepting the statistical studies that documented the existence of racial discrimination. As Scalia wrote,

I disagree with the argument that the inferences that can be drawn from the Baldus study are weakened by the fact that each jury and trial is unique, or by the large number of variables at issue. And I do not share the view, implicit in [Powell's draft opinion], that an effect of racial factors upon sentencing, if it could be shown by sufficiently strong statistical evidence, would require reversal. Since it is my view that the unconscious operation of irrational sympathies and antipathies, including racial, upon jury decisions and (hence) prosecutorial [ones] is real, acknowledged by the [cases] of this court and ineradicable, I cannot honestly say that all I need is more proof. I expect to write separately on these points, but not until I see the dissent. (Dorin 1994, 1038)

Thus Scalia's vote to reject the discrimination claim clearly indicated that he would support the continuation of death sentences based on "irrational [racial] antipathies" evinced by prosecutors and jurors. In Professor Dorin's view, Scalia "trivializ[ed] [racist practices] by saying, in a single-paragraph memo, that they were merely an unavoidable and legally unassailable, part of life for African-Americans" (1077). Moreover, Dorin concluded that "[a]pparently for Scalia, the capital punishment system's valuing [of] a white life significantly above a black one did not implicate any constitutional provisions" (1077). In light of Scalia's memo about the inevitability and acceptability of racial discrimination in capital punishment, it is difficult to escape the conclusion that his commitment to the continuation of capital punishment reflected a paramount priority, one even greater than the constitutional command of "equal protection of the laws."

In other cases, Scalia indicated his strong support for interpreting the Constitution in a manner that gives broad authority to the states to make their own choices about imposing the death penalty. When the Rehnquist Court majority declared that the imposition of the death penalty on mentally retarded offenders violated the Eighth Amendment, Scalia objected (*Atkins v. Virginia* 2002). In a characteristically blunt and strongly worded dissent, Scalia argued that a national consensus did not exist on the issue and thus states should not be deprived of their authority to implement criminal punishments as they see fit. Scalia's opinion accused the majority of bowing to personal preferences and ignoring the law and the Constitution:

Today's decision is the pinnacle of our Eighth Amendment death-is-different jurisprudence. Not only does it, like all of that jurisprudence, find no support in the text or history of the Eighth Amendment; it does not even have support in current social attitudes regarding the conditions that render an otherwise just death penalty inappropriate. Seldom has an opinion of this Court rested so obviously upon nothing but the personal view of its members. (337-38)

Scalia's dissent reflected both his support for the preservation of capital punishment and his originalist objections to the Court's flexible, evolving approach for interpreting the Eighth Amendment's Cruel and Unusual Punishments Clause.

Support for Liberal Outcomes

Although subsequent sections of this chapter will focus on Scalia's influence in limiting the extent of constitutional rights in criminal justice, it must be recognized that Scalia's priorities and approach did not lead inevitably to support for conservative outcomes. For example, Scalia takes a "plain-meaning" approach to statutory interpretation that led him to focus on the words and avoid reliance on the legislative history (Scalia 1997). This approach led him to write the Supreme Court's majority opinion declaring that prisoners were included under the federal Americans with Disabilities Act and could therefore file actions against corrections officials under that statute (*Pennsylvania Department of Corrections v. Yeskey* 1998).

Similarly, with respect to constitutional interpretation, Scalia's approach led to his support for strong declarations about specific rights when he believed that police officers' and prosecutors' actions clashed with the text and original meaning of provisions within the Bill of Rights (Yarbrough 2000). In cases concerning the Confrontation Clause, for example, Scalia wrote majority opinions insisting that the Sixth Amendment guarantees a live, face-to-face confrontation between the defendant and his accusers (*Cruz v. New York* 1987; *Coy v. Iowa* 1988). When his conservative colleagues reshaped the confrontation right in a more flexible way to accommodate concerns about avoiding psychological trauma for juvenile sex crime victims by, for example, permitting closed circuit television testimony, Scalia wrote a vigorous dissent (*Maryland v. Craig* 1990). According to Scalia, the confrontation right is presented in the Sixth Amendment with "unmistakable clarity" and he said of the majority's diminution of that right, "Seldom has this Court failed so conspicuously to sustain a categorical guarantee of the Constitution against the tide of prevailing current opinion" (860-61).

In another example of his support for rights in criminal justice contexts, Scalia joined the Court's three most liberal justices in protesting the majority's decision endorsing the reasonableness of holding arrestees in jail for forty-eight hours prior to a probable cause hearing (*County of Riverside v. McLaughlin* 1991). Scalia and the other dissenters argued in favor of a long-standing tradition to hold probable cause hearings within twenty-four hours so that people could not be held in jail for longer periods without evidence of criminal conduct.

In Fourth Amendment cases, Scalia wrote the Court's majority opinion that rejected the warrantless use of thermal imaging devices to examine heat sources within houses as a means to detect whether marijuana was being cultivated indoors under grow-lights (*Kyllo v. United States* 2001). He objected to the suspicionless drug testing of U.S. Customs Service employees in *National Treasury Employees Union v. Von Raab* (1989). With Justice Stevens joining his opinion, Scalia used his talent for penning pointed, memorable criticisms in order to declare in *Von Raab* that "the Customs Service rules are a kind of immolation of privacy and human dignity in symbolic opposition to drug use" (681).

Justice Scalia also voted with his liberal colleagues Stevens, Ginsburg, and Souter in cases that supported the jury's key fact-finding role under the Sixth Amendment and thereby diminished the authority of both judges and sentencing guidelines schemes to incorporate unproven facts into the determination of criminal sentences (*Apprendi v. New Jersey* 2000; *United States v. Booker* 2005). Later, in the Roberts Court era, he even criticized Stevens and Ginsburg for failing to extend the right to fact-finding by a jury to additional sentencing contexts (*Oregon v. Ice* 2009).

Justice Scalia's most striking use of originalism to support constitutional rights came during the Rehnquist Court's examination of the applicability of constitutional rights to suspects detained in the post-9/11 "war on terrorism." Because of his outspoken, off-the-bench public comments, Scalia eventually established a reputation as a harsh critic of those who would scrupulously apply constitutional rights in determining the fates of terrorism suspects. For example, he personalized his opposition to the granting of procedural rights by making reference to his son, a U.S. Army officer who served in Iraq: "I had a son on that battlefield and they were shooting at my son, and I'm not going to give this man who was captured in a war a full jury trial. I mean it's crazy" (Biskupic 2009, 322). He also made public statements that seemed to accept the permissibility of torture in some circumstances related to anti-terrorism efforts (338-40). Yet, when confronted with a case concerning a terrorism suspect who was an American citizen held on American soil, Scalia's view of originalism and textualism led him to write the most strongly pro-rights opinion of any justice on the Court. In *Hamdi v. Rumsfeld* (2004), Scalia's dissenting opinion, joined by Stevens, demanded that the federal government either release the suspect or proceed with a formal criminal prosecution that would include the full range of constitutional rights for criminal defendants. Scalia rejected the Bush Administration's assertion that the president possessed the authority to hold American terrorism suspects in indefinite incommunicado detention without any prospect of representation by counsel or an appearance in court, let alone a trial to determine the suspect's guilt. According to Scalia's opinion, "The very core of liberty secured by our Anglo-Saxon system of separated powers has been freedom from indefinite imprisonment at the will of the Executive" (*Hamdi v. Rumsfeld* 2004, 554-555). By contrast, because Scalia did not regard the U.S. Constitution as applicable overseas, especially to foreigners held in custody by the United States outside of its borders, he was strongly supportive of other assertions of power by the Bush Administration and Congress that would diminish terrorism suspects' access to American courts and preclude the recognition of legal rights.

Scalia's Influence

Through his coherent judicial philosophy, active engagement in oral argument, blunt opinions, and sharp criticism of his colleagues' viewpoints, Scalia established a reputation as a conservative visionary with contempt for justices who compromise their principles or engage in pragmatic thinking (Brisbin 1997). Indeed, Scalia's outspokenly undiplomatic style may have undercut his efforts to shift the direction of Supreme Court decisions on abortion and establishment of religion as he may have effectively alienated rather than cultivated the votes of potential allies (Smith 1993). In the realm of criminal justice, however, Scalia had a profound impact on several specific issues during the Rehnquist Court era through his ingenuity in finessing the characterization and use of precedents as he persuaded a majority of his colleagues to adopt his views. Even when he was not successful in gaining majority support, he could assert ideas into constitutional discourse as a means to potentially shape future developments in the Supreme Court's development of legal doctrine.

Justice Scalia had an especially powerful impact on prisoner litigation through his majority opinion in the case of *Wilson v. Seiter* (1991). In that case, a prisoner in an Ohio prison filed a civil rights lawsuit alleging various unconstitutional conditions of confinement related to overcrowding, sanitation, nutrition, and ventilation. Scalia's opinion changed the standards by which judges evaluate whether conditions of confinement in correctional institutions violate the Eighth Amendment prohibition on cruel and unusual punishments. Scalia appropriated the subjective "deliberate indifference" test that liberal Justice Thurgood Marshall had articulated for a prior Supreme Court decision about prisoners' limited right to medical care in *Estelle v. Gamble* (1976). Under the test, prisoners' right to medical care existed only to the extent of protecting them from corrections officials being deliberately indifferent to the prisoners' serious medical needs. Thus the test focused on a subjective assessment of corrections officials' knowledge and motives rather than looking objectively at whether and what medical care was provided in response to prisoners' needs. Although Marshall developed the test for the purpose of expanding rights for prisoners, Scalia apparently recognized the opportunity to apply that test to a new context in order to sharply limit lower court judges' ability to order prison officials to make improvements in conditions of confinement (Smith 2001).

In *Wilson*, Scalia's majority opinion declared that the subjective test for medical care actually applied to all claims concerning conditions of confinement in prisons that allegedly violated the Eighth Amendment's prohibition on cruel and unusual punishments. This new standard suddenly posed a significant challenge for prisoners seeking judicial orders that would force prison officials to create more humane conditions, correct problems with ventilation and sanitation, and ensure the provision of nutritious food. As prominent scholars observed,

> *Wilson* appears to raise a substantial barrier to Eighth Amendment suits against state prisons; it is conceivable that the case could preclude most conditions of confinement suits on the grounds that conditions are the result of an insufficiently trained staff [or] an insufficiently funded operational budget. (Feeley and Rubin 1998, 49)

Another scholar saw Scalia's opinion in *Wilson v. Seiter* as the centerpiece of a series of Rehnquist Court decisions affecting prisoners that "encourage lower federal courts to yield to the authority of state and local officials in prison and jail administration [thereby creating] a significant retreat" from the federal judiciary's prior interventionist posture (Fliter 2001, 174).

In marshaling precedent to support the subjective standard, Scalia cited the Supreme Court's opinion in *Whitley v. Albers* (1986). Whitley, however, concerned the narrow issue of corrections officials' potential liability for injuring a prisoner through the use of force during a disturbance. In that context, the Court limited liability to situations in which the prisoner could make a showing of the officials' subjective intent in using force "maliciously" and for the very purpose of causing harm (322). Scalia did not use the Court's precedents concerning general conditions of confinement that had been applied in the contexts most similar to that of *Wilson v. Seiter*. Scalia's opinion was conspicuously devoid of reliance on the Supreme Court's two decisions that actually concerned living conditions within prisons: *Rhodes v. Chapman* (1981) and *Hutto v. Finney* (1978). In those cases, the Court had emphasized an objective assessment of conditions of confinement in order to determine whether any Eighth Amendment violations existed. These decisions by the Supreme Court did not focus on the corrections officials' state of mind. Four justices in *Wilson v. Seiter* warned that Scalia's new emphasis on a subjective test would permit corrections officials to defeat prisoner lawsuits merely by claiming that they had inadequate funds to correct inhumane conditions. Moreover, on behalf of these critics, Justice White's opinion noted that Scalia's new test would be unworkable when applied to inhumane prison conditions that are produced through "cumulative actions and inactions by numerous officials inside and outside a prison, sometimes over a long period of time" (310).

Justice Scalia's position in other cases indicated that his opinion in *Wilson* was not merely intended to limit prisoners' opportunities to present Eighth Amendment claims as well as attendant opportunities for judges to intervene in correctional administration. *Wilson* represented an indirect step toward Scalia's ideal goal: the elimination of any recognition of Eighth Amendment protections for prisoners. Justice Scalia's opposition to prisoners' Eighth Amendment rights was made clear when he joined two post-*Wilson* dissenting opinions by Justice Thomas (*Hudson v. McMillian* 1992; *Helling v. McKinney* 1993). These opinions relied on originalism to assert that prisoners should not receive any protection from the Eighth Amendment because the authors and ratifiers of the Cruel and Unusual Punishments Clause did not intend to affect the treatment of people held in government custody. With support from Scalia, Thomas expressed "serious doubts about th[e] premise" that "deprivations suffered by a prisoner constitute 'punishmen[t]' for Eighth Amendment purposes" (*Helling v. McKinney* 1993, 37). Justices Thomas and Scalia believed that the Eighth Amendment was only relevant to the sentence announced by the judge, which was the "punishment" referred to by the Eighth Amendment, rather than to the implementation and administration of the sentence by corrections officials. Thomas, joined by

Scalia, asserted that there is "substantial doubt that the Eighth Amendment proscribes a prison deprivation that is not inflicted as part of the sentence" (42).
Moreover, they emphasized that the Supreme Court had never applied the
Eighth Amendment to conditions in prisons until 1976 (*Estelle v. Gamble*) in
order to demonstrate their interpretation of the original intention as merely prohibiting judges' announcement of "cruel and unusual" sentences rather than any
limitation on how a sentence of incarceration was subsequently carried out. Justice Thomas made reference to the specific intentions of the Eighth Amendment's authors and ratifiers as well as early American judges in claiming that
prison conditions can never violate the Eighth Amendment (*Hudson v. McMillian* 1992, 19):

> Surely prison was not a more congenial place in the early years of the Republic
> than it is today; nor were our judges and commentators so naive as to be una-
> ware of the often harsh conditions of prison life. Rather, they simply did not
> conceive of the Eighth Amendment as protecting inmates from harsh treatment.

The position presented by Thomas and Scalia attracted scholarly criticism
asserting that they had misapplied originalism because prisons did not exist
when the Eighth Amendment was ratified and therefore the framers could not
have had any specific intentions with respect to such institutions (Smith 1997).
In response to those criticisms, a decade later in a concurring opinion, Thomas,
still joined only by Scalia, acknowledged that prisons were not developed until
the nineteenth century (*Overton v. Bazzetta* 2003). He presented a new historical
justification for denying any constitutional protections for prisoners, except for a
limited right of access to the courts, based on a more complex argument about
state officials' authority to define the meaning of incarceration and the rights
retained by those who are imprisoned. In sum, Thomas and Scalia continued to
maintain that the provisions of the U.S. Constitution, including the Eighth
Amendment, generally do not provide any prisoners' rights.

In light of what these subsequent opinions indicated about Scalia's actual
views on prisoners' rights, it appeared that a straightforward presentation of
Scalia's views in *Wilson v. Seiter* (1991) would have required him to state forthrightly that he does not believe that the Eighth Amendment should apply at all to
conditions of confinement. If he had done so, however, no justices other than
Thomas would have joined his opinion. Even the other consistently conservative
justice, Chief Justice Rehnquist, acknowledged the necessity of judicial intervention to remedy unconstitutional conditions of confinement (*Bell v. Wolfish*
1979). Rehnquist did not join any of the Thomas-Scalia dissents that demonstrated their opposition to the application of Eighth Amendment rights to inhumane conditions within prisons. Thus Scalia's majority opinion in *Wilson* was
able to reshape constitutional law as it affected prisoners' rights to humane conditions of confinement by deceptively purporting to agree that the Eighth
Amendment applies to such conditions.

The Prison Litigation Reform Act of 1996 (PLRA), a congressional effort to limit federal judges' ability to order remedies for constitutional rights violations in correctional settings, contained several provisions that made it more difficult for prisoners to file lawsuits successfully. One such provision barred filing-fee waivers for prisoners who have had three prior lawsuits "dismissed on the grounds that [they were] frivolous, malicious, or fail[ed] to state a claim upon which relief may be granted, unless the prisoner is under imminent danger of serious physical injury." Scalia's opinion in *Wilson* made it significantly more difficult for prisoners to successfully prove violations of conditions of confinement and, therefore, made such actions susceptible to dismissal for failing to state a claim if there were insufficient allegations and evidence of "deliberate indifference." In the aftermath of the PLRA, despite growing prison populations and larger numbers of potential prisoner-litigants, there was significant reduction in the number of constitutional rights lawsuits filed by prisoners (Scalia 2002). Justice Scalia's *Wilson* opinion may have contributed to that decline both on its own and in conjunction with the later PLRA.

Justice Scalia affected prisoners' access to the courts through his majority opinion in *Lewis v. Casey* (1996). In that case, the Court rejected a district judge's remedial order designed to ensure access to law library resources and legal assistance for illiterate prisoners, non-English-speaking prisoners, and prisoners confined to their cells for rules infractions. Under the doctrine of *Bounds v. Smith* (1977), prisoners are entitled to access to a prison law library to enable them to prepare appeals, habeas corpus petitions, and civil lawsuits. The district judge concluded, however, that these prisoners need legal assistance beyond merely access to a law library in order to effectuate their right of access to the courts. The "locked down" prisoners could not go to the prison law library and the illiterate and non-English-speaking prisoners could not make effective use of the law library to gain access to the courts. In examining the lower court decision, Scalia emphasized the Supreme Court's precedent in *Bounds v. Smith* that stated that access to a law library is sufficient to fulfill the requirements of court access. In using the *Bounds* precedent, Scalia selectively trumpeted Thurgood Marshall's defense of prisoners' ability to use law libraries and thereby undervalued and obscured the fundamental message of Marshall's *Bounds* opinion: "'Meaningful access' to the courts is the touchstone" (823). Marshall's intention was clearly to look at the fulfillment of meaningful access and not to limit prisoners' resources if those resources did not, in fact, provide meaningful access for all prisoners (Smith 2001).

According to Scalia, a prisoner must provide very specific proof about the inadequacy of a law library as a means of court access in order to permit judges to require additional forms of legal assistance. In imposing this requirement, Scalia relied on the concept of standing, a jurisdictional element that he made central to his jurisprudence as a means of limiting judges' involvement in various cases and legal issues (Scalia 1983). In the context of prisoners' access to the court, such an emphasis on proof of injury for standing purposes creates the risk of a "catch-22" situation: in order to prove that they are unable to present a case in court without special legal assistance, they must first effectively present a case in court without legal assistance to prove their special need. If they were able to go to court to attempt to prove that special need, it would seem to negate the claim that the special need exists. Those truly in need of additional legal assistance, such as illiterate prisoners, would be unable to use the courts success-fully on their own in order to prove that need. Instead, those who genuinely need legal assistance could be forced to suffer deprivations of rights that will never be remedied through judicial action (Hellerstein 2002). Justice Scalia's opinion in *Lewis*, like his opinion in *Wilson v. Seiter*, had the effect of advancing his goal of reducing the number of cases filed in the federal courts and diminishing op-portunities for judges to order remedies for rights violations in correctional con-texts, which was a form of undesirable judicial activism in Scalia's eyes.

Scalia's opinion also may have effectively sent a message to lower court judges that the Supreme Court intended to rein them in if they were actively involved in identifying and remedying rights violations in prisons. The results of this message and the standing requirement appeared to advance Scalia's policy preference for a diminution of rights for prisoners.

Justice Scalia made an additional significant impact on prisoners' rights through a free exercise of religion opinion that did not involve prisoners. In 1990 Scalia wrote the majority opinion in *Employment Division of Oregon v. Smith*, a free exercise case that attracted enormous attention from the legal community. The case concerned the eligibility for unemployment compensation of Native American substance abuse counselors who lost their jobs for ingesting peyote as a well-established component of their traditional religious services. Scalia shocked many scholars by concluding that "[w]e have never held that an individual's religious beliefs excuse him from compliance with an otherwise valid law prohibiting conduct that the State is free to regulate" (*Employment Division of Oregon v. Smith* 1990, 878-79). His opinion, supported by only four other justices (Justice O'Connor filed a separate opinion concurring in the judgment), relegated the protection of free exercise of religion to the minimal protections of a rational basis test rather than the protection of strict scrutiny analysis that so many legal authorities had understood to be the prevailing theme of prior Court precedents (McConnell 1990). In reaching this result, Scalia re-characterized prior free exercise of religion precedents, which appeared to apply strict scrutiny analysis, as actually concerning narrow sub-issues, such as unem-ployment compensation for Sabbatarians, rather than establishing guiding prin-ciples for judges' analyses of free exercise issues (Hensley, Smith, and Baugh 1997).

At the time of the *Smith* decision in 1990, the Supreme Court was already applying a rational basis test to free exercise claims by prisoners (*O'Lone v. Estate of Shabazz* 1987). The application of the rational basis test was based on the seminal decision in *Turner v. Safley* (1987) that established a standard that required judges to be very deferential to corrections officials when examining prisoners' claims concerning a variety of rights (Smith 2009). However, a political backlash against Scalia's opinion in *Smith* affected prisoners' rights and, in effect, Scalia unintentionally expanded free exercise protections for prisoners.

Religious and civil rights groups across the political spectrum banded together to support congressional efforts to enact legislation that would counteract the diminished protection for free exercise of religion mandated by Scalia's opinion in *Employment Division of Oregon v. Smith* (1990). Congress enacted the Religious Freedom Restoration Act (RFRA) in 1993 that sought to mandate legislatively the application of a strict scrutiny-type "compelling interest" test for religious free exercise claims. This legislation had the potential to affect prisoners' free exercise claims because Congress specifically rejected an effort to exclude prisoners from coverage by the RFRA. Thus the political reaction to Scalia's opinion provided a basis for additional claims about and increased judicial protection of prisoners' religious rights. Subsequently, the Supreme Court invalidated the RFRA's application to state prisons and other state and local contexts by concluding that Congress exceeded its constitutional authority under section five of the Fourteenth Amendment in enacting such a statute (*City of Boerne v. Flores* 1997).

Congress reacted again with the enactment of the Religious Land Use and Institutionalized Persons Act of 2000 (RLUIPA). This statute was enacted under congressional authority from the Spending and Commerce Clauses. Thus its applicability to state prisons was premised on congressional authority to impose conditions on recipients of federal funds, such as state governments and their corrections departments. Unlike the RFRA, which covered prisoners by implication, the RLUIPA explicitly sought to expand the religious free exercise rights of prisoners (Smith and McCall 2003). In the final year of the Rehnquist Court era, the justices unanimously upheld the RLUIPA against a constitutional challenge (*Cutter v. Wilkinson* 2005). Although Justice Scalia, along with Justice Thomas, were on record as opposing the recognition of most rights for prisoners, by supporting the Court's decision they stayed true to their purported philosophical preference for deferring to decisions of elected officials. Thus Scalia's majority opinion in *Employment Division of Oregon v. Smith* (1990), with its controversial re-characterization of prior Supreme Court precedents concerning free exercise of religion, ultimately expanded religious rights for prisoners by triggering a political and legislative backlash against the decision.

Justice Scalia's ingenuity and selectivity in using precedent to shape constitutional law in the foregoing cases apparently reflected the fact that he has no particular reverence for precedent, especially if he thinks prior cases were wrongly decided. For more than two decades, he forthrightly advocated overturning *Roe v. Wade* (1973) and other precedents with which he disagreed (e.g., *Webster v. Reproductive Health Services* 1989). In one important example in criminal justice, Scalia saw his adamant opposition to established precedent lead to a quick reversal when the Court's composition changed through the retirement of Justice William Brennan and the appointment of Justice David Souter in 1990. Prior to Brennan's departure, a majority of justices opposed the use of Victim Impact Statements at capital sentencing hearings. They perceived a risk that such statements might exacerbate racial and social class discrimination, including the kinds of problems revealed in *McCleskey v. Kemp* (1987) in which prosecutorial and sentencing decisions could place differing values on the lives of victims with white victims' lives valued more highly than those of African American victims. The Court examined the issue and barred the use of such impact statements in 1987 (*Booth v. Maryland*) and 1989 (*South Carolina v. Gathers*). In both cases, Scalia wrote dissenting opinions in which he argued strongly for overturning the Court's precedents. He even indicated that he merely awaited a change in the Court's composition in order to see doctrine move in his preferred direction: "Overrulings of precedent rarely occur without a change in the Court's personnel" (824). Immediately after Brennan's retirement, in *Payne v. Tennessee* (1991), a new majority of justices formed to reverse the recently established precedents from *Booth* and *Gathers* and thereby permit the introduction of victim impact statements.

Unfulfilled Goals

As an especially outspoken and influential member of the Supreme Court, Scalia was credited for his ability to put his theories and ideas into circulation for discussion by scholars and application by judges. His ability to disseminate and promote ideas stemmed not only from his proactive effort to write concurring and dissenting opinions but also from his busy schedule of public speeches at law schools and judges' conferences. The expansion of originalism's familiarity and legitimacy in the eyes of scholars and judges has been attributed to Scalia's effectiveness in promoting this theory of constitutional interpretation (Biskupic 2009). On a smaller scale, Scalia also promoted his ideas about specific legal issues, even in cases in which his ideas could not command majority support.

In several cases, Justice Scalia pushed forward and kept afloat arguments for new directions in constitutional doctrine without seeing his ideas come to fruition during the Rehnquist Court era. Although he did not succeed in influencing these issues directly, his opinions provide ammunition for future justices who may revisit these matters.

For example, Scalia was unable to persuade his Rehnquist Court colleagues to give government greater flexibility for imposing the death penalty. Scalia consistently criticized the Supreme Court's requirements for judges and juries to focus on aggravating and mitigating factors in capital cases in order to make individualized decisions. Indeed, Scalia advocated the constitutionality of mandatory death sentences for murderers, a policy forbidden by the Supreme Court's decision in *Woodson v. North Carolina* (1976). According to Scalia, mandatory death sentences for murder or other crimes historically punished by execution

> cannot possibly violate the Eighth Amendment because it will not be "cruel" (neither absolutely nor for a particular crime) and it will not be "unusual" (nei-

ther in the sense of being a type of penalty that is not traditional nor in the sense of being rarely or "freakishly" imposed). (*Walton v. Arizona* 1990, 671)

Such arguments make justices susceptible to criticism for naively failing to recognize that mandatory death sentences will do nothing to alleviate the problem of discrimination because such sentences are the cumulative product of a series of discretionary and potentially discriminatory decisions (Smith 1990). In Scalia's case, however, he had already demonstrated his lack of concern about the existence of discrimination in the imposition of the death penalty through the memorandum he wrote regarding *McCleskey v. Kemp* (1987). Thus the argument appeared to reflect Scalia's goal of preserving and expanding the application of capital punishment, notwithstanding highly publicized evidence concerning the risks of racial discrimination and mistaken capital sentences for innocent people. Could Scalia's arguments gain majority support in the Roberts Court and subsequent Supreme Court eras? Because constitutional doctrines are affected by changes in the Court's composition as well as by developments in social history, it is difficult to predict whether a future event, such as a major terrorist attack, or other future developments, such as the judicial philosophies of new Supreme Court justices, might shift decisions about capital punishment. However, Scalia laid the groundwork for future justices to draw from his arguments and reasoning if they are inclined to move death penalty jurisprudence in a permissive direction.

In another example, Scalia wrote the majority opinion in *Harmelin v. Michigan* (1991), an Eighth Amendment challenge to Michigan's draconian mandatory sentences for cocaine crimes. Under Michigan law at that time, anyone convicted of possessing 650 or more grams of cocaine was subject to a mandatory sentence of life in prison without possibility of parole. Because Michigan did not have the death penalty, this was the most severe sentence possible in the state's criminal justice system, the same sentence imposed on offenders convicted of multiple counts of first-degree murder. The mandatory sentencing law was alleged to violate the Eighth Amendment's prohibition on cruel and unusual punishments by imposing a punishment disproportionate to the crime when applied to non-violent, first offenders who were given murder-equivalent sentences for possessing specific quantities of cocaine. Justice Scalia wrote the majority opinion that rejected the Eighth Amendment argument and permitted such severe mandatory incarcerative sentences in non-capital cases. However, Scalia went even farther and wrote a section of the opinion that was joined by only Chief Justice Rehnquist, which argued that the Eighth Amendment should not be interpreted to provide any proportionality protection in non-capital cases. Justice Byron White's dissenting opinion sharply criticized the "dangers [that] lurk" in Scalia's argument:

First, he provides no mechanism for addressing a situation such as that proposed in *Rummel* [*v. Estelle* 1980], in which a legislature makes overtime parking a felony punishable by life imprisonment. He concedes that "one can imagine extreme examples"—perhaps such as the one described in *Rummel*— "that no rational person, in no time or place, could accept," but attempts to offer reassurance by claiming that "for the same reason these examples are easy to decide, they are certain never to occur." This is cold comfort indeed, for absent a proportionality guarantee, there would be no basis for deciding such cases should they arise. (*Harmelin v. Michigan* 1991, 1018)

Again, it is difficult to predict whether and how Scalia's effort to eliminate the Eighth Amendment's non-capital proportionality protection might gain support from future Supreme Court justices. As with Scalia's argument in favor of mandatory sentences in capital contexts, he articulated justifications and made them available for use by future justices.

Conclusion

Justice Antonin Scalia was an important figure on the Rehnquist Court. Although Scalia was one of the justices least likely to support individuals' claims in criminal justice cases, his originalist interpretive approach and concern for the text of the Constitution led him to join his liberal colleagues in a variety of specific cases. He demonstrated his ability to have a broad impact on policy issues through judicial opinions that sought to reshape constitutional law. In criminal justice cases, his influence was exceptionally potent in the Supreme Court's decisions affecting prisoners' rights. Scalia had a profound impact on prisoners' rights through his seminal opinions concerning Eighth Amendment conditions-of-confinement litigation (*Wilson v. Seiter*) and access to legal resources (*Lewis v. Casey*). He also affected free exercise of religion (*Employment Division of Oregon v. Smith*), although his major opinion on free exercise triggered a backlash from Congress that led to greater protection for that particular right.

Overall, Scalia advanced his preference for a diminution of constitutional protections for incarcerated offenders, a reduction in case filings in federal courts, and fewer opportunities for judges to intervene into corrections contexts by issuing remedial orders. With respect to the death penalty, Scalia's commitment to the continuation and expansion of capital punishment appeared to outweigh other values, including normally important constitutional values such as equal protection rights against racial discrimination and the detection of erroneous convictions.

Justice Stevens, the Court's most outspoken liberal during the second decade of the Rehnquist Court era and a frequent opponent of Scalia in criminal justice cases, acknowledged Scalia's influential role by saying, "He's made a huge difference, some of it constructive, some of it unfortunate" (Biskupic 2009, 362). As one of the most prolific opinion writers during the Rehnquist Court era, Scalia disseminated his arguments and ideas about a variety of issues. In doing so, he created the possibility that his influence over constitutional interpretation will continue even after he retires. The Roberts Court era saw the addition of a third self-described originalist on the Supreme Court, Justice Samuel Alito (Biskupic 2009). Thus it is possible that Scalia's Rehnquist Court era opinions may continue to have influence in the future, especially if there are future appointments of new justices who share Scalia's philosophy and interpretive approach.

References

Biskupic, Joan. *American Original: The Life and Constitution of Supreme Court Justice Antonin Scalia*. New York: Farrar, Straus & Giroux, 2009.

Brisbin, Richard A., Jr. *Justice Antonin Scalia and the Conservative Revival*. Baltimore, MD: Johns Hopkins University Press, 1997.

Dorin, Dennis D. "Far Right of the Mainstream: Racism, Rights, and Remedies From the Perspective of Justice Antonin Scalia's McCleskey Memorandum." *Mercer Law Review* 45 (1994): 1035-88.

Epstein, Lee, Jeffrey A. Segal, Harold J. Spaeth, and Thomas G. Walker. *The Supreme Court Compendium*, 4th edition. Washington, DC: CQ Press, 2007.

Feeley, Malcolm, and Edward L. Rubin. *Judicial Policy Making and the Modern State*. New York: Cambridge University Press, 1998.

Fliter, John. *Prisoners' Rights: The Supreme Court and Evolving Standards of Decency*. Westport, CT: Greenwood Press, 2001.

Hellerstein, William E. "No Rights for Prisoners." Pp. 71-81 in *The Rehnquist Court: Judicial Activism on the Right*, edited by Herman Schwartz. New York: Hill & Wang, 2002.

Hensley, Thomas R., Christopher E. Smith, and Joyce A. Baugh. *The Changing Supreme Court: Constitutional Rights and Liberties*. St. Paul, MN: West, 1997.

Jeffries, John C., Jr. *Justice Lewis F. Powell, Jr.: A Biography*. New York: Scribner, 1994.

McConnell, Michael W. "Free Exercise Revisionism and the *Smith* Decision." *University of Chicago Law Review* 57 (1990): 1109-53.

Rossum, Ralph. "Text and Tradition: The Originalist Jurisprudence of Antonin Scalia." Pp. 34-69 in *Rehnquist Court: Under the Court Dynamic*, edited by Earl M. Maltz. Lawrence, KS: University Press of Kansas, 2003.

Scalia, Antonin. "The Doctrine of Standing as an Essential Element of Separation of Powers." *Suffolk University Law Review* 17 (1983): 881-99.

———. "Originalism: The Lesser Evil." *Cincinnati Law Review* 57 (1989): 849-65.

———. *A Matter of Interpretation: Federal Courts and the Law*. Princeton, NJ: Princeton University Press, 1997.

———. "Forward." Pp. 43-45 in *Originalism: A Quarter-Century of Debate*, edited by Steven G. Calabresi. Washington, DC: Regnery, 2007.

Scalia, John. "Prisoner Petitions Filed in U.S. District Courts, 2000, with Trends 1980-2000." Pp. 1-8 in *Bureau of Justice Statistics Special Report*, January 2002.

Schultz, David A. and Christopher E. Smith. *The Jurisprudential Vision of Justice Antonin Scalia*. Lanham, MD: Rowman & Littlefield, 1996.

Smith, Christopher E. "The Supreme Court and Ethnicity." *Oregon Law Review* 69 (1990): 797-845.

————. *Justice Antonin Scalia and the Supreme Court's Conservative Moment.* Westport, CT: Praeger, 1993.

————. *The Rehnquist Court and Criminal Punishment.* New York: Garland, 1997.

————. "The Malleability of Constitutional Doctrine and Its Ironic Impact on Prisoners' Rights." *Boston University Public Interest Law Journal* 11 (2001): 73-96.

————. "Justice Sandra Day O'Connor and Corrections Law." *Hamline Law Review* 32 (2009): 477-97.

Smith, Christopher E. and Madhavi McCall. "Justice Scalia's Influence on Criminal Justice." *University of Toledo Law Review* 34 (2003): 535-57.

Taylor, Stuart. "Scalia Proposes Major Overhaul of U.S. Courts." *New York Times*, February 16, 1987, 1A.

Yarbrough, Tinsley E. *The Rehnquist Court and the Constitution.* New York: Oxford University Press, 2000.

Cases Cited

Apprendi v. New Jersey, 530 U.S. 466 (2000)
Atkins v. Virginia, 536 U.S. 304 (2002)
Bell v. Wolfish, 441 U.S. 520 (1979)
Booth v. Maryland, 482 U.S. 496 (1987)
Bounds v. Smith, 430 U.S. 817 (1977)
City of Boerne v. Flores, 521 U.S. 507 (1997)
County of Riverside v. McLaughlin, 500 U.S. 44 (1991)
Coy v. Iowa, 487 U.S. 1012 (1988)
Cruz v. New York, 481 U.S. 186 (1987)
Cutter v. Wilkinson, 544 U.S. 709 (2005)
Employment Division, Department of Human Resources of Oregon v. Smith, 494 U.S. 872 (1990)
Estelle v. Gamble, 429 U.S. 97 (1976)
Furman v. Georgia, 408 U.S. 238 (1972)
Hamdi v. Rumsfeld, 542 U.S. 507 (2004)
Harmelin v. Michigan, 501 U.S. 957 (1991)
Helling v. McKinney, 509 U.S. 25 (1993)
Herrera v. Collins, 506 U.S. 390 (1993)
Holland v. Illinois, 493 U.S. 474 (1990)
Hudson v. McMillian, 503 U.S. 1 (1992)
Hutto v. Finney, 437 U.S. 678 (1978)
In re Davis, 557 U.S. ____ (2009)
Kyllo v. United States, 533 U.S. 27 (2001)
Lewis v. Casey, 518 U.S. 343 (1996)
Maryland v. Craig, 497 U.S. 836 (1990)
McCleskey v. Kemp, 481 U.S. 279 (1987)
National Treasury Employees Union v. Von Raab, 489 U.S. 656 (1989)
O'Lone v. Estate of Shabazz, 482 U.S. 342 (1987)
Oregon v. Ice, 555 U.S. 160 (2009)
Overton v. Bazzetta, 539 U.S. 126 (2003)
Payne v. Tennessee, 501 U.S. 808 (1991)
Pennsylvania Department of Corrections v. Yeskey, 524 U.S. 206 (1998)
Printz v. United States, 521 U.S. 898 (1997)

Rhodes v. Chapman, 452 U.S. 337 (1981)
Roe v. Wade, 410 U.S. 113 (1973)
Rummel v. Estelle, 445 U.S. 263 (1980)
South Carolina v. Gathers, 490 U.S. 805 (1989)
Trop v. Dulles, 356 U.S. 86 (1958)
Turner v. Safley, 482 U.S. 78 (1987)
United States v. Booker, 543 U.S. 220 (2005)
United States v. Lopez, 514 U.S. 549 (1995)
United States v. Morrison, 529 U.S. 598 (2000)
Walton v. Arizona, 497 U.S. 639 (1990)
Webster v. Reproductive Health Services, 492 U.S. 490 (1989)
Whitley v. Albers, 475 U.S. 312 (1986)
Wilson v. Seiter, 501 U.S. 294 (1991)
Woodson v. North Carolina, 428 U.S. 280 (1976)

Chapter 9
Anthony Kennedy:
Conservatism & Independence

John D. Burrow

Anthony Kennedy began his career as a justice on the U.S. Supreme Court at the dawn of the Rehnquist Court era. As a result, he was a key member of the Court who participated in decisions shaping criminal justice throughout the era of Chief Justice Rehnquist's leadership. Kennedy was educated at Stanford University and Harvard Law School. Working in Sacramento, California, Kennedy practiced law, lobbied the state legislature, and taught constitutional law at the University of the Pacific before being appointed to serve on the U.S. Court of Appeals for the Ninth Circuit in 1975. Justice Kennedy's tenure on the Supreme Court began in 1988 when the U.S. Senate confirmed him after being appointed by President Ronald Reagan. President Reagan selected Kennedy after enduring political controversies in two prior unsuccessful nominations to fill the same vacancy. The U.S. Senate rejected Judge Robert Bork's nomination, and Judge Douglas Ginsburg was forced to withdraw after revelations about his use of marijuana. Reagan did not want to face the embarrassment of a third unsuccessful nomination so he selected Kennedy as a respected, noncontroversial nominee whom he believed shared his conservative principles.

While Kennedy's early voting record suggested that he would adopt a conservative judicial approach, his later opinions demonstrated a liberal perspective on certain issues, including specific criminal justice issues (Smith 1992). Because Kennedy's voting record in constitutional rights cases tended to be less conservative than those of his fellow Reagan and Bush appointees, he and Justice Sandra O'Connor were often characterized as the "swing" or "middle" justices who periodically parted company with their more consistently conservative colleagues, Chief Justice William Rehnquist and Justices Antonin Scalia and Clarence Thomas (Schmidt and Yalof 2004). These departures created opportunities for the Court's more liberal justices to gain a needed fifth vote for some decisions endorsing or expanding the recognition of constitutional rights for individuals in the criminal justice process. Thus one source of Kennedy's influence over criminal justice in Rehnquist Court era criminal justice cases came through his votes that helped to determine case outcomes. The other source of influence came through his written judicial opinions. It should be noted, however, that the infrequency of opportunities to author majority opinions on criminal justice limits the direct influence that Kennedy had in shaping criminal justice policy nationwide (Smith 2006). In this chapter, the primary focus will be on Kennedy's judicial opinions concerning specific criminal justice topics that illuminate both his judicial perspective and his influence in shaping law and policy. He played an important role in a number of cases that have profoundly influenced criminal justice.

For many years, judicial scholars have documented the centrality of Supreme Court justices' judicial philosophies in shaping law and policy (Edelman 1984; Maltz 1999; Whittington 1999). While a number of justices are guided in their decision making by their professed belief in originalism or by a rights-protecting, flexible approach to constitutional interpretation, certain justices cannot be easily classified (Bibas 2005; Kersch 2006). Justice Kennedy was an exceptionally important member of the Rehnquist Court, as he provided the pivotal vote on a number of important cases, yet scholars have been challenged to analyze and classify the constitutional philosophy that guided his decision making. Two book-length analyses of Justice Kennedy's approach to judicial philosophy both focused on Kennedy's emphasis on his sense of "liberty" under the Constitution (Colucci 2009; Knowles 2009). One author characterized Kennedy as "modestly libertarian" (Knowles 2009, 196) and another author wrote of Kennedy's "moral conception of liberty" and "individualistic conception of human dignity" (Colucci 2009, 170). Yet, in-depth analyses of Justice Kennedy never concentrated on his votes and opinions affecting criminal justice, except insofar as his opinions on First Amendment and privacy issues intersected with criminal laws (Maltz 2003). Instead, analyses of Kennedy's judicial philosophy rested on his most prominent opinions concerning freedom of speech, racial discrimination, abortion, and laws affecting gays and lesbians. In the realm of criminal justice, for which Kennedy did not receive majority opinion-writing assignments for many prominent cases, Kennedy's judicial philosophy remained more elusive.

Decisional Orientation

Justice Kennedy was appointed by President Reagan to fill a vacancy on the Court that was created with the retirement of Justice Lewis Powell. Because Powell was perceived to be the centrist justice on a Court equally divided between judicial conservatives and liberals, many observers expected the appointment of Justice Kennedy to strengthen the conservative wing of the Court. This expectation was borne out immediately in his early years on the Court when Kennedy voted with the majority in many cases that expanded the authority of criminal justice officials and limited the scope of individuals' constitutional rights. During the Rehnquist Court era, Kennedy supported the government in 70.5 percent of cases classified as "Criminal Procedure" cases in the Supreme Court Judicial Database, a percentage that made him slightly more liberal than four other justices (Rehnquist, Thomas, Scalia, O'Connor) but significantly more conservative than the other Rehnquist Court justices (Epstein, Segal, Spaeth, and Walker 2007, 535). For example, Kennedy voted with a six-member majority in *Arizona v. Youngblood* (1988) that denied a due process claim when police failed to preserve physical evidence that, if properly saved and tested, may have exonerated a defendant who was convicted of rape. Some forensic scientists and defense attorneys consider *Youngblood* to be one of the most harmful criminal justice decisions ever made by the Supreme Court because it has been applied to excuse police officers' and prosecutors' intentional destruction of evidence that might have proven an offender's innocence (Greene and Moffeit 2007).

In the criminal justice cases listed by the *New York Times* as the "major" cases of the Rehnquist Court era (Epstein et. al 2007), Kennedy supported the government in most of them, including: *Penry v. Lynaugh* (1989) and *Stanford v. Kentucky* (1989) (capital punishment); *Michigan Department of State Police v. Sitz* (1990) (police use of suspicionless sobriety stops at highway checkpoints); *Arizona v. Fulminante* (1991) (confession not coerced); *Herrera v. Collins* (1993) (consideration of newly-discovered evidence); *United States v. Ursery* (1996) (no double jeopardy in civil property forfeiture related to drug crime); *United States v. Bajakajian* (1998) (excessive fines); *Kyllo v. United States* (2001) (warrantless examination of home with thermal imaging device); and *Ewing v. California* (2003) ("three strikes" mandatory life sentences).

If one examines the same *New York Times* list of "major" cases to determine when Kennedy supported the claims of individuals for issues related to criminal justice, one can see evidence of scholars' conclusions that Kennedy emphasizes his conception of liberty for certain issues (Colucci 2009; Knowles 2009). For example, in *City of Chicago v. Morales* (1999), Justice Kennedy joined the majority in striking down Chicago's Gang Congregation Ordinance because, in Kennedy's view, its overly broad and vague language could subject innocent citizens to arrest for merely going about their daily lives and conversing with other citizens on the sidewalk. One particularly notable pattern is evident in these cases as Justice Kennedy typically supported individuals' claims for the cases in which First Amendment free speech issues intersected with criminal laws. In *Texas v. Johnson* (1989) and *United States v. Eichman* (1990), Kennedy voted to protect symbolic speech against criminal laws that sought to punish those who burned the American flag as a means of political expression. In his concurring opinion in *Texas v. Johnson* (1989, 420-21), Justice Kennedy penned one of the most famous lines from any of his judicial opinions: "The hard fact is that sometimes we must make decisions we do not like. We make them because they are right, right in the sense that the law and the Constitution, as we see them, compel the result." Similarly, in *Simon & Schuster v. New York State Crime Victims Board* (1991) and *R.A.V. v. City of St. Paul* (1992), Justice

Kennedy joined large Court majorities that voted to invalidate, respectively, a law limiting criminal offenders' ability to profit from writing books and a local bias-crime ordinance that criminalized the use of expressive symbols. Justice Kennedy joined two of the Court's most liberal justices as a dissenting minority against the majority's endorsement of Virginia's law criminalizing cross burning conducted with intent to intimidate (*Virginia v. Black* 2003).

As indicated by the foregoing examples, Justice Kennedy's support for the government in criminal justice-related cases did not appear to be ideological or reflexive. While he tended to support police and prosecutors in cases concerning the Fourth and Fifth Amendments and prisoners' rights, for several other issues he made specific determinations that could lead him to support the claims of individuals, especially for matters in which he identified intrusions on his conception of liberty.

Explaining His Views

During Kennedy's initial terms on the Rehnquist Court, his jurisprudential voice was obscured because he was assigned a limited share of the Court's majority opinions. His lack of opinion authorship was attributable to the fact that the chief justice assigns majority opinions when voting as a member of the majority (Brenner and Spaeth 1988). Chief justices, including Rehnquist, typically try to distribute opinion assignments relatively evenly among the justices. However, this does not mean that each issue area, such as criminal justice, is evenly distributed because chief justices may pursue various organizational and policy goals in determining who shall write for the majority (Maltzman and Wahlbeck 2004). As with other newcomers to the Court, Kennedy did not immediately receive enough majority opinion assignments to create opportunities to use majority opinions as the means to reveal his approach to deciding criminal justice issues. Eventually, he looked for ways to explain his positions through concurring opinions and, less frequently, dissenting opinions. He did not stand out as a prolific author of dissenting opinions in criminal justice cases because he so often voted with the majority. However, his proactive effort to explain himself in these concurring and dissenting opinions helped to reveal his perspective on specific issues.

For example, in *Harmelin v. Michigan* (1991), the Court ruled that the Eighth Amendment did not prohibit mandatory life terms of imprisonment for non-violent, first-time drug offenders. The case concerned a Michigan law that imposed a mandatory sentence of life without parole for offenders convicted of carrying a specific quantity of cocaine. Michigan's mandatory sentence was far more severe than mandatory drug sentences for similar offenses in other states. Indeed, because Michigan is a not a capital punishment state, its mandatory cocaine sentence treated these offenders in an identical fashion to offenders convicted of first-degree murder. Justice Kennedy agreed that there was no constitutional violation in Michigan's imposition of its severe mandatory sentence on a first-time offender. However, he did not endorse the argument put forward by Justice Scalia and Chief Justice Rehnquist that the Eighth Amendment contains no proportionality requirement in non-capital cases. Instead, Kennedy wrote a concurring opinion on behalf of himself and Justices O'Connor and Souter that articulated a very limited proportionality principle applicable to Eighth Amendment excessive-sentence claims in non-capital cases. In Kennedy's approach, proportionality limitations existed for non-capital sentences, but few sentences would fail to pass constitutional muster.

Justice Kennedy's concurring opinion recognized that the exact dimensions of the proportionality principle were uncertain, in part, because it was so rarely used. He concluded that there were four general principles that should guide the Court's proportionality review: (1) the determination of criminal sentences is the province of state legislatures; (2) the penological or philosophical justification for a punishment or sentence is variable (varies from state to state) rather than fixed (uniform); (3) principles of federalism empower the states to mete out sentences or punishments that vary from offender to offender; and (4) a proportionality review of sentences should be governed by objective standards (*Harmelin v. Michigan* 1991, 998-1000). These guiding principles espoused by Kennedy demonstrated his conservative orientation toward generally deferring to states' authority to control the definition of criminal sentences within their own jurisdictions (Gibbs 1992).

Justice Kennedy expressed his views in other cases about sentencing issues. In *Ring v. Arizona* (2002), Kennedy authored a concurrence in which he wrote that principles of federalism should be respected when it comes to criminal justice because, in his view, it is at the state level where sentencing reform is most likely to occur and it is the states that are best equipped to address issues of sentencing disparity. *Ring* concerned the distribution of authority between judges and juries in making determinations about whether to impose the death penalty.

Justice Kennedy also asserted that sentencing guidelines do not completely divest judges of discretion. These ideas would coalesce in his dissenting opinion in *Blakely v. Washington* (2004), a case in which he indicated that the Court had misunderstood the intimate connection between federalism and the demands of criminal justice. In *Blakely*, a narrow five-member majority invalidated state sentencing guidelines that permitted judges to increase sentences based on factual determinations, such as the purported cruelty of the defendant's actions, that were not proven and found to be true by the jury during trial. Justice Scalia, in writing for the majority, claimed that the history of the Sixth Amendment counseled against permitting judges to usurp the role of the jury. Thus, Scalia believed that the sentencing judge exceeded his authority in imposing a sentence beyond the statutory maximum.

Justice Kennedy's dissent, on the other hand, outlined a number of troubling issues with the majority's reasoning. Foremost among these was the concern that the majority was short-circuiting the ongoing dialogue between the federal courts and the states. In Kennedy's view, this decision would have the effect of

shutting down experimentation and innovation at the state level. Though he recognized that mistakes would occur along the way, even mistakes of constitutional proportions, states should nevertheless be given the opportunity to resolve,
remedy, and modify criminal justice issues as they arise. To Kennedy, the net
effect of the Court's ruling would be that many state-level sentencing reforms
would be deemed unconstitutional because that they would run afoul of the
Court's truncated view of the Sixth Amendment. Moreover, Kennedy agreed
with many of the concerns raised by Justice O'Connor in her dissent, particularly related to the monopolization of sentencing authority by the courts rather than
centering that authority in the legislatures where it historically resided. The
sense of foreboding contained in the dissenting opinions of Justices Kennedy
and O'Connor was echoed in the writings of many legal experts who commented on the potential destructiveness of the majority's decision to sentencing
guidelines at both the federal and state levels (e.g., Bowman 2004).

In *Kentucky v. Thompson* (1989), Justice Kennedy voted with the six-
member majority in declining to recognize a right for prisoners to receive visitors under the Due Process Clause or the state's regulations governing prison
visitations. However, Kennedy provided an indication that his views could differ
from those of other conservative justices because he took the opportunity to
make clear that he had not rejected the possibility that a right to visitation could
be recognized in a future case that arose under different circumstances. In this
case, the visitors who were barred from the prison were suspected of bringing
contraband or were in the company of people previously caught bringing contraband into the visiting room. Kennedy's concurring opinion implied that he
would be open to considering a challenge to a prison's practices if that prison
banned visitors generally or otherwise imposed visitation restrictions in circumstances unconnected with rules violations by the excluded visitors. In the later
case of *Overton v. Bazzetta* (2003), Kennedy maintained this position when he
wrote the majority opinion on behalf of a unanimous Court that rejected a rights-
violation claim when prisoners were denied visitors for violating prison rules
related to drug tests. Consistent with his earlier concurring opinion, Kennedy
wrote, "If the withdrawal of all visitation privileges were permanent or for a
much longer period, or if it were applied in an arbitrary manner to a particular
inmate, the case would present different considerations" (137). By contrast, Justice Thomas's concurring opinion in *Overton*, joined by Justice Scalia, indicated
that permanent or arbitrary removal of visiting privileges would not necessarily
violate any right.

Shaping the Law

Although Justice Kennedy was not generally regarded as a primary author of
majority opinions in criminal justice cases during the Rehnquist Court era, he
received multiple opinion assignments that enabled him to shape the law con-

cerning specific important issue areas. Moreover, with respect to some of these issues, he asserted his deep interest and developing expertise through additional concurring and dissenting opinions in other cases.

Much like Kennedy's attention to First Amendment free speech issues in cases that intersected with criminal laws, his most monumental majority opinion came in a case that is taught in law schools as concerning the issues of privacy and equality. The decision's greatest importance does not stem from its effect on criminal justice cases. In fact, it affected very few of such cases. Instead, its importance and renown came because it involved a major shift in Supreme Court doctrine concerning a highly-debated issue that divided large segments of the American public. In *Lawrence v. Texas* (2003), two men were arrested in a private home for engaging in noncommercial, consensual sexual conduct that violated the Texas criminal statute aimed at punishing people of the same sex for engaging in intimate acts forbidden by law. The prevailing precedent on the issue at the time of the case was *Bowers v. Hardwick* (1986) in which Justice White's majority opinion upheld Georgia's criminal statute and declared that people do not have a constitutional right to engage in sodomy. By contrast, the dissenters in *Bowers* argued that the real issue was about the right to privacy for adults to make their own choices about consensual sexual conduct in their own homes. Justice Kennedy, who had not been on the Court at the time of the *Bowers* case, wrote a majority opinion on behalf of himself and four other justices that focused on liberty interests and privacy rights under the Due Process Clause. Justice O'Connor wrote a separate concurring opinion on equal protection grounds. Justice Kennedy's majority opinion overruled *Bowers* and declared that

> [t]he petitioners are entitled to respect for their private lives. The State cannot demean their existence or control their destiny by making their private sexual conduct a crime. Their right to liberty under the Due Process Clause gives them the full right to engage in their conduct without intervention of the government. (*Lawrence v. Texas* 2003, 578)

Previously, Justice Kennedy had written a majority opinion striking down on equal protection grounds an amendment to Colorado's state constitution that purported to bar any antidiscrimination laws and ordinances in that state which would protect gays and lesbians. Thus when Kennedy received the majority opinion assignment from Justice Stevens in *Lawrence*, it may have been due to his prior experience in researching and writing about issues concerning the rights of gays and lesbians. The assignment may also have been motivated by a desire to increase the acceptance and legitimacy of the controversial decision by having a generally conservative justice appointed by revered President Ronald Reagan write on the behalf of the Court rather than one of the justices who was regularly vilified by political conservatives for consistently espousing liberal constitutional doctrines.

The majority opinion assignment in *Lawrence* gave Kennedy the opportunity to write in lofty terms about the importance of individual liberty, an issue of great importance to him (Knowles 2009). For example, he wrote in *Lawrence* that "Liberty protects the person from unwarranted governmental intrusions into a dwelling or other private place. . . . Liberty presumes an autonomy of self that includes freedom of thought, belief, expression, and certain intimate conduct" (*Lawrence v. Texas* 2003, 562). Despite his generally conservative voting record, this majority opinion cemented Kennedy's reputation in the eyes of political conservatives as an undependable conservative who was President Reagan's "mistake." The opinion not only narrowed the scope of permissible criminal statutes, it also reinforced a recognition of the significant issues for which Kennedy's independent viewpoints were substantially different from those of the Rehnquist Court's most conservative justices.

Justice Kennedy distinguished himself as especially interested and influential in issues concerning juries in criminal cases. Initially, Justice Kennedy relied on concurring opinions to distinguish himself from his most conservative colleagues in examining issues about fair practices in jury trials. For example, early in his Supreme Court career, Justice Kennedy wrote a concurring opinion in support of the liberal justices' ruling against limitations placed by a state on jurors' consideration of mitigating evidence in capital cases (*McKoy v. North Carolina* 1990). During that same term, Kennedy endorsed a Scalia-authored majority opinion rejecting a Sixth Amendment fair cross-section claim from a white defendant who objected to prosecutors' actions in using peremptory challenges to exclude African Americans from his jury (*Holland v. Illinois* 1990). However, Justice Kennedy wrote a concurring opinion to state forthrightly that "I write this separate concurrence to note that our disposition of the Sixth Amendment claim does not alter what I think to be the established rule, which is that exclusion of a juror on the basis of race, whether or not by use of a peremptory challenge, is a violation of the *juror's* constitutional rights" (emphasis supplied) (488). *Holland* was a 5-4 decision so Kennedy's concurrence, in effect, explicitly encouraged attorneys to raise the same kind of case, but recast it in the form of an alleged Fourteenth Amendment equal protection violation of an African American juror's right to be free from having racial discrimination used to block her participation in the jury process. Because the encouragement came from Kennedy, one of the justices in the five-member, pro-government majority, attorneys could feel optimistic that an equal protection claim might lead Kennedy to switch sides and thereby produce a new five-member majority deciding in favor of the rights-claimant.

The following term, the Supreme Court accepted a case to address the issue that Kennedy had effectively invited attorneys to present. In *Powers v. Ohio* (1991), a white murder defendant objected when the prosecutor used peremptory challenges to exclude African Americans from the jury. The Supreme Court decided in favor of the defendant by concluding that defendants of a different race can challenge race-based juror exclusions. Because Chief Justice Rehnquist joined Justice Scalia's dissenting opinion that argued for rejecting the defendant's claim, the senior justice in the majority, Justice White, was able to select which justice in the majority would write the opinion on behalf of the Court. Justice White chose Justice Kennedy for that task. Justice Kennedy wrote,

> We hold that the Equal Protection Clause prohibits a prosecutor from using the State's peremptory challenges to exclude otherwise qualified and unbiased individuals from the petit jury solely by reason of their race, a practice that forecloses a significant opportunity to participate in civil life. (*Powers* 1991, 409)

Kennedy further explained that racial discrimination by a prosecutor in jury selection "condones violations of the United States Constitution within the very institution entrusted with its enforcement" and it also "invites cynicism respecting the jury's neutrality and its obligation to adhere to the law" (412). Justice Kennedy's majority opinion took a strong stand against interfering with individuals' opportunities to participate as citizens in governmental processes. He also demonstrated his concern for elements in the judicial process that might detract from the image and legitimacy of the courts.

Justice Kennedy's opinion rejected Scalia's claim that such racial discrimination was permissible because it was not necessarily aimed at a single racial group, since in different cases and with different prosecutors other racial groups may be subject to exclusion. As noted by Colucci (2009, 120), Kennedy's opinion in this and other jury cases demonstrated that he was different from justices such as Scalia, Rehnquist, and, sometimes, O'Connor, who "employ the rhetoric of the color-blind Constitution" which could, in jury selection cases, lead to acceptance of discrimination as long as it *might* be applied against any racial group. Instead, Kennedy thought that discriminatory classifications based on race "must be exterminated from the law" (120).

During that same term, Justice White again assigned to Kennedy the responsibility for writing the majority opinion in another case about jury discrimination. *Edmonson v. Leesville Concrete* (1991) raised the issue of whether race-based peremptory challenges may be used by attorneys in civil cases. *Edmonson* was arguably an important criminal justice-related case, despite its focus on civil litigation, because civil lawsuits have such an important impact on the criminal justice system. In particular, civil lawsuits against police officers, corrections officers, and other criminal justice officials serve as primary drivers of policy change with respect to criminal justice policies and practices. Police and corrections agencies change their training, policies, and procedures in response to being sued or to their fears of civil liability from the law-violating actions of their officers (Smith and Hurst 1997). Thus jury selection rules for civil cases have important impacts on the criminal justice system. Kennedy's majority opinion again took a strong stand against racial discrimination in the judicial process:

> [T]he injury caused by the discrimination is made more severe because the government permits it to occur within the courthouse itself. Few places are a more real expression of constitutional authority of the government than the

courtroom, where the law itself unfolds. . . . Race discrimination within the
courtroom raises serious questions as to the fairness of the proceedings conducted there. Racial bias mars the integrity of the judicial system, and prevents
the idea of democratic government from becoming a reality. (*Edmonson v.
Leesville Concrete* 1991, 628)

In *Edmonson*, Kennedy's conclusions on the behalf of the majority required him
to take an expansive view of "state action" under the Fourteenth Amendment.
Because the Equal Protection Clause only applies to state action, the concept of
state action was necessarily interpreted through a flexible approach in order to
attribute to private attorneys and their decisions the quality of state action that is
the target and textual focus of the Fourteenth Amendment's limitations. Justice
Kennedy's conclusion about this issue faced vigorous disagreement from Chief
Justice Rehnquist and Justices Scalia and O'Connor, conservative colleagues
with whom Kennedy agreed in most other criminal justice-related cases during
the Rehnquist Court era. Thus this issue of discrimination in jury selection
served to differentiate Kennedy from his colleagues who had similar rates of
supporting the government in cases concerning justice system issues.

Justice Kennedy subsequently wrote another concurring opinion on this
issue when he supported the Court's decision in *J.E.B. v. Alabama ex rel. T.B.*
(1994), the case in which the justices barred the use of sex discrimination in jury
selection. Kennedy later wrote an additional majority opinion that articulated the
reasons for extending the Court's reasoning to cases in which a white defendant
objected to racial considerations in the selection of a grand jury member (*Campbell v. Louisiana* 1998). Throughout these cases, Kennedy expressed both his
opposition to tolerating racial discrimination and his protective concerns for the
image and integrity of court processes. These law-shaping opinions can also be
seen as connected to Kennedy's concern for the preservation of his conception
of liberty and human dignity. As Colucci (2009, 117-18) has observed, Kennedy
emphasized the "profound personal humiliation" in a public setting suffered by
an excluded potential juror who is denied the opportunity to participate as a citizen in important civic processes.

The foregoing examples do not demonstrate that Justice Kennedy's opinions about jury issues necessarily favored claims of individuals. For example,
in *Tuilaepa v. California* (1994), Justice Kennedy's majority opinion for the
Rehnquist Court concluded that a "common sense" approach is often necessary
when juries are asked to interpret the meaning of words describing eligibility
requirements for the death penalty. At issue in this case was whether the various
special circumstances that could justify the death penalty described in a state
capital punishment statute were too vague in that they were insufficiently defined and too difficult for jurors to apply. The Court rejected the defendant's
claim that the California statute violated the Eighth Amendment prohibition on
cruel and unusual punishments. In Kennedy's view, however, one cannot assure
mathematical precision in crafting selection and eligibility requirements for the
death penalty. Thus it was permissible to bring the "common sense" judgments

of the jury to bear on these issues as it allows them to exercise the discretion that is necessary to individualize sentences in capital cases. Similarly, in *Johnson v. Texas* (1993), Kennedy rejected an Eighth Amendment challenge and wrote the majority opinion approving procedures in Texas for instructing juries on the consideration of aggravating and mitigating factors in death penalty cases.

Justice Kennedy also had the opportunity to shape the law with respect to mental capacity issues in criminal justice, another topic of apparent interest to him. He spoke for the Court in *Washington v. Harper* (1990), a case that addressed whether prisoners possessed the right to refuse the administration of antipsychotic drugs. Justice Kennedy's majority opinion held that due process rights are not violated when antipsychotic drugs are forcibly administered to prisoners, provided that two conditions are met: first, they are mentally disabled and second, they are a danger to themselves or others. In addition, Justice Kennedy found that the requirements of due process are met whenever the prisoners receive notice, are provided with the opportunity to be heard, and have the opportunity to present evidence on their behalf including calling witnesses. Central to Justice Kennedy's analysis was the state's interest in maintaining the safety of inmates and the security of correctional facilities. In balancing these interests against those of prisoners and their resistance to taking antipsychotic medications, he found that the state's interest in prison safety and security must prevail. To Kennedy, the uniqueness of the prison environment made it necessary for prisons to have at their disposal methods to address and control the continuum of problems posed by traditional prisoners and other special populations:

> There are few cases in which the state's interest in combating the danger posed by a person to both himself and others is greater than in a prison environment, which, by definition, is made up of persons with a demonstrated proclivity for antisocial, criminal, and often violent conduct. (225)

As a result, the rights of prisoners, including certain liberty interests, such as the desire to remain medication-free, must give way to the interests of the state in maintaining a threat-free, safe environment for prison staff and the prisoners themselves.

In 1992, Justice Kennedy revisited the issue of state powers over the minds and bodies of troubled individuals in the custody of criminal justice officials by writing a concurring opinion in *Riggins v. Nevada*. The case concerned a criminal defendant who was forcibly medicated to control his behavior during trial. Justice Kennedy argued that there was a clear distinction between rendering prisoners harmless to maintain the safety and security of an institution and the state's desire to render defendants competent to stand trial. Kennedy stated that the state bears the burden of making "an extraordinary showing" that the forcible use of such medications is essential (138). Justice Kennedy seemed most concerned about the consequences, both long- and short-term, associated with the use of these antipsychotic medications. In particular, he was sensitive to the issue of how the medications may affect the defendant's ability to interact with the defense attorney and the image of the defendant in the eyes of the jury, especially if the defendant was experiencing visible side effects from medications: "The side effects of antipsychotic drugs can hamper the attorney-client relation, preventing effective communication and rendering the defendant less able or willing to take part in his defense. The state interferes with this relation when it administers a drug to dull cognition" (144).

Although Kennedy was concerned about the imposition of psychiatric medications upon defendants at trial, he joined the conservatives in imposing burdens of proof upon those who claimed to lack sufficient mental competence to face criminal charges. In *Medina v. California* (1992), Justice Kennedy wrote the majority opinion that said a state could require a defendant to prove his incompetence by a preponderance of evidence. By contrast, Justices Blackmun and Stevens argued in dissent that the right to due process requires that the state bear the burden of proving the defendant's competence to stand trial.

Justice Kennedy also wrote a concurring opinion in *Kansas v. Hendricks* (1997), the case in which the Court held that the post-imprisonment civil commitment of dangerous sex offenders did not violate the Constitution. In the case, an offender with a long record of multiple sex offenses served his entire prison sentence and then was immediately transferred to a high-security medical facility for indefinite detention and treatment. His post-imprisonment transfer was conducted under the authority of a statute enacted after he had committed his crimes and while he was serving his prison sentence. According to the majority opinion by Justice Thomas, the potentially indefinite duration of confinement did not transform this civil proceeding into punishment because psychiatric detainees are allowed to petition for release every year, and the state must prove beyond a reasonable doubt that they remain a danger to the public. Thus the involuntary detention and treatment of the ex-offender did not violate the constitutional protections against either double jeopardy or ex post facto laws.

Despite his support for the case outcome in favor of the state, Justice Kennedy believed that there was an inherent danger in using civil commitment procedures in this manner. Foremost among his concerns was the real possibility that defendants would be committed for life despite the uncertainty and unsettled state of scientific and medical knowledge about the psychological problems affecting sex offenders. However, his deeper reservations concerned who should make these decisions. Justice Kennedy seemed to allude to the fact that these civil commitment proceedings may be nothing more than a pretext for further post-imprisonment punishment. Justice Kennedy also expressed concern that courts may be unwilling to second-guess and undo the harms that were generated by these civil commitment proceedings.

The concerns of Justice Kennedy have been echoed by a number of legal commentators who have reiterated the possibility that legislatures will overreach in their zeal to protect the public from the menace of sex offenders (Pollock 1998). Commentators have repeatedly expressed concerns about the pretextual nature of these civil commitment schemes (Gillespie 1998). An especially dire concern stems from the likelihood that states may not actually provide treatment to these offenders (Dorsett 1998; Zonana 1997). Justice Kennedy warned that scientific and medical knowledge might not be advanced enough to develop treatment regimens for sex offenders that would prove to be effective over long periods of time. Indeed, his concerns have been substantiated by, for example, studies showing that assessment instruments that are used to make commitment decisions may not be reliable indicators of future dangerousness (Levenson 2004). However, this concern was lost on the majority of justices who advanced the position that treatment was, at best, a concern of secondary importance when compared to protecting the public from these presumptively dangerous offenders.

It should be noted that the reservations expressed by Justice Kennedy in *Kansas v. Hendricks* (1997) did not necessarily make him a strong advocate for skepticism about states' authority to detain outside of criminal sentences those individuals whose behavior and self-control were demonstrably questionable. Justice Kennedy dissented against the Supreme Court's decision in *Foucha v. Louisiana* (1992), in which the Court said that the state had not adequately justified the continued detention of an insanity acquittee who was no longer insane. In that case, Kennedy accused the majority of confusing civil commitment standards with the criminal insanity defense, undervaluing the procedural protections of the criminal process and giving insufficient attention to the individual's risk of dangerousness. Thus Kennedy concluded in that context that the state possessed "the constitutional authority to incarcerate petitioner for the protection of society" (102).

Justice Kennedy's most controversial majority opinion that included consideration of mental capacity came at the end of Rehnquist Court era. In *Roper v. Simmons* (2005), Justice Stevens, the senior justice in the majority, assigned to Kennedy the responsibility for writing the opinion on behalf of the five-member majority. The Court ruled that the imposition of death sentences on juvenile offenders violated the Eighth Amendment's prohibition on cruel and unusual punishments.

When the justices had previously addressed the issue early in Kennedy's career on the Rehnquist Court in *Stanford v. Kentucky* (1989), he had joined Justice Scalia's majority opinion that found no constitutional violation in imposing death sentences for capital crimes committed by sixteen- and seventeen-year-old offenders. The majority opinion acknowledged that most justices evaluate Eighth Amendment violations according to contemporary conceptions of "evolving standards of decency," as guided by the precedent in *Trop v. Dulles* (1958). However, Scalia argued that there was no clear national consensus about whether or not this punishment should be imposed on older teens. Scalia argued for individualized assessments of culpability and harm; such assessments may include consideration of age, maturity, and rehabilitative potential. Despite Kennedy's acceptance of these views in 1989, his position changed sixteen years later. In *Roper v. Simmons* (2005), Justice Kennedy's majority opinion was guided by a reassessment of whether a national consensus had formed which would prohibit the imposition of this punishment on juvenile offenders. Recognizing that there was a trend among the states, albeit at a slow pace, to make the death penalty inapplicable to juveniles, he found that there was significant change occurring that warranted a reconsideration of the Court's prior precedent. He concluded that there was a consistent movement at the state legislative level to prohibit the application of the death penalty to juveniles and there was no evidence that the opposite trend was occurring in any states. The implication, as he viewed it, was that the states did not view this type of punishment as appropriate for juveniles.

In addition, Justice Kennedy brought forward the issue of mental capacity with respect to juveniles and cited a variety of scholarly studies on the subject. He wanted to convey the point that historically the death penalty has always been reserved for the "worst of the worst" among criminal offenders. Such a label, as he saw it, could not apply to juveniles because not only are they less culpable than their adult counterparts, they are not even "fully formed." Thus they should not be considered miniature adults solely for the sake of punishment. Rather than summarize this mental capacity issue as a single argument, Kennedy put so much emphasis on its importance that he subdivided it into separate rationales in support of his conclusion favoring abolition. He cited psychological and sociological studies to support each of the following points:

> Three general differences between juveniles under 18 and adults demonstrate that juvenile offenders cannot with reliability be classified among the worst offenders. First, as any parent knows and as scientific and sociological studies respondent and his *amici* cite tend to confirm, "[a] lack of maturity and an underdeveloped sense of responsibility are found in youth more often than in adults. . . . These qualities often result in impetuous and ill-considered actions and decisions" . . . . The second area of difference is that juveniles are more vulnerable or susceptible to negative influences and outside pressures, including peer pressure . . . . This is explained in part by the prevailing circumstance that juveniles have less control, or less experience with control, over their own environment . . . . The third broad difference is that the character of a juvenile is not as well formed as that of an adult. The personality traits of juveniles are more transitory, less fixed. (*Roper v. Simmons* 2005, 569-70)

Justice Kennedy used these rationales to assert his conclusions about the "diminished culpability of juveniles" and how these mental capacity issues undercut deterrence purposes underlying capital punishment statutes (*Roper v. Simmons* 2005, 571). His conclusions dovetailed with a large body of scholarly analysis and commentary that was highly critical of applying the death penalty to juveniles, a practice that existed in only a handful of countries around the world (Fagan 2003; Streib 1998). In light of the interest expressed in Kennedy's prior opinions about scientific issues affecting society's understanding of mental capacity, including his concerns about the use of psychotropic medications and the difficulties in predicting the dangerousness of sex offenders, the proliferation of scientific studies about developmental aspects of adolescents' brains and thinking may have helped to shift Kennedy's position on the issue after the prior decision in *Stanford v. Kentucky* (1989).

Justice Kennedy's majority opinion in *Roper* provided additional points of differentiation between himself and the other Rehnquist Court conservatives who usually supported the government in criminal justice cases. Kennedy openly adopted the flexible, evolutionary *Trop v. Dulles* (1958) standard for evaluating Eighth Amendment cruel and unusual punishment claims, an approach that clashed very directly with the originalist approach to constitutional interpretation espoused by Justices Scalia and Thomas. Moreover, Kennedy demonstrated his willingness to incorporate consideration of social science research, another element that clashed with the viewpoints of Scalia, Thomas, and Rehnquist, justices who viewed themselves more along the lines of strict constructionists who look primarily at the Constitution's words, history, purpose, and role within the democratic governing system. In addition, Kennedy's willingness in his *Roper* opinion to consider international law, as he had done in an unprecedented fashion in several prior opinions, attracted scathing criticism from Justice Scalia, joined by Chief Justice Rehnquist and Justice Thomas, justices who categorically reject such references points and sources of evidence for interpreting the U.S. Constitution (Toobin 2005). Thus Kennedy's groundbreaking opinion in *Roper* not only had a major impact on law, it confirmed Kennedy's independence of thought and special role in writing about issues of mental capacity for the Court.

The Voice of a Divided Court

Justice Kennedy's controversial opinion in *Roper,* a 5-4 decision, also helped to illuminate another aspect of his important role on the Rehnquist Court: the decisive voter when the Court was deeply divided. During the Rehnquist Court era, many observers commented on the role of Justices O'Connor and Kennedy in providing the pivotal fifth vote on controversial issues that deeply divided the Court (Maveety 2008). O'Connor frequently determined outcomes in divided cases during the Rehnquist Court era, and Kennedy took sole control over the outcomes of divided cases in the early Roberts Court era after O'Connor's retirement (Lane 2006). Yet, a former Supreme Court law clerk who served during the Rehnquist Court era acknowledged influence of Kennedy in that era by saying, "[T]he Court remains, as it was in my day, a creature of Justices O'Connor and Kennedy, one or the other of whom holds sway in every major area of law" (Lazarus 1998, 515). It is easy to think of many examples of cases in which five-member majorities, including Kennedy's decisive vote, determined the Court's decision in notable criminal justice cases of the Rehnquist Court era: *United States v. Dixon* (1993) (conservative relaxation of the standard applied to evaluate double jeopardy claims); *Pennsylvania Board of Probation and Parole v. Scott* (1998) (prohibition on the application of the exclusionary rule for Fourth Amendment violations that produced evidence to be used in parole revocation proceedings); *Illinois v. Wardlow* (2000) (expansion of police stop-and-frisk authority); and *Atwater v. City of Lago Vista* (expanded authority for police to make arrests for traffic offenses punishable only by small fines).

Of importance for Kennedy's influence on the Rehnquist Court was the common strategy of the chief justice (or the senior justice in the majority when the chief justice dissented) who often sought to solidify support for the case by assigning the majority opinion to the "middle justice" (Brenner and Spaeth 1988). This strategy was assumed to help maintain the narrow and presumptively fragile five-member majority by producing a moderate majority opinion that would not alienate any justice who initially voted with the majority. Alternatively, the assignment could help the middle justice convince him- or herself about the correctness of the majority's position as the justice developed the arguments and reasoning in support of that position (Smith 1997). Thus, in several criminal justice cases, much like the situation in *Roper*, Kennedy was given several opportunities to shape the law by writing majority opinions when the Court was closely divided.

For example, in *National Treasury Employees Union v. Von Raab* (1989), Justice Kennedy wrote the majority opinion in a Fourth Amendment case challenging the U.S. Customs Service's program for suspicionless drug-testing of employees. Kennedy justified the Customs Service program under the "special needs" exception to the Fourth Amendment's warrant requirement. According to Kennedy,

> The purposes of the program are to deter drug use among those eligible for promotion to sensitive positions within the Service, and to prevent the promotion of drug users to those positions. These substantial interests . . . present a special need that may justify departure from the ordinary warrant and probable cause requirements. (666)

The opinion reflected the fact that Kennedy's votes and opinions on Fourth Amendment issues typically showed deference to asserted governmental interests and thereby endorsed expanded law enforcement authority over the claims of individuals. By contrast, Justice Scalia, not typically a supporter of individuals' claims in Fourth Amendment cases, complained in dissent that "I think it is obvious that this is a type of search particularly destructive to privacy and offensive to personal dignity" (680). Indeed, Scalia was so angrily contemptuous of the government's flimsy justifications, which did not cite a single instance of an employee using drugs, that he condemned these drug tests as a "kind of immolation of privacy and human dignity in symbolic opposition to drug use" (681). Kennedy's opinion prevailed, however, as he had four other colleagues in agreement with his balancing approach for this Fourth Amendment issue.

In another important contested case raising both Fourth and Fifth Amendment issues, Justice Kennedy's majority opinion addressed a novel issue and, in effect, endorsed an expansion of law enforcement authority. *Hiibel v. Sixth Judicial District Court* (2004) concerned a man who refused to provide his identification upon request when an officer responded to a witness's call about a possible assault inside a vehicle. After the man, who was found standing next to the vehicle matching the one in the witness report, repeatedly refused to show his identification, the man then began taunting the officer and telling the officer to arrest him. Eventually the officer placed him under arrest and he was charged with willfully resisting, delaying, or obstructing a public officer attempting to discharge his duties. The case arose under a Nevada statute that is sometimes referred to as a stop-and-identify law. In previous cases, the Supreme Court had invalidated some other states' versions of these laws for being too vague or for encouraging arbitrary and abusive police practices (*Brown v. Texas* 1979; *Kolender v. Lawson* 1983). In this case, which differed from the precedents because reasonable suspicion existed to stop the individual based on the witness's report to the police, Kennedy concluded that "[a] state law requiring a suspect to disclose his name in the course of a valid *Terry* [*v. Ohio* 1968] stop is consistent with Fourth Amendment prohibitions on unreasonable searches and seizures" (*Hiibel v. Sixth Judicial District Court* 2004). Justice Kennedy justified this conclusion by declaring that the "request for identity has an immediate relation to the purpose, rationale, and practical demands of the *Terry* stop." The opinion also rejected an asserted Fifth Amendment claim because Kennedy concluded that the privilege against compelled self-incrimination prohibits only compelled testimony that is incriminating, not a needed disclosure of identity. In dissent, Justice Stevens saw the statute as creating a Fifth Amendment violation while Justices Breyer, Souter, and Ginsburg argued that the situation constituted a Fourth Amendment violation because prior precedents clearly said that individuals are not required to respond to officers' questions during such stops. In this context implicating Fourth and Fifth Amendment rights, Kennedy was receptive to law enforcement arguments about the need for flexibility and expanded authority.

In other divisive cases, Justice Kennedy separated himself from the Rehnquist Court's most conservative justices and wrote majority opinions favoring individuals' claims. For example, in *Gentile v. State Bar of Nevada* (1991), Kennedy's sensitivity to free speech issues led him to invalidate a Nevada Supreme Court rule through which lawyers were sanctioned for pretrial public statements about cases. In *United States v. James Daniel Good Real Property* (1993), Justice Kennedy's majority opinion found a due process violation in a governmental property seizure as part of a forfeiture action related to a criminal drug case in which the property owner had inadequate prior notice and no opportunity to respond. Justice Kennedy also wrote a majority opinion protecting a defendant's Fifth Amendment privilege against compelled self-incrimination in sentencing hearings. On behalf of his four most liberal colleagues (Justices Stevens, Souter, Ginsburg, and Breyer), Kennedy's majority opinion concluded that the entry of a guilty plea does not waive a defendant's Fifth Amendment rights at the sentencing proceeding and that the sentencing judge may not draw adverse inferences from the defendant's silence (*Mitchell v. United States* 1999).

Conclusion

Although he was not known for being a prominent figure in the development of constitutional law for criminal justice, Justice Kennedy wrote several significant opinions that shaped criminal justice during the Rehnquist Court. In some instances, these opinions are generally regarded as focusing on his special interests in freedom of speech and liberty aspects of privacy rather than criminal justice. In fact, however, several of these opinions address the permissibility of certain criminal statutes and ordinances. In particular, Kennedy's monumental majority opinion in the controversial case of *Lawrence v. Texas* (2003) made a strong declaration about the privacy rights of gays and lesbians and thereby limited states' ability to target these individuals with criminal statutes concerning adults' private, noncommercial sexual conduct. Justice Kennedy was also especially influential in cases concerning juries as well as issues of mental capacity in criminal cases because he wrote multiple opinions, including several important majority opinions, on each of these issues.

Interestingly, Justice Kennedy's two most famous and controversial criminal justice-related majority opinions of the Rehnquist Court era affected very few criminal defendants. Relatively few people nationwide were prosecuted under the statutes invalidated by the decision in *Lawrence v. Texas* (2003). Similarly, the death penalty was sought against a relatively small number of teenage defendants prior to Kennedy's opinion in *Roper v. Simmons* (2005) that barred states from imposing capital punishment for crimes committed by offenders while under the age of eighteen. Both cases produced an outpouring of public debate, political commentary, and scholarly analyses because they concerned issues that define emotional fault lines in the American polity, and they have symbolic implications for the changing values and policy directions of the country. Justice Kennedy's critical vote and landmark opinions in these dramatic, doctrine-changing decisions made clear that, despite a voting record similar to other conservatives in criminal justice-related cases, he applied an independent interpretive perspective to many issues.

References

Bibas, Stephanos. "Originalism and Formalism in Criminal Procedure: The Triumph of Justice Scalia, the Unlikely Friend of Criminal Defendants?" *Georgetown Law Journal* 94 (2005): 183-204.

Bowman, Frank O. "Train Wreck? Or Can the Federal Sentencing System Be Saved? A Plea for Rapid Reversal of *Blakely v. Washington*." *American Criminal Law Review* 41 (2004): 217-265.

Brenner, Saul and Harold J. Spaeth. "Majority Opinion Assignments and the Maintenance of the Original Coalition on the Warren Court." *American Journal of Political Science* 32 (1988): 72-81.

Colucci, Frank J. *Justice Kennedy's Jurisprudence: The Full and Necessary Meaning of Liberty*. Lawrence, KS: University Press of Kansas, 2009.

Dorsett, Kimberley. *"Kansas v. Hendricks*: Marking the Beginning of a Dangerous New Era in Civil Commitment." *DePaul Law Review* 48 (1998): 113-28.

Edelman, Martin. *Democratic Theories and the Constitution*. Albany, NY: State University of New York Press, 1984.

Epstein, Lee, Jeffrey A. Segal, Harold J. Spaeth, and Thomas G. Walker. *The Supreme Court Compendium*, 4th edition. Washington, DC: CQ Press, 2007.

Fagan, Jeffrey. *"Atkins*, Adolescence, and the Maturity Heuristic: Rationales for the Categorical Exemption of Juveniles from Capital Punishment." *New Mexico Law Review* 33 (2003): 207-54.

Gibbs, Margaret R. "Eighth Amendment: Narrow Proportionality Requirement Preserves Deference to Legislative Judgments." *Journal of Criminal Law and Criminology* 82 (1992): 955-78.

Gillespie, Anne. "Constitutional Challenges to Civil Commitment Laws: An Uphill Battle for Sexual Predators after *Kansas v. Hendricks*." *Catholic University Law Review* 47 (1998): 1145-63.

Greene, Susan and Miles Moffeit. "Bad Faith Difficult to Prove," *Denver Post*, July 22, 2007. http://www.denverpost.com/ci_6429277 (accessed October 20, 2010).

Kersch, Ken. "Everything Is Enumerated: The Development Past and Future of an Interpretive Problem." *University of Pennsylvania Journal of Constitutional Law* 8 (2006): 957-82.

Knowles, Helen J. *The Tie Goes to Freedom: Justice Anthony M. Kennedy on Liberty*. Lanham, Md.: Rowman & Littlefield, 2009.

Lane, Charles. "Kennedy Reigns Supreme on Court," *Washington Post*, July 2, 2006.

Lazarus, Edward. *Closed Chamber*. New York: Times Books, 1998.

Levenson, Jill. "Reliability of Sexually Violent Predator Civil Commitment Criteria in Florida." *Law and Human Behavior* 28 (2004): 357-68.

Maltz, Earl M. "Anthony Kennedy and the Jurisprudence of Respectable Conservatism." Pp. 140-56 in *Rehnquist Justice: Understanding the Court Dynamic*, edited by Earl M. Maltz. Lawrence, KS: University Press of Kansas, 2003.

Maltz, Michael. *Rethinking Constitutional Law: Originalism, Interventionism, and the Politics of Judicial Review*. Lawrence, KS: University Press of Kansas, 1999.

Maltzman, Forrest, and Paul J. Wahlbeck. "A Conditional Model of Opinion Assignment on the Supreme Court." *Political Research Quarterly* 57 (2004): 551-62.

Maveety, Nancy. *Queen's Court: Judicial Power in the Rehnquist Court Era*. Lawrence, KS: University Press of Kansas, 2008.

Pollock, Brian. *"Kansas v. Hendricks*: A Workable Standard for 'Mental Illness' or a Push Down the Slippery Slope Toward State Abuse of Civil Commitment?" *Arizona Law Review* 40 (1998): 319-36.

Schmidt, Patrick D. and David A. Yalof. "The 'Swing Voter' Revisited: Justice Anthony Kennedy and the First Amendment Right of Free Speech." *Political Research Quarterly* 57 (2004): 209-17.

Smith, Christopher E. "Supreme Court Surprise: Justice Anthony Kennedy's Move Toward Moderation." *Oklahoma Law Review* 45 (1992): 459-76.

———. *Courts, Politics, and the Judicial Process*, 2nd ed. Chicago: Nelson-Hall, 1997.

———. "The Roles of Justice John Paul Stevens in Criminal Justice Cases." *Suffolk University Law Review* 39 (2006): 719-44.

Smith, Christopher E. and John Hurst. "The Forms of Judicial Policy Making: Civil Liability and Criminal Justice Policy." *Justice System Journal* 19 (1997): 341-54.

Streib, Victor. "Moratorium on the Death Penalty for Juveniles." *Law and Contemporary Problems* 61 (1998): 55-87.

Toobin, Jeffrey. "Swing Shift: How Anthony Kennedy's Passion for Foreign Law Could Change the Supreme Court." *New Yorker,* September 12, 2005. http://www.new-yorker.com/archive/2005/09/12/050912fa_fact (accessed June 10, 2010).

Whittington, Keith. *Constitutional Interpretation: Textual Meaning, Original Intent, and Judicial Review.* Lawrence, KS: University Press of Kansas, 1999.

Zonana, Howard. "The Civil Commitment of Sex Offenders." *Science* 278 (1997): 1248-49.

Cases Cited

Arizona v. Fulminante, 499 U.S. 279 (1991)

Arizona v. Youngblood, 488 U.S. 51 (1988)

Atwater v. City of Lago Vista, 532 U.S. 318 (2001)

Blakely v. Washington, 542 U.S. 296 (2004)

Bowers v. Hardwick, 478 U.S. 186 (1986)

Brown v. Texas, 443 U.S. 47 (1979)

Campbell v. Louisiana, 523 U.S. 392 (1998)

City of Chicago v. Morales, 527 U.S. 41 (1999)

Edmonson v. Leesville Concrete Company, 500 U.S. 614 (1991)

Ewing v. California, 538 U.S. 11 (2003)

Foucha v. Louisiana, 504 U.S. 71 (1992)

Gentile v. State Bar of Nevada, 501 U.S. 1030 (1991)

Harmelin v. Michigan, 501 U.S. 957 (1991)

Herrera v. Collins, 506 U.S. 390 (1993)

Hiibel v. Sixth Judicial District Court of Nevada, Humboldt County, 542 U.S. 177 (2004)

Holland v. Illinois, 493 U.S. 474 (1990)

Illinois v. Wardlow, 528 U.S. 119 (2000)

J.E.B. v. Alabama ex rel T.B., 511 U.S. 127 (1994)

Johnson v. Texas, 509 U.S. 350 (1993)

Kansas v. Hendricks, 521 U.S. 346 (1997)

Kentucky Dept. Of Corrections v. Thompson, 490 U.S. 454 (1989)

Kolender v. Lawson, 461 U.S. 352 (1983)

Kyllo v. United States, 533 U.S. 27 (2001)

Lawrence v. Texas, 539 U.S. 558 (2003)

McKoy v. North Carolina, 494 US 433 (1990)

Medina v. California, 505 U.S. 437 (1992)

Michigan Department of State Police v. Sitz, 496 U.S. 444 (1990)

Mitchell v. United States, 526 U.S. 314 (1999)

National Treasury Employees Union v. Von Raab, 489 U.S. 656 (1989)

Overton v. Bazzetta, 539 U.S. 126 (2003)

Pennsylvania Bd. of Probation and Parole v. Scott, 524 U.S. 357 (1998)

Penry v. Lynaugh, 492 U.S. 302 (1989)

Powers v. Ohio, 499 US 400 (1991)

R. A. V. v. City of St. Paul, 505 U.S. 377 (1992)

Riggins v. Nevada, 504 U.S. 127 (1992)

Ring v. Arizona, 536 U.S. 584 (2002)

Roper v. Simmons, 543 U.S. 551 (2005)

Simon & Schuster, Inc. v. Members of N. Y. State Crime Victims Bd., 502 U.S. 105 (1991)
Stanford v. Kentucky, 492 U.S. 361 (1989)
Terry v. Ohio, 392 U.S. 1 (1968)
Texas v. Johnson, 491 U.S. 397 (1989)
Trop v. Dulles, 356 U.S. 86 (1958)
Tuilaepa v. California, 512 U.S. 967 (1994)
United States v. Bajakajian, 524 U.S. 321 (1998)
United States v. Dixon, 509 U.S. 688 (1993)
United States v. Eichman, 496 U.S. 310 (1990)
United States v. James Daniel Good Real Property, 510 U.S. 43 (1993)
United States v. Ursery, 518 U.S. 267 (1996)
Virginia v. Black, 538 U.S. 343 (2003)
Washington v. Harper, 494 U.S. (1990)

Chapter 10
David H. Souter:
Unexpected Independent

Scott P. Johnson

David Souter was nominated to the U.S. Supreme Court on July 25, 1990, by President George H. W. Bush at the suggestion of U.S. Senator Warren Rudman (R-NH) and former New Hampshire Governor John Sununu, a high-ranking official in the Bush Administration. Souter was educated at Harvard Law School and, after his graduation in 1966, he worked as an associate at the law firm of Orr & Reno in Concord, New Hampshire, where he practiced in a variety of legal areas, including corporate law and criminal litigation. In 1968, Souter was hired by the state of New Hampshire as an assistant attorney general in the criminal division and was later appointed to serve as attorney general. Next, Souter served as a trial and appellate judge in New Hampshire from 1978 to 1990. President Bush appointed him to the federal court of appeals in Boston where he served briefly until Bush nominated him to the U.S. Supreme Court to replace Justice William Brennan, a liberal who was retiring after thirty-four years of service (Yarbrough 2005, 17-93).

It was widely assumed that Souter would provide another conservative vote in a long line of appointments by Republican presidents (Johnson and Smith 1992, 239). These assumptions were based on aspects of Souter's performance over the course of his legal and judicial careers, as well as on the descriptions of Souter by Rudman, Sununu, and other Republicans. For example, on the New Hampshire state supreme court, Souter had a record of ruling conservatively by respecting precedent and interpreting the law in a fairly technical fashion (Jordan 1992, 492). As a trial judge, Souter also had a reputation for issuing harsh punishments during the sentencing of defendants (Yarbrough 2005, 120). Moreover, prior to his appointment to the U.S. Supreme Court, Souter had not published anything about his legal views and refused to make public speeches about his own constitutional philosophy (Greenhouse 1990). Hence, he was able to appear as a "stealth" candidate for the U.S. Supreme Court and was easily confirmed by a vote of 90-9 in the U.S. Senate despite the assumptions about his conservatism (Yarbrough 2005, 123).

It is now widely acknowledged by contemporary commentators that Souter's performance on the U.S. Supreme Court disappointed the Bush Administration and its Republican supporters. He was more supportive of rights for individuals than anyone predicted that he would be. In retrospect, a closer examination of Souter's pre-U.S. Supreme Court record may have provided clues that Souter would not necessarily decide cases in a predictable or ideological fashion. Despite the evidence of conservatism in Souter's performance as a New Hampshire judge, Souter also had a reputation among both Republicans and Democrats in New Hampshire for promoting a fair trial in the interests of justice, even if this meant ruling in favor of criminal defendants who had committed horrendous crimes (Yarbrough 2005, 55-56). During Senate confirmation hearings, Souter surprisingly endorsed a limited right to privacy and spoke respectfully about the liberal decisions of the Warren Court in the 1960s which had expanded the rights of criminal defendants (Hensley, Smith, and Baugh 1997, 76). Moreover, Souter praised Justice William Brennan, the staunch liberal who he was replacing, as one of the greatest protectors of the Bill of Rights (Greenhouse 1990; Smith and Johnson 1992, 24).

During the Rehnquist Court era, Souter proved himself to be anything but an ideological appointment (Yarbrough 2005, 259). While he did appear to align more often with conservative justices in his earlier years on the Court, he cannot be easily categorized according to the liberal-conservative continuum employed by contemporary scholars of the judiciary (Smith 1992, 11; Segal and Spaeth 1993). Eventually, Souter became a moderating influence on the U.S. Supreme Court (Yarbrough 2005, 168). In criminal justice cases, an area where Souter displayed the most conservatism during his earlier years with a tendency to support the authority of police and prosecutors, he clearly did not behave as an ideological conservative (185). In fact, during his tenure on the Court, Souter demonstrated independent thinking and thereby frequently disappointed political conservatives in criminal justice cases (Hensley et al. 2007, 77). Souter never adopted the original intent theory of constitutional interpretation espoused by ideological conservatives. He favored a more practical application of precedent and flexible interpretation of the law in deciding criminal justice issues (77).

This chapter's examination of Souter's opinions and votes in the Rehnquist Court era reveals that he clearly evolved into a more moderate, or even liberal, jurist than ideological conservatives would have preferred in the area of criminal justice (Baum 2007, 122-27). Over the course of his judicial career, Souter gained commentators' respect as an intellectual scholar by attempting to understand both sides of a dispute completely and apply precedent and legal rules in a flexible, albeit technical, manner in the hope of achieving justice (Yarbrough 2005, 198). As a result, Souter played an important role in thwarting the goals of political conservatives who wished to see the Rehnquist Court reverse the Warren Court's rights-expanding decisions in the field of criminal justice. Many of the Rehnquist Court's decisions limited the definitions of rights for criminal suspects and defendants. However, such limitations were far less extensive than they would have been if Souter had fulfilled the Bush Administration's original expectations that he would be a doctrinaire judicial conservative.

Career Prior to U.S. Supreme Court Appointment

David Souter's career included service as attorney general of New Hampshire and time on the bench as both a state trial and appellate judge. Prior to his selection as a U.S. Supreme Court nominee, he also served for a few months on the First Circuit U.S. Court of Appeals as an appointee of President Bush, but he participated in only one decision (*United States v. Waldeck* 1990, 555). As attorney general, Souter displayed conservatism in his support for the use of the death penalty in New Hampshire (Yarbrough 2005, 36). After the U.S. Supreme Court ruled in 1976 that the use of capital punishment by the states was legal and did not violate the Eighth Amendment's protection against cruel and unusual punishment, Souter testified before the New Hampshire House of Representatives and argued that a lifetime sentence was not sufficient punishment for the capital crime of first-degree murder (36). Souter based his death penalty views largely upon the argument that capital punishment served as a deterrent. Eventually, New Hampshire reinstated the use of death sentences.

As associate justice on the New Hampshire superior court from 1978 to 1983, Souter was renowned for being tough in the sentencing of defendants (Yarbrough 2005, 55). This was exemplified in a 1981 case when he rejected attempts by defense lawyers and prosecutors to use plea bargaining to reduce a sentence for a felony conviction. The plea bargain had involved granting only probation for a female defendant after she had stolen a .357 magnum revolver. Souter scolded the prosecutors for accepting the plea bargain and ordered the defendant to serve nine months in prison (Garrow 1994, 41).

Although Souter was a tough trial judge, he consistently respected precedents that expanded the rights of criminal suspects and even showed sympathy at times for defendants (Marcus 1990). For example, he once refused a plea bargain accepted by a defendant over the objections of defense counsel to serve two years in prison for stealing one dollar. Souter stated that "it was cruel and inhumane to sentence someone to two years for stealing a dollar" (Yarbrough 2005, 55). In addition, Souter was not averse to suppressing evidence. In a case involving charges of arson and second-degree murder, Souter ruled evidence inadmissible when it was revealed that police had tampered with the evidence and had also coerced a confession from the defendant by threatening to take away the defendant's child if she refused to cooperate with police (Yarbrough 2005).

Souter served as an associate justice of the New Hampshire Supreme Court from 1983 to 1990 (Greenhouse 1990). As a state supreme court justice, he respected precedent and interpreted the language of legal provisions and the intent of those who framed the laws in a technical manner (Jordan 1992, 530; Marcus 1990). While serving on the New Hampshire Supreme Court, Souter's opinions focused mainly upon interpretations of state law in such areas as negligence, family law, and criminal procedure (Greenhouse 1990). In the area of criminal justice, Souter was generally known as a conservative judge who rarely voted in favor of criminal defendants' rights (Devroy 1990). In fact, Souter voted on behalf of criminal defendants' rights only nine times out of eighty-two votes, roughly 11 percent of the time (Yarbrough 2005, 92). Though Souter was largely viewed as a traditional conservative, he eventually developed a flexible interpretation of constitutional law. Hence, Souter came to be respected by Democrats in New Hampshire because, although he had a reputation as a conservative judge, he ruled in the interests of promoting a fair trial for defendants (93).

Souter appeared disinclined to vote in favor of criminal defendants regarding *Miranda* rights during his years on the state high court. In *State v. Denney* (1987), Souter dissented when the majority held that the refusal of a defendant to submit to a blood alcohol test could not be admitted by prosecutors because police had not warned the defendant that such a refusal could be used against him at trial (Jordan 1992, 512). Souter argued that the arresting officers had issued the *Miranda* warnings to the defendant and the defendant should have understood that the warnings implied that the refusal to submit to the test could be used against him in court. Interestingly, Souter had prevailed in an earlier case involving a prosecutor using a refusal to submit to a blood alcohol test as evidence of guilt. Souter maintained that the Fifth Amendment privilege against compelled self-incrimination applied only to testimonial evidence, not physical evidence. Souter continued a trend of conservative voting in *Miranda* cases when he allowed a defiant statement made by a defendant to be introduced at trial. In *State v. Coppola* (1987), Vincent Coppola had boasted to police that they could not get him to confess to a rape of an elderly woman. In writing the opinion for the unanimous court, Souter contended that this statement by Coppola was not within the protection of the Fifth Amendment's right to remain silent and it could be admitted by prosecutors as evidence of guilt.

When Souter was selected by President George H. W. Bush to replace Justice William Brennan who was retiring from the U.S. Supreme Court at the age of eighty-four, Souter's prior record in criminal justice cases led observers to conclude that he would strengthen the Rehnquist Court's conservative wing (Broder and Dewar 1990). Because he was replacing one of the most liberal holdovers from the Warren Court era, there was speculation that Souter would have an immediate impact in tilting the Court's criminal justice decisions further in the direction of limiting the scope of constitutional rights and expanding the authority of police and prosecutors.

Policy Impact of a Freshman Justice

During Souter's first year on the U.S. Supreme Court, he immediately had an impact in replacing Justice William Brennan, particularly in the area of criminal justice (Smith 1992, 40). During his first term, Souter had provided the decisive vote in seven different 5-4 decisions where the Court established new "conservative" precedents that limited the rights of criminal defendants. If these cases had been argued the previous term, Justice Brennan most likely would have voted in favor of the rights of the criminal suspects. Hence, Souter's impact in one year on the Court served to have broad policy implications in the area of criminal justice (Johnson and Smith 1992, 239). In *Arizona v. Fulminante* (1991), Souter provided the pivotal vote to allow coerced confessions as harmless error and, in *County of Riverside v. McLaughlin* (1991), Souter also provided the swing vote to allow persons placed under arrest to be held for two days or more before a magistrate was required to determine probable cause. In regard to prisoners' rights, Souter voted with the conservative bloc to make it more difficult for prisoners to challenge their conditions of confinement and also to provide states the power to mandate life sentences without the possibility of parole for drug convictions (*Wilson v. Seiter* 1991; *Harmelin v. Michigan* 1991). Finally, Souter voted against the rights of criminal defendants in three cases involving jury selection and jury instructions during criminal trials (*Mu'min v. Virginia* 1991; *Peretz v. United States* 1991; *Schad v. Arizona* 1991).

It should be noted that Souter did break with the conservative bloc on a few occasions such as his opinion for the Court in *Yates v. Evatt* (1991) that held the harmless error doctrine did not extend to jury instructions. Hence, he was able to separate himself at times from the conservative bloc and began to establish a streak of independence, even during his first term.

Overall, while Souter proved to be a decisive vote for the conservative members, he did not author any "important" opinions during his first year on the Court (Johnson and Smith 1992, 241). In fact, he authored an extremely low number of opinions relative to the other justices (Jordan 1992, 522). Souter wrote only eight majority opinions and two concurring and dissenting opinions each, for a total of twelve during the entire 1990-91 Term (Smith 1992, 21). No other justice authored fewer than twenty-one opinions during Souter's first year (Johnson and Smith 1992, 241). In addition, Souter's first year saw the Court undergo severe gridlock at the end of the term. A former clerk attributed this to a "breakdown in one chamber" and speculated that Souter's insistence upon composing his own opinions rather than relying upon his law clerks to prepare drafts and his refusal to use a word processor had caused the backlog (*Newsweek* 1991, 4). In fact, Souter described the workload as overwhelming during his first year on the Court and conveyed to *The Boston Globe* that he felt as if he had "walk[ed] through a tidal wave" (Yarbrough 2005, 160).

Search and Seizure Cases

In search and seizure cases, Souter generally voted with the government during his career on the Court, although he did exhibit a trend toward defending the rights of criminal defendants toward the end of the Rehnquist Court era. An examination of Souter's opinions as well as his voting behavior confirms a conservative trend; however, it also reveals a willingness to separate from the conservative bloc and rely upon a flexible and pragmatic approach to constitutional interpretation. In short, unlike Chief Justice William Rehnquist and Justices Antonin Scalia and Clarence Thomas, Souter was inclined to place limits on the amount of discretion given to government officials in conducting searches and seizing evidence.

Souter's first majority opinion in a search and seizure case was not assigned until after he had served over a decade on the Court, but it would prove to be one of his most controversial. In writing for a five-person majority in *Atwater v. City of Lago Vista* (2001), Souter led a majority composed of conservative justices, namely Chief Justice Rehnquist and Justices Scalia, Thomas, and Kennedy, in ruling that the Fourth Amendment does not prohibit a warrantless arrest for a misdemeanor seat belt violation. The controversy in the *Atwater* case involved the arrest of a woman, Gail Atwater, by a police officer in Lago Vista, Texas, for failing to secure her two small children with seat belts in the front seat of her pickup truck. A statute in Texas prohibited passengers, particularly small children, from riding in the front seat without seat belts. The Texas statute authorized police to arrest Atwater and charge her with a misdemeanor, although police could have simply issued her a citation instead of arresting her.

Atwater's legal counsel argued that when the Constitution was drafted, authorities prohibited warrantless arrests under common law for misdemeanor offenses, except where someone had disturbed the peace or committed some type of violent act. Justice Souter's majority opinion for the Court conceded that, although there was some substance to the argument presented by Atwater's counsel, ultimately it failed. Souter countered that a close examination of English common law at the drafting of the Constitution revealed that police were authorized to arrest persons for night walking and negligent carriage driving without a warrant. In short, the historical evidence provided by common law rules and the subsequent development of American law did not support Atwater's position. In sum, Souter concluded for the Court that an officer may arrest an individual without violating the Fourth Amendment if there is "probable cause to believe that an individual has committed even a very minor criminal offense in the officer's presence" (*Atwater v. City of Lago Vista* 2001, 354).

Two years later, in *United States v. Banks* (2003), Justice Souter wrote a unanimous opinion in a Fourth Amendment case concerning whether police officers may execute a search warrant by knocking on a suspect's door and then waiting for only a brief period of time before entering the home by way of force. In this case, North Las Vegas police officers and FBI agents obtained a warrant to search the apartment of Lashawn Lowell Banks for cocaine. After knocking on Banks' apartment door loudly and shouting "police search warrant," the law enforcement officials waited fifteen to twenty seconds and then broke the door down with a battering ram. Banks contended that he was in the shower and did not hear the knock on the door or the officers announce their presence with the search warrant. Banks' legal counsel sought to suppress the crack cocaine, weapons, and other evidence of drug dealing secured by police officials at Banks' residence.

Souter's unanimous opinion held that the forcible entry by law enforcement after knocking and waiting fifteen to twenty seconds was not a violation of the Fourth Amendment. Souter's opinion concluded that it was reasonable for the law enforcement officials to assume that fifteen to twenty seconds was enough time for a suspect to destroy evidence. The search and seizure of evidence by police officers must be analyzed in light of exigent circumstances. If police officers have reasonable suspicion to believe that exigent circumstances exist such as the possible destruction of evidence, then authorities are allowed to enter a residence forcibly without violating the Search and Seizure Clause of the Fourth Amendment.

In other search and seizure cases during the Rehnquist Court era, Souter's voting record and opinions, both concurring and dissenting, illustrated the flexibility and independence in his judicial decision making as well as a later trend toward favoring the preservation of rights for criminal defendants. For example, during his first term, Souter joined a conservative majority in *Florida v. Bostick* (1991) where the Court held that the Florida Supreme Court had applied an incorrect legal analysis in holding that the questioning of bus passengers by police had constituted an unreasonable search and seizure of drug evidence. In 1995, Souter also voted conservatively to extend the "good faith" exception to the exclusionary rule in cases where a computer error caused an illegal search and seizure of evidence, although he expressed concern in a separate concurrence that it might be necessary to apply the exclusionary rule as a deterrent against other governmental employees, not simply police officers, to keep false arrests and the illegal seizures of evidence to a minimum (*Arizona v. Evans* 1995). However, Souter dissented against a conservative majority in *United States v. Drayton* (2002) when the Court decided a case similar to *Bostick* involving the pat-down of bus passengers by police. Souter argued in his dissenting opinion that the pat-down by police was not a consensual exercise, and the passengers were given every indication by police that they did not have a free choice to refuse the search. In 2005, Souter also dissented from the conservative majority in a search and seizure case where a drug-sniffing police dog was used to examine the trunk of an automobile and the Court determined that such an examination did not constitute a "search" that was limited by the Fourth Amendment's requirements (*Illinois v. Caballes* 2005).

In other areas of search and seizure, Souter also appeared to employ a flexible approach in his decision making. For example, even though Souter endorsed sobriety checkpoints as a state supreme court justice, he voted to strike down a police roadblock designed to discover and arrest drug offenders in *Indianapolis v. Edmond* (2000). He also joined an opinion concurring in part and dissenting in part written by Justice Stevens in *Illinois v. Lidster* (2004) where the Court ruled that police could stop motorists for the purpose of obtaining information about a past crime committed in the community. Stevens and Souter maintained that local judges would have been more capable of deciding the constitutionality of the roadblocks based upon the local conditions and practices of a community. Finally, Souter voted against the conservative bloc in cases of suspicionless drug testing for high school students participating in athletics and a hospital's voluntary revelations to law enforcement officials about pregnant women's medical tests that showed evidence of drug abuse (*Vernonia v. Acton* 1995; *Ferguson v. City of Charleston* 2001). While Souter remained moderately conservative in the area of search and seizure, he deviated from the conservative bloc more frequently during his later years on the Court. In short, Souter's case-by-case approach in search and seizure cases made him one of the less predictable justices on the Court.

Compelled Self-incrimination and *Miranda* Warnings

In *Withrow v. Williams* (1993), Justice Souter wrote his first opinion involving *Miranda* warnings, specifically the Fifth Amendment's privilege against compelled self-incrimination. Souter's opinion in *Withrow* also dealt with the question of whether to extend a conservative precedent from the Burger Court era established in *Stone v. Powell* (1976). In *Stone,* the Burger Court refused to allow state prisoners to challenge search and seizure claims in federal habeas proceedings if the defendant had a fair chance during trial and on appeal to raise such issues. The Court concluded that any attempt during post-appeal federal proceedings to exclude evidence based upon an illegal search and seizure would not advance the intended purpose of the exclusionary rule, which was designed to prevent misconduct by police officers.

In *Withrow,* Souter wrote for a unanimous Court in deciding whether to extend the *Stone* precedent to state convictions based upon confessions that may have been obtained in violation of the *Miranda* warnings. Souter wrote in his opinion that the defendant did have a right to federal habeas corpus review and his incriminating statements should have been thrown out of court because his right to remain silent under the Fifth Amendment had been violated. This case involved the questioning of Robert Allen Williams by the Michigan police about a double murder case. Williams implicated himself by admitting that he had furnished the weapon for the shooter. Police officers had not issued a *Miranda* warning to Williams and had threatened to "lock him up" if he refused to talk. The trial court had refused to exclude his statements and Williams was convicted of first-degree murder. Prosecutors had argued that Williams' claim of a violation of *Miranda* rights was not reviewable in federal court based upon the precedent established in *Stone v. Powell.* However, Souter reasoned that *Miranda* warnings were a fundamental right during the trial stage of the criminal justice process that prevented the use of unreliable confessions at trial, while claims to exclude evidence based upon an illegal search and seizure were not a fundamental trial right.

In *United States v. Balsys* (1998), Souter issued another opinion for the Court on the privilege against self-incrimination in a case involving the federal government's investigation of the World War II-era activities in Europe of an individual who later became a resident of the United States. Aloyzas Balsys had claimed a Fifth Amendment privilege against self-incrimination because he was afraid of being prosecuted by a foreign nation. While Balsys did not fear prosecution by the United States, he was afraid that his statements about his wartime activities could subject him to prosecution in Lithuania, Germany, or Israel. In writing for a seven-person majority composed of Chief Justice Rehnquist and Justices Scalia, Thomas, O'Connor, Stevens, and Kennedy, Souter held that the Balsys' refusal to provide information in the U.S. because he feared prosecution by a foreign nation was beyond the scope of the Fifth Amendment's privilege against self-incrimination. Souter asserted that the Fifth Amendment privilege against self-incrimination cannot be applied beyond criminal proceedings in the United States.

In 2000, Souter voted with a seven-person majority to reaffirm the basic principles of *Miranda v. Arizona* (1966) by striking down a lower court's interpretation of the Omnibus Crime Control Act of 1968 that had asserted that federal law enforcement officers are not bound by the requirements of *Miranda* (*Dickerson v. United States* 2000). Four years later, Souter continued to demonstrate support for the *Miranda* precedent and the privilege against compelled self-incrimination when he wrote for a liberal 5-4 majority in *Missouri v. Seibert* (2004). Here, Souter and the Court's majority held that a confession to murder was inadmissible because police used a two-step tactic through which officers would secure a confession from a suspect without *Miranda* warnings. Then, *Miranda* warnings would be issued to gain the confession by asking the suspect to repeat his or her statements for a second time. Souter wrote that the "midstream recitation of warnings after interrogation and unwarned confession could not effectively comply with *Miranda* warnings" (*Seibert*, 604). Souter furthered maintained that the purpose of the police tactic in question was "to get a confession the suspect would not make if he understood his rights at the outset" (613). Souter argued that *Miranda* warnings cannot function effectively in such a scenario and it deprives the defendant of understanding his or her Fifth Amendment rights and the ramifications of waiving such protections.

Finally, Souter expressed further support for *Miranda* and the protection against compelled self-incrimination near the end of the Rehnquist Court era when he dissented from the majority decision in *United States v. Patane* (2004). In *Patane*, the Court ruled that physical evidence secured by police does not necessarily have to be suppressed, even if it was discovered because of incriminating statements obtained without providing *Miranda* warnings. Souter's dissenting opinion, joined by Justices Stevens and Ginsburg, accused the majority of "closing their eyes to the consequences of giving an evidentiary advantage to those who ignore *Miranda*" (630). Moreover, he added that the decision would provide an incentive for interrogators to ignore *Miranda*.

"Fair Trial" Rights

During Souter's second term on the Court (1991-92), he demonstrated a liberal trend in deciding criminal justice cases concerning certain issues. Souter's first significant opinion in the area of Sixth Amendment trial rights involved a 5-4 decision overturning the conviction of a defendant who had been denied a right to a speedy trial. In the case of *Doggett v. United States* (1992), Marc Doggett had been indicted on federal drug charges in 1980, but he left the United States for Panama before federal agents could arrest him. After leaving Panama for Colombia, Doggett returned to the United States in 1982 where he lived for six years before the U.S. Marshal Service discovered him when a credit check revealed an outstanding warrant for his arrest.

In *Doggett*, the Rehnquist Court was deeply divided. Souter and Justices White, Stevens, Kennedy, and Blackmun formed a liberal bloc ruling in favor of criminal defendants' rights, while Chief Justice Rehnquist, and Justices O'Connor, Scalia, and Thomas established a conservative bloc in favor of the U.S. government's position. In Souter's majority opinion, he concluded that the eight-year lag between the indictment and arrest was sufficient to raise the Sixth Amendment question about the fulfillment of the right to a speedy trial. Souter asserted that the U.S. government was negligent in pursuing Doggett and, in fact, Doggett did not know of his indictment in 1980, and the negligent delay between indictment and arrest hindered Doggett in preparing his legal defense. Souter noted that a lengthy delay in a trial can cause a number of unidentifiable problems for a defendant in his attempt to secure a fair trial, and it is irrelevant that Doggett failed to cite specifics concerning how his trial would be prejudiced by the excessive delay. In short, the lengthy delay itself caused a presumption of prejudice against the defendant.

In a dissenting opinion, Justice Sandra Day O'Connor argued that Doggett should have been required to show that specific prejudice had occurred because of the delay. O'Connor maintained that the lag between indictment and trial did not limit Doggett's freedom in any way. In a separate dissent joined by Chief Justice Rehnquist and Justice Scalia, Justice Clarence Thomas argued that the purpose of Sixth Amendment's right to speedy trial was to prevent a person from being unnecessarily incarcerated for a long period of time and to avoid the anxiety of disrupting a person's life by having an unresolved criminal charge hanging over a defendant for an extended period of time. In addition, a lengthy period of time between indictment and a trial may cause problems for the defense because evidence might be lost, the memory of witnesses may fade, and persons associated with the case could disappear or die. Thomas concluded that Doggett could not claim that any of these issues related to his right to a speedy trial. In short, Doggett suffered none of the harms that the speedy trial right was intended to protect. The dissenters presented rational arguments that were consistent with other types of cases in which individuals bear the burden of demonstrating that they were harmed by a governmental action. Yet Souter's more expansive view of Sixth Amendment protections led him to favor the arguments of a criminal defendant when he saw the government as failing in its obligation to vigorously pursue prosecutions that it had initiated.

Souter's concern for fair processes was also evident in *Kyles v. Whitley* (1995). Souter wrote for a five-person majority in ordering a new trial for a defendant who had been sentenced to death in Louisiana for first-degree murder. Souter's opinion, joined by Justices Ginsburg, Breyer, Stevens, and O'Connor, concluded that the defendant was entitled to a new trial after it was revealed that the state of Louisiana had withheld evidence favorable to the defense that may have produced a different result.

Souter did not, however, consistently place legal burdens on the government in criminal cases. Ten years later, Souter wrote for the majority in a right to counsel case that involved the interpretation of a federal rule. Federal Rule of Criminal Procedure 11, also referred to as Rule 11, outlines the process that must be followed by a judge in ensuring that a guilty plea is understood and voluntarily accepted by a defendant. If the judge deviates from this procedure, a guilty plea still may be upheld if the actions by the judge did not violate any substantial rights of the defendant and an appellate court concludes that the judge's deviation constituted only a "harmless error." In the case of *United States v. Vonn* (2002), Alphonso Vonn had been charged with armed robbery and informed by a magistrate that he had a right to counsel. However, at later stages of the criminal proceedings when Vonn entered a plea of guilty, the court informed him of his basic rights but failed to indicate that he had a right to counsel. Souter's opinion for the unanimous Court held that Vonn could not benefit from the error by the court because he had raised the issue of Rule 11 after the trial court phase, hence, the burden of proving that the error affected substantial rights had shifted from the government to the defendant. Under federal rules, if a defendant is negligent in raising a Rule 11 objection, then the burden shifts to the defendant who must then establish that the error was plain.

Two years later, Souter relied upon the precedent that he had established in *Vonn* in a similar case involving the application of Rule 11. In *United States v. Dominguez Benitez* (2004), Souter again wrote for a unanimous Court in a case involving a defendant who had pled guilty to conspiracy. When the court rejected the plea offered by the government because Dominguez had three prior convictions, he was sentenced to a mandatory ten-year prison term and instructed that he could not withdraw the guilty plea. Dominguez maintained that he was not informed by the court that he was prevented from withdrawing the plea and raised a Rule 11 claim. Relying upon precedent established in the *Vonn* case, Justice Souter asserted in his opinion that, because the Rule 11 claim was not filed in a timely fashion, the defendant must demonstrate that a different outcome in the trial would have occurred, if not for the error committed by the court.

In *Rompilla v. Beard* (2005), Justice Souter's majority opinion contributed to a trend by the Court since 2000 of ruling in favor of certain capital defendants who had received inadequate representation by legal counsel. Souter's majority opinion focused upon the right to counsel for Ronald Rompilla, a criminal defendant who had received a death sentence for murder based upon a number of aggravating circumstances. One of the aggravating circumstances presented by prosecutors to justify a sentence of death was the fact that Rompilla had a history of felony convictions. Souter held for the five-person majority that Rompilla's defense attorneys should have introduced evidence that he had a limited mental capacity, was a victim of child abuse, and was diagnosed with fetal alcohol syndrome and schizophrenia. Such evidence was readily available to his legal counsel and had been introduced when Rompilla was convicted of felony rape almost a decade-and-a-half earlier. Hence, Souter concluded that Rompilla had received inadequate counsel based upon standards set by the American Bar Association (ABA). In overturning the death sentence for Rompilla, Souter quoted from the ABA standards:

> It is the duty of the lawyer to conduct a prompt investigation of the circumstances of the case and to explore all avenues leading to facts relevant to the merits of the case and the penalty in the event of conviction. The investigation should always include efforts to secure information in the possession of the prosecution and law enforcement authorities. The duty to investigate exists regardless of the accused's admissions or statements to the lawyer of facts constituting guilt or the accused's stated desire to plead guilty. (*Rompilla*, 387)

In short, Rompilla's legal counsel should have provided evidence from his prior rape conviction as mitigating factors in the capital sentencing phase. Because of the Supreme Court's decision in *Rompilla*, the state of Pennsylvania was required to provide Rompilla with a new capital sentencing hearing or a life sentence for the murder conviction.

Justice Souter also wrote a majority opinion in 2005 concerning the Sixth Amendment and the issue of racial discrimination. Relying upon precedent from *Batson v. Kentucky* (1986) in which the Court ruled that prosecutors could not issue peremptory challenges in a racially discriminatory manner, Souter wrote the opinion in *Miller-El v. Dretke* (2005) where the Court held by a 6-3 vote that the Dallas County District Attorney's office had discriminated by race in using peremptory challenges to exclude potential jurors in a capital murder case. Souter led a majority of six justices in holding that the Dallas District Attorney had violated the Equal Protection Clause of the Fourteenth Amendment and Miller-El's right to fair trial by an impartial jury found in the Sixth Amendment. Souter wrote that "prosecutors used peremptory strikes to exclude 91 percent of the eligible black venire panelists, a disparity unlikely to have been produced by happenstance" (241).

In *Dretke*, Souter clearly aligned himself with the liberal bloc of justices concerned about the fair trial rights of a defendant amidst serious concerns about the racial composition of a jury. As will be shown, Justice Souter also broke with the more conservative members of the Court in cases raising certain sentencing issues.

Sentencing

At the final stage of the criminal justice process, Souter demonstrated a penchant for siding with criminal defendants during the sentencing phase. Justice Souter's majority opinions in sentencing cases have involved technical applications of federal law to disputes involving the authority of the federal district courts, the sentencing of juveniles for serious offenses, carjacking, and firearm possession. In these opinions, Souter provided support for the claims of criminal defendants.

In *Wade v. United States* (1992), Souter wrote for a unanimous Court in holding that the district courts can reduce a sentence beyond the minimum sentence established by the federal government through the U.S. Sentencing Commission but only if the federal government filed a motion requesting such a reduction. During this same term, Souter also wrote for the Court in *United States v. R. L. C.* (1992) which involved a juvenile sentenced to three years detention for involuntary manslaughter where the law would appear to have sentenced an adult to a shorter prison sentence for the same act. Souter held that, after applying federal sentencing guidelines, the federal law prohibited the sentencing of a juvenile to a longer sentence than an adult.

Souter again ruled in favor of a defendant during the sentencing phase in *Jones v. United States* (1999). This case concerned federal legislation that established serious penalties for the crime of carjacking. The federal law increased the number of years in prison based upon the seriousness of the offense. For example, the sentence for carjacking would be enhanced if bodily injury occurred to a victim and enhanced further if the death of a victim resulted from the carjacking. The U.S. district court sentenced Nathaniel Jones to twenty-five years in prison based upon the fact that serious bodily injury had occurred to a victim. However, the district court did not note serious bodily injury in the indictment nor did the district court prove serious bodily injury before the jury. Souter's opinion for the six-member majority held that the district court must introduce separate elements that affect the sentencing within the indictment, the element must be proven beyond a reasonable doubt, and it must be submitted to the jury for a verdict.

During the 2005 Term, Souter issued two majority opinions for the Court in favor of defendants raising claims during their sentencing stages. In one majority opinion, Souter held that a defendant could challenge his sentencing under U.S. Sentencing Commission Guidelines if a prior state conviction used to enhance his federal sentence had been vacated (*Johnson v. United States* 2005). In another majority opinion, Souter held that a sentencing court could not examine police reports or other information to determine whether a prior guilty plea constituted a generic burglary for the purpose of mandating a fifteen-year minimum sentence for possessing a firearm after three prior convictions (*Shepard v. United States* 2005).

Death Penalty Cases

As noted above, Souter was a staunch supporter of the death penalty during his days as attorney general and state judge in New Hampshire (Yarbrough 2005, 36). The first case for Souter on the U.S. Supreme Court involving the death penalty was *Payne v. Tennessee* (1991). In *Payne*, Souter joined a conservative majority in a 6-3 vote that upheld the admission of victim impact statements during the sentencing stage of a death penalty case. Souter authored a concurring opinion in *Payne* in which he argued that withholding victim impact statements would be unfair and provide an advantage to the defendant. Souter wrote, "Indeed, given a defendant's option to introduce relevant evidence in mitigation . . . sentencing without such evidence of victim impact may be seen as a significantly imbalanced process" (839).

Souter, however, did depart from the majority in his concurrence when he expressed concern that the *Payne* decision had overturned two precedents established only a few years earlier (*Booth v. Maryland* 1987; *South Carolina v. Gathers* 1989). Souter discussed the "fundamental importance" of stare decisis to the rule of law in his concurring opinion, whereas Rehnquist's majority opinion and Scalia's separate concurrence gave far less weight to the importance of precedent. Hence, even in his early years on the Court, Souter began to demonstrate a streak of independence from his colleagues that would grow even stronger during his later years on the Court (Yarbrough 2005, 162).

Souter's initial opinion for the Court in the area of the death penalty occurred in *Sochor v. Florida* (1992). *Sochor* involved a death sentence recommended by a jury that was instructed to decide upon four aggravating factors, including such vague factors as "heinousness" and "coldness." While the jury recommendation did not specify which aggravating factors existed, the judge found all of the aggravating factors to have existed and found no mitigating factors in issuing the death sentence. Souter's complex opinion for the Court held that the U.S. Supreme Court did not have the jurisdiction to rule on the state of Florida's "heinous" factor. But, the justices did find that the Florida Supreme Court committed an Eighth Amendment error because it did not possess enough evidence to uphold the "coldness" factor and should have reviewed the judge's decision regarding the aggravating and mitigating factors in an independent fashion. Souter's opinion for the Court resulted in a unanimous ruling on the "heinousness" factor, while the ruling on the "coldness" factor divided the justices in a non-ideological manner.

Souter wrote a majority opinion in a capital punishment case decided late in the Rehnquist Court era (*Kelly v. South Carolina* 2002). Here, Souter wrote for a six-person majority holding that a defendant was entitled to have the judge or legal counsel instruct the jury that he would be ineligible for parole if he received a life sentence. Instead of a life sentence without the possibility of parole, the defendant was given a death sentence by the jury in the absence of such jury instruction. Souter argued in his opinion that due process required the jurors to be informed through jury instructions or through arguments presented by legal counsel.

In the more recent and publicized cases involving the death penalty, Souter sided with the liberal bloc on the Court. In *Atkins v. Virginia* (2002), Souter voted with a liberal majority to prohibit the use of the death penalty for offenders classified as "mentally retarded." He also voted with a liberal majority in *Roper v. Simmons* (2005) to raise the minimum age of eligibility for capital punishment from sixteen to eighteen. As in the *Kelly* decision, Souter disagreed with his most conservative colleagues, Chief Justice Rehnquist and Justices Scalia and Thomas, as the Court overturned precedents and incrementally diminished capital punishment in a manner that seemed consistent with a growing national trend against executions (*Washington Post* 2007).

These decisions that limited the scope of capital punishment and looked closely at the fairness of trial processes were consistent with the previously discussed opinion that Souter wrote for a liberal majority in *Rompilla v. Beard* (2005) in which he held that a defendant had received inadequate legal counsel in a death penalty case. The *Rompilla* case dealt more directly with the Sixth Amendment right to counsel; however, it also involved the death penalty issue.

Even though Souter was supportive of the death penalty since his early years as a state judicial officer, he established a liberal voting record in this area. Souter consistently voted to limit the application of the death penalty when due process rights had been violated and to abolish the use of the death penalty in cases involving the mentally retarded and defendants under the age of eighteen (Yarbrough 2005, 238). With the exception of his initial vote on the Court in *Payne*, Souter voted in favor of defendants in nearly every claim involving the death penalty.

Prisoners' Rights & Cruel and Unusual Punishment

Souter's opinions in prisoners' rights cases also demonstrated his independence, although Souter wrote only four opinions in this area of law. Early in Souter's career on the Court, he wrote for a conservative majority in *Rowland v. California Men's Colony* (1993). Here, Souter was joined by Chief Justice Rehnquist and Justices White, O'Connor, and Scalia in holding that only natural persons may qualify as indigents in the filing of in forma pauperis petitions. This case dealt with a representative association known as the California Men's Colony that served as an advisory council for the warden of a prison. The organization, composed of prisoners, tried to file an in forma pauperis petition in federal court claiming that the California Department of Corrections had violated its members' Eighth Amendment right against cruel and unusual punishment. However, Souter held that only individual persons as defined by the plain meaning of a federal law could file suit in federal court as indigents, and the organization it-self did not constitute a person under federal law.

Souter's next opinion on the topic of prisoners' rights was significant as it became controlling precedent in the area of inmate-on-inmate rape, as well as sexual misconduct by prison officials against inmates. In *Farmer v. Brennan* (1994), Souter wrote a unanimous opinion for the Court establishing a two-part test to determine a violation of the Eighth Amendment's Cruel and Unusual Punishment Clause. The first part of the test required that a prisoner objectively demonstrate that an injury was sufficiently serious, and the second part required a showing that prison officials were deliberately indifferent to the safety of an inmate. If the two-part test was satisfied, then prison officials could be held liable in a civil lawsuit. The circumstances surrounding this case involved a trans-vestite prisoner who was transferred to a prison holding violent offenders and placed in the general population where the prisoner was sexually assaulted. The prisoner claimed that prison officials deliberately ordered the transfer with knowledge that such an assault would occur. Souter's opinion ordered the district court to reconsider both the discovery motion that had been denied to the prisoner and the allegations against the prison officials in light of the two-part test.

In *Booth v. Churner* (2001), Souter also wrote for a unanimous Court in holding that the Prisoner Litigation Reform Act of 1995 required a prisoner to exhaust the administrative remedies available in order to attempt a resolution before a complaint over prison conditions could be filed in federal court. Souter's opinion focused on the statutory intent of Congress in defining the words "administrative remedies" and "available." Hence, Souter's opinion was written in a fairly technical manner with regard to the Court's interpretation of a congressional statute.

Souter's additional opinion touching upon prisoners' rights arose later in the Rehnquist Court era in *Roell v. Withrow* (2003). In *Roell*, Souter wrote for a five-justice majority in favor of a prisoner who had sued based upon an allegation that prison officials ignored his medical needs in violation of his right against cruel and unusual punishment. The main issue concerned whether prison officials consented to have the case heard before a U.S. magistrate judge instead of a U.S. district court judge. Prison officials did not object until after the U.S. magistrate judge ruled in favor of the prisoner. Souter's opinion held that consent could be inferred based upon the behavior of the prison officials who had participated in the entire litigation process without objection.

Conclusion

Justice David Souter's written opinions and voting behavior in the Rehnquist Court's criminal justice cases highlighted two trends. First, Souter evolved from a conservative state judge and a U.S. Supreme Court justice who initially voted with Chief Justice Rehnquist and Justices Scalia and Thomas into a jurist who later aligned more frequently with the liberal bloc comprised of Justices Stevens, Ginsburg, and Breyer (Hensley et al. 1997; Baum 2007). Souter was nominated by President George H. W. Bush with the expectation that he would provide another conservative vote on a Court in the midst of a conservative revolution. John Sununu told political conservatives that Souter would be a "home run" for conservatives (Garrow 1994). However, legal scholars have recognized that Souter practiced moderate pragmatism on the Court and directly challenged conservative justices such as Scalia in intellectual debates about a number of issues (Garrow 1994).

Second, Justice David Souter's decision making in the Rehnquist Court's criminal justice cases appeared consistent with the Court's historical trend in the twentieth century of providing increasing protection for defendants at the later stages of the criminal justice process (see Hensley et al. 1997). Evidently, Souter was sensitive to the fact that the Court has historically expressed serious concerns about the power of government brought to bear upon one individual who moves closer to punishment in the form of a loss of liberty or the death penalty (Hensley et al. 1997). In sum, the two decision-making patterns displayed by Souter established him as a moderately liberal justice who favored a measured and balanced approach in his opinion writing and voting behavior in criminal justice cases (Garrow 1994). This characterization of Souter is supported by a review of his opinions and votes.

In search and seizure cases, Souter's opinions for the Court in *Atwater v. City of Lago Vista* (2001) and *United States v. Banks* (2003) as well as his votes in *Florida v. Bostick* (1991) and *Arizona v. Evans* (1995) illustrated a conservative orientation toward the scope of rights in the early investigative stages of the criminal justice process. Cases raising such issues led Souter to side with the interests of law enforcement on a regular basis. Souter clearly was more conservative in search and seizure cases than in any other area of criminal justice. However, Souter later showed greater sensitivity to Fourth Amendment rights, particularly with his majority opinion in the Roberts-era case of *Georgia v. Randolph* (2006), concerning a homeowner's rejection of a consent search overriding a co-owner's previously expressed consent. In addition, his liberal votes in such landmark cases as *Indianapolis v. Edmond* (2000) and *Illinois v. Lidster* (2004), as well as in drug testing cases (*Vernonia School District v. Acton* 1995; *Ferguson v. City of Charleston* 2001) show that there were specific contexts in which Souter saw individuals' reasonable expectations of privacy as having priority over law enforcement interests. Hence, Souter's behavior can best be characterized as moderate in the area of search and seizure with a more liberal pattern of siding with the rights of criminal defendants during his later years on the Court (Hensley et al. 1997).

In contrast to Souter's decision-making behavior in search and seizure cases, Souter later demonstrated a more liberal pattern by supporting greater protection for the rights of criminal defendants during the latter stages of the criminal justice process. In regard to Fifth Amendment rights, Souter demonstrated strong support for the privilege against compelled self-incrimination in his opinions in *Withrow v. Williams* (1993) and *Missouri v. Seibert* (2004). He wholeheartedly supported the preservation of the *Miranda* precedent with his votes in such cases as *Dickerson v. United States* (2000) and *United States v. Patane* (2004).

With respect to trial rights for defendants, Souter lived up to his reputation as a "pro-fair trial" judge that was established during his years as a state court judge. Souter's opinions for the Court in *Doggett v. United States* (1992), *Rompilla v. Beard* (2005), and *Miller-el v. Dretke* (2005) caused sharp ideological divisions as Souter wrote for liberal majorities in each case. Although Souter did write two opinions with conservative outcomes involving trial rights in *United States v. Vonn* (2002) and *United States v. Dominguez Benitez* (2004), these cases were less controversial as all of the justices joined together to support unanimous decisions on the specific issues under consideration by the Court.

Finally, Souter reserved his strongest support for defendants at the final stage of the criminal justice process. With the exception of a few cases early in the Rehnquist Court era such as *Payne v. Tennessee* (1991) and *Rowland v. California Men's Colony* (1993), handed down during Souter's earlier terms on the Court, his written opinions and votes favored the claims of convicted offenders in the sentencing process, in death penalty cases, and in prisoners' rights disputes. In fact, Souter voted regularly in favor of claims by criminal defendants and convicted offenders in Eighth Amendment cases even during his initial terms on the Court (1991-1994), a period which saw him side more frequently with the conservative bloc in all other areas of criminal justice (Hensley et al. 1997). While Souter had supported tough sentences for criminal defendants, as well as the use of the death penalty as a state attorney general and state judge, he clearly distinguished his view from those of his most conservative colleagues such as Justices Antonin Scalia and Clarence Thomas, and he sought out a middle ground in these areas. While Scalia and Thomas consistently sided with the government in criminal justice cases, Souter demonstrated independence of thought and a non-ideological orientation that began during his years as a state judge and which drew praise from Republicans and Democrats in his home state (Hensley et al. 1997). In the area of criminal justice, Souter's behavior of distributing justice based upon a more practical and flexible interpretation of the law earned him the respect of legal scholars and disappointed political conservatives who had hoped that he would provide the additional vote needed to solidify the conservative bloc of justices appointed by Republican presidents Richard Nixon, Ronald Reagan, and George H. W. Bush (Garrow 1994). Souter's impact in the area of criminal justice cannot be understated and perhaps can be summed up best by Linda Greenhouse, a Pulitzer Prize winning reporter for the *New York Times*, who was quoted as saying that Souter's evolution toward the liberal end of the ideological spectrum "is probably as responsible as any single factor for the failure of the conservative revolution" in American constitutional law (Garrow 1994).

References

Baum, Lawrence. *The Supreme Court*. Washington, DC: CQ Press, 2007.

Broder, David S., and Helen Dewar. "Bush Opens Drive for Court Nominee: Confirmation Hearings Set for September," *Washington Post*, July 25, 1990.

Devroy, Ann. "President Selects Souter, 50, for 'Intellect and Ability': Court Nominee Called Classic Conservative," *Washington Post*, July 24, 1990.

Dowd, Maureen. "A Swift Nomination: Questions on Abortion to Be Left for Hearings on Confirmation," *New York Times*, July 24, 1990.

Garrow, David J. "Justice Souter Emerges." *New York Times Magazine,* September 25, 1994. http://query.nytimes.com/gst/fullpage.html?res=9A01EFDD103BF936A1575-AC0A962958260 (accessed October 22, 2010).

Greenhouse, Linda. "An Intellectual Mind: David Hackett Souter." *New York Times*, July 24, 1990.

Hensley, Thomas R., Christopher E. Smith, and Joyce A. Baugh. *The Changing Supreme Court: Constitutional Rights and Liberties*. Belmont, CA: Wadsworth, 1997.

Johnson, Scott, and Christopher E. Smith. "David Souter's First Term on the Supreme Court: The Impact of a New Justice." *Judicature* 75, 5 (1992): 238-43.

Jordan, William S. III. "Justice David Souter and Statutory Interpretation." *University of Toledo Law Review* 23 (1992): 491-530.

Lewis, Neil A. "Combing the Past for Clues on Souter," *New York Times*, September 2, 1990. I.

Marcus, Ruth. "Souter: Conservative Mindset, Careful Jurist," *Washington Post*, July 25, 1990.

Newsweek. "Souter: Slow Off the Mark." May 27, 1991. http://www.newsweek.com/1991/05/26/souter-slow-off-the-mark.html (accessed January 10, 2011).

Segal, Jeffrey A., and Harold J. Spaeth. *The Supreme Court and the Attitudinal Model Revisited.* Cambridge: Cambridge University Press, 1993.

Smith, Christopher E., and Scott P. Johnson. "Newcomer on the High Court: Justice David Souter and the Supreme Court's 1990 Term." *South Dakota Law Review* 37 (1992): 21-43.

Smith, Robert H. "Justice Souter Joins the Rehnquist Court: An Empirical Study of Supreme Court Voting Patterns." *Kansas Law Review* 41 (1992): 11-95.

Washington Post. "Death Penalty in Review: Capital Punishment Loses Ground, For Good Reasons." December 23, 2007, 6(B).

Yarbrough, Tinsley E. *David Hackett Souter: Traditional Republican on the Rehnquist Court.* Oxford: Oxford University Press, 2005.

Cases Cited

Arizona v. Evans, 514 U.S. 1 (1995)

Arizona v. Fulminante, 499 U.S. 279 (1991)

Atkins v. Virginia, 536 U.S. 304 (2002)

Atwater v. City of Lago Vista, 532 U.S. 318 (2001)

Batson v. Kentucky, 476 U.S. 79 (1986)

Booth v. Churner, 532 U.S. 731 (2001)

Booth v. Maryland, 482 U.S. 496 (1987)

County of Riverside v. McLaughlin, 500 U.S. 44 (1991)

Dickerson v. United States, 530 U.S. 428, 2000

Doggett v. United States, 505 U.S. 647 (1992)
Farmer v. Brennan, 511 U.S. 825 (1994)
Ferguson v. City of Charleston, 532 U.S. 67 (2001)
Florida v. Bostick, 501 U.S. 429 (1991)
Georgia v. Randolph, 547 U.S. 103 (2006)
Harmelin v. Michigan, 501 U.S. 957 (1991)
Illinois v. Caballes, 543 U.S. 405 (2005)
Illinois v. Lidster, 540 U.S. 419 (2004)
Indianapolis v. Edmond, 531 U.S. 32 (2000)
Johnson v. United States, 544 U.S. 295 (2005)
Jones v. United States, 526 U.S. 227 (1999)
Kelly v. South Carolina, 534 U.S. 236 (2002)
Kyles v. Whitley, 514 U.S. 419 (1995)
Miller-El v. Dretke, 545 U.S. 231 (2005)
Miranda v. Arizona, 384 U.S. 436 (1966)
Missouri v. Seibert, 542 U.S. 600 (2004)
Mu' min v. Virginia, 500 U.S. 415 (1991)
Payne v. Tennessee, 501 U.S. 808 (1991)
Peretz v. United States, 501 U.S. 923 (1991)
Roell v. Withrow, 538 U.S. 580 (2003)
Rompilla v. Beard, 545 U.S. 374 (2005)
Roper v. Simmons, 543 U.S. 551 (2005)
Rowland v. California Men's Colony, 506 U.S. 194 (1993)
Schad v. Arizona, 501 U.S. 624 (1991)
Shepard v. United States, 544 U.S. 12 (2005)
Sochor v. Florida, 504 U.S. 527 (1992)
South Carolina v. Gathers, 490 U.S. 805 (1989)
State v. Coppola, 536 A.2d 1236 (1987)
State v. Denney, 130 N.H. 217 (1987)
Stone v. Powell, 428 U.S. 465 (1976)
United States v. Balsys. 524 U.S. 666 (1998)
United States v. Banks, 540 U.S. 31 (2003)
United States v. Dominguez Benitez, 542 U.S. 74 (2004)
United States v. Drayton, 536 U.S. 194 (2002)
United States v. Patane, 542 U.S. 630 (2004)
United States v. R. L. C., 503 U.S. 291 (1992)
United States v. Vonn, 535 U.S. 55 (2002)
United States v. Waldeck, 909 F.2d 555 (1990)
Vernonia School District v. Acton, 515 U.S. 646 (1995)
Wade v. United States, 504 U.S. 181 (1992)
Wilson v. Seiter, 501 U.S. 294 (1991)
Withrow v. Williams, 507 U.S. 680 (1993)
Yates v. Evatt, 500 U.S. 393 (1991)

Chapter 11
Clarence Thomas:
Consistent, Conservative, & Contrarian

Joyce A. Baugh

When federal appeals court judge Clarence Thomas arrived on the U.S. Supreme Court in October of 1991, he succeeded Thurgood Marshall, a justice revered by the nation's most prominent civil liberties and civil rights activists. Marshall was one of the Court's strongest advocates of due process protections for criminal defendants and incarcerated offenders. He was a staunch opponent of the death penalty, and he consistently voted to uphold two of the Court's most controversial Warren Court era judicial policies—the exclusionary rule and *Miranda* warnings. In addition, Marshall consistently sought to eradicate racial and class discrimination in the criminal justice system. In *Furman v. Georgia* (1972) during the Burger Court era, Marshall joined four colleagues in holding that the death penalty, as it was then being applied, constituted cruel and unusual punishment in violation of the Eighth Amendment. Moreover, he called for the complete abolition of the death penalty, a position maintained throughout his tenure on the high court. In Marshall's view, not only had capital punishment been imposed in discriminatory and arbitrary ways, but also he argued that it was an "excessive and unnecessary punishment" that "wreaks havoc with our entire criminal justice system" (364). In 1982, when the Court gave police officers significant discretion in conducting automobile searches without warrants issued by a judge, he complained that the new rule masked "the startling assumption that a policeman's determination of probable cause is the functional equivalent of the determination of a neutral and detached magistrate" (*United States v. Ross* 1982, 833). And, as the Court repeatedly created exceptions to the exclusionary rule and *Miranda* warnings, Marshall protested vigorously. Inevitably, new appointees to the Supreme Court are compared to the departing justices whom they are replacing. Thomas's arrival at the Supreme Court placed him in a context to be compared to one of the Court's most consistent supporters of individual rights in criminal justice cases.

Clarence Thomas was born in 1948 near Savannah, Georgia. As an African American growing up in Georgia during the 1950s, he experienced first-hand the harsh aspects of racial segregation and discrimination. He earned his university degrees from Holy Cross College in Massachusetts and Yale Law School. After working for Republican Senator John Danforth of Missouri, he served in President Ronald Reagan's Administration as an official in the U.S. Department of Education and later as the Chairman of the Equal Employment Opportunity Commission. Thomas served briefly as an appointee of President George H.W. Bush on the U.S. Court of Appeals for the District of Columbia Circuit before Bush nominated Thomas to succeed Marshall on the Supreme Court. Since Marshall was the first and only African American justice on the Supreme Court, it was widely recognized that Bush chose Thomas from among available conservatives, despite his relatively young age and the fact that most of his professional experience had been in administration rather than legal practice or judging, because Bush did not want to be accused of making the high court all-white again.

Before being nominated to the Supreme Court, Thomas had not written much about criminal justice issues. But, given his service in the Reagan and Bush Administrations that had strongly criticized the pro-defendant decisions of the Warren Court and, to a more limited extent, the Burger Court, Thomas's critics feared that he would help to undermine liberal doctrines and rulings. Despite his service in these conservative administrations, however, Judge Thomas made statements during his confirmation testimony that led some observers to suggest that he, like Marshall, possessed an empathic understanding of criminal defendants and might work to ensure due process in the criminal justice system. In a dramatic moment when asked why he wanted to serve on the Court, Thomas replied,

> You know, on my current court I have occasion to look out the window that faces C Street, and there are converted buses that bring in the criminal defendants to our criminal justice system, busload after busload. And you look out, and you say to yourself, and I say to myself almost every day, "But for the grace of God there go I." So you feel that you have the same fate, or could have, as those individuals. So I can walk in their shoes, and I can bring something different to the Court. And I think it is a humbling responsibility; and it is one that, if confirmed, I will carry out to the best of my ability. (U.S. Congress, Committee on the Judiciary 1991, vol. 1, 260)

Later, in response to a question from Senator Strom Thurmond regarding proposals to limit death row appeals, Thomas emphasized, "the death penalty is the harshest penalty that can be imposed, and it is certainly one that is unchangeable. And we should be most concerned about providing all the rights and all the due process that can be provided and should be provided to individuals who face that kind of consequence" (133).

Justice Thomas's actual performance, however, has been quite the opposite. From the very beginning of his tenure, he joined Chief Justice Rehnquist and Justice Scalia as the justices least likely to vote to support criminal defendants' rights (see Hensley, Smith, and Baugh 1997; Smith 1996), and this pattern has continued throughout his tenure on the high court (see Smith and McCall 2003,

2004; Smith, McCall, and McCall 2007). One scholarly analysis of his first seven terms reported that he supported defendants' claims primarily only in unanimous or nearly-unanimous cases and, when the Court was closely divided, Thomas generally sided with the government (Smith and Baugh 2000). The author of another comprehensive study of Thomas's Supreme Court record also underscored his conservatism in this area, noting that when he writes separate opinions in criminal justice cases, his opinions reflect "a distinctive liberal strain" only in one aspect of criminal law: "strict interpretation of criminal statutes" (Graber 2003, 77).

While Thomas's conservatism is consistent across a range of criminal justice issues, he has written most extensively in two areas: the Eighth Amendment's Cruel and Unusual Punishments Clause, particularly concerning prison conditions and capital punishment; and habeas corpus appeals in death penalty cases. This chapter examines a number of these cases, along with several notable opinions involving Fourth Amendment search and seizure matters, Fifth Amendment self-incrimination issues, and Sixth Amendment jury trial concerns. The primary focus is on his concurring and dissenting opinions, as they most clearly reveal his judicial philosophy and approach. Several of his majority and plurality opinions also are discussed. The overall themes in Thomas's writings reflect an emphasis on promoting efficiency in the criminal justice process and deferring to state officials' decision making, even when those officials may be responsible for the rights' violations being challenged.

In addition, Thomas claims to follow the philosophy of original intent, or originalism, in deciding cases. "Strict adherence to this [originalist] approach is essential if we are to fulfill our constitutionally assigned role of giving full effect to the mandate of the Framers without infusing the constitutional fabric with our own political views" (*Lewis v. Casey* 1996, 367). The extent to which he actually relies on originalist theory in his decision making is debatable, however.

Prison Conditions & Prisoners' Rights

Thomas's very first dissent concerned the issue of prison conditions, an area of jurisprudence in which Justice Marshall had made a major contribution. In 1976, Marshall wrote the majority opinion in *Estelle v. Gamble* (1976), endorsing the idea that prisoners could sue for deprivation of medical care and setting a subjective standard to be used in evaluating such claims. He concluded that "deliberate indifference to serious medical needs of prisoners constitutes the 'unnecessary and wanton infliction of pain' . . . proscribed by the Eighth Amendment" (104). Two years later, the Court created an objective standard for deciding cases concerning the actual conditions of confinement (e.g., food, cell size, disciplinary issues). According to this ruling, courts are to examine the conditions and practices themselves to determine if they violate concepts of "dignity, civilized standards, humanity, and decency" (*Hutto v. Finney* 1978, 685). The Burger

Court reaffirmed this standard three years later: conditions were cruel and unusual "if they violate[d] contemporary standards of decency, involve[d] wanton
and unnecessary infliction of pain, or result[ed] in unquestioned and serious
deprivation of basic human needs" (*Rhodes v. Chapman* 1981, 347).

Thomas almost immediately took a different approach, one seriously at
odds with these established precedents. The case involved an inmate who had
been beaten by guards in a correctional facility in Angola, Louisiana. In *Supreme Discomfort: The Divided Soul of Clarence Thomas* (2007, 238), Kevin
Merida and Michael Fletcher contend that "[n]o case did more to define Clarence Thomas in many people's minds than one brought by Keith Hudson." Two
prison guards had placed Hudson in restraints and then punched him in the
mouth, eyes, chest, and stomach—one of them had had previous run-ins with
Hudson. Reportedly, their supervisor watched the beating from nearby and told
them "not to have too much fun." About two months after his injuries healed,
Hudson filed a civil rights lawsuit in federal court for damages from the beating,
which had resulted in bruises, bleeding, loose teeth, and a cracked partial dental
plate. He prepared his own petition, following the formats contained in a book
he borrowed from another inmate. The district court ruled in his favor, but Louisiana appealed. A three-judge appellate court rejected his suit, concluding that
his injuries were "minor" and did not demonstrate the "significant injury" required to proceed with such litigation. After his request for an *en banc* hearing
by the appeals court was rejected, he petitioned the Supreme Court for review.

The high court granted his petition and, by a 7-2 vote, ruled in Hudson's
favor. Writing for the majority, Justice O'Connor overruled the "significant injury" requirement, holding instead that Eighth Amendment physical force cases
required courts to determine "whether force was applied in a good-faith effort to
maintain or restore discipline, or [was applied] maliciously and sadistically to
cause harm" (*Hudson v. McMillian* 1992, 7). Moreover, O'Connor addressed the
appropriate standards for review in cases concerning practices and conditions
inside correctional institutions. O'Connor looked to the subjective standard established in *Whitley v. Albers* (1986) that asks whether a use of force by corrections officers is "malicious" or applied for the purpose of causing pain.

By contrast, Thomas not only criticized O'Connor's interpretation of the
appropriate standard of review, but he argued vehemently that the framers never
intended for the Eighth Amendment to apply to practices and conditions inside
correctional facilities. "Surely prison was not a more congenial place in the early
years of the Republic than it is today; nor were judges and commentators so
naïve as to be unaware of the often harsh conditions of prison life. Rather, they
simply did not conceive of the Eighth Amendment as protecting inmates from
harsh treatment" (*Hudson v. McMillian* 1992, 19-20). Thus Thomas would impose a "significant injury" requirement in such cases, although Thomas's interpretive approach indicates that he would prefer to decline to recognize the existence of any rights for prisoners in the use-of-force context.

Thomas's attempt to use original intent to analyze this issue evoked criticism from scholars who questioned his historical analysis. In *First Principles:*

The Jurisprudence of Clarence Thomas, Scott Gerber analyzed Thomas's first five terms, including discussions of *Hudson* and two additional prison condition cases (*Helling v McKinney* 1993; *Farmer v. Brennan* 1994). Gerber maintained that Thomas "was *correct* [emphasis in original] in his reading of the [Eighth Amendment's] text and history" (128), and he chastised those who questioned the justice's interpretation. These critics noted, however, that the Framers did not even speak to the issue of whether the Eighth Amendment applied to prison conditions, likely because "the concept of the prison as an institution for serving significant criminal sentences was essentially born in the nineteenth century—after the Eighth Amendment had been drafted and ratified" (Smith and Baugh 2000, 91; see also Friedman 1993). Indeed, the oldest prison in the United States—New Jersey's Trenton State Prison—did not open until 1798, seven years after the Bill of Rights was ratified (Clear, Cole, and Reisig 2006). Finally, as Smith (2000, 227) pointed out, "How can original intent be applied as an approach to constitutional interpretation when discussing an institution—the modern prison—that was unknown to the Eighth Amendment's authors and ratifiers? How can anyone know what the Eighth Amendment's framers would have thought about the issue of prison conditions when they only had knowledge of conditions in local jails that were used for short-term confinement?"

Thomas's *Hudson* dissent also illustrated his willingness to leave matters of prison conditions and prisoners' rights in the hands of state officials rather than permitting federal judicial supervision of these problems. Joined only by Scalia, Thomas wrote,

> Today's expansion of the Cruel and Unusual Punishment Clause beyond all bounds of history and precedent is, I suspect, yet another manifestation of the pervasive view that the Federal Constitution must address all ills in our society. Abusive behavior by prison guards is deplorable conduct that properly evokes outrage and contempt. But that does not mean that it is invariably unconstitutional. The Eighth Amendment is not, and should not be turned into, a National Code of Prison Regulation. *(Hudson v. McMillian* 1992, 28)

His opinion elicited scorn from many corners, including his colleagues. Justice Harry Blackmun labeled Thomas's position on the "significant injury" requirement to be seriously misguided and, according to Merida and Fletcher (2007), was stunned after seeing an early draft of Thomas's dissent. O'Connor objected, "To deny, as the dissent does, the difference between punching a prisoner in the face and serving him unappetizing food is to ignore the concepts of dignity, civilized standards, humanity, and decency that animate the Eighth Amendment" (*Hudson v. McMillian* 1992, 11; internal citation omitted). Several authors have noted that a *New York Times* editorial referred to Thomas as the "youngest, cruelest justice" while a columnist for the *Washington Post* called the dissent "bizarre" (Merida and Fletcher 2007; Greenburg 2007; Tushnet 2006).

In defending Thomas against these charges, Gerber chastised scholars and "liberal members of the popular press" for engaging in "ad hominem attacks upon his character" and misrepresenting his views. According to Gerber, these analysts accused Thomas of condoning the torture of prisoners when Thomas had simply argued that prisoners should turn to state law to redress their grievances or, if need be, perhaps a remedy might be available under the Fourteenth Amendment's Due Process Clause. Gerber's argument failed to recognize a critical point. This approach could place a prisoner in the position of asking for relief from the very government system whose officials are responsible for the alleged rights violation.

The severe criticisms directed at Thomas's *Hudson* dissent did not deter the justice. In two subsequent cases, he adhered to the claim that the Eighth Amendment does not apply to prison conditions, and he rebuked his colleagues for interfering with state and local officials in exercising their authority to administer correctional facilities as they saw fit. Justice White's majority opinion in *Helling v. McKinney* (1993) ruled that a non-smoking prisoner could file an Eighth Amendment claim on the grounds that prison officials showed deliberate indifference to his health when they placed him in a cell with another inmate who smoked five packs of cigarettes per day. But Thomas, again citing original intent, argued that "the text and history of the Eighth Amendment, together with pre-*Estelle* [v. *Gamble*] precedent, raise substantial doubt in my mind that the Eighth Amendment proscribes a prison deprivation that is not inflicted as part of the sentence" (*Helling v. McKinney* 1993, 42). This was particularly striking because it was a direct assault on Marshall's earlier opinion. Thomas wrote, "Because I seriously doubt that *Estelle* was correctly decided, I decline to join the Court's holding" (42).

One year later, *Farmer v. Brennan* (1994) involved a transsexual prisoner who was assaulted after being placed in the general population of a maximum security prison. The majority applied the deliberate indifference test, holding that prison officials are liable in such cases if they know that the inmate faces a substantial risk of harm and they fail to take action to reduce the risk. Predictably, Thomas rejected this approach, contending that the appropriate standard was "significant injury" rather than the *risk of injury* to the prisoner. He continued to assert that the Eighth Amendment should not be applied to cases concerning excessive force, medical treatment, conditions of confinement, or any other matters in correctional institutions. This is an approach that even the other conservative justices—with the exception of Scalia—could not abide.

At his confirmation hearings, when Thomas uttered the words "But for the grace of God there go I" in describing the busloads of criminal defendants that he saw from his office window, some interpreted this as a sign that he would show empathy towards defendants and prisoners in future cases. Tushnet (2006, 93), however, had a different interpretation of what Thomas meant by the statement:

> For liberals and moderates, "But for the grace of God there go I" is a statement about the speaker's empathy for people caught up in circumstances in which the speaker could just as easily have found himself. For Thomas, however, the

statement may have been deeply theological. Thomas said that the grace of God had been visited upon him and made him different from—no longer the same as—the defendants he saw from his office window. There may have been no discernible reason for the fact that God's grace had fallen on him rather than them, but the fact that it had done so separated him from the criminal defendants, rather than connected him to them. The "grace of God" statement, then, really shouldn't have given hope to skeptics about Thomas.

Tushnet certainly has a plausible theory, but it would be more plausible had Thomas not followed "the grace of God" statement with "So I can walk in their shoes, and I can bring something different to the Court" (U.S. Congress, Committee on the Judiciary 1991, 260).

In his criminal justice opinions during the Rehnquist Court era, Thomas focused primarily on preserving the autonomy and discretion of corrections officials and on highlighting technical details to raise doubts about the legitimacy of prisoners' claims. A 2002 case from Alabama, *Hope v. Pelzer* (2002), is illustrative. Prison guards had twice handcuffed Larry Hope to a hitching post in the hot sun outside the prison. His hands were placed above shoulder level that caused pain and injuries to his arms. The first episode lasted for two hours and occurred because of Hope's altercation with another prisoner on his work squad. The guard captain released Hope after determining that the other inmate had caused the altercation. The second episode, however, was the result of an altercation between Hope and a guard following a bus ride to a work site. This time, in an incident involving four guards, Hope was subdued, handcuffed, placed in leg irons, and returned to the prison. Back at the prison, the guards cuffed him, shirtless, to a hitching post for seven hours without bathroom breaks and very little water, and they verbally taunted him.

Hope filed suit in federal district court against three of the guards from the first incident, one of whom apparently was also involved in handcuffing him in the second incident. A U.S. magistrate judge in the district court entered a finding of qualified immunity for the guards without determining whether their conduct violated the Eighth Amendment. Under the doctrine of qualified immunity, specific government officials may be held liable for constitutional violations only if it was clearly established at the time the conduct occurred that the officials' actions were illegal. The district court and court of appeals affirmed the U.S. magistrate judge's judgment. Although the judges found that the use of the hitching post violated the Eighth Amendment because the purpose was punitive rather than to restore order or suppress a threat, the appellate court nonetheless affirmed. The court concluded that, based on existing law and precedents, the guards would not have known that their conduct violated an established constitutional right.

The Supreme Court recognized an Eighth Amendment violation and, more importantly, rejected the guards' qualified immunity defense. Writing for a six-member majority, Justice Stevens concluded that use of the hitching post "unnecessarily and wantonly inflicted pain" and, based on Supreme Court and circuit precedents, the Alabama corrections department's regulations, and a U.S. Department of Justice report, the guards' conduct "violated clearly established statutory or constitutional rights of which a reasonable person would have known" (*Hope v. Pelzer* 2002, 742). Thomas, joined by Rehnquist and Scalia, criticized the majority for not focusing more attention on the specific allegations Hope asserted against the three guards. Thomas noted allegations that other guards were involved and he claimed that the record was not clear as to which guards were involved in the two incidents. Most importantly, he rejected the majority's conclusion that the precedents and other documents clearly established that handcuffing Hope to the hitching post violated the Eighth Amendment. "It is far from obvious," Thomas wrote, "that respondents, by attaching petitioner to a restraining bar, acted with 'deliberate indifference' to his health and safety" (758-59). In addition, unlike the majority which viewed the hitching post incident as primarily retributive, he saw a legitimate penological purpose— encouraging compliance with prison rules while on work duty.

Thomas's penchant for following rules may be connected to his childhood experiences which included being reared by a strict, disciplinarian grandfather and attending Catholic schools. In his memoir, *My Grandfather's Son*, Thomas recounted what his grandfather told him and his younger brother when they were sent to live with him in Savannah, Georgia. Myers Anderson, whom Thomas called "Daddy," emphasized that the boys would be expected to have "manners and behavior" and follow "rules and regulations" (Thomas 2007, 12). Thomas continued, "Whenever we failed to obey . . . punishment was swift, sure, and painful. Daddy didn't whip us regularly, but our encounters with his belt or a switch were far from infrequent, and it soon became clear that he meant to control every aspect of our lives" (12). He described his grandfather as possessing an "iron will" and "unbending rules." Myers Anderson sent Thomas to St. Benedict the Moor Catholic School, one of the three black Catholic elementary schools in Savannah, where the strict discipline complemented his efforts at home. Merida and Fletcher (2007, 60) noted that he "thrived under the Franciscan sisters' tough-love approach," and he "was especially fond of his eighth-grade teacher . . . whom he singled out during his confirmation hearings and who testified on his behalf." In his memoir, Thomas offered this assessment of the strong discipline meted out by his grandfather and the nuns: "Sometimes their strict rules chafed, but they also gave me a feeling of security, and above all they opened doors of opportunity leading to a path that took me far from the cramped world into which I had been born" (Thomas 2007, 27).

Thomas's dissent in *Hope v. Pelzer* (2002) demonstrated his tendency to give more credence to the claims of corrections officials over those made by incarcerated offenders. Again, not only are his views at odds with the majority, but his views would represent a dramatic shift in the Court's jurisprudence regarding prisoners' rights and conditions inside correctional institutions. In addition, he simply did not seem to have an appreciation of the human element underlying these cases, namely the risks of inhumane suffering and physical harm.

Instead, the efficient operation of the penal system seemed to be paramount in Thomas's assessment of prison practices.

Capital Punishment:
Procedural Issues & Habeas Corpus

In the decade before Thomas arrived, the Court's jurisprudence regarding both the death penalty in general and, more specifically, the extent of habeas corpus relief available to capital defendants, underwent significant turmoil. In 1982, the justices initially refused to permit capital punishment to be inflicted on accomplices to felony murder who had not actually participated in the killing (*Enmund v. Florida* 1982). The decision was based on the Eighth Amendment's proportionality principle, the concept that a punishment is cruel and unusual if it is disproportionate to the crime committed. Five years later, however, the Court held that such accomplices could be sentenced to death if they "acted with reckless disregard for human life" (*Tison v. Arizona* 1987). Similarly, by 5-4 votes, the Court initially rejected the use of victim impact statements in sentencing proceedings in capital cases, concluding that such statements are irrelevant and risk causing capricious applications of the death penalty (*Booth v. Maryland* 1987; *South Carolina v. Gathers* 1989). But after David Souter was appointed to succeed William Brennan, the Court reversed itself and decided to permit juries to consider victim impact statements (*Payne v. Tennessee* 1991).

Although these cases addressed important constitutional issues in the application of capital punishment, death penalty proponents directed some of their harshest criticism at judicial decisions granting habeas corpus relief to capital defendants. Conservatives in Congress, the executive branch, state capitols, and think tanks had long complained of the "excesses" of the Warren Court in expanding due process for criminal defendants, especially decisions that granted federal habeas review of state criminal convictions. They criticized these decisions for creating inordinate delays between the imposition of a death sentence and the actual execution of the convicted offender. They also asserted that successive habeas appeals made a mockery of the criminal justice system by allowing convicted offenders to escape the consequences of their actions and by permitting federal judges to improperly intrude upon state criminal justice proceedings.

Campaigning for the presidency in 1968, President Nixon pledged to appoint justices who would restore "law and order" to the criminal justice system and side with the "peace forces" against the criminals. Although Nixon, like the 1980s president Ronald Reagan, was successful in appointing conservatives, including Chief Justice Warren Burger, the Burger Court was unable to quickly repudiate the Warren Court's decisions and shift the Court in a strong, conservative direction. Initial efforts in Congress to alter the law on habeas corpus also did not bear much fruit. Finally, in 1996 Congress passed the Antiterrorism and

Effective Death Penalty Act (AEDPA) to curb habeas corpus appeals in general—not just in capital punishment cases.

As Congress worked on legislation to reform habeas corpus law, the Rehnquist Court began to issue decisions revising the rules regarding federal constitutional claims brought by state prisoners (see Yackle 1993, 1994). In 1991, the Court held that offenders are normally limited to filing only one habeas petition, and that one petition must include all of their claims (*McClesky v. Zant* 1991). Under this ruling, they may not file additional petitions even if they later discover new information indicating a potential violation of rights in their cases. That same year the justices concluded that when procedural errors, such as missing a filing deadline, cause claims to be forfeited in state courts, those claims are also barred from federal habeas review (*Coleman v. Thompson* 1991). Two years earlier in *Teague v. Lane* (1989), a majority had held that offenders who demonstrate a violation of a federal constitutional right may obtain a new trial only if they can show that the right was clearly recognized at the time of their initial trials. These cases went a long way toward reducing the role of the federal courts in preserving due process in criminal cases, especially those involving capital punishment.

Justice Thomas's confirmation testimony suggested that he might disagree with legislative proposals and Court decisions limiting federal habeas review. When he was asked by Senator Strom Thurmond about limiting the number of appeals provided to death row inmates, he said, "I believe that there should be reasonable restrictions at some point, but not to the point that an individual is deprived of his constitutional rights" (U.S. Congress, Committee on the Judiciary 1991, 133). Responding to Senator Patrick Leahy's question about whether the Court's decisions limiting habeas in cases such as *McClesky v. Zant* (1991) were appropriate exercises of its power to alter precedents, Thomas said, "I think that activism, going beyond either the legislation or beyond the law on either side is inappropriate. I don't think that any brand, whether it is conservative activism or liberal activism . . . is appropriate" (U.S. Congress, Committee on the Judiciary 1991, 352-53).

Thomas's votes and opinions on these issues during the Rehnquist Court era were in the opposite direction, however. His positions in death penalty cases, especially those regarding habeas relief, reflected both a desire to defer to the judgments of lower court judges and state officials, as well as technical applications of rules that promote efficiency in criminal justice processes over the rights of individuals to due process. In addition, when writing separately in these cases, he often went farther than even his most conservative colleagues; he urged the Court to reexamine and overrule longstanding precedents. *Graham v. Collins* (1993) was a prime example. Thomas joined Justice White's majority opinion rejecting a federal habeas claim pertaining to Texas's capital sentencing procedures that barred juries from considering certain mitigating evidence in deciding whether to issue a death sentence. The defense counsel had pointed to evidence of the defendant's abusive childhood, but Texas law instructing the jury to consider three "special issues" did not permit consideration of this evidence. Graham's conviction and sentence became final in 1984, and he unsuccessfully sought review in the Texas courts, federal district court, and a federal appellate court in 1987 and 1988. He petitioned the Supreme Court for review and, while his petition was pending there, the high court found a rights violation in *Penry v. Lynaugh* (1989), another case involving Texas's capital sentencing framework. In *Penry*, mitigating evidence of the defendant's mental retardation and childhood abuse had not been given proper consideration by the jury. Therefore, the Court remanded Graham's petition to the federal appellate court for reconsideration in light of its *Penry* ruling, but the appellate court rejected it once again. When the case returned to the Supreme Court, the majority held that, in relying upon *Penry*, Graham was seeking a "new rule" not available to him because of the 1989 *Teague* decision.

Thomas not only joined the majority in *Graham*, but he took the additional step of calling for *Penry* to be overruled altogether. In doing so, he first recalled the 1972 decision in *Furman v. Georgia* in which the Court ruled 5-4 that the death penalty violated the Eighth Amendment because of the way it was applied. Thomas claimed incorrectly that the main reason for the decision was the justices' conclusion that excessive jury discretion had resulted in racial discrimination in capital punishment. While some of the justices did indeed express concerns about racial discrimination in the application of the death penalty, their discussions were much broader. There was no majority opinion, and each of the five members who voted to strike the death penalty issued a separate opinion. Brennan and Marshall argued that the death penalty itself, not just its application under the procedures in existence at that time, was always cruel and unusual punishment in violation of the Eighth Amendment, and each offered his own explanation for this conclusion. Justices William O. Douglas, Potter Stewart, and Byron White focused on the idea that death sentences were meted out based on the discretion of judges and juries and that this resulted in arbitrary, capricious, and discriminatory decisions. These three expressed a common theme:

> They each suggested that the death-sentencing systems under scrutiny in *Furman* were unconstitutional because of two factors: the infrequency with which juries actually imposed the death penalty, and the lack of any legitimate explanation of why some persons among those convicted of atrocious crimes received life sentences, while others convicted of atrocious crimes were sentenced to death. (Baldus, Woodworth, and Pulaski 1990, 12-13)

In *Graham*, Thomas stressed, nonetheless, that concern about racial discrimination by juries was the overriding factor in *Furman*. Consequently, he claimed that the requirement for juries to consider *any* mitigating factors in deciding whether to impose a death sentence actually exacerbates the problem of racial discrimination. A bewildered Stevens wrote in dissent, "I do not see how permitting full consideration of a defendant's mental retardation and history of childhood abuse, as in *Penry*, or of a defendant's youth, as in this case, in any way increases the risk of race-based or otherwise arbitrary decisionmaking"

(*Graham* 1993, 504). Finally, invoking his usual deference to state officials, Thomas admonished the dissenters to "leave it to elected state legislators 'representing organized society,' to decide which factors are 'particularly relevant' to the sentencing decision" (499).

In Thomas's view, making the death penalty mandatory for certain crimes would solve the problem of juries making arbitrary, capricious, and discriminatory decisions. The Court rejected statutes providing mandatory death sentences in *Woodson v. North Carolina* in 1976, ruling instead that capital sentencing requires careful, individualized decision making. Thomas's position that mandatory sentences would eliminate discriminatory decisions failed to recognize the effect of discretionary decision making in the steps leading up to the sentencing phase of a capital case. As Smith, DeJong, and Burrow (2003, 65) noted, "Death sentences are the product of cumulative discretionary decisions beginning with the prosecutor's discretionary decision to seek the death penalty through a judge's or jury's imposition of capital punishment, and including indictment decisions by prosecutors and defense attorneys, and evidentiary and other rulings by trial judges."

In some respects, Thomas's mischaracterization of the *Furman* decision in *Graham* is not that surprising. A year earlier, he had drawn criticism from his colleagues for his opinion in *Wright v. West* (1992), another case involving habeas review. Here, however, Thomas turned what should have been a routine, unanimous decision into a controversial one. As Jan Crawford Greenburg (2007) recounted the story, the case involved Frank Robert West, a state defendant who had been convicted of a burglary. West was unsuccessful in challenging his conviction in state courts, but a federal appeals court granted his habeas petition and ruled that the evidence used to convict him was insufficient. The Bush Administration weighed in, urging the justices to use this case to cut back dramatically on federal habeas review of state convictions. When the case was discussed in conference, the justices were unanimous in concluding that the appellate court was wrong and that, in fact, the evidence supported West's conviction.

Chief Justice Rehnquist assigned the opinion to Thomas, but when Thomas submitted his draft, most of his colleagues refused to join it. And when the decision became final, they assailed his historical analysis of habeas law, including his description of earlier cases, as grossly inaccurate and misleading. Greenburg (2007, 136) noted that it is rare for justices to single out each other by name in their written opinions, but she said that O'Connor's separate concurrence in the outcome "eviscerated Thomas, mentioning him by name eighteen times." Greenburg continued: "O'Connor was brutal, paragraph after paragraph. She didn't disagree with Thomas on the outcome, but she delivered a stinging lecture on how he'd summarized the law. 'Justice Thomas errs in describing the history of habeas corpus law,' she said. 'Justice Thomas quotes Justice Powell's opinion out of context,' she said. 'Justice Thomas errs in characterizing a 1953 case'. . . . On and on, eighteen times." Justices Blackmun and Stevens joined O'Connor's opinion, which concurred only in the result. In the end, although the vote remained 9-0 against West, there was no majority opinion, with only Rehnquist and Scalia joining Thomas. Justices Souter, Kennedy, and White, like Justice O'Connor, also wrote separate concurrences. Gerber (1999, 137) offered a somewhat more charitable interpretation of the events in *West*, but in the end he acknowledged that Thomas "advance[d] a questionable reading of habeas corpus decisions."

O'Dell v. Netherland (1997), similar to *Graham v. Collins* (1993), questioned the retroactive application of rules for federal habeas review. In 1994, the Court required in *Simmons v. South Carolina* (1993) that in capital sentencing proceedings, when prosecutors present as evidence arguments about the future dangerousness of defendants, the offenders must be permitted to inform their sentencing juries that they are ineligible for parole. Otherwise, the Court reasoned, juries could incorrectly conclude that their failure to recommend a death sentence might result in the defendant eventually being released from prison. O'Dell, whose death sentence became final in 1988, six years before the *Simmons* ruling, filed a habeas petition asserting that his death sentence was faulty because he had not been permitted to inform the jury of his parole ineligibility. Thomas's opinion for a five-member majority rejected O'Dell's claim, holding that the rule established in *Simmons* was a new rule under the criteria established in *Teague* for retroactivity and, therefore, O'Dell was not entitled to a new sentencing hearing. The dissenters disputed that the rule in *Simmons* was new, and they argued that even if it were "it is of such importance to the accuracy and fairness of a capital sentencing proceeding that it should be applied consistently to all prisoners whose death sentences were imposed in violation of the rule," whether they were sentenced before *Simmons* was decided or afterward (*O'Dell v. Netherland* 1997, 173).

Despite the Court's rejection of O'Dell's claim that *Simmons* should have been retroactively applied to his case, in 2001 the Court reiterated the requirement that juries in capital sentencing proceedings be informed about parole ineligibility when the defendant's future dangerousness is raised by the prosecutor. *Shafer v. South Carolina* (2001) involved a dispute between the prosecution and defense about whether the prosecution had put future dangerousness at issue, and the trial judge accepted the prosecutor's claim that he had not done so. The judge instructed the jury that "life imprisonment means until the death of the offender" and "parole ineligibility or eligibility is not for your consideration" (43, 45). The South Carolina Supreme Court determined that because the state's statutory scheme permitted a second alternative to death—a mandatory minimum thirty-year sentence—the *Simmons* rule no longer applied. Justice Ginsburg's majority opinion, joined by six other justices, rejected this conclusion. She said that in practice, the only two choices available to jurors were: 1) death; or 2) life imprisonment without the possibility of parole because, under the statute, the thirty-year mandatory minimum is available only if the jury finds no aggravating factors in the case. Thus Ginsburg concluded that the trial judge's instructions "did nothing to ensure that the jury was not misled and may well have been taken to mean 'that parole was available but that the jury for some unstated reason, should be blind to this fact'" (*Shafer* 2001, 53).

In a solo dissent, Thomas scolded the majority for "micromanag[ing] state sentencing proceedings" and "interfere[ing] with matters that the Constitution leaves to the States" (Shafer 2001, 59). For Thomas, the trial judge's instructions to the jury and statements made by the defense counsel were sufficient to inform the jury of the meaning of life imprisonment. Again, concerns about federalism and deference to state officials took priority over potential violations of due process. One year later, Thomas went further, appearing to encourage the Court to simply overrule *Simmons*: "[T]he Court was wrong, in the first instance, to hold that the Due Process Clause requires the States to permit a capital defendant to inform the jury that he is parole ineligible in cases where the prosecutor argues future dangerousness" (*Kelly v. South Carolina* 2002, 262).

Thomas's approach to these cases involving various aspects of the death penalty is in marked contrast to that of his predecessor. Justice Marshall was consistently skeptical about the death penalty and deeply suspicious about the undesirable consequences, such as rights violations and discrimination that can flow from various procedures in capital cases. This view was reflected in his pattern of voting to accept every petition that arrived at the Court concerning death penalty cases. Thomas was inclined in a different direction. As noted by Merida and Fletcher (2007, 274), "Two former clerks for other justices say that Thomas almost always votes against death penalty appeals—'reflexively,' says one—even in cases that appear to be close calls." The authors conceded that this "clerk's view is impossible to quantify," but they noted that he is "among the justices most reluctant to throw out death sentences that come under Supreme Court review" (274).

In *McFarland v. Scott* (1994), Justice Blackmun's majority opinion sought to give meaning to a defendant's statutory right to appointed counsel in post-conviction proceedings. Blackmun interpreted relevant federal statutes to authorize a federal district court to appoint counsel to assist an impoverished capital defendant in filing his habeas petition and to stay the defendant's execution in the meantime. According to Blackmun, "By providing indigent capital defendants with a mandatory right to qualified legal counsel in these proceedings, Congress has recognized that federal habeas corpus has a particularly important role to play in promoting fundamental fairness in the imposition of the death penalty" and the "district court has jurisdiction to enter a stay of execution where necessary to give effect to that statutory right" (859). Thomas, however, joined by Rehnquist and Scalia, interpreted the relevant statutes to limit the appointment of counsel until after the habeas petition is filed and to prevent the lower court from granting a stay of execution until then.

Had Thomas's view prevailed, defendants in such cases would be put in a precarious position. Given the Court's earlier decision in *McClesky v. Zant* (1991) limiting defendants to one habeas petition, indigent inmates would be forced to proceed without the assistance of counsel to make their only claim of a rights violation. This would be a Herculean task for most people, even those who are well-educated but not trained in the law. Thus, Thomas's view would have had a devastating impact on death row inmates, most of whom are indigent and poorly educated. He insisted, nevertheless, "I agree that legal assistance prior to the filing of a federal habeas petition can be very valuable to a prisoner. That such assistance is valuable, however, does not compel the conclusion that Congress intended the Federal Government to *pay* [emphasis in original] for it" (*McFarland v. Scott* 1994, 868-69). He would have left the provision of such assistance to legal assistance organizations and to the states themselves, despite the fact that these organizations lack sufficient funding and, in periods of tight budgets, state officials are highly unlikely to devote scarce resources for this purpose. Finally, he chided the majority for sanctioning federal intervention that "disturbs the State's significant interest in repose for concluded litigation, denies society the right to punish some admitted offenders, and intrudes on state sovereignty to a degree matched by few exercises of federal judicial authority" (872).

The Rehnquist Court decided several additional noteworthy cases involving capital defendants and habeas corpus review from 2003 to 2005. Prosecutorial misconduct was at the core of these disputes. Two of them, *Miller-El v. Cockrell* (2003) and *Miller-El v. Dretke* (2005), concerned a Texas prosecutor's use of race-based peremptory challenges in jury selection. In *Batson v. Kentucky*, a landmark Burger Court-era case from 1986, the Court had used the Fourteenth Amendment's Equal Protection Clause to prohibit prosecutors from using racial reasons to systematically exclude potential jurors, and the majority established a process to evaluate defendants' claims of such violations. When Thomas Joe Miller-El, whose trial occurred shortly before the *Batson* decision, moved to invalidate the selection and composition of his jury on the grounds that the prosecution had improperly used peremptory challenges to exclude African Americans, the trial judge denied the motion. Miller-El was tried, convicted, and sentenced to death. Following *Batson*, the trial court held another hearing and concluded that Miller-El had not offered sufficient evidence of racial motivation by the prosecution; the state appellate court then denied his appeal and the U.S. Supreme Court denied certiorari in 2003.

As Miller-El's case was progressing through the state courts, Congress passed AEDPA, which substantially altered the federal habeas statute. Under AEDPA, a state prisoner seeking federal habeas review does not have an automatic right to appeal a federal district court's denial of relief, but instead must file a certificate of appealability (COA). To receive a COA, the prisoner must also "demonstrate a substantial showing of the denial of a federal constitutional right." After unsuccessfully seeking habeas review in state courts, Miller-El's COA requests were denied by the federal district court and circuit court of appeals. These lower courts deferred to the trial judge's determination that the prosecutor had provided sufficient race-neutral reasons for striking the jurors. By an 8-1 vote, the Supreme Court reversed, holding that the court of appeals should have issued the COA (*Miller-El v. Cockrell* 2003). Justice Kennedy's majority opinion directed the appellate court to give full consideration to the defendant's substantial evidence of race discrimination, rather than accepting the trial judge's conclusions without question. Thomas dissented, arguing that Miller-El did not merit a COA because he had not provided clear and convincing evidence that the prosecutor had used peremptory challenges in a racially discriminatory fashion; therefore, the lower federal courts were correct to accept the state trial court's findings of no purposeful discrimination.

On remand, the federal appellate court again rejected Miller-El's federal habeas corpus claim, but in the second phase, the high court concluded that he should, in fact, prevail. This time, the vote was 6-3, with Thomas joined in dissent by Rehnquist and Scalia. Writing for the majority in *Miller-El v. Dretke* (2005, 265), Justice Souter said that the evidence presented—statistical disparities, side-by-side comparisons of black panel members who were struck with white jurors who were not, the county's decades-long policy of systematically excluding blacks from juries, and other patterns—"was too powerful to conclude anything but discrimination." By contrast, Thomas accused the majority of relying on evidence that had not been presented to the state courts and claimed that Miller-El had not even come close to showing that the state had racially discriminated against potential jurors. In yet another example of his propensity to defer to the judgments of state courts on these kinds of issues, he accepted the prosecution's claims that its peremptory strikes against blacks could be explained on nonracial grounds. In rejecting what appeared to be strong evidence of racial discrimination in Miller-El's case, Thomas's position was ironic in light of his earlier statements in the *Penry* cases about the potential discriminatory effects of jury discretion in capital sentencing hearings.

At the same time, Thomas's general position on the use of peremptory strikes to exclude potential jurors on the basis of race was unusual. Although concurring in the Court's extension of the *Batson* ruling to defense attorneys in *Georgia v. McCollum* (1992), he did so only on the grounds that precedent necessitated the result. Most importantly, he viewed these decisions as primarily protecting jurors rather than ensuring that defendants will have juries inclusive of members of their race who presumably would help to prevent racial bias in their trials. Thomas wrote, "I am certain that black criminal defendants will rue the day that this court ventured down this road that inexorably will lead to the elimination of peremptory strikes" (60). He insisted that peremptory strikes could cut both ways. Although prosecutors may use them to exclude potential black jurors in cases involving black defendants, attorneys for black defendants could also use them to remove white jurors who harbor racial animus against blacks.

Yet another case involving a death row inmate in Texas was decided the year between the two decisions concerning Miller-El. The ruling in *Banks v. Dretke* (2004) upheld Delmar Banks's claim to federal habeas relief on the basis that the prosecution's concealment of important evidence had violated his right to due process in accordance with the precedent established forty years earlier in *Brady v. Maryland* (1963). Under *Brady*, a due process violation occurs when evidence favorable to the accused and requested by the accused is suppressed, and such evidence is material to his or her guilt or punishment. The suppression is deemed as a violation, whether or not the prosecution acted in bad faith. In Banks's case, the disclosure of evidence would have allowed him to discredit two essential prosecution witnesses, one of them, a paid police informant. Prosecutors and law enforcement officers coached the other witness intensively in preparation for his trial testimony. Ginsburg's majority opinion held that Banks was entitled to habeas relief on the basis of his *Brady* claim with respect to the first witness, and the federal district and appellate courts also erred in rejecting his *Brady* claim with respect to the second witness. Thomas issued an opinion concurring and dissenting in part, in which he accepted the conclusion regarding the second witness but disagreed with granting habeas relief regarding the *Brady* claim for the first witness. Joined by Scalia, he said that it was "a very close question," but he did not view the concealment of the witness's status as a paid police informant as prejudicial to the defendant.

Fourth, Fifth, and Sixth Amendment Issues

Fourth Amendment search and seizure issues have long been a staple on the Court's agenda. As previous chapters have noted, the exclusionary rule has been highly controversial since the Court incorporated it to apply to state governments in *Mapp v. Ohio* (1961). Similarly, the Court has identified several contexts in which warrantless searches are reasonable, including plain view, stop and frisk, hot pursuit, search incident to a lawful arrest, vehicles, and consent searches. Thomas has not written nearly as much on the Fourth Amendment as he has on Eighth Amendment and habeas corpus issues, but a conservative approach characterizes his performance in this area as well. His votes and opinions in this area show that he is skeptical about extending the exclusionary rule to new situations and is willing to expand the contexts in which law enforcement officers may conduct searches without warrants.

Early in his tenure on the high court, Thomas wrote for a unanimous Court in a case involving a longstanding principle from common law—the "knock and announce" requirement. *Wilson v. Arkansas* (1995) posed the question of whether police officers who have a valid search warrant must knock and announce their presence prior to conducting a search. After being arrested for delivery and possession of illegal drugs, Wilson sought to suppress the evidence because police had entered his residence through an unlocked screen door without announcing their presence. The trial court denied his motion and the state supreme court upheld his conviction on grounds that the Fourth Amendment did not require the common law "knock and announce" principle. In reversing the state high court's decision, Thomas's opinion for a unanimous Court relied upon founding-era commentaries, constitutional provisions, statutes, and cases espousing or supporting the "knock and announce" principle to conclude there was little doubt that the Framers "thought that the method of an officer's entry into a dwelling was among the factors to be considered in assessing a search's reasona-

bleness" (934). Graber (2003, 76) noted that "[w]hen Justice Thomas uses originalist rhetoric in a majority opinion, he usually reaches more liberal conclusions," citing this case as an example. Thomas stopped short of characterizing
the "knock and announce" principle as an inflexible rule, noting instead that
concerns about officers' physical safety and the destruction of evidence might
make it constitutionally permissible to enter without knocking and announcing.
Wilson's case, therefore, was remanded to the state courts to determine whether
the unannounced entry to his home was reasonable under the circumstances.

A 1998 case involving the exclusionary rule found Thomas in his usual position in criminal justice cases—siding with the government over the defendant's claims. He wrote the majority opinion in a 5-4 decision limiting the application of the exclusionary rule so it would not bar improperly obtained evidence
from use in parole revocation hearings. In *Pennsylvania Board of Probation v.
Scott* (1998), the Pennsylvania Supreme Court had ruled that parole officers
violated Scott's Fourth Amendment right by conducting a search of his home
without obtaining his mother's consent (she owned the home) and without reasonable suspicion. Thomas accepted the state court's finding that a Fourth
Amendment violation had occurred but rejected any application of the exclusionary rule because: 1) the costs of excluding evidence would detract from the
truth-finding process and thus would hinder the functioning of state parole systems; 2) the rule would lead to extensive litigation which would tax the flexibility of the administrative process for parole revocation proceedings; and 3) any
deterrence benefits would not outweigh the costs, and the deterrent effect is already provided by applying the rule in the trial itself.

Justice Souter's dissent took issue with Thomas's characterization of the
deterrent effect, maintaining that parole revocation hearings function in much
the same way as criminal trials. According to Souter (*Scott* 1998, 379):

> [W]ithout a suppression remedy in revocation proceedings, there will often be
> no influence capable of deterring Fourth Amendment violations when parole
> revocation is a possible response to new crime. Suppression in the revocation
> proceeding cannot be looked upon, then, as furnishing merely incremental or
> marginal deterrence over and above the effect of exclusion in criminal prosecu-
> tion. Instead, it will commonly provide the only deterrence to unconstitutional
> conduct when the incarceration of parolees is sought, and the reasons that sup-
> port the suppression remedy in prosecution therefore support it in parole revo-
> cation.

Thomas's reasoning in this case was similar to that in his opinions regarding
federal habeas review—a desire to promote finality and efficiency in the operation of the criminal justice system.

One year later in *Florida v. White* (1999), the Court addressed the validity
of a warrantless search that occurred when a vehicle had been seized in a public
parking lot, after the vehicle's owner had been arrested. Under Florida law, "certain forms of contraband, including motor vehicles used in violation of the Act's
provisions, may be seized and potentially forfeited." Police officers reportedly

had observed White's vehicle being used to deliver narcotics over a two-month period, and they assumed that it was subject to forfeiture under the state contraband law. Several months after these initial observations, they arrested him at his workplace on charges unrelated to the previously observed transactions. Subsequently, without a search warrant, they seized the vehicle in the parking lot and conducted a search that produced evidence of crack cocaine. The Florida Supreme Court ruled that the warrantless search violated the Fourth Amendment. The state court determined that the Fourth Amendment requires the police to obtain a warrant prior to seizing property used in violation of the contraband law unless exigent circumstances exist. The U.S. Supreme Court, however, in a majority opinion written by Thomas, reversed the Florida high court. Thomas wrote for a seven-member majority, holding that the Fourth Amendment does not require that police officers obtain a warrant before seizing a vehicle from a public place if and when the police have probable cause to believe that the vehicle is forfeitable contraband. He said that this ruling was based on federal law enforcement practices that existed at the time the Fourth Amendment was adopted. Graber (2003, 76) cited this as "the only majority opinion where Justice Thomas reached a conclusion partly on original grounds" and continued "No other sentence in a Thomas majority opinion supports a conservative conclusion on historical grounds."

As previous chapters have noted, the Warren Court's due process revolution extended rights under the Fifth and Sixth Amendments, including the protection against self-incrimination, the right to counsel, and various fair trial guarantees. Following its landmark 1963 decision in *Gideon v. Wainwright* which required states to provide attorneys for indigent defendants charged with serious crimes, the Warren Court issued several decisions that required states to make these attorneys available at earlier points in the criminal process (see *Malloy v. Hogan* 1964; *Escobedo v. Illinois* 1964; *Massiah v. United States* 1964). These decisions ultimately led to the Court's famous decision in *Miranda v. Arizona* (1966) that combines the protection against self-incrimination and the right to counsel. *Miranda* requires law enforcement officers to inform suspects held in custody of their rights, including their rights to remain silent and to be provided an attorney, before police questioning begins. Critics of the Warren Court immediately and continuously thereafter assailed *Miranda* for allegedly handcuffing the police in their investigative work and for protecting the rights of criminals over those of victims and other law-abiding citizens.

While later Supreme Court decisions have not overturned *Miranda*, the justices have issued rulings that limited or reduced its application (see *Harris v. New York* 1971; *Michigan v. Tucker* 1974; *Oregon v. Hass* 1975; *New York v. Quarles* 1984; *Oregon v. Elstad* 1985; *Moran v. Burbine* 1986; *Duckworth v. Eagan* 1989). Following his 'arrival on the high court, Thomas also joined in decisions limiting *Miranda*'s applicability and also calling for the rights-granting precedent to be overturned. In addition, he wrote an opinion that would have severely undercut the general protection provided in the Fifth Amendment against compelled self-incrimination.

In a case decided early in his tenure, *Thompson v. Keohane* (1995), a state defendant brought a habeas corpus claim to federal court for a determination of whether his interrogation was improper because the police had failed to give him *Miranda* warnings. The state courts had determined that there was no violation because Thompson was not in custody at the time of the interrogation, and therefore his confession was admissible. The federal district and appellate courts held that whether the defendant was "in custody" was a factual question and the state courts' answer was entitled to a presumption of correctness. Seven members of the Court disagreed, however. Ginsburg's majority opinion held that the custody issue involved a mixed question of law and fact and was not presumed to be correct, thus warranting independent habeas review by a federal court.

Thomas, joined only by Rehnquist, reached the opposite conclusion, declaring that "the Alaska trial judge—who first decided this question . . . was in a far better position than a federal habeas court to determine whether Thompson was 'in custody' for purposes of *Miranda* v. *Arizona*" (*Thompson v. Keohane* 1995, 116). His reasoning was not very surprising, given his calls in other criminal justice cases for deference to the judgments of state officials, including state judges, on questions of violations of federal constitutional rights. While rejecting the majority's analysis of the "in custody" question, Thomas went further, arguing that remand was unnecessary because the defendant could not prevail even upon *de novo* review. And yet again, his anxiety about placing undue burdens on the state outweighed concerns for due process. "I would resolve that [in custody] question now, and avoid putting the State of Alaska to the uncertainty and expense of defending for the sixth time in nine years an eminently reasonable judgment secured against a confessed murderer" (121).

Questions raised in cases about *Miranda* included whether it was a constitutional decision and whether it merely established "prophylactic rules" to prevent improper police misconduct. The case of *Michigan v. Tucker* (1974) decided during the Burger Court era, for example, seemed to indicate the latter. Chief Justice Rehnquist was a strong proponent of this viewpoint but, despite expressing this position in a number of cases, he wrote for the majority in a 7-2 ruling, in *Dickerson v. United States* (2000), establishing *Miranda* as a constitutionally-based precedent.

> Whether or not we would agree with *Miranda*'s reasoning and its resulting rule, were we addressing the issue in the first instance, the principles of stare decisis weigh heavily against overruling it now . . . *Miranda* has become embedded in routine police practice to the point where warnings have become part of our national culture. . . . [O]ur subsequent cases have reduced the impact of the *Miranda* rule on legitimate law enforcement while reaffirming the decision's core ruling that unwarned statements may not be used as evidence in the prosecution's case in chief. . . . In sum, we conclude that *Miranda* announced a constitutional rule that Congress may not supersede legislatively. Following the rule of stare decisis, we decline to overrule the *Miranda* decision ourselves. (*Dickerson* 2000, 443-44)

Thomas joined what Jeffrey Toobin (2007, 124) described as one of Scalia's "classic fire-breathing dissents." Scalia accused the majority of "judicial arrogance" in "imposing its Court-made code upon the States" (*Dickerson* 2000, 465) and, in characteristically harsh language, he wrote:

> Far from believing that stare decisis compels this result, I believe we cannot allow to remain on the books even a celebrated decision—especially a celebrated decision—that has come to stand for the proposition that the Supreme Court has the power to impose extraconstitutional constraints upon Congress and the States. This is not the system that was established by the Framers, or that would be established by any sane supporter of government by the people.

Four years later, in *United States v. Patane* (2004), Thomas wrote a plurality opinion limiting the effect of *Miranda*, despite the *Dickerson* ruling. Joined by Rehnquist and Scalia, he held that police officers' failure to give a suspect his *Miranda* warnings did not trigger the suppression at trial of physical evidence found by the officers as a result of the suspect's voluntary statements. He said that *Miranda* protects against violations of the Self-Incrimination Clause, but that the Clause was not implicated by the introduction at trial of nontestimonial evidence resulting from a voluntary statement. In language similar to that used when he criticized the application of the Eighth Amendment to prison conditions cases, Thomas wrote, "The *Miranda* rule is not a code of police conduct, and police do not violate the Constitution (or even the *Miranda* rule, for that matter) by mere failure to warn" (*United States v. Patane* 2004, 637). The dissenters warned, however, that the decision would invite police misconduct. Souter wrote, "There is no way to read this case except as an unjustifiable invitation to law enforcement officers to flout *Miranda* when there may be physical evidence to be gained" (647).

One year before establishing the *Miranda* warnings as a way to give teeth to the protection against self-incrimination, the Warren Court had held that individuals' exercise of that right cannot be used against them at trial (*Griffin v. California* 1965). Thirty-four years later, the Court extended this principle to sentencing hearings. In *Mitchell v. United States* (1999), a five-member majority held first that a guilty plea in a federal criminal case does not waive a defendant's self-incrimination privilege at her sentencing hearing. Furthermore, Justice Kennedy wrote, the Fifth Amendment prevents a sentencing court from drawing a negative inference from the defendant's failure to testify about the crime. Scalia's dissent, which Thomas joined, called for the Court to reconsider the longstanding *Griffin* precedent.

> [T]he text and history of the Fifth Amendment give no indication that there is a federal *constitutional* prohibition on the use of the defendant's silence as demeanor evidence. Our hardy forebears, who thought of compulsion in terms of the rack and oaths forced by the power of law, would not have viewed the drawing of a commonsensical inference as equivalent pressure. And it is implausible that the Americans of 1791, who were subject to adverse inferences

for failing to give unsworn testimony, would have viewed an adverse inference for failing to give sworn testimony as a violation of the Fifth Amendment. *(Mitchell v. United States* 1999, 335)

Scalia stopped short, however, of explicitly calling for *Griffin* to be overturned. "To my mind, *Griffin* was a wrong turn—which is not cause enough to overrule it, but is cause enough to resist its extension" (336). Thomas disagreed. In a separate opinion, he insisted that *Griffin* "should be reexamined" because it "fail[s] to withstand a proper analysis" and "lacks foundation in the Constitution's text, history, or logic" (341-42).

Thomas's and Scalia's disagreement over how to deal with *Griffin* may seem surprising. Toobin (2007, 102) argued, however, that Thomas, unlike Scalia and the other justices, "fundamentally [does] not believe in stare decisis, the law of precedent." Merida and Fletcher (2007, 334) reported that Scalia has confirmed this observation, stating that he is more willing than Thomas to "let sleeping dogs lie."

Conclusion

During his fifteen years on the Rehnquist Court, Justice Thomas clearly established himself as a consistent and reliable member of the conservative wing in criminal justice cases. On a range of issues, from Fourth Amendment search and seizure to Eighth Amendment cruel and unusual punishment to the interpretation of federal criminal statutes, he supported the interests of government over the claims of criminal defendants and prisoners in the overwhelming majority of cases. He often berated his colleagues for interfering in matters he believed should be left to the discretion of state officials and for making decisions that create lengthy delays in administering justice to criminal offenders. Gerber (1999, 63) suggested that Thomas's approach to the rights of criminal defendants stems from his recognition of their "free will and moral responsibility." He points to a 1994 speech Thomas gave to the Federalist Society and Manhattan Institute.

> I am convinced that there can be no freedom and opportunity for many in our society if our criminal law loses sight of the importance of responsibility. Indeed, in my mind, the principal reason for a criminal justice system is to hold people accountable for the consequences of their actions. Put simply, it is to hold people's feet to the fire when they do something harmful to individuals or society as a whole. (Thomas quoted in Gerber 1999, 63)

Gerber cited Thomas's approach in a positive light, but Merida and Fletcher (2007, 90) were less charitable, accusing him of "mocking those who show empathy for the less fortunate in legal cases." They pointed to these statements presumably drawn from Thomas's speeches:

Once our legal system accepted the general premise that social conditions and upbringing could be excuses for harmful conduct, the range of causes that might prevent society from holding anyone accountable for his actions became potentially limitless. Do we punish the drunk driver who has a family history of alcoholism? A bigoted employer reared in the segregationist environment who was taught that blacks are inferior? . . . A thief or drug pusher who was raised in a dysfunctional family and who received a poor education? A violent gang member, rioter, or murderer who attributes his rage, aggression, and lack of respect for authority to a racist society that has oppressed him since birth? Which of these individuals, if any, should be excused for their conduct? (90-91)

And what of Thomas's claims that originalism drives his decisions? Gerber (1999, 193) saw him as a "conservative originalist" in civil liberties cases who appeals to "the Framer's specific intentions—as manifested in the text and historical context of the Constitution." By contrast, Graber (2003, 87-88) contended that his "separate opinions in constitutional cases reveal an erratic originalist," one who may be "originalist in theory" but fails to be a "consistent originalist" in practice." Tushnet (2006, 89) observed that "his natural law approach to the Constitution sometimes [comes] into conflict with his originalist approach" and that his jurisprudence which includes "originalist, natural law, and conservative components" does not "hang together all that well."

Finally, at this point, Thomas's influence on the Court's criminal justice jurisprudence appears rather limited. He has taken positions in some cases that are too radical, even for his most conservative colleagues. In a number of opinions, he has gone beyond what is necessary to decide the case at hand, exhorting the Court to overturn longstanding precedents, even if doing so would potentially create unfairness, chaos, and confusion in the criminal justice system. Future personnel changes may provide him with greater opportunities to realize his vision through the acquisition of additional allies, but only time will tell if he ultimately will be regarded as an influential justice.

References

Baldus, David, George Woodworth, and Charles Pulaski. *Equal Justice and the Death Penalty: A Legal and Empirical Analysis*. Boston: Northeastern University Press, 1990.

Clear, Todd R., George F. Cole, and Michael D. Reisig. *American Corrections*, 7th ed. Belmont, CA: Thomson Wadsworth, 2006.

Friedman, Lawrence M. *Crime and Punishment in American History*. New York: Basic Books, 1993.

Gerber, Scott. *First Principles: The Jurisprudence of Clarence Thomas*. New York: New York University Press, 1999.

Graber, Mark. "Clarence Thomas and the Perils of Amateur History." Pp. 70-102 in *Rehnquist Justice: Understanding the Court Dynamic*, edited by Earl M. Maltz. Lawrence, KS: University Press of Kansas, 2003.

Greenburg, Jan Crawford. *Supreme Conflict: The Inside Story of the Struggle for Control of the United States Supreme Court*. New York: Penguin Books, 2007.

Hensley, Thomas R., Christopher E. Smith, and Joyce A. Baugh. *The Changing Supreme Court: Constitutional Rights and Liberties*. Belmont, CA: West/Wadsworth, 1997.

Merida, Kevin, and Michael A. Fletcher. *Supreme Discomfort: The Divided Soul of Clarence Thomas*. New York: Doubleday, 2007.

Smith, Christopher E. "Criminal Justice and the 1995-96: U.S. Supreme Court Term." *University of Detroit-Mercy Law Review* 74 (1996): 1-25.

———. *Law and Contemporary Corrections*. Belmont, CA: Wadsworth/West, 2000.

Smith, Christopher E. and Joyce A. Baugh. *The Real Clarence Thomas: Confirmation Veracity Meets Performance Reality*. New York: Peter Lang, 2000.

Smith, Christopher E., Christina DeJong, and John D. Burrow. *The Supreme Court, Crime, and the Ideal of Equal Justice*. New York: Peter Lang, 2003.

Smith, Christopher E. and Madhavi McCall. "Criminal Justice and the 2001-2002 U.S. Supreme Court Term." *Michigan State DCL Law Review* (2003): 413-46.

———. "Criminal Justice and the 2002-2003 U.S. Supreme Court Term." *Capital University Law Review* 32 (2004): 859-99.

Smith, Christopher E., Michael McCall, and Madhavi McCall. "Criminal Justice and the 2005-2006 U.S. Supreme Court Term." *Quinnipiac Law Review* 25 (2007): 495-546.

Thomas, Clarence. *My Grandfather's Son: a Memoir*. New York: HarperCollins, 2007.

Toobin, Jeffrey. *The Nine: Inside the Secret World of the Supreme Court*. New York: Doubleday, 2007.

Tushnet, Mark. *A Court Divided: The Rehnquist Court and the Future of Constitutional Law*. New York: Norton, 2006.

U.S. Congress. Senate. Committee on the Judiciary. *Hearings on the Nomination of Clarence Thomas to be an Associate of the Supreme Court of the United States*. 102nd Congress, 1st session, September 10-27, 1991.

Yackle, Larry W. "The Habeas Hagioscope." *Southern California Law Review* 66 (1993): 2331-2431.

———. *Reclaiming the Federal Courts*. Cambridge, MA: Harvard University Press, 2004.

Cases Cited

Banks v. Dretke, 540 U.S. 668 (2004)
Batson v. Kentucky, 476 U.S. 79 (1986)
Booth v. Maryland, 482 U.S. 496 (1987)
Brady v. Maryland, 373 U.S. 83 (1963)
Coleman v. Thompson, 501 U.S. 722 (1991)
Dickerson v. United States, 530 U.S. 428 (2000)
Duckworth v. Eagan, 492 U.S. 195 (1989)
Enmund v. Florida, 458 U.S. 782 (1982)
Escobedo v. Illinois, 378 U.S. 438 (1964)
Estelle v. Gamble, 429 U.S. 97 (1976)
Farmer v. Brennan, 511 U.S. 825 (1994)
Florida v. White, 526 U.S. 559 (1999)

Furman v. Georgia, 408 U.S. 238 (1972)
Georgia v. McCollum, 505 U.S. 42 (1992)
Gideon v. Wainwright, 372 U.S. 335 (1963)
Graham v. Collins, 506 U.S. 461 (1993)
Griffin v. California, 380 U.S. 609 (1965)
Harris v. New York, 401 U.S. 222 (1971)
Helling v. McKinney, 509 U.S. 25 (1993)
Hope v. Pelzer, 536 U.S. 730 (2002)
Hudson v. McMillian, 503 U.S. 1 (1992)
Hutto v. Finney, 437 U.S. 678 (1978)
Kelly v. South Carolina, 534 U.S. 246 (2002)
Lewis v. Casey, 518 U.S. 343 (1996)
Malloy v. Hogan, 378 U.S. 1 (1964)
Mapp v. Ohio, 367 U.S. 643 (1961)
Massiah v. United States, 377 U.S. 201 (1964)
McClesky v. Zant, 499 U.S. 467 (1991)
McFarland v. Scott, 512 U.S. 849 (1994)
Michigan v. Tucker, 417 U.S. 433 (1974)
Miller-El v. Cockrell, 537 U.S. 322 (2003)
Miller-El v. Dretke, 545 U.S. 231 (2005)
Miranda v. Arizona, 384 U.S. 436 (1966)
Mitchell v. United States, 526 U.S. 314 (1999)
Moran v. Burbine, 475 U.S. 412 (1986)
New York v. Quarles, 467 U.S. 649 (1984)
O'Dell v. Netherland, 521 U.S. 151 (1997)
Oregon v. Elstad, 470 U.S. 298 (1985)
Oregon v. Hass, 420 U.S. 714 (1975)
Payne v. Tennessee, 501 U.S. 808 (1991)
Pennsylvania Board of Probation v. Scott, 524 U.S. 357 (1998)
Penry v. Lynaugh, 492 U.S. 302 (1989)
Rhodes v. Chapman, 452 U.S. 337 (1981)
Shafer v. South Carolina, 532 U.S. 36 (2001)
Simmons v. South Carolina, 512 U.S. 154 (1994)
South Carolina v. Gathers, 490 U.S. 805 (1989)
Teague v. Lane, 489 U.S. 288 (1989)
Thompson v. Keohane, 516 U.S. 99 (1995)
Tison v. Arizona, 481 U.S. 137 (1987)
United States v. Patane, 542 U.S. 630 (2004)
United States v. Ross, 456 U.S. 798 (1982)
Whitley v. Albers, 475 U.S. 312 (1986)
Wilson v. Arkansas, 514 U.S. 927 (1995)
Woodson v. North Carolina, 428 U.S. 280 (1976)
Wright v. West, 505 U.S. 277 (1992)

Chapter 12
Ruth Bader Ginsburg:
Careful Defender of Individual Rights

Christina DeJong

Ruth Bader Ginsburg joined the Rehnquist Court in August 1993 as the first of two justices nominated by President Bill Clinton. She previously served for a dozen years as a judge on the U.S. Court of Appeals for the District of Columbia Circuit, where one of her colleagues for six years was future Supreme Court Justice Antonin Scalia. Ginsburg was only the second woman to ever serve on the U.S. Supreme Court, and prior to her nomination had been described as "the nation's foremost legal advocate for constitutional gender equality" (Smith, Baugh, Hensley, and Johnson 1994).

Justice Ginsburg received her legal education during a time when women rarely enrolled (or were accepted) in law school—her first-year law class at Harvard Law School had nine female students out of 500, and she frequently felt as if she were "answering for [her] entire sex" (Bazelon 2009). After transferring to and graduating from Columbia Law School, she realized that her gender would pose significant professional challenges, and she struggled to find work in a world that did not take women seriously. To wit, she was turned down for a clerkship in 1960 by Supreme Court Justice Felix Frankfurter, who was reluctant to break the tradition of only hiring male clerks (Halberstam 2005).

Prior to her nomination on the Court, Ginsburg was an outspoken advocate for women's rights. In 1970, while a faculty member at Rutgers University, she founded the Women's Rights Law Reporter (WRLR 2010). She later took a position at Columbia University, where she became the first tenured female professor there thanks to then President Nixon's affirmative action initiatives (Bazelon 2009). Her scholarly publications and speeches in the 1970s focused predominantly on equal protection, gender, and the Equal Rights Amendment (see Ginsburg 1970; 1971; 1975; 1977; 1979). In 1972 she took a leadership role in the American Civil Liberties Union (ACLU) Women's Right's Project (ACLU 2006) and began arguing cases before the Supreme Court. In all, she argued six cases before the Supreme Court, all focused on matters of equal protection (Morris 2002).

One of the cases she argued as counsel for the ACLU involved a criminal justice issue: *Duren v. Missouri* (1978). At that time in Missouri and several other states, jury duty was optional for women. Ginsburg believed that this law sent the wrong message to women—specifically, that their service was not required to ensure the fair functioning of the justice system (Von Drehle 1993). In that same year, Ginsburg noted that Thomas Jefferson's intent in "all men are created equal" really did refer to all men—Jefferson had stated in other writings that women had to be excluded from political deliberations in order to prevent their degradation and subsequent immorality (Ginsburg 1978b, 451). In addition to reinforcing the traditional roles of women and rendering their participation "unnecessary," the realistic implications of such laws were to create juries that were entirely male (Ginsburg 1978b). The Court decided in Duren's favor in a 7-1 vote, striking down the Missouri law that made jury service optional for women. The sole dissenter, however—Chief Justice William Rehnquist—failed to see the decision as helping achieve equality for women. In his view, "The short of it is that the only winners in today's decision are those in the category of petitioner, now freed of his conviction of first-degree murder" (*Duren v. Missouri* 1978, 377).

Ginsburg's dedication to issues of fairness and gender equality for both women and men is apparent when examining her criminal justice decisions as a justice. Unfortunately, an analysis of her criminal justice decisions must omit her most notable written opinion—that of *United States v. Virginia* (1996), in which the Court declared the male-only admissions policy of the Virginia Military Institute unconstitutional. In this decision, Ginsburg wrote the opinion for the Court and denied Virginia's argument that a program designed specifically for women was acceptable by being "separate but equal." In her opinion, Ginsburg wrote:

> [T]he Court has repeatedly recognized that neither federal nor state government acts compatibly with the equal protection principle when a law or official policy denies to women, simply because they are women, full citizenship stature—equal opportunity to aspire, achieve, participate in and contribute to society based on their individual talents and capacities. (*United States v. Virginia* 1996, 515)

While not a criminal justice case, Ginsburg's authorship of this opinion reflected her core beliefs in gender equality (Merritt and Lieberman 2004; Pressman 1997; Walsh 1998). In fact, her commitment to equality led to decisions that benefited men as well as women (Merritt 1998; Morris 2002; Walsh 1998). As an advocate, she frequently selected sex discrimination cases to argue in court that were brought by men in order to demonstrate that gender equality was not an issue only for women (Morris 2002). Her most significant victory as a lawyer for the cause of gender equality came in a case concerning a state law that set a higher drinking age for men than for women. This case, *Craig v. Boren* (1976), led to the Supreme Court's firm declaration that the Equal Protection

Clause provides protection against sex discrimination. As a justice, she supported the Court's decision against permitting the removal of all males from a jury in a child custody case. The Court concluded that such actions violated the Equal Protection Clause of the Fourteenth Amendment (*J.E.B. v. Alabama* 1994).

Judicial Philosophy

Those speculating on Ginsburg's judicial philosophy prior to her appointment as a federal judge had little doubt she would be a champion for equal rights—less was known about her philosophy regarding criminal justice cases. Her appointment to the federal appellate court by President Jimmy Carter and her appointment to the Supreme Court by President Bill Clinton, both Democratic presidents, certainly implied liberal leanings in her viewpoints. She claimed during her Supreme Court confirmation hearings, however, that her approach to jurisprudence was "neither liberal nor conservative" (Lewis 1993). Given that she had been described as a moderate on criminal justice issues (Harring and Kirchmeier 2004) and her nomination was endorsed by both Democratic and key Republican senators during confirmation (Baugh, Smith, Hensley, and Johnson 1994), there was little evidence that she espoused a strong liberal ideology. In fact, Clinton believed she would serve as a "consensus-builder" and reduce conflict on the Court (Ray 2003).

Ginsburg typically voted with the liberal justices on the Court in criminal justice cases (Smith 2003). Presumably, the values she possessed, as represented in her prior work for the ACLU, predisposed her to vote in favor of the individual in civil liberties cases (Smith 2003). However, the addition of Ginsburg to the Rehnquist Court in 1993 did not change the percentage of constitutional rights cases decided in the liberal direction (Smith and Hensley 2005). Overall, according to the Supreme Court Judicial Database, Ginsburg supported individuals' claims in 60.9 percent of cases classified as "Criminal Procedure" during the Rehnquist Court era (Epstein, Segal, Spaeth, and Walker 2007, 534). Among Rehnquist Court justices with whom she served, only Justice Stevens voted more frequently in support of individuals in criminal justice cases. Despite being one of the most liberal justices in these cases during the later years of the Rehnquist Court era, Ginsburg arguably fulfilled her claimed judicial reputation for moderation because her voting record was not nearly as liberal as those of her predecessors on the Rehnquist Court, Justices William Brennan and Thurgood Marshall, or several of the earlier justices who served during the Warren Court era.

For a snapshot example of Ginsburg's performance as relatively liberal justice in the later Rehnquist Court era, an analysis of the Court's decisions in 1999-2000—a year in which the Court decided a high percentage of criminal justice decisions—indicated that the Court was most likely to issue criminal justice decisions with a 5-4 vote (in ten cases) or a unanimous vote (in nine cases) (Smith 2001). In the 5-4 decisions, the conservative and liberal "groups" of justices tended to vote together—Ginsburg routinely dissented with the other liberal justices in those cases (Justices Stevens, Souter, and Breyer). However, there were some cases in which she voted with the conservative justices (Rehnquist, Thomas, O'Connor, Kennedy, and Scalia) (Smith 2001). It is important to note that Ginsburg's support for individuals in criminal justice cases increased in 1999-2000 from her first year on the Court (Baugh et al. 1994; Smith 2001). Indeed, by 1999 Ginsburg was most likely to vote with Stevens and Breyer (Smith 2001, 10).

Justice Ginsburg's judicial philosophy has been described as adhering to judicial restraint, minimalism, and incrementalism (Baugh et al. 1994; Morris 2002). She believed strongly in moderation. She also believed that judicial decisions should not engender major change, but should be narrowly focused to allow precise interpretation (Ray 2003). As an example, in 1992 she stated her belief that *Roe v. Wade* (1973) went too far, and that the Court should have stopped at striking down the Texas criminal law about which "Jane Roe" filed her lawsuit—instead, the Court fashioned "a regime blanketing the subject, a set of rules that displaced virtually every state law then in force" (Ginsburg 1992, 1199).

Ginsburg avoided broad, sweeping resolutions, concerning herself more with focused issues of law (Ray 2003). In her first term on the Supreme Court, she delivered on President Clinton's belief that she would serve as a consensus builder, mediating between the liberal and conservative factions of the Court (Baugh et al. 1994, 11).

Ginsburg's written opinions during the Rehnquist era have been described as collegial, focused on consensus rather than criticism (Ray 2003), and consistent with her own beliefs about how a judge should write opinions for a court (Ginsburg 1992). Justice Ginsburg underscored that the importance of making a point must be balanced with maintaining a professional atmosphere and a collegial relationship between justices (Ginsburg 1990). This theme of collegiality reflected a sentiment expressed prior to her nomination for the Supreme Court by Justice Antonin Scalia, her colleague during her early years on the Court of Appeals and a frequent opponent of Ginsburg's in judicial decisions. Referring to the two front-runners for the appointment to the high court, Scalia was asked by a reporter, "If you had to spend the rest of your life on a desert island with Laurence Tribe or Mario Cuomo, which would you choose?" He replied, "Ruth Bader Ginsberg" (Rosen 1993).

Case law is built on the principle of stare decisis, or reliance on case precedent. Court decisions are normally expected to follow precedent unless judges can justify that a case under consideration differs in a meaningful way from prior decisions (Kuo and Wang 1998). The Supreme Court, however, overrules precedent when the justices find that the prior decisions, including those of their own Court, violate the Constitution. While lower courts generally follow precedent, the Supreme Court can overrule precedent as the court of last resort

(Kuo and Wang 1998). Prior to her appointment, Ginsburg noted that decisions should be based on precedent and such behavior keeps a judge from infusing his or her own beliefs in decisions (Ginsburg 1992). Analysis of her decisions indicates she has been reluctant to overrule precedent (Kuo and Wang 1998).

On Concurring & Dissenting
Criminal Justice Opinions

In evaluating Justice Ginsburg's criminal justice decisions, her written opinions—especially dissents and concurrences written at her own initiative—presumably illuminate issues about which she felt strongly. With respect to concurrences, Ginsburg has said a concurring opinion can add significantly to the majority opinion. "What do separate opinions contribute to the improvement or progress of the law? Most immediately, when drafted and circulated among the judges, they may provoke clarifications, refinements, modifications in the Court's opinion" (Ginsburg 1990, 143).

She placed similar emphasis on the benefits of dissenting opinions. Ginsburg wrote and spoke often about the importance of well-written dissents. She noted that as a federal appellate judge in Washington, D.C., she tried to write her dissents ". . . as affirmative statements of my reasons, drafted before receiving the Court's opinion, and later adjusted, as needed, to meet the majority's presentation" (Ginsburg 1992, 1196). According to Ginsburg, "an impressive dissent [improves] an opinion for the Court. A well-reasoned dissent will lead the author of the majority opinion to refine and clarify her initial circulation." She added that "[o]n rare occasions, a dissent will be so persuasive that it attracts the votes necessary to become the opinion of the Court" (Ginsburg 2007).

Underscoring her belief in collegiality, she also stressed the importance of writing clear dissents that state the legal reasoning for the dissent without resorting to personal attacks or condemnation. This method of analyzing dissents and concurrences seemed especially relevant for Ginsburg, who strongly believed that judge's individual viewpoints should be suppressed in order to "examine all arguments objectively" (Ellington 1998).

After looking at cases in which Ginsburg asserted herself in concurring and dissenting opinions, three issues emerge that help to illuminate her values and reasoning. These issues, namely jury instructions in capital cases, due process, and search and seizure, all demonstrate Ginsburg's concern for the protection of individual rights in the criminal justice process. The remainder of this chapter will review the major cases that appeared before the Court on these issues, and discuss how Ginsburg's opinions on these issues of particular interest to her provide valuable insight into her judicial philosophy.

Juror Instructions in Death Penalty Cases

Because she served as counsel for the ACLU, some members of Congress assumed Ginsburg would be philosophically opposed to capital punishment. However, she wrote no opinions on the topic while serving as a federal appellate judge for the District of Columbia Circuit, so her record could not speak to this issue (Harring and Kirchmeier 2004). After her appointment to the Supreme Court, Justice Ginsburg authored several dissents in death penalty cases, most of which focused on jury instructions. These cases were characterized by instances when the state statute or the judge failed to provide sufficient and clear information to juries regarding mitigating circumstances when considering the death penalty.

In *Romano v. Oklahoma* (1994), Romano was charged with two counts of first-degree murder for separate offenses occurring in 1985 and 1986. He was tried first for the 1986 robbery-homicide and sentenced to death. He subsequently stood trial for the 1985 homicide. During the sentencing phase of the second trial, the prosecution introduced evidence to the jury that the petitioner had been sentenced to death in the first trial. This served as an aggravating factor against the defendant, and the second jury returned with a death sentence for Romano. Romano appealed, arguing that introducing the first death sentence to the jury violated his rights under the Eighth and Fourteenth Amendments.

The five-member majority of the Court ruled that the admission of this evidence was not a violation of Romano's constitutional rights. Writing for the Court, Rehnquist explained that the evidence did not mislead the jury and the case did not violate the standards that were set in the earlier case of *Caldwell v. Mississippi* (1985). In *Caldwell*, another capital case, the defense attorney reminded the jury of their "awesome responsibility" when deliberating whether to sentence the defendant to death. The prosecution responded by telling the jury that the final responsibility for imposing the death penalty was not theirs, but the job of the Mississippi Supreme Court, which would review the case for errors. Therefore, the prosecution attempted to relieve the jury of the "awesome responsibility" placed upon them by sentencing the petitioner to death.

In *Caldwell*, Justice Marshall's majority opinion held that "[i]t is constitutionally impermissible to rest a death sentence on a determination made by a sentencer who has been led to believe, as the jury was in this case, that the responsibility for determining the appropriateness of the defendant's death rests elsewhere" (*Caldwell v. Mississippi* 1985, 320). Justice Marshall also underscored the "awesome responsibility" held by the sentencer, whether judge or jury, and the importance of the sentencer's understanding of the gravity of the decision. He declared these elements to be indispensible to the Eighth Amendment's protection against cruel and unusual punishment.

In *Romano*, however, the Court determined that the decision in *Caldwell* had no relevance to this case. The majority opinion in this case was written by Rehnquist, who wrote the dissent in *Caldwell*. The Court also found that the evidence of the prior death sentence, while irrelevant, did not violate the Eighth Amendment, and "did not so infect the trial with unfairness as to render the jury's imposition of the death penalty a denial of due process . . . " (*Romano v. Oklahoma* 1994, 2). Essentially, the Court stated that in Romano's case, the information provided to the jury was truthful and accurate and thus did not bias the jury's decision.

Writing for the dissenters, Justice Ginsburg argued that because the jury knew the defendant had already been sentenced to death, knowledge of that prior decision relieved them of responsibility for imposition of the death penalty. Ginsburg stated in her dissent:

> The risk of diminished jury responsibility was also grave in Romano's case. Revealing to the jury that Romano was condemned to die for the [prior] Thompson murder signaled to the jurors in the [current] Safarty murder case that Romano faced execution regardless of their life or death decision in the case before them. Jurors so informed might well believe that Romano's fate had been sealed by the previous jury, and thus was not fully their responsibility. (*Romano v. Oklahoma* 1994, 19)

Ginsburg wrote that the majority did not consider the concept of "diminished jury responsibility" as a pivotal issue in the case, but rather focused on the other aggravating factors that led to the imposition of the death penalty. This dissent may underscore Ginsburg's orientation toward collegiality—she did not state that her fellow justices were incorrect, only that the Court failed to give sufficient weight to an issue she viewed as pivotal (*Romano v. Oklahoma* 1994, 21).

In that same Supreme Court term, Ginsburg addressed a related issue in *Simmons v. South Carolina* (1994). According to the South Carolina statute, juries must be informed when conviction for a crime will make the offender ineligible for parole; that is, even if the defendant were to be sentenced to life imprisonment, he could not be released on parole. The de facto sentence for crimes in this category is life without possibility of parole. In *Simmons*, the trial court refused to instruct the jury on defendant's parole eligibility when the jury requested clarification on the meaning of "life imprisonment." In fact, the court ordered the jurors *not* to consider petitioner's parole eligibility in making their decision. The jury subsequently sentenced Simmons to death.

At issue in *Simmons* was the concept of *future dangerousness*. According to the South Carolina statute, if the state argued that the defendant posed a danger to society, the jury must be notified that he or she is ineligible for parole. This allows the jury to select either life imprisonment without parole or death as a possible sentence. During trial, the state argued that petitioner's future dangerousness provided evidence that the death penalty was the correct sentence for his crime. Witnesses for both the prosecution and defense testified during trial that Simmons posed a threat to elderly women, and the defense presented evidence that he would not likely pose a threat in prison. In the majority opinion,

Justice Blackmun, joined by Ginsburg, expressed concern that the jury instructions were misleading. In his own words:

> Far from ensuring that the jury was not misled, however, this instruction actually suggested that parole was available but that the jury, for some unstated reason, should be blind to this fact. Undoubtedly, the instruction was confusing and frustrating to the jury, given the arguments by both the prosecution and the defense relating to petitioner's future dangerousness, and the obvious relevance of petitioner's parole ineligibility to the jury's formidable sentencing task. (*Simmons v. South Carolina* 1994, 170-71)

The majority concluded that, therefore, the petitioner's due process rights had been violated and they remanded the case back to the state.

In addition to joining with Blackmun, Ginsburg authored a concurrence focusing on one of the core values of due process—the right to be heard. For Ginsburg, the heart of the issue in *Simmons* was his lack of ability to inform the jury of his parole eligibility and thereby rebut the prosecutor's argument that his future dangerousness should be used as evidence in favor of a death sentence. She also noted that not only did the trial judge refuse to instruct the jury about defendant's parole eligibility, he also ordered defense counsel not to mention the parole issue during his remarks. For Ginsburg, these factors led to a violation of Simmons' due process rights.

In another capital case dealing with jury instructions, *Shafer v. South Carolina* (2001), Shafer argued that his jury was not instructed that some criminal offenses were not eligible for parole. Similar to the issue in *Simmons*, the petitioner requested that the jury be informed that he would not be eligible for parole—the sentencing judge declined to give that instruction, finding that the prosecution never presented evidence that the petitioner posed a danger to the community in the future. Thus, the judge believed that *Simmons* did not apply.

The South Carolina Supreme Court affirmed the sentence, stating that a change to South Carolina's sentencing scheme meant that *Simmons* no longer applied to capital cases heard in the state. To wit, at the time petitioner Simmons was tried, the only sentencing options available to the jury were (1) death or (2) life imprisonment. Unfortunately, the term "life imprisonment" can be used to mean a long period of incarceration followed by parole, or life imprisonment without the possibility of parole. In Simmons' 1993 sentencing, this distinction was not clear. By 2001, however, South Carolina had changed its sentencing structure to allow for three sentencing options in capital cases: (1) death, (2) life imprisonment without parole, or (3) imprisonment for a mandatory minimum of thirty years. According to the South Carolina Supreme Court, adding the final option of thirty years incarceration nullified the rule from the *Simmons* case, namely the requirement to notify juries when defendants are not eligible for parole.

In Ginsburg's majority opinion on behalf of seven justices, with only Thomas and Scalia dissenting, she concluded that the additional third sentencing option did not invalidate the *Simmons* case requirement for trial judges to inform the jury of the lack of parole eligibility. Some scholars have noted that Ginsburg's collegial style of writing was evident in this decision. Rather than scold South Carolina for failing to apply a previous rule created by the Supreme Court, Ginsburg's neutral manner of writing simply pointed out the constitutional issues and reversed South Carolina's decision (Ray 2003). It is also worth noting that this case regarding jury instructions in capital cases had the largest majority of any similar Supreme Court case regarding these types of issues. In *Jones v. United States* (1999), the petitioner kidnapped, raped, and murdered a woman in San Angelo, Texas. Due to two aggravating factors, the jury found the offender to be death-eligible and the sentencing phase began. Prior to sentence deliberations, the defendant requested that the court provide instructions to the jury that if they deadlocked on the sentencing decision, the judge would be required to sentence the defendant to life imprisonment without parole. The judge denied the request, and the jury came back with a death sentence. In his appeal, petitioner argued that his rights under the Eighth Amendment were violated in that the jury might incorrectly assume that the judge could impose a lesser sentence in the event of a deadlock and thus risk meting out a "slap on the wrist" to the defendant.

In an opinion written by Justice Thomas, the Court decided that the Eighth Amendment does not require that a jury be instructed about the potential consequences in the event of a deadlock. In addition, the majority concluded that there was no reason to think the jury would believe a lesser sentence was possible in the event that they deadlocked.

Ginsburg's dissent focused on the fact that the jury was wrongly instructed in being told that a lesser sentence, something other than life imprisonment, could be imposed on the defendant. The jury may have been swayed in favor of the death penalty in light of the possible alternative that the defendant may "get off easy" with a limited sentence if they were not unanimous. In her dissent, Ginsburg quoted the landmark case of *Gregg v. Georgia* (1976), in which the Court referred to accurate sentencing information as the "indispensible prerequisite" for a jury's decision to impose death. Again, Ginsburg stressed the importance of accurate jury instructions to ensure a fair outcome for the defendant.

In addition to the cases discussed above, Justice Ginsburg joined several others during the Rehnquist era in the area of jury instruction. These cases included *Buchanan v. Angelone* (1998) and *Brown v. Payton* (2005), in which both petitioners argued that the jury was not correctly instructed to consider mitigating factors relevant to their cases; and *Weeks v. Angelone* (1999), in which the petitioner argued that the judge's instructions to the jury were unclear. In these cases, Ginsburg continued to side with defendants and in favor of providing clear and comprehensive instructions to juries.

Ginsburg's majority opinions, dissents, and concurrences in cases related to capital juries highlighted her view that defendants are entitled to clear and understandable jury instructions in order to receive the benefits of their full due process rights. Whether juries are relieved of their significant responsibility when deciding capital cases (*Romano*) or incorrectly instructed on what their decisions realistically mean for defendants (*Simmons, Schafer,* and *Jones*), Ginsburg sent the message that a fair process means juries are adequately informed about their responsibilities.

Remarks Made to Juries

Related to issues surrounding jury instruction, Justice Ginsburg established a record of writing dissents in other matters concerning juries. In the cases discussed below, her focus was not on jury instructions but rather on the evidence presented to the jury and the defendant's constitutional rights.

In *Gray v. Netherland* (1995), Gray was accused of murdering the manager of a local department store. During the sentencing phase, the prosecution presented evidence that Gray committed another murder (which was still unsolved) in order to demonstrate that the modus operandi of the two crimes were similar. Gray's attorney argued he did not have sufficient notice to prepare a rebuttal to this evidence, but he did not request a formal continuance. Gray was subsequently sentenced to death by the jury.

Gray's case was brought to the Supreme Court on two occasions and justices denied certiorari both times. In a third action filed in the federal courts, the district court found in Gray's favor, concluding that the insufficient notice of evidence violated Gray's due process rights. The Supreme Court later agreed to hear the case, based on Gray's argument that the prosecution withheld evidence showing that he had not committed the Sorrell murders, namely that the police investigation had focused heavily on the spouse of Mrs. Sorrell, who had motive and opportunity. Gray also argued he was misled into believing that only eyewitness evidence would be presented when in fact crime scene photos and expert testimony were presented.

At the core of the debate between the majority and the minority in a close 5-4 decision was the issue of a "new rule:" that is, the majority argued that by finding in the petitioner's favor a "new rule" would be created that did not then exist in constitutional doctrine. Justice Ginsburg, along with Justices Stevens, Souter, and Breyer, argued in a dissenting opinion that no "new rule" would be created by finding in favor of Gray, and that, in fact, his due process rights were violated because of the insufficient notice provided by the prosecutor. Her dissent focused on the basic issue of due process and the denial of such in Gray's case. In her words, "There is nothing 'new' in a rule that capital defendants must be afforded a meaningful opportunity to defend against the State's penalty phase evidence" (*Gray v. Netherland* 1995, 181).

Ginsburg also veered from her typical diplomatic collegiality in writing opinions by accusing the majority of misrepresenting Gray's claim: "This Court also restates and reshapes Gray's claim. The Court first slices Gray's whole claim into pieces; it then deals discretely with each segment of it. . . . His own claim is more basic and should not succumb to artificial endeavors to divide and conquer it" (*Gray v. Netherland* 1995, 181). In another case focusing on prosecutor's remarks to the jury, the defendant appealed his conviction for sexual assault because the State accused him of manipulating his own testimony to fit the physical evidence presented in court and the testimony given by the witnesses (*Portuondo v. Agard* 2000). Specifically, the prosecutor stated the following in his closing remarks: "You know, ladies and gentlemen, unlike all the other witnesses in this case, the defendant has a benefit and the benefit that he has, unlike all the other witnesses, is he gets to sit here and listen to the testimony of all the other witnesses before he testifies" (*Portuondo v. Agard* 2000, 64). Agard claimed that these statements violated his rights to be present at trial and face his accusers, as well as his rights to due process. Essentially, the prosecutor used Agard's rights to be present and to confront his accusers against him; therefore, the weight of his own testimony was diminished. The respondent also claimed that his due process rights were violated, as New York law requires that he attend his own trial. The prosecutor's comments allegedly served to make his required attendance work against him and thereby violated due process.

The Court's majority claimed no precedents existed to guarantee the rights asserted by the respondent. They also claimed that the case cited by the respondent, *Griffin v. California* (1965) was not relevant. The landmark *Griffin* decision guaranteed that a defendant who refuses to testify cannot have that fact used against her in court. However, the majority, with Scalia writing the opinion, noted that Agard did not *refuse* to testify, as was the case in *Griffin*. Agard also cited *Doyle v. Ohio* (1976), which found that defendants who refuse to talk to the police after being *Mirandized* cannot have that fact held against them in court. However, the Court rejected the claim that *Doyle* applied in his case. Scalia also noted that the jury must weigh the credibility of any statements made by the defendant when it is very clear to the jurors that the defendant has had the privilege of attending the trial and hearing all other witnesses up to the point of his own testimony. Finally, Agard's claim that his right to due process was violated was also rejected by the Court.

Ginsburg's dissent began with an uncharacteristically sharp note: "The Court today transforms a defendant's presence at trial from a Sixth Amendment right into an automatic burden on his credibility" (*Portuondo v. Agard* 2000, 76). By finding against Agard, the Court allowed a prosecutor to impugn the defendant if he chooses to exercise his right to be present at his trial and face his accusers. She indicated that the relevant cases cited by the defendant as precedents are rooted in the same principle as that raised by Agard:

> In *Griffin* . . . we held that a defendant's refusal to testify at trial may not be used as evidence of his guilt. In *Doyle*, we held that a defendant's silence after receiving Miranda warnings did not warrant a prosecutor's attack on his credibility. Both decisions stem from the principle that where the exercise of constitutional rights is "insolubly ambiguous" as between innocence and guilt . . . a

prosecutor may not unfairly encumber those rights by urging the jury to construe the ambiguity against the defendant. (*Portuondo v. Agard* 2000, 76-77)

As in *Gray*, Ginsburg called the majority to task for complicating what she viewed as a simple issue—the rights of a defendant to face his accusers and be present at his trial.

In *Montana v. Egelhoff* (1996), the defendant was charged with the "deliberate homicide" of two friends with whom he became intoxicated. After drinking a considerable amount of alcohol that led his blood alcohol level to be 0.36 one hour after his arrest, the defendant shot his two friends with a handgun. Part of the defense's argument in court was that extreme intoxication meant that he had no memory of killing his companions and he could not have committed the intent-based crimes for which he was charged. In accordance with Montana state law, the jury was instructed that evidence of extreme intoxication could not be considered when deciding whether respondent was guilty of the crime. They found him guilty and sentenced him to eighty-four years in prison.

Egelhoff appealed by claiming that his due process rights were violated and he was not able to present all relevant information about intoxication, a traditional defense to intent-based crimes. The Montana Supreme Court agreed and reversed this finding of guilt, indicating that in order to fully enjoy due process rights, the defendant must be allowed to present all relevant evidence to rebut the state's charges. In the U.S. Supreme Court's majority opinion on this case, Justice Scalia pointed out that defendants do not have an absolute right to present any and all evidence relevant to a case—in some cases, relevant evidence can be excluded if it is found to be privileged, procedurally flawed, or misleading. In this case, evidence of extreme intoxication would be used to diminish or eliminate the defendant's ability to form mens rea and commit the crime with intent. Thus, Scalia's majority opinion reversed the decision of the Montana Supreme Court. Unlike the prior cases discussed in this section, Justice Ginsburg did not prepare a dissent in this case; in fact, she was one of five justices forming the majority, along with Rehnquist, Scalia, Kennedy, and Thomas. Ginsburg's concurrence begins by clarifying the issue: "Can a State, without offense to the Federal Constitution, make the judgment that two people are equally culpable where one commits an act stone sober, and the other engages in the same conduct after his voluntary intoxication has reduced his capacity for self control?" (*Montana v. Egelhoff* 1996, 57). Indeed, Justice Ginsburg concluded that couching this issue in mens rea terms rather than evidentiary terms kept it from violating the Due Process Clause of the U.S. Constitution. The majority opinion deferred to the original state statute that was bypassed by the state supreme court's decision when they declared that it was proper to allow the people of Montana to "resurrect the rule of an earlier era, disallowing consideration of voluntary intoxication when a defendant's state of mind is at issue" (*Montana v. Egelhoff* 1996, 56).

Prior to reading the opinion of Court and armed with the knowledge of which presidents appointed each justice, one would not expect Scalia, Rehnquist, Kennedy, Thomas, and Ginsburg to be in agreement on this issue. This case demonstrates an example of Justice Ginsburg's minimalist philosophy—leaving state legislatures with the decisions as to how to define crimes, rather than have excessive judicial intrusion into matters that she did not see as clearly implicating constitutional rights.

Search and Seizure

Ginsburg's dissents in search and seizure cases indicated that she believed that the power of the federal and state governments should be limited when law enforcement officials sought to intrude on persons and property in the pursuit of criminal evidence. In the cases discussed below, her philosophies of minimalism and judicial restraint can be seen quite clearly.

A Phoenix police officer observed respondent Evans driving the wrong way on a one-way street. A warrant check indicated that Evans had an outstanding misdemeanor warrant and suspended driver's license, leading to his arrest. During the arrest process, officers found marijuana in Evans' car and he was charged with marijuana possession. Further investigation revealed that the misdemeanor warrant had been quashed two weeks prior to Evans' arrest, yet a miscommunication between the court clerk's office and the sheriff's office resulted in a failure to remove the warrant from Evans' record.

During his trial, Evans argued that the exclusionary rule should apply and the drug evidence should be excluded from consideration because the search incident to arrest was actually based on a nonexistent warrant and unlawful arrest. He also argued that excluding the evidence would send a message to courts and law enforcement about the importance of removing past warrants from the record-keeping system in a timely manner. The trial court agreed and the evidence was suppressed. The Arizona Court of Appeals reversed that decision. Evans subsequently appealed to the Arizona Supreme Court. The state supreme court agreed with Evans that applying the exclusionary rule would send a strong message to criminal justice actors and underscore the importance of keeping such records accurate.

Writing for the U.S. Supreme Court in *Arizona v. Evans* (1995), Chief Justice Rehnquist declared that the search was permissible and appropriate. He emphasized that the police acted in good faith when making the arrest and conducting the search in reliance upon the no-longer-valid misdemeanor warrant that appeared in court records. He went on to state that there was no reason to believe a finding in Evans' favor would improve law enforcement practices because the error was apparently made by a court clerk.

In her dissent, Justice Ginsburg expressed concern about the increasing use of technology to store records and noted that unintentional errors can have grave consequences for citizens. Ginsburg pointed out that the Arizona Supreme Court was not merely concerned with a single computer error made by a court clerk, but rather "the potential for Orwellian mischief" brought about by an increased reliance on technology (*State v. Evans* 1994, 872). In her dissent, Ginsburg noted several cases in which faulty technology resulted in the arrest of innocent citizens, thereby demonstrating that small "unintentional" errors can accumulate to harm citizens.

In *Minnesota v. Carter* (1998), Carter and others were bagging cocaine in an apartment when a police officer observed their behavior through a small opening in a closed blind. After leaving the apartment, Carter's vehicle was searched and drugs, money, and weapons were found. Carter claimed that the search was unreasonable under the Fourth Amendment because it was based on a police officer standing at the window and looking through a thin opening in closed blinds that were intended to protect interior privacy. However, the trial court disagreed. The Minnesota Supreme Court concluded that the respondent had a reasonable expectation of privacy in the apartment and reversed this decision. The U.S. Supreme Court reversed the decision by the Minnesota Supreme Court, finding that the search was not unreasonable.

A substantial part of the discussion of this case revolved around the status of the respondent as a guest in another's home. The lessee of the apartment gave use of her home to Carter and another individual for the purpose of bagging cocaine. In return, she was paid with a small amount of cocaine for her personal use. The Court had previously decided that overnight guests in a home have a reasonable expectation of privacy (*Minnesota v. Olson*, 1990). In this case, however, Carter was not an overnight guest and was at the residence for only two and a half hours to prepare cocaine for distribution. According to the Court, this did not give Carter standing to make a Fourth Amendment claim. The apartment was not a "home away from home" for Carter, as it would have been for an overnight guest, but rather a place to do business. The Court based its decision on the premise that Carter had no reasonable expectation of privacy, and thus the issue of whether the police officer conducted a search was moot.

Ginsburg argued in her dissent that even short-term guests in a home have a reasonable expectation of privacy. She used the language from the Fourth Amendment itself to justify her position, "As I see it, people are not genuinely 'secure in their . . . houses . . . against unreasonable searches and seizures,' if their invitations to others increase the risk of unwarranted governmental peering and prying into their dwelling places" (*Minnesota v. Carter* 1998, 108). As with *Evans*, she favored protecting the rights of the individual and opposed expanded intrusions by the state.

At the end of the Rehnquist Court era, Ginsburg was an outspoken dissenter in *Illinois v. Caballes* (2005), a case that confirmed broader police authority to investigate crimes. Respondent Caballes had been stopped for speeding by the state police. Upon hearing the call, a member of the State Police Drug Canine Unit proceeded to the location on his own initiative. The drug interdiction officer walked his drug-sniffing dog around Caballes' car, and the dog indicated that there were drugs in the trunk. After a brief search, marijuana was found in the trunk. Caballes was later convicted of drug trafficking. He subsequently argued that the officers did not have probable cause to search his car. The Illinois Supreme Court agreed, and reversed the conviction because there was no reason for the officers to think that Caballes had drugs in his car.

The U.S. Supreme Court reversed the decision in an opinion by Justice Stevens declaring that the use of drug-sniffing dogs does not invade the defendant's reasonable expectation of privacy. If no reasonable expectation of privacy is violated in the police officers' investigative actions, then no search has occurred and the question of "reasonableness" under the Fourth Amendment cannot be raised. In the view of the Court majority, a dog walking around the outside of the car is not an intrusion and, furthermore, individuals do not have a reasonable expectation of privacy against the non-intrusive detection of drug aromas when their automobiles are in public.

Justices Souter and Ginsburg filed separate dissents on this issue. Ginsburg argued that the Illinois State Police did need "reasonable suspicion" to believe drugs were in the car, such as smelling marijuana, before the intrusion of the dog could be permitted. She expressed concern that the Court's decision might expand the powers of the police such that all traffic stops could now be subject to drug-sniffing dog examinations. She continued this line of thought, supposing that this decision may pave the way for suspicionless drug sweeps conducted among parked cars and along sidewalks. Thus, she raised a warning about the risks of expanding law enforcement authority in ways that may impact a wide array of citizens in their daily lives.

Conclusion

If one sought to characterize Justice Ginsburg's role in criminal justice cases during the Rehnquist Court era, any accurate characterization would need to focus on her assertiveness in presenting her views about the need to protect certain individual rights. Her voting record was more liberal than most of her colleagues' records in the latter stages of the Rehnquist Court era, but it was not exceptionally liberal when compared to the records of her liberal predecessors, such as Justices Brennan and Marshall. Thus, her support for individuals in criminal justice cases did not appear to be ideological, but rather based on her own careful assessment of individual cases and issues.

Ginsburg was not noted as a majority opinion author who defined particular areas of law in criminal justice because she was dependent on the decisions of others, Chief Justice Rehnquist and Justice Stevens in particular, for using their opinion-assignment authority to give her opportunities to speak on behalf of the Court. Although she received her fair share of majority opinion assignments, those assignments were not necessarily in cases about criminal justice issues. Thus, Ginsburg's role and reputation in criminal justice emerged through her own proactive assertiveness in writing concurring and dissenting opinions on issues of particular concern to her. Most often, those opinions emphasized the need for greater protection of rights instances in which the Rehnquist Court majority had decided to limit or diminish constitutional rights. As indicated in this chapter, Ginsburg distinguished herself in defending rights concerning jury instructions, trial issues, and search and seizure. For the most part, she sought to write diplomatic opinions that enhanced the collegial atmosphere on the Court. However, she also demonstrated that she was willing to forthrightly criticize those majority opinions that she found most threatening to the rights of criminal defendants in the trial process as well as to the rights of citizens throughout society who are susceptible to excessive investigative intrusions by law enforcement officers.

References

American Civil Liberties Union. "Tribute: The Legacy of Ruth Bader Ginsburg and WRP Staff." 2006. http://www.aclu.org (accessed February 16, 2010).

Baugh, Joyce A., Christopher E. Smith, Thomas R. Hensley, and Scott P. Johnson. "Justice Ruth Bader Ginsburg: A Preliminary Assessment." *University of Toledo Law Review* 26 (1994): 1-34.

Bazelon, Emily. "The Place of Women on the Court," *New York Times*, July 7, 2009. http://www.nytimes.com (accessed February 16, 2010).

Ellington, Toni. J. "Ruth Bader Ginsburg and John Marshall Harlan: A Justice and Her Hero." *University of Hawaii Law Review* 20 (1998): 797-834.

Epstein, Lee, Jeffrey A. Segal, Harold J. Spaeth, and Thomas G. Walker. *The Supreme Court Compendium.* Washington, DC: CQ Press, 2007.

Ginsburg, Ruth. B. "Treatment of Women by the Law: Awakening Consciousness in the Law Schools." *Valparaiso University Law Review* 5 (1970): 480-88.

———. "Sex and Unequal Protection: Men and Women as Victims" (speech). *Journal of Family Law* 11 (1971): 347-62.

———. "Gender and the Constitution." *University of Cincinnati Law Review* 44 (1975): 1-42.

———. "Some Thoughts on Benign Classification in the Content of Sex." *Connecticut Law Review* 10 (1977): 813-27.

———. "Ratification of the Equal Rights Amendment: A Question of Time." *Texas Law Review* 57 (1978a): 918-46.

———. "Sex Equality and the Constitution." *Tulane Law Review* 52 (1978b): 451-75.

———. "Sexual Equality Under the Fourteenth and Equal Rights Amendments." *Washington University Law Quarterly* (1979): 161-78.

———. "Remarks on Writing Separately." *Washington Law Review* 65 (1990): 133-50.

———. "Speaking in a Judicial Voice." *New York University Law Review* 67 (1992): 1185-1209.

———. "The Role of Dissenting Opinions." The 20th Annual Leo and Barry Eizenstat Memorial Lecture (Given October 21, 2007). http://www.supremecourtus.gov/ (accessed July 22, 2009).

Greenhouse, Linda. "Women Suddenly Scarce Among Justices' Clerks," *New York Times*, August 30, 2006. http://www.nytimes.com (accessed July 16, 2009).

Halberstam, Malvina. "Ruth Bader Ginsburg." In *Jewish Women: A Comprehensive Historical Encyclopedia* (2005). http://jwa.org/encyclopedia (accessed July 16, 2009).

Harring, Sidney, and Jeffrey L. Kirchmeier. "Scrupulous in Applying the Law: Justice Ruth Bader Ginsburg and Capital Punishment." *New York City Law Review* 7 (2004): 241-73.

Jamieson, Kathleen. H. *Beyond the Double Bind: Women and Leadership.* New York: Oxford University Press, 1995.

Kuo, Mei-Fei, and Kai Wang. "When is Innovation in Order? Justice Ruth Bader Ginsburg and Stare Decisis." *University of Hawaii Law Review* 20 (1998): 835-94.

Legal Information Institute (LLI). 2009. http://topics.law.cornell.edu/wex (accessed July 18, 2009).

Lewis, Neil A. "The Supreme Court: Ginsburg Promises Judicial Restraint if She Joins Court," *New York Times,* July 21, 1993. http://www.nytimes.com (accessed February 18, 2010).

Merritt, Deborah J. "Hearing the Voices of Women and Men: Justice Ruth Bader Ginsburg." *Hawaii Law Review* 20 (1998): 635-46.

Merritt, Deborah J. and David M. Lieberman. "Ruth Bader Ginsburg's Jurisprudence of Opportunity and Equality." *Columbia Law Review* 104 (2004): 39-48.

Morris, Melanie K. "Ruth Bader Ginsburg and Gender Equality: A Reassessment of Her Contribution." *Cardozo Women's Law Journal* 9 (2002): 1-25.

Pressman, Carol. "The House that Ruth Built: Justice Ruth Bader Ginsburg, Gender and Justice." *New York Law School Journal of Human Rights* 14 (1997): 311-37.

Ray, Laura K. "Justice Ginsburg and the Middle Way." *Brooklyn Law Review* 68 (2003): 629-82.

Rosen, Jeffrey. "The List." *New Republic,* May 10, 1993. http://www.tnr.com (accessed February 18, 2010).

Smith, Christopher. E. "Criminal Justice and the 1999-2000 U. S. Supreme Court Term." *North Dakota Law Review* 77 (2001): 1-26.

———. "The Rehnquist Court and Criminal Justice." *Journal of Contemporary Criminal Justice* 19 (2003): 161-81.

Smith, Christopher. E., Joyce A. Baugh, Thomas R. Hensley, and Scott P. Johnson. "The First-term Performance of Justice Ruth Bader Ginsburg." *Judicature* 78 (1994): 74-80.

Smith, Christopher E., and Thomas R. Hensley. "Decision-making Trends of the Rehnquist Court Era: Civil Rights and Liberties Cases." *Judicature* 89 (2005): 161-85.

Smith, Sheila. "Justice Ruth Bader Ginsburg and Sexual Harassment Law: Will the Second Female Supreme Court Justice Become the Court's Women's Rights Champion?" *University of Cincinnati Law Review* 63 (1995): 1893-1945.

Von Drehle, David. "Redefining Fair with a Simple Careful Assault," *Washington Post,* Monday, July 19, 1993. http://www.washingtonpost.com (accessed July 3, 2009).

Walsh, Amy. "Ruth Bader Ginsburg: Extending the Constitution." *Marshall Law Review* 32 (1998): 197-225.

Women's Rights Law Reporter. 2010. http://pegasus.rutgers.edu/~wrlr/index.html.

Yip, Elijah., and Eric. K. Yamamoto. "Justice Ruth Bader Ginsburg's Jurisprudence of Process and Procedure." *Hawaii Law Review* 20 (1998): 647-98.

Cases Cited

Arizona v. Evans, 514 U.S. 1 (1995)
Brown v. Payton, 544 U.S. 133 (2005)
Buchanan v. Angelone, 522 U.S. 269 (1998)

Caldwell v. Mississippi, 472 U.S. 320 (1985)
Craig v. Boren, 429 U.S. 190 (1976)
Doyle v. Ohio, 426 U.S. 610 (1976)
Duren v. Missouri, 439 U.S. 357 (1978)
Gray v. Netherland, 518 U.S. 152 (1995)
Gregg v. Georgia, 428 U.S. 153 (1976)
Griffin v. California, 380 U.S. 609 (1965)
Illinois v. Caballes, 543 U.S. 405 (2005)
J.E.B. v. Alabama, 511 U.S. 127 (1994)
Jones v. United States, 527 U.S. 373 (1999)
Minnesota v. Carter, 525 U.S. 83 (1998)
Minnesota v. Olson, 495 U.S. 91 (1990)
Montana v. Egelhoff, 518 U.S. 37 (1996)
Portundo v. Agard, 529 U.S. 61 (2000)
Roe v. Wade, 410 U.S. 113 (1973)
Romano v. Oklahoma, 512 U.S. 1 (1994)
Shafer v. South Carolina, 531 U.S. 36 (2001)
Simmons v. South Carolina, 512 U.S. 154 (1994)
State v. Evans, 177 Ariz. 204 (1994)
United States v. Virginia, 518 U.S. 515 (1996)
Weeks v. Angelone, 528 U.S. 225 (1999)

Chapter 13
Stephen G. Breyer:
Judicial Modesty & Pragmatic Solutions

Charles F. Jacobs

According to an anecdote recounted in Jeffrey Toobin's recent examination of the United States Supreme Court, a couple approached Justice David Souter as he ate lunch at a Massachusetts restaurant and asked if he was a member of the Court. He replied that he was, and, pressed again by the pair, was asked if he was Stephen Breyer. Making light of what was a somewhat awkward situation, Souter replied that he was but added that the greatest reward he received from working on the high court was the pleasure of serving with David Souter (Toobin 2007). This story, although amusing and somewhat endearing, reflects how generally unacquainted the American public is with the members of the Supreme Court, its work, and the impact of the justices' decisions on the politics of the age. This absence of knowledge is particularly glaring in the case of Justice Stephen Breyer, who is among the least well-known members of the Supreme Court. In a July 2005 public opinion poll, a mere 3 percent of respondents could name Breyer as a sitting justice, tying him with Justice John Paul Stevens as the most anonymous member of the nation's highest court (Deeney 2006). In a similar poll conducted in 2003, 75 percent of respondents admitted that they had too little information about Breyer even to form an opinion about him or his work (Epstein, Segal, Spaeth, and Walker 2007, 766). This dearth of knowledge is notable considering that Breyer had served on the Court for more than a decade and made contributions to many of the most controversial opinions delivered by the Court since the mid-1990s.

Although it would be easy to heap criticism upon those too inattentive to learn the membership of the high court, even for scholars who study the Court there exist glaring holes in what we know about the jurisprudence of individual justices. Justice Breyer's approach to resolving questions of law related to criminal justice is among the unexplored topics that deserve closer examination. Although a number of authors have offered analyses of Breyer's work on the Court (Yarbrough 2000; Baugh 2002; Greenburg 2007), their focus tends to examine him as "techno-judge" whose legal expertise rests in the area of administrative law and regulatory behavior (Kersch 2003, 267). Little, however, has been written regarding his contribution in the area of criminal law. Unlike his colleagues on the Court, Breyer is usually not recognized as a leading light helping to define the rights of the criminally accused. This chapter seeks to examine the contributions of Justice Breyer to the Supreme Court's criminal justice decisions during the Rehnquist Court era. The discussion begins with a brief review of Breyer's early career and selection and confirmation to the bench, followed by an examination of his judicial philosophy, which Breyer himself explains in his treatise on decision making, *Active Liberty* (Breyer 2005). The analysis will conclude with an assessment of the application of this philosophy in opinions authored by Breyer from the Rehnquist Court's body of decisions affecting criminal justice.

Early Career & Arrival on the Rehnquist Court

The U.S. Senate's confirmation of Justice Breyer in the summer of 1994 marked the sixth and final addition to the Supreme Court during the tenure of William H. Rehnquist as chief justice. Breyer's arrival established a cohort of nine justices who would serve together for a period of more than eleven years—a term of stability unrivaled in modern Court history. Although this period of stable composition and interactions among a fixed set of justices certainly had ramifications for the development of legal doctrine, there existed professional ramifications for Breyer as well. The absence of any change in the membership of the Court meant that he was consigned to the position of junior justice for more than a decade. More than just a titular role, the junior justice by tradition is required to fulfill a number of duties on behalf of the other members, including answering the door during the private meetings of the Conference to retrieve missing documents or, on occasion, a cup of coffee (Cushman 2007). Despite these obligations, Breyer has remarked that the job is "neither onerous nor humiliating" and the position does not necessarily disadvantage a justice in influencing other members of the Court (285).

Breyer came to this position after serving on the First Circuit Court of Appeals in Boston for nearly fourteen years. A graduate of Stanford University and Harvard Law School, Breyer spent much of his early career as a professor of law at Harvard. He also held posts with the Justice Department and Senate Judiciary Committee and served as its Chief Counsel from 1979 to 1980 (Yarbrough 2000, 32). He continued to offer his expertise to the federal government even after his appointment to the appeals court by President Jimmy Carter, serving as a member of the United States Sentencing Commission from 1985 to 1989. His work outside the courtroom earned him a reputation as a policy wonk and a technocrat. During his time with the Administrative Practices Subcommittee of the Senate Judiciary Committee, he helped create a blueprint for deregulation of the airline and trucking industries. Breyer also helped to shape the contours and content of the federal sentencing guidelines during his years on the Sentencing Commission (Baugh 2002).

Breyer's elevation to the Supreme Court came about almost by happenstance. After twelve years of Republican control of the White House that resulted in the appointment of five new members to the high court, Democrats hoped that the election of President Bill Clinton would provide an opportunity to recalibrate the philosophical orientation and composition of a Court perceived by political liberals as far too conservative. Justice Byron White provided that opportunity when he announced his retirement from the bench in March of 1993. Clinton himself indicated he hoped to hit a "home run" with any appointment to the Supreme Court by seeking a nominee with "a fine mind, good judgment, wide experience in the law and in the problems of real people, and someone with a big heart" (Silverstein 2007, 114). Swinging for the fences, however, proved difficult for the Clinton Administration. Conservatives in the Senate and among the public cautioned against the nomination of anyone perceived as too liberal, a forewarning of a possible bitter partisan fight. As a result, the president focused his sights on more ideologically moderate candidates. Although Clinton briefly considered Breyer for White's seat on the Court, the president's apprehensions about potential confirmation issues, including reports about an oversight by Breyer related to the payment of Social Security taxes for a household employee, led to the nomination of Ruth Bader Ginsburg.

A second opportunity for Clinton to shape the Supreme Court's membership came with the announcement in April 1994 of Justice Harry Blackmun's impending retirement. Again Clinton sought to make a mark on the Court but was rebuffed by his first choice, Senator George Mitchell of Maine. Other candidates, such as Interior Secretary Bruce Babbitt, were removed from consideration when Republicans in the Senate suggested that the confirmation of any nominees perceived as liberal would again be unlikely. Breyer, a "noncandidate throughout the entire torturous process," became Clinton's choice in large measure because the president's initial choices were eliminated (Silverstein 2007, 121). Breyer's experience and qualifications, coupled with his familiarity with the Judiciary Committee and many of its members, insured a relatively easy path to confirmation. A judicial moderate, Breyer also lacked the partisan baggage that would galvanize opposition from Republicans bent on keeping a liberal off the bench.

As a result, Breyer's confirmation hearings before members of the Senate Judiciary Committee were anticlimactic. The only controversy that merited any attention during the proceedings involved Breyer's decision while serving on the appellate court to refuse recusal from a case in which he had an apparent financial stake, an issue raised repeatedly by Democratic Senator Howard Metzenbaum of Ohio (see *United States v. Ottati & Goss* 1990). Like Ginsburg the previous year, Breyer received a rather warm welcome from the committee, fielding typical questions regarding judicial temperament, privacy rights, and statutory interpretation. An area that received scant attention during the hearing was that of criminal justice and criminal law. Of more than 350 questions posed

by the eighteen members of the committee, fewer than thirty were directly related to the rights of suspects, criminal defendants, and convicted offenders
(U.S. Congress, Committee on the Judiciary 1994). The availability of Breyer's
decisions in criminal cases during his years on the appellate bench may explain
the committee's relative disinterest in the subject. The senators did, however,
press Breyer on his views regarding capital punishment—an area of law on
which Breyer had likely written little. Of the states in the First Circuit, only New
Hampshire permitted the imposition of the death penalty, although not a single
person had been executed since before the Second World War. For observers
seeking illumination of Breyer's beliefs about criminal law, these few queries
offered little insight into an area that constitutes an important portion of the Supreme Court docket.

The Judicial Philosophy of Stephen Breyer

Although the confirmation hearings provided few firm clues about how Breyer
would decide specific criminal justice issues as a Supreme Court justice, his
responses to questions regarding his judicial philosophy provided a window into
the general approach he would employ in the interpretation of both constitutional and statutory cases. At the time of his nomination to the high court, scholars
characterized his legal mien as pragmatic—a label that is consistently applied to
his judicial analysis (U.S. Congress, Committee on the Judiciary, Sullivan
1994). Many credit Oliver Wendell Holmes as the father of American legal
pragmatism, a theory that is connected to the legal realist and sociological jurisprudence movements of the early twentieth century (Cardozo 1949; Holmes
1963; Fisher, Horowitz, and Reed 1993). Although no single definition exists to
describe this approach (Dworkin 1986; Horowitz 1992; Schwartz 1993), the
term is generally understood as a method "that is practical and instrumental rather than essentialist—interested in what works and what is useful rather than in
what '*really*' is. It is therefore *forward-looking*, valuing continuity with the past
only so far as such continuity can help us cope with the problems of the present
and of the future" (Posner 1995, 4). Additional descriptors for the method include activist and progressive as well as fact-based and skeptical. Those who
employ the approach view the law as a means to an end, leveraging case outcomes with a general purpose in mind but without suggesting that there exists a
specific legal telos.

Although evidence concerning Breyer's judicial philosophy existed in both
his appellate record and academic writings (Breyer 1988, 1992), a comprehensive exposition of his decision making came only after Clinton elevated him to
the Supreme Court bench. Published in 2005, *Active Liberty* is a short treatise in
which Breyer offers his thesis about the proper approach to judicial interpretation. The title of the book is borrowed from the writings of French thinker Benjamin Constant who drew distinctions in his philosophy between the liberty of

the moderns and the liberty of the ancients. Constant argued that the former concerns civil liberties and the ability of citizens to exercise rights and freedoms without undue interference of government or tyrannical majorities. If liberty of the moderns is freedom *from* government, then liberty of the ancients, as described by Constant, is freedom *to* engage in the "sharing of a nation's sovereign authority among that nation's citizens" (Breyer 2005, 4). This active liberty demands public participation in the exercise of democratic power and responsibility. Although distinct, Constant indicated these two liberties were necessary and complementary components of a well-functioning democracy. Breyer argues that too little emphasis is placed on the need for active liberty by those empowered to rule from the bench. His thesis suggests "that courts should take greater account of the Constitution's democratic nature when they interpret constitutional and statutory text" (5). Hence, the responsibility of judges is to offer interpretations in cases that promote active liberty. The result of such an approach, he contends, is a type of judicial modesty that will serve as a restraint on judges while also serving as "a source of judicial authority and an interpretive aid to more effective protection of ancient and modern liberty alike" (6). Breyer is quick to note that he is not presenting a comprehensive theory of judicial decision making. Instead, he offers a theme of democracy and the Constitution that provides guidance and structure to the process of resolving disputes and interpreting legal texts.

The tools employed in the endeavor differ little from those already used by judges. The basic elements used in evaluating the Constitution or statutes remain the same and include reference to language, history, tradition, precedent, and consequences (Breyer 2005, 8). For Breyer, the difference between his method and the method of other jurists is one of emphasis. Critical to his approach is a focus on the final two criteria. His interpretive approach "sees texts driven by purposes" (17). In evaluating the content of law, the analysis begins with the question: "What was the purpose to be achieved?" Judges must be careful, claims Breyer, to investigate closely the reasons that motivated the creation of a particular text and attempt to meet the conditions set by the public in their creation of law. As a secondary step, judges must evaluate the consequences of the interpretive process on economic, social, political, and community conditions (18). The ultimate goal is to focus case outcomes on the "Constitution's democratic imperative" by restraining judges from replacing the judgment of the people with that of judges, especially when those judicial actors are ill-equipped to offer appropriate evaluation of democratic will (34). The objective becomes not one of fealty to a particular and rigid judicial philosophy but instead the wise and restrained use of legal resources to promote the interests of society while also strengthening the democratic process. In this way, Breyer's thesis demonstrates its debt to realist thinkers and association with pragmatism by the manner in which it sustains and strengthens active liberty through practical and instrumental legal analysis.

In support of his argument, Breyer explores a number of hypothetical examples of the thesis in action. He applies his purposeful and consequential method to the areas of free speech, federalism, privacy, affirmative action, statutory interpretation, and administrative law, always cognizant of the caution that must be exercised in order to protect what he calls the "'conversational' lawmaking process" (Breyer 2005, 71). The result is the use of balancing tests in most circumstances to protect, as Constant recommended, both ancient and modern liberty. Inherent in all of these discussions is a thinly-veiled contempt for the text-based approach advocated by the likes of Breyer's Supreme Court colleague Justice Antonin Scalia (Scalia 1997). Textualists, Breyer argues, rely far too heavily on language "divorcing law from life" and eroding democracy (Breyer 2005, 85). He recognizes the complaint lobbed by advocates of textualism that a purposive approach itself might be undemocratic because judges will exercise a subjective judgment about the purpose or consequence of the law. In Breyer's estimation, the process of deciding the type of information useful to a textual analysis is not more or less subjective than carefully imputing a purpose or consequence to the law or Constitution. In fact, Breyer would claim that the cramped, literal approach of textualists has the effect of foreclosing democratic choice by applying such narrow definitions to the law that avenues of public participation may be closed.

Despite presenting a detailed account of purposive decision making and a tidy rebuttal to the textual alternative, Breyer offers scant insight into the application of his approach in the area of criminal justice and the constitutional rights of the criminally accused. The closest he comes to shedding light on this significant area of constitutional adjudication comes in a brief discussion of Fourth Amendment search and seizure jurisprudence in relation to personal privacy. He makes specific mention of the case of *Kyllo v. United States* (2001) in which the Court reviewed the use of thermal imaging cameras by law enforcement agents. Breyer also offered an examination of the somewhat ambiguous federal habeas corpus statute to demonstrate the utility of his approach for the sensible application of muddled statutory language in circumstances when a text-based approach might pervert the implied intent of the law's drafters (Breyer 2005, 95-98, 101).

What is lacking in Breyer's own discussion of his analytical approach, however, is a more detailed accounting of how active liberty operates in an area of constitutional law where modern liberty, more than liberty of the ancients, is implied. The protections of liberties enumerated in the Fourth, Fifth, Sixth, and Eighth Amendments are aimed squarely at providing relief from government imposition upon the individual—a clear imperative for the liberty *from* government control and state power. This begs a question regarding the extent to which Breyer can or does utilize his active liberty analysis in the area of criminal justice. The following section seeks to shed light on this issue by examining select opinions penned by Breyer during the Rehnquist Court era. The evidence suggests that although Breyer applies the interpretive approach he articulates in *Active Liberty* consistently, the results he reaches do not necessarily promote the enhancement of democracy in all circumstances.

Select Opinions of Justice Stephen Breyer

Under the leadership of Chief Justice Rehnquist, Breyer penned a total of ninety-three majority opinions for the Court (Epstein et al. 2007, 653-55). Like new justices before him, Breyer shared with his colleagues the burden of writing decisions from the moment he joined the Court, receiving the job of composing the majority opinion eight times during his first term (Bowen and Scheb 1993). That same year, he contributed an additional eight opinions, six in dissent and two concurring with the majority (Smith, Baugh, and Hensley 1995, 76). Although not obvious during his first year on the Court, Breyer would become noted for the frequency with which he wrote concurring opinions, recording a higher proportion of this type of opinion than any other justice who served under Rehnquist (Segal and Spaeth 2004, 385-86). In total, Breyer wrote sixty-three concurrences and eighty-four dissents during the Rehnquist Court era (Epstein et al. 2007, 638).

Breyer's appointment to the Court did not significantly alter the ideological dynamic among the justices. Breyer took the seat of Justice Harry Blackmun who was one of the Court's most liberal justices at the time of his retirement. Clinton had hoped his appointments to the federal judiciary would alter the content of the Court's decisions and the shape of its jurisprudence for years into the future. However, what he accomplished with the selection of Breyer was the installation of a "centrist and legal technician" (O'Brien 2005, 83). Although Breyer is frequently, and correctly, described as a pragmatist, pragmatism is not necessarily synonymous with judicial moderation (Smith, Baugh, and Hensley 1995, 75). In the case of Breyer, however, these two descriptors of judicial behavior and temperament appear to correlate. Of the fourteen justices who served during the Rehnquist era, Breyer ranks eighth in the percentage of liberal votes in civil rights and civil liberties cases. His 62 percent voting record is significantly higher than the 44 percent average for the Court during this period. Thus, among liberal-leaning justices, his overall voting record placed him closer to the ideological middle ground between his sets of colleagues who voted more consistently to either support or oppose individuals' rights claims (Smith and Hensley 2005, 164).

Breyer contributed his unique perspective on criminal law and procedure in a total of seventy-two cases, including twenty-eight majority opinions, twenty-four dissents, eighteen concurrences, and two special concurrences. This total, however, does not include cases that may have related to, or referenced, issues of criminal law and rights of the criminally accused, but were more directly related to a different area of constitutional or statutory interpretation. As an example, see *Printz v. United States* (1997) and the Court's interpretation of federalism jurisprudence as it relates to the Brady Handgun Prevention Act of 1993 (18 U.S.C. 921). Similar to his voting behavior across a range of civil rights and civil liberties questions, Breyer was moderate in his treatment of criminal justice issues. Of the 214 cases argued before the Rehnquist Court, Breyer recorded liberal votes in 53.7 percent of the criminal procedure cases, defined as litigation related to "the rights of persons accused of a crime except for the due process rights of prisoners" (Epstein et al. 2007, 537). This tendency placed him among his more liberal colleagues on the bench including Justices Souter, Ginsburg, and Stevens who opposed conservative outcomes in 54.3, 60.9 and 65.4 percent of the cases respectively (536). Due to Breyer's prolific opinion-writing performance, he wrote opinions concerning a panoply of constitutional issues related to protections afforded the criminally accused. However, his ability to impact Court doctrine directly through majority opinions was limited to a small number of notable cases. These included Fourth Amendment search and seizure cases, for which he wrote a pair of opinions (*Illinois v. McArthur* 2001; *Illinois v. Lidster* 2004), a case concerning the double jeopardy protection provided by the Fifth Amendment (*United States v. Lara* 2004), and selected fair trial rights guaranteed by the Fifth and Sixth Amendments (*Gray v. Maryland* 1998; *United States v. Ruiz* 2002; *Sell v. United States* 2003). Breyer also employed the expertise he gained on the U.S. Sentencing Commission by writing four majority opinions regarding federal sentencing guidelines and protections afforded defendants by the Sixth Amendment during the sentencing phase of a criminal prosecution (*Almendarez-Torres v. United States* 1998; *Edwards v. United States* 1998; *Buford v. United States* 2001; *United States v. Booker* 2005).

Breyer made additional contributions to the Rehnquist Court's impact on criminal justice through majority opinions interpreting federal law, including civil rights and habeas corpus statutes. The breadth of Breyer's writing—covering both constitutional and statutory themes—and the numerous majority, concurring and dissenting opinions provides the opportunity to explore in detail the application of his active liberty concept to criminal justice cases. In order to provide an illuminating focus, the examination offered here provides a review of Breyer's interpretation of various constitutional protections afforded by the Sixth Amendment, with particular attention to the Court's treatment of sentencing practices at both the state and federal levels. Additionally, Breyer's opinions related to Fourth Amendment search and seizure cases will be explored.

Sixth Amendment, Right to Jury Trial, & Sentencing Schemes

In 1984 Congress passed the Sentencing Reform Act that ended the use of indeterminate sentencing at the federal level by replacing the use of parole with a structured system of punishment that sought to provide a measure of uniformity and fairness across the system. This method of sentencing, although novel in federal courts, was already in use in nine states prior to implementation of the federal version in 1987 (Frase 1995). Michael Tonry claims "few outside the federal commission [empowered to write the guidelines] would disagree that the federal guidelines have been a disaster" (1995, 171). By contrast, Breyer, a former member of that commission, is among those fiercely dedicated to sustaining the policy that guides incarceration decisions and in apparent denial about its deficiencies. The first opportunity that Breyer had to resolve a challenge to the guidelines came in the *Almendarez-Torres* case in 1998. Breyer, writing for the five-member majority, addressed whether an amendment to the sentencing guidelines authorized by Congress defined a separate crime or merely created the possibility of an enhanced penalty for recidivists. Hugo Almendarez-Torres faced two years in prison for returning to the United States illegally after being deported. That term of incarceration, however, was enhanced to eighty-five months because the deportation order related to his previous conviction for three aggravated felonies. In approaching the defendant's challenge to the sentence enhancement, Breyer wrote, "we look to the statute's language, structure, subject matter, context and history—factors that typically help courts determine a statute's objectives and thereby illuminate its text" (*Almendarez-Torres v. United States* 1998, 228). He found few questions about the intent of Congress—it sought to enhance penalties rather than establish a new offense. In doing so, he focused almost exclusively on the intent of Congress and the precedents that support the constitutionality of longer sentences for recidivists. He expressed a specific worry that if the intent of Congress was read to suggest the creation of a new crime, the government would need to prove the existence of previous criminal activity as part of the indictment. This, Breyer claimed, would likely prejudice the jury and undermine the fairness of the trial.

Scalia's dissent in *Almendarez-Torres* hinted at the division that existed on the Court regarding guidelines and other methods that increased sentences based upon facts that were either not presented to a jury or raised in an indictment—questions that introduced fundamental Sixth Amendment questions regarding the fairness of jury proceedings. In a number of cases over the next several years, Breyer found himself fighting to sustain the interpretation he offered in *Almendarez-Torres* and to preserve the vitality of the sentencing guidelines. In three subsequent cases, *Apprendi, Blakely,* and *Booker,* Breyer offered strongly-stated opinions that challenged the contention of the Court's majority that "any fact that increases the penalty for a crime beyond the prescribed statutory maximum, other than the fact of a prior conviction, must be submitted to a jury and proved beyond a reasonable doubt" (*Apprendi v. New Jersey* 2000, 466).

In *Apprendi,* the Court reviewed a challenge to a New Jersey law that created an enhanced sentence if a judge determines that a defendant committed a crime with "a purpose to intimidate a person or group because of . . . race" (*Apprendi v. New Jersey* 2000, 466). Apprendi faced a maximum term of ten years imprisonment after his conviction for firing a gun into the home of a neighbor. However, the trial judge added two years to this total based upon evidence presented at sentencing that the offense was racially motivated. Apprendi argued that the decision by the judge, while permitted under a New Jersey hate law provision, denied Sixth Amendment guarantees that required prosecutors to present every element of a crime to a jury to be proved beyond a reasonable doubt. The majority agreed. In an opinion authored by Justice John Paul Stevens, the Court held that common law tradition suggests limits on discretion exercised by judges at sentencing. Distinguishing between sentencing factors and elements of the crime, Stevens argued that a sentencing decision is limited by statutorily prescribed maximum sentences as they relate to the crimes for which a jury found a defendant guilty. In dissent, Breyer claimed the Court's attempt to create this procedural nicety was unworkable given the myriad sentencing factors that would need to be submitted to a jury. In his estimation, "the rationale that underlies the Court's rule suggests a principle—jury determination of all sentencing-related facts—that, unless restricted, threatens the workability of every criminal justice system . . . or threatens efforts to make those systems more uniform, hence more fair" (565). Beyond this issue of process, Breyer worried whether the holding would have the additional effect of limiting choices made by legislatures. He argued "New Jersey has determined that one motive—racial hatred—is particularly bad and ought to make a difference in respect to punishment for a crime" (565). The result of the holding, he suggested, would be a limitation on the right of a democratic institution to make a reasonable determination about what constitutes an appropriate punishment for committing a particular crime.

Breyer also questioned why the majority could tacitly accept the existence of sentencing guidelines, an issue not before them in the *Apprendi* case, but then find it necessary to limit the discretion of a sentencing judge. He asked, somewhat rhetorically "if the Constitution permits Guidelines, why does it not permit Congress similarly to guide the exercise of a judge's sentencing discretion?" (*Apprendi v. New Jersey* 2000, 561). Breyer received a response to this question in a pair of cases regarding punishments imposed under guideline systems. In *Blakely v. Washington* (2004) and *United States v. Booker* (2005), petitioners asked the Court to evaluate sentencing enhancements that were permitted by statute but exceeded the sentences prescribed by guidelines. Scalia wrote for the majority that in the spirit of the *Apprendi* decision, judicially determined facts that were not presented to the jury for determination, and served to increase the length of sentences, were prohibited under the Sixth Amendment. The majority noted that the Court's holding did not invalidate guideline systems *per se* but simply demanded that when employed, these systems respect the responsibility of a jury to determine all relevant facts. Breyer disagreed, claiming as he did in *Apprendi* that the Court was interfering with the ability of a legislature to choose how to define and describe elements of a crime and establish statutory factors that influence sentencing. He argued that the case is "ultimately about the limitations that the court imposes upon legislatures' ability to make democratic legislative decisions" (*Blakely v. Washington* 2004, 345).

Breyer found himself again defending sentencing guidelines in the case of *United States v. Booker* (2005). On this occasion, however, the petitioner attacked the constitutionality of sentences prescribed under the federal guidelines that Breyer himself had helped shape. As in *Blakely*, the Court held that enhanced sentences under the federal system violated the Sixth Amendment if the judge based the enhancement on facts not presented to the jury. As expected, Breyer dissented from this portion of the opinion, citing objections similar to those voiced in previous cases. However, Breyer authored the portion of the opinion that announced the Court's remedy. He wrote that the best way to maintain the basic intent of Congress was not to retain the guideline system as it existed while also, as Justice Stevens suggested, mandating a jury trial requirement for all facts influencing sentencing. Instead, Breyer reviewed the history and purpose for creating the guidelines system. His conclusion was that Congress intended to provide a sentencing system that was both fairer and more uniform by guiding the discretion of judges. To insure this basic purpose, the Court announced a remedy that made the guidelines advisory rather than mandatory.

Central to Breyer's criticism of the Court's holdings in both *Blakely* and *Booker* was the practical possibility that such decisions would force the states and federal government to create jury trial processes and sentencing systems that upended what he perceived as the fundamental purpose behind the creation of the guidelines—insuring the equitable treatment of those convicted of crimes by providing comparable penalties for comparable offenses. A shift away from guideline sentencing, he surmised, would shift that discretion to other actors in the criminal justice system and create disparities in sentencing based upon prejudicial factors such as race or gender.

As he argued in *Active Liberty*, Breyer approached this line of cases with an eye toward the *purposes* of legislative institutions responsible for regulating the sentencing of those found guilty of crimes. Yet, he failed to adequately consider the *consequences* of his uncompromising support of sentencing guidelines systems. As the majorities in *Apprendi*, *Blakely*, and *Booker* argued, permitting sentencing decisions based upon facts that were not introduced at trial serves to grant very significant discretion to sentencing judges. Although guidelines limit that discretion, its existence places defendants in jeopardy of significantly longer sentences, including sentences that exceed the underlying purposes of the punishment. Hence, resulting sentences may not reflect the intent of the legislature that created the penalties and thereby serve to undermine the democratic process.

Breyer's support for vesting discretionary authority over sentencing with judges effectively advocates a diminution of jurors' role as fact-finders at trial. Fundamental to the arguments of the majority in *Apprendi* and its progeny is the notion that Sixth Amendment liberties are best protected when juries exercise their judgment about all facts that may impact the length of incarceration of a criminal defendant. The jury, as Alexis de Tocqueville noted in his treatise *Democracy in America*, is not merely an institution of law but "is pre-eminently a political institution; it should be regarded as one form of the sovereignty of the people" (283). Limiting the participation of the jury, as Breyer would permit, diminishes the ability of citizens to exercise a component of their democratic power.

Breyer's failure to acknowledge this tension between his active liberty concept and his approach to sentencing guidelines is odd when considered in light of the justification he offered for joining the majority opinion in *Miller-El v. Dretke* (2005). The case, although not directly related to sentencing decisions, required the Court to determine the fairness of jury selection for Miller-El's trial on capital murder charges. The petitioner challenged his conviction by arguing that the prosecutor in Dallas County, Texas, had systematically excused African Americans during jury selection. Breyer, who supported the majority's holding that the use of peremptory challenges to strike ten of eleven black venire members entitled Miller-El to a new trial, went so far as to argue that peremptory challenges are arbitrary and capricious and should be eliminated entirely. In his concurring opinion, he reasoned, "peremptory challenges betray the jury's democratic origins and undermine its representative function" (*Miller-El v. Dretke* 2005, at 8 of concurring opinion). Breyer's *Miller-El* opinion applies the philosophy espoused by the justice's book *Active Liberty* but is in tension with his opinions concerning the related matter of the jury's role during the use of sentencing guidelines.

Breyer was similarly supportive of the role of the jury in *Ring v. Arizona* (2002), a case in which the seven-member majority applied the *Apprendi* holding to overturn an Arizona sentencing procedure that allowed a judge to determine, without jury input, the existence of aggravating factors that would sustain a sentence of execution for murder. Concurring in judgment only, Breyer distanced himself from the line of cases that began with *Apprendi*. He relied on precedent from the Court's Eighth Amendment decisions to contend that jury sentencing in capital cases is always required. In making his case, Breyer considered the jury's ability to "reflect more accurately the composition and experiences of the community as a whole" and "translate a community's sense of capital punishment's appropriateness in a particular case" (*Ring v. Arizona* 2002, 616). This argument acknowledged and endorsed the essential role juries play as democracy-enhancing institutions of government. Yet Breyer does not employ the same reasoning to support the Court's decision regarding sentencing enhancement, creating an evident and somewhat puzzling contradiction as noted by Scalia in his concurring opinion in *Ring*. He wrote that "while . . . pleased to travel in Justice Breyer's company, the unfortunate fact is that today's judgment has nothing to do with jury sentencing. . . . There is really no way in which Justice Breyer can travel with the happy band that reaches today's result unless he says yes to *Apprendi*. Concisely put, Justice Breyer is on the wrong flight; he should either get off before the doors close, or buy a ticket to *Apprendi*-land" (612-13).

Breyer's unwillingness to "book the flight" with Scalia may suggest that he is hesitant to apply his democracy-enhancing theme of active liberty to cases that would undo the system of federal sentencing guidelines that he helped to craft. Yet Breyer's experience on the U.S. Sentencing Commission may not be the sole factor that creates a tension between his espoused approach to constitutional decision making and his willingness to diminish the jury's role within sentencing guidelines systems. Breyer also suggested denying to majorities the ability to participate in the democratic dialogue in other circumstances implicating constitutional rights in criminal justice. In *Ewing v. California* (2003), a convicted offender challenged California's three-strikes law that provided for a sentence of twenty-five years to life in prison upon conviction for three serious felonies. Ewing claimed that under the Eighth Amendment Cruel and Unusual

Punishment Clause, such a long term of imprisonment was disproportional to his third offense—the theft of three golf clubs—and hence unconstitutional. In her majority opinion, Justice Sandra Day O'Connor reflected on the Court's precedents and concluded "Ewing's is not 'the rare case in which a threshold comparison of the crime committed and the sentence imposed leads to an inference of gross disproportionality'"(30). Fundamental to O'Connor's analysis was her conclusion that Californians had made a policy decision regarding the most appropriate approach to remedying the problem of crime in the state. This decision about sentencing policy, she concluded, "is generally a policy choice to be made by state legislatures, not federal courts" (25).

Breyer, however, disagreed. Although he paid lip service to the need to recognize and defer to legislative will, his dissenting opinion second-guessed the California Assembly's stated purpose of deterrence, or any other imperative, as a rationale for creating the three-strikes penalty. He rather dismissively claimed that "the upshot is, in my view, the State cannot find in its three strikes law a special criminal justice need sufficient to rescue a sentence that other relevant consideration indicate is unconstitutional" (*Ewing v. California* 2003, 52). Breyer's claim that the three-strikes law, as established, was in a constitutional gray area that required close scrutiny by the justices did little to distract from the fact that he rather easily dismissed the will of the public in his dissent. His interpretation and conclusions bore little resemblance to the deferential approach advocated by realist thinkers who provide the foundation for his thesis regarding active liberty.

Confrontation Clause, Effective Counsel, & Fair Trials

Breyer also weighed in on issues of the Sixth Amendment protection associated with the right to confront witnesses and the assistance of counsel at trial. Although his contribution in the latter area during the Rehnquist Court era came only through dissenting opinions, his writing offered insight into his assessment of these guarantees. In *Texas v. Cobb* (2001), Breyer's dissent challenged the Court's conclusion that the Sixth Amendment right to counsel was not violated by authorities when they conducted a custodial interrogation of Raymond Cobb regarding a pair of murders linked to a burglary for which he had already been charged. Cobb, who had exercised his rights under the Fifth and Sixth Amendments after his arrest in the burglary case, argued that police should not have conducted any questioning related to the murders without the presence of his attorney because the two offenses were factually related. Breyer, quoting precedent, focused his analysis on "the purpose of the Sixth Amendment counsel guarantee [which] is to protect the unaided layman at critical confrontations with his expert adversary" (180, internal quotation omitted). In his estimation, the "technical" evaluation of the facts by the majority produced a holding that overlooked the fundamental principle related to the necessity of counsel—to provide for fair criminal proceedings. He pondered the likely abuses that could arise, in particular the ability of police to conduct wide-ranging questioning of an individual charged with a crime. If a prosecutor failed to list in the indictment all related crimes, then officials would be free to continue questioning a suspect on these additional offenses outside of the presence of counsel with near impunity. The decision of the majority, argued Breyer, not only lacked common sense, but also would "undermine the lawyer's role as 'medium' between the defendant and the government" (183).

In two additional cases, Breyer echoed this basic theme of fairness. In *Mickens v. Taylor* (2002), he objected to the conflict created by the state of Virginia when it assigned counsel to Walter Mickens for a capital murder trial. It was revealed later that the attorney appointed to represent Mickens was available to serve in that capacity only because his last indigent case had been dismissed when the defendant had been murdered—allegedly at the hands of Mickens himself. Despite the apparent conflict, the majority held that Mickens had not demonstrated the existence of any actual prejudice that impacted his defense. Breyer argued for a categorical rule in this type of circumstance, maintaining a defendant should not need to prove bias when it is so apparent on its face. Breyer commented on issues related to legal counsel again in a brief concurring opinion in *Martinez v. Court of Appeals of California, 4th Appellate District* (2000). He agreed with the Court's conclusion that pro se representation is not a constitutional right on appeal. But again, his analysis began and ended with a consideration of fairness. He wrote, "I have found no empirical research that might help determine whether, in general, the right to represent oneself furthers or inhibits the Constitution's basic guarantee of fairness" (164).

Prejudice is also central to Breyer's opinion in his lone majority opinion regarding the confrontation of witnesses. The case of *Gray v. Maryland* (1998) involved the use of a confession during the joint trial of two men charged with murder. Jurors were read the confession of one of the accused that the police elicited from him before trial. Redacted from the confession was any specific mention of the co-defendant, Kevin Gray, or the implication of him in the crime. Gray claimed a violation of his right to cross-examine an adverse witness when prosecutors substituted his name with the word "deletion" throughout the police officer's reading of the co-defendant's confession to the jury. Breyer and the Court agreed. In reviewing precedent, Breyer focused on the prejudicial effect such a reading would have on the outcome of the trial, leading jurors to presume that the redacted material "refers specifically to the defendant" (193). Such a conclusion, Breyer surmised, would be inescapable with the co-defendant seated next to the confessor and would likely taint the verdict.

The cases described above indicate Breyer's willingness to recognize specific constitutional protections for the criminally accused in several Sixth Amendment contexts. However, in other cases the application of the balancing test that undergirds his analytical approach often resolved the question of fairness to the benefit of the state. In *Sell v. United States* (2003), the Court held that the government could forcibly administer anti-psychotic drugs to a mentally ill criminal defendant in order to proceed to trial. Breyer's majority opinion argued that as long as the protocol was medically appropriate, served an important government interest in a manner less intrusive than other approaches, and was "substantially unlikely to have side effects that undermine the fairness of the trial," a defendant could be compelled to take medication (179). In the case of *United States v. Ruiz* (2002), similar questions regarding the fairness of criminal proceedings were raised regarding the obligation of federal prosecutors to disclose "impeachment information relating to any informants or other witnesses" during the plea bargaining process (625). Although Breyer, writing for a unanimous Court, recognized the constitutional necessity of a fair trial, he was quick to note that some rights are abrogated when you choose to plea bargain. One of those is acquiring from the prosecutor information potentially useful to the defense in the case. In concluding his analysis, he posited that "we cannot say that the Constitution's due process requirement demands so radical a change in the criminal justice process in order to achieve so comparatively small a constitutional benefit" (632). Such a conclusion, Breyer observed, would lead to higher costs, a slower process, and inefficiencies that would negatively impact the entire criminal justice system.

Search and Seizure & the Fourth Amendment

Breyer also offered his interpretive perspective in a small number of cases involving the protections offered by the Fourth Amendment. In *Illinois v. Lidster* (2004), the respondent challenged his conviction for drunk driving by arguing that the traffic stop that revealed his intoxication violated his right against unreasonable searches and seizures. In this instance, police were stopping motorists seeking information regarding a recent hit-and-run accident that had left a bicycle rider dead. Breyer, again writing for the majority, examined the purpose of the stop to determine its lawfulness. Law enforcement agents established the checkpoint not in an attempt to uncover a crime, he argued, but instead with the intent of gathering information to conclude an investigation of a prior crime. That context makes all the difference to the majority. Employing a reasonableness test, Breyer argued that the public concern regarding the crime, paired with the narrow objective of discovering specific information about a known crime, must be balanced against the liberty protected by the Fourth Amendment. The application of that test prompted the Court to conclude that there existed only a minimal intrusion that did not create a constitutional violation.

Breyer accepted a similar application of a reasonableness test in *Board of Education v. Earls* (2002). The majority opinion written by Justice Clarence Thomas supported an Oklahoma school district's policy of conducting random drug tests of students who chose to participate in extracurricular activities. The Court approved the suspicionless searches because the approach was a "reasonable means of furthering the School District's important interest in preventing and deterring drug use among its schoolchildren" (822). Breyer's concurrence supported this general conclusion but suggested additional justifications for the outcome. Of particular note was his recognition that the policy did not apply to the entire student body and that even those who participated in extracurricular programs had the opportunity to refuse the test and resign from the activity. He admitted that there was a price exacted if a student chose this path—the inability to participate in choirs, debate teams, and other activities—but the existence of this choice, in Breyer's assessment allowed for the protection of privacy and the maintenance of the purposes of Fourth Amendment rights.

Breyer's Purpose-Driven Jurisprudence & Criminal Justice

The written opinions penned by Breyer during his tenure on the Rehnquist Court reflected the moderation that is evident in his overall voting record. The balancing test that he often employed suggests that he is wedded to the idea of determining the purposes of constitutional and statutory language and understanding the consequences that will result from the decisions in a discrete case. This purpose-driven approach, however, is not divorced from facts, history, language, or precedent. Rather than limit his legal analysis to a single interpretive thread, Breyer weaves these elements together to provide a more fulsome tapestry that captures the detail of a particular case.

In evaluating Breyer's contributions to the Rehnquist Court, one cannot avoid asking whether his conception of active liberty, the pursuit of "law that helps a community of individuals democratically find practical solutions to important contemporary social problems," is achieved through the Court's decision making related to the rights of the criminally accused (Breyer 2005, 6). These rights are, by their nature, intended to limit democratic choice by restricting the power of government, including choices made by elected legislators and executive officials, such as county sheriffs and district attorneys, concerning investigation and case-processing procedures in criminal cases. Hence, majorities should not be permitted to wield significant influence in this area of public policy in order for criminal justice-related rights to serve their purposes.

Breyer, it appears, overcomes this legal conundrum by utilizing fairness as a surrogate for democracy when he considers the objective to be met by a judge. As a result, Breyer weighs the needs of the community against the rights of the accused. This rough calculus, it seems, provides a guidepost for his evaluation of the results in specific cases. When possible, Breyer draws as directly as possible a line between the achievement of a fair result and the consequence of that result for democratic choice. Sometimes this connection is rather subtle and attenuated, as in the case of *Board of Education v. Earls*. In his concurring opinion, he noted that the random drug-testing policy achieved a fair balance between the policy concerns of the community and the privacy concerns of students. The policy additionally protected personal decision making when it permitted students to choose whether or not they would participate in the school's extracurricular activities. In Breyer's view, fairness, or put another way, the balancing of interests, provides greater opportunity for both individuals and communities to shape policy or make choices regarding the meaning and application of rights related to the criminal process.

Of course, fairness is in the eye of the beholder, and Breyer appears on occasion to hold contradictory visions, especially as it relates to the promotion of democracy and the community. In *Ring*, Breyer celebrated the role of the jury in projecting the sense of the community through a verdict or decision. In capital cases, this process permits the public to validate the punishment through its participation as the final arbiter in the disposition of a case. As Justice Scalia notes, however, Breyer is somewhat inconsistent in the amount of deference that he shows to juries. When evaluating fairness in other sentencing environments, particularly those in which sentencing guidelines are employed, Breyer is much more willing to vest a judge with sentencing discretion while limiting the sovereign authority of the jury. Breyer would likely argue that the community, in endowing a legislature with the authority to create a sentencing system, has exercised its democratic function by directing the establishment of a mode of punishment. Hence, the community at large determines fairness, which in this context Breyer would argue is uniformity in sentencing, rather than the community represented through the jury. As a result, fairness is achieved and the imperative of active liberty is also met.

However, it does seem as if Breyer holds a special place in his jurisprudence for sentencing guideline systems, for in at least one other instance he is less inclined to defer to the public's will in sentencing decisions. In *Ewing*, he offered no hesitation in suggesting that the citizens of California were simply wrong when they created a three-strikes provision for criminal sentences, a provision endorsed directly by voters through a statewide ballot issue. His dissection of the law not only challenged the policy on constitutional grounds, arguing that the punishment, twenty-five years to life, was unconstitutionally disproportionate, but that the justification for the penalty was unsupportable. He went on to suggest that there existed *no* legitimate basis or purpose for a sentence of this duration. This was a particularly dismissive conclusion from an advocate of active liberty.

Beyond these few anomalous decisions, Breyer appeared to make a significant effort to apply the general theme of active liberty, even in cases where its use may seem inapt. The pursuit of democratic objectives in the area of criminal justice seems an impossible goal considering the purpose of the rights established in the Fourth, Fifth, Sixth, and Eighth Amendments. Breyer's search for equitable outcomes in this class of cases seems to parallel the theme that he promotes in *Active Liberty*, balancing the rights of a defendant against the impact a decision will have on both the immediate issues related to law enforcement and the larger democratic purposes articulated by the community. Any contradictions inherent in Breyer's criminal justice analysis are less a result of the careless application of his theme and more a consequence of how he chooses to focus the theme.

References

Baugh, Joyce A. *Supreme Court Justices in the Post-Bork Era: Confirmation Politics and Judicial Performance.* New York: Peter Lang, 2002.

Bowen, Terry, and John M. Scheb II. "Reassessing the 'Freshman Effect': The Voting Bloc Alignment of New Justices on the United States Supreme Court, 1921-90." *Political Behavior* 15, 1 (1993): 1-14.

Breyer, Stephen. "The Federal Sentencing Guidelines and the Key Compromises Upon Which They Rest." *Hofstra Law Review* 17 (1988): 1-50.

———. "The 1991 Justice W. Roth Lecture: On the Uses of Legislative History in Interpreting Statutes." *Southern California Law Review* 65 (1992): 845-74.

———. *Active Liberty: Interpreting Our Democratic Constitution.* New York: Alfred A. Knopf, 2005.

Cardoza, Benjamin. *The Nature of the Judicial Process.* New Haven, CT: Yale University Press, 1949.

Cushman, Clare. "Rookie on the Bench: The Role of the Junior Justice." *Journal of Supreme Court History* 32, 1 (2007): 282-96.

Deeney, Chris. "Most Americans Can't Name Any Supreme Court Justices, Says FindLaw.com Survey." *Ipsos in North America,* January 10, 2006. http://www.Ipsos-na.com/news/pressrelease.cfm>id=2933 (accessed April 2, 2008).

Dworkin, Ronald. *Law's Empire.* Cambridge, MA: Belknap Press of Harvard University Press, 1986.

Epstein, Lee, Jeffrey A. Segal, Harold J. Spaeth, and Thomas G. Walker. *The Supreme Court Compendium: Data Decisions & Developments.* 4th edition. Washington DC: CQ Press, 2007.

Fisher, William W. III, Morton J. Horowitz, and Thomas A. Reed, eds. *American Legal Realism.* New York: Oxford University Press, 1993.

Frase, Richard S. "State Sentencing Guidelines: Still Going Strong." *Judicature* 78, 4 (1995): 173-79.

Greenburg, Jan Crawford. *Supreme Conflict: The Inside Story of the Struggle for Control of the United States Supreme Court.* New York: Penguin Press, 2007.

Holmes, Oliver Wendell. *The Common Law,* edited by Mark DeWolfe Howe. Boston: Little, Brown, 1963.

Horowitz, Morton J. *The Transformation of American Law, 1870-1960: The Crisis Of Legal Orthodoxy.* New York: Oxford University Press, 1992.

Kersch, Ken I. "The Synthetic Progressivism of Stephen G. Breyer." Pp. 241-76 in *Rehnquist Justice: Understanding the Court* Dynamic, edited by Earl M. Maltz. Lawrence, KS: University Press of Kansas, 2003.

O'Brien, David M. *Storm Center: The Supreme Court in American Politics.* New York: Norton, 2005.

Posner, Richard A. *Overcoming Law.* Cambridge, MA: Harvard University Press, 1995.

Scalia, Antonin. *A Matter of Interpretation: Federal Courts and the Law.* Princeton, NJ: Princeton University Press, 1997.

Schwartz, Bernard. *Main Currents in American Legal Thought.* Durham, NC: Carolina Academic Press, 1993.

Segal, Jeffrey A., and Harold J. Spaeth. *The Supreme Court and the Attitudinal Model Revisited.* Cambridge, England: Cambridge University Press, 2004.

Silverstein, Mark. *Judicious Choices: The Politics of Supreme Court Confirmations.* 2nd edition. New York: Norton, 2007.
Smith, Christopher E., Joyce A. Baugh, and Thomas R. Hensley. "The First-Term Performance of Justice Stephen Breyer." *Judicature* 79, 3 (1995): 74-79.
Smith, Christopher E., and Thomas R. Hensley. "Decision-Making Trends of the Rehnquist Court Era: Civil Rights and Liberties Cases." *Judicature* 89, 3 (2005): 161-67, 184-85.
Tocqueville, Alexis de. *Democracy in America.* Edited by Phillips Bradley. New York: Vintage Books, 1990 [1831, 1840].
Tonry, Michael. "Twenty Years of Sentencing Reform: Steps Forward, Steps Backward." *Judicature* 78, 4 (1995): 169-72.
Toobin, Jeffrey. *The Nine: Inside the Secret World of the Supreme Court.* New York: Doubleday, 2007.
U.S. Congress. Senate. Committee on the Judiciary. *Hearings on the Nomination of Stephen G. Breyer to be an Associate of the Supreme Court of the United States. 103rd Congress, 2nd session,* July 12-15, 1994.
Yarbrough, Tinsley E. *The Rehnquist Court and the Constitution.* New York: Oxford University Press, 2000.

Cases Cited

Almendarez-Torres v. United States, 523 U.S. 224 (1998)
Apprendi v. New Jersey, 530 U.S. 466 (2000)
Blakely v. Washington, 542 U.S. 296 (2004)
Board of Education v. Earls, 536 U.S. 822 (2002)
Buford v. United States, 532 U.S. 59 (2001)
Edwards v. United States, 523 U.S (1998)
Ewing v. California, 538 U.S. 11 (2003)
Gray v. Maryland, 523 U.S. 185 (1998)
Illinois v. Lidster, 540 U.S. 419 (2004)
Illinois v. McArthur, 531 U.S. 326 (2001)
Kyllo v. United States, 533 U.S. 27 (2001)
Martinez v. Court of Appeals of Cal., Fourth Appellate District, 528 U.S. 162 (2000)
Mickens v. Taylor, 535 U.S. 162 (2002)
Miller-El v. Dretke, 545 U.S. 231 (2005)
Printz v. United States, 521 U.S. 898 (1997)
Ring v. Arizona, 536 U.S. 584 (2002)
Sell v. United States, 539 U.S. 166 (2003)
Texas v. Cobb, 532 U.S. 162 (2001)
United States v. Booker, 543 U.S. 220 (2005)
United States v. Lara, 541 U.S. 193 (2004)
United States v. Ottati & Goss, 900 F.2d 429 (1990)
United States v. Ruiz, 536 U.S. 622 (2002)

Case Index

Subject Index

Contributors

Joyce A. Baugh
Professor of Political Science, Central Michigan University
Ph.D. (Kent State University)

John D. Burrow
Associate Professor of Criminal Justice, University of South Carolina
Ph.D. (Michigan State University), J.D. (University of Wisconsin)

Christina DeJong
Associate Professor of Criminal Justice, Michigan State University
Ph.D. (University of Maryland)

Mark S. Hurwitz
Associate Professor of Political Science, Western Michigan University
Ph.D. (Michigan State University), J.D. (Brooklyn Law School)

Charles F. Jacobs
Assistant Professor of Political Science, St. Norbert College
Ph.D. (University of Connecticut)

Scott P. Johnson
Associate Professor of Political Science, Frostburg State University
Ph.D. (Kent State University)

Ashlyn Kuersten
Associate Professor of Political Science, Western Michigan University
Ph.D. (University of South Carolina)

Madhavi M. McCall
Professor of Political Science, San Diego State University
Ph.D. (Washington University in St. Louis)

Michael A. McCall
Associate Professor of Sociology, San Diego State University
Ph.D. (Washington University in St. Louis)

Christopher E. Smith
Professor of Criminal Justice, Michigan State University
Ph.D. (University of Connecticut), J.D. (University of Tennessee)

Lee Ruffin Wilson
Attorney-at-Law, Columbia, South Carolina
J.D. (University of South Carolina)